THE DECLINE AND FALL OF THE HABSBURG EMPIRE 1815–1918

The Decline and Fall of the Habsburg Empire 1815–1918

Alan Sked

Longman
London and New York

Longman Group UK Limited,
Longman House, Burnt Mill, Harlow,
Essex CM20 2JE, England
and Associated Companies throughout the world

Published in the United States of America
by Longman Inc., New York

First published 1989

British Library Cataloguing in Publication Data

Sked, Alan, *1947–*
The decline and fall of the Habsburg Empire 1815–1918.
1. Habsburg Empire. Political events, 1815–1918
I. Title
940.2′8

ISBN 0-582-02530-3 CSD
ISBN 0-582-02531-1 PPR

Library of Congress Cataloging-in-Publication Data

Sked, Alan, 1947–
The decline and fall of the Habsburg Empire, 1815–1918/Alan Sked.

p. cm.
Includes index.
ISBN 0-582-02530- 3. ISBN 0-582-02531-1 (pbk.)
1. Austria – History – 1815–1848. 2. Austria – History – 1848–1867. 3. Austria – History – 1867–1918. 4. Habsburg, House of. I. Title.
DB80.S58 1989
943.6′04–dc19

88-9003
CIP

Set in Linotron 10/12 pt Bembo

Produced by Longman Singapore Publishers (Pte) Ltd.
Printed in Singapore

Contents

List of Maps

To Jessie and Family,
and to George and Tom in memoriam

Introduction

The Habsburgs were Europe's greatest dynasty. Between the thirteenth century and the twentieth they provided rulers for empires, kingdoms, duchies and principalities in modern-day Germany, Austria, Spain, Italy, Belgium, Holland, Czechoslovakia, Yugoslavia, Romania, Poland and Hungary. The German Crown, for example, was held continuously by them from 1452 to 1806, with the exception of the years 1740 to 1745, when it was in the temporary possession of a Wittelsbach. The Habsburg itself, on the other hand, the possession from which the dynasty derived its name, was lost as early as 1635 by the Emperor Ferdinand II.

In the nineteenth century, imperial possessions were still vast. When Franz Joseph acceded to the throne in 1848 they included (1) the Austrian lands (the Archduchies of Lower and Upper Austria; the Duchies of Styria, Carniola and Carinthia; the Counties of Tyrol and Vorarlberg, Gorizia and Gradisca; plus the Margraviate of Istria and the City of Trieste); (2) the lands of the Hungarian Crown (the Kingdoms of Hungary, Croatia and Slavonia, with the city of Fiume; the Grand Duchy of Transylvania; plus the Croatian–Slavonian and Servian–Hungarian military frontiers); (3) the lands of the Bohemian Crown (the Kingdom of Bohemia; the Margraviate of Moravia; and the Duchy of Upper and Lower Silesia); (4) the Kingdom of Lombardy-Venetia; (5) the Kingdom of Galicia and the Grand Duchy of Cracow; (6) the Duchy of the Bukovina; (7) the Kingdom of Dalmatia; and (8) the Duchy of Salzburg.

The total area covered by these possessions was 257,478 m^2, making them, when taken together, the largest country in Europe after Russia, and only 10,000 m^2 smaller than Texas. Their total population amounted to 37.5 million souls. This included (8 million)

Germans, (5.5 million) Magyars, (5 million) Italians, (4 million) Czechs, (3 million) Ruthenes, (2.5 million) Romanians, (2 million) Poles, (almost 2 million) Slovaks, (1.5 million) Serbs, (almost 1.5 million) Croats, over 1 million Slovenes, 0.75 million Jews, plus over half a million others (including Gypsies, Armenians, Bulgars and Greeks).

If all this were insufficient an inheritance, Franz Joseph also claimed to rule territories which were no longer in his possession or which no longer even existed – for example, Upper and Lower Lusatia, Lorraine, Kyburg and Habsburg, not to mention the Kingdom of Jerusalem, which had ceased to exist in 1291.

Nevertheless, it will be immediately apparent that with so many lands in Central Europe (not to mention Austria's Presidency of the German Confederation and junior branches of the Habsburg family ruling in Tuscany, Parma and Modena), European history would still revolve around the dynasty. And so it proved. It was Franz Joseph's ultimatum to Serbia in 1914 which would begin the First World War; the downfall of the empire four years later would end an era of European history.

In spite of all this, few people today know or care to know very much about the Habsburgs. History students rush towards doors or even windows when the subject is mentioned. The names involved are too difficult; the geography no less so; the evolution of events apparently complicated. The story, in any case, is one of retreat and dissolution, and therefore lacks appeal. A most distinguished historian of the dynasty's foreign policy has recently lent academic support to this outlook, writing: 'The Habsburg Monarchy offers no classical cases to the investigator of world history . . . the historian . . . is unable to discover, however well intentioned he may be, anything that was pioneering in Austrian history. All that happened in the Monarchy was nothing but a belated, second hand, and often distorted variant of Western European developments. Nor is Austrian history rich in decisive events transcending national boundaries.'[1] Is there any point at all, therefore, in studying Habsburg history?

The answer to that question is a resounding yes. All history is rewarding to study not only as a background to the present but in order to see how people lived under different conditions and thought systems. Besides, it does not require a very great deal of imagination to see that the historian quoted above was obviously wrong. The history of Western Europe is not so stereotyped after all that one can talk about variants of it; Habsburg history, in any case, forms an intrinsic part of that history, not some mere reflection of it. Finally, at a time when Europe is making attempts, however feeble, to unite, it takes a brave man indeed (or an East European) to dismiss the history of its greatest supra-national empire as meaningless. On the contrary, given recent debates concerning Europe's bureaucracy, two-tier Europes and the need for a European voice independent of the superpowers, it is extremely difficult not to be reminded of Habsburg themes – Josephinism, Dualism, the Monarchy as a European necessity, for example. The European Idea, in short, recalls the Austrian one, the so-called *oesterreichisches Staatsidee*. European statesmen, therefore, would be well advised to ponder the fate of the Monarchy. To study it after all is not merely to investigate a variety of problems common to other European states, but to study the problems involved in ruling a large number of peoples of disparate and often mutually hostile cultures, in finding some bond of loyalty between them, and in retaining that loyalty in a world full of internal and external challenges. The Habsburgs did, moreover, rule more of Europe, and for a longer period, than anyone else in modern times. Hence if Europe is to unite it may still prove possible to learn from their mistakes. This is not to suggest that history is an infallible guide. But if statesmen are expected to negotiate a sensible path towards the future, it would do them little harm and perhaps some good to know exactly which territories have already been traversed and with what results in the past.

The purpose of this book is *not* to provide yet another narrative account of the dynasty's demise. It is intended, rather, to be an extended essay on its decline as analysed by modern historians, particularly those concerned with the period 1815 to 1918, and mostly those of British, American, Austrian and Hungarian nationality. It will not attempt a comprehensive survey of all the specialist literature, but will limit itself to the principal themes with which students should be familiar. In this way the author hopes that it will fill a gap in the existing literature.

The fundamental question which has lain behind nearly all the work discussed in this book has been 'at what point did the collapse of the Habsburg Empire become inevitable?' although its corollary, 'could anything have been done to avoid this?' has also been present. The result has been that Habsburg historiography has been marked by a distinctive, counter-factual streak, a feature which has been enhanced in the work, particularly of American authors by their belief that everything would have been for the better had the Monarchy survived.[2] This is because the majority of these historians have been refugees or sons of refugees from the successor regimes of the Dual Monarchy and compare it favourably with the authoritarian and communist regimes which replaced it. They share, in other words, the view which was recently expressed by the distinguished American scholar, George Kennan, namely that, 'The Austro-Hungarian Empire still looks better as a solution to the tangled problems of that part of the world than anything that has succeeded it.'[3] If only the dynasty had produced a fairer system for governing all the peoples it ruled over; if only it had produced statesmen capable of meeting the internal and external challenges to its rule; if only the other powers had seen the advantages to Europe's balance of power of preserving a supra-national empire between West and East; if only, in short, the dynasty had survived, then how much better off the world would now be as a whole. Perhaps so, perhaps not. Others have been less nostalgic in their viewpoint, preferring to adopt a very different perspective. These historians, the majority of them British or East European, have argued that the Monarchy was less a 'multi-national empire'[4] than a *Hausmacht*, that is to say, a political or territorial vehicle which enabled a particular family, the Habsburgs, to pursue their quest for power and prestige. The Habsburg Monarchy, in other words, was quintessentially a proprietorial affair, a way of preserving a collection of family estates on an international scale, and not in A. J. P. Taylor's words 'a device for enabling a number of nationalities to live together'.[5] From this perspective, therefore, it was not so much the difficulties involved in creating a 'well-balanced federalism'[6] within the Monarchy, or even the lack of statesmanship applied to this task, which was responsible for the Monarchy's demise, but the insistence of the Habsburg emperors on retaining their autocratic powers and maintaining and expanding their territorial possessions, which brought about their ruin. In all the historical explanations which follow, therefore, the student should take care to distinguish between what might be described as federalist or counter-factual interpretations on the one hand, and dynastic or imperialist ones on the other.

But where does one begin? At what point can it be argued that the Monarchy began its decline? When precisely did its collapse become inevitable? One prominent British historian of the dynasty, C. A. Macartney, has argued: 'The turning point in the central Monarchy . . . can without extravagance be dated to a day: 28 January 1790.'[7] That was the day on which, according to Macartney, 'the tide turned in Central Europe.'[8] Joseph II had been forced to revoke most of his reforms and, thereafter, the Habsburg Monarchy entered a long period of decline. To quote Macartney yet again: '. . . the territorial advance gives way to a retreat in which one outpost after another is lost. At the same time, the forces of absolutism and centralism are driven back on the defensive until at last the peoples of the monarchy allied with its foreign enemies repudiate not only the character of the Monarch's rule, but the rule itself. The end has come.'[9]

The whole period 1789–1815 has been singled out by Austrian historians as portentous for the Monarchy's decline. Professor Wandruszka, for example, has discussed the death of Joseph II as a turning point although, as the biographer of Leopold II, he has laid more emphasis on the death of that monarch in 1792.[10] Not only did this usher in the reactionary rule of Francis I which, combined with the outbreak of war against revolutionary France and the discovery in 1794–5 of the 'Jacobin Plot' in Hungary and Vienna, put paid to Leopold's plans for reform; the year 1792, Wandruszka also reminds us, witnessed that resumption of diplomatic relations between Austria and Turkey which ended three centuries of hostility and warfare.[11] Yet with the resumption of normal relations between these two states, it can be argued, the House of Austria had fulfilled its historic mission, which had been to protect Europe from the Turks. Danilevski and other Russian Panslavs were certainly to maintain that on this ground alone, the Monarchy had forfeited its right to survive. The Habsburgs, for their part, however, found a new mission to pursue – protecting Central Europe from French and Russian aggression as an essential part of the European balance of power.

The period 1790–1815 has been invested by historians with even more turning points – 1804, for example, with the assumption of Francis I of the simple title 'Emperor of Austria' or 1806 with the end of the Holy Roman Empire. The Austrian historian, Berthold Sutter, has pointed out that the Archduke John believed that the 'fatal day for the young Austrian Empire' was in July 1809 when Napoleon won the battle of Wagram.[12] There is certainly something in this, because it was with Wagram that the only attempt to defeat Napoleon by rousing the German and European peoples under Austrian leadership was thwarted, and it was after Wagram that the reform party at the Vienna court, led by the brothers Stadion and the Archdukes Charles and John, had to relinquish their control of Austrian policy to Metternich.

The fact remains, however, that the Monarchy emerged from the Napoleonic Wars victorious and that the Congress of Vienna gave

Austria the leadership of Germany and Italy. Metternich played a distinguished role in that settlement and helped produce a peace which not only left the Monarchy more consolidated territorially than hitherto, but allied militarily against any threat of future revolution from France. It is difficult to believe, therefore, that a process of decline had already set in by 1815. Historians as a result have been prone to stress the nineteenth century as marking the real beginning of the Monarchy's decline. Hence Metternich's refusal to compromise with the rising tide of liberalism and nationalism before 1848; the 1848 revolutions; the loss of leadership in Italy and Germany; the Compromise of 1867; the Monarchy's Balkan diplomacy; and its decision to start a war with Serbia in 1914 at a time when it was relatively weak in European terms, both militarily and economically, are seen as the real milestones on the road to disaster. The following chapters of this book will, therefore, concentrate on the period 1815 to 1918.

One fundamental point, however, has to be made clear now. The fact that one talks about the *decline and fall* of the Monarchy does not mean that it had to decline and fall at a steady pace. The phrase has simply become common currency. Indeed, the fact that the Monarchy *fell* does not logically have to imply any *decline* at all. As will become clear, the pattern was a rather different one. What happened was that in 1848 the Monarchy almost fell apart but thereafter recovered and in many ways *rose* rather than *declined* before 1914. It can even be argued that there was no domestic or even foreign threat to its integrity until 1918.

The final point which should be made in this introduction is that because on so many issues in Habsburg history – including most of the big ones – there is still so much work to be done, it has been necessary very often to discuss important themes without being able to point to any major or recent work of research. (Conversely, some themes which have been relatively well treated by historians – for example, the history of the Jews inside the Monarchy – have had to be left out, since they do not pertain to the book's theme.) This is extremely unfortunate. It may allow room for the author to sketch out questions and suggest answers in an easy and superficial fashion, but it is a cause for regret, none the less, that more solid bases of judgement should remain unavailable. Given the trouble, moreover, that so many potential doctoral students appear to find in searching for research topics, it is a matter of some bewilderment that there is still no modern monograph on Franz Joseph's system of government, no modern biography of him, no thorough account of

Metternich's German or Russian policy, no overview of the development of parliamentary politics in the Monarchy, no study of the bureaucracy or court, no up-to-date synthesis of 1848, etc. etc. etc. It is my hope, therefore, that this book might encourage others to help fill the gaps.

NOTES AND REFERENCES

1. István Diószegi (1983) *Hungarians in the Ballhausplatz, Studies on the Austro-Hungarian Common Foreign Policy*. Budapest, p. 9.
2. For more on this theme, see Alan Sked (1981) Historians, the nationality question and the downfall of the Habsburg Empire, *Transactions of the Royal Historical Society*, 5th series, Vol. 31, pp. 175–93.
3. George Kennan (1979) *The Decline of Bismarck's European order. Franco-Russian Relations, 1875–1890*. Princeton, p. 423.
4. As in Robert A. Kann (1950) *The Multinational Empire, 1848–1918*, 2 vols. New York. But see A. J. P. Taylor's devastating review (1967), The failure of the Habsburg Monarchy, in his *Europe: Grandeur and Decline*. Harmondsworth, pp. 127–132.
5. Taylor, *op. cit.*, p. 132.
6. See the discussion in Sked, *op. cit.*, pp. 184–5.
7. C. A. Macartney (1978) *The House of Austria: The Later Phase, 1790–1918*. Edinburgh, p. 1.
8. C. A. Macartney (1968) *The Habsburg Empire, 1790–1918*. London, p. 1.
9. *Ibid.*
10. A. Wandruszka (1968) Finis Austriae? Reformpläne und Untergangsahnungen in der Habsburger Monarchie, in *Der österreichische Ausgleich von 1867. Seine Grundlagen und Auswirkungen*, Buchreihe der Südostdeutschen Historischen Kommission, Vol. 20. Munich.
11. *Ibid.*
12. B. Sutter (1963) Erzherzog Johanns Kritik an Osterreich, *Mitteilungen des Oesterreichischen Staatsarchivs*, Vol. 16, p. 165 ff.

CHAPTER ONE
Metternich and his System, 1815–48

The most prominent figure in nineteenth-century Habsburg history was, of course, Prince Metternich, Foreign Minister between 1809 and 1848 and House, Court and State Chancellor from 1821. Historians occasionally refer to the period 1815–48 as the 'Age of Metternich' and often it is said to have been dominated by 'the Metternich System'. The implication is that Metternich not only formulated the foreign policy of the Habsburg Monarchy, but through that controlled the destiny of Europe. For this reason he is considered a major historical figure and like all such figures is surrounded by controversy. Judgements of him, however, have on the whole been negative. Most textbook writers see him as a reactionary figure whose obsession with suppressing revolution – the Revolution, with a capital R from his point of view – frustrated the establishment of moderate, constructive, reforming regimes in Central Europe. Had it not been for the Metternich System, these writers imply, Europe as a whole might have developed along general liberal lines and perhaps have been spared all sorts of wars and catastrophies. In particular, the *Deutscher Sonderweg*, that is to say, Germany's peculiar path of historical development, might never have occurred, Bismarck might never have been necessary, and European history might have taken on an altogether different character. Likewise, if it had not been for Metternich, the Habsburg Empire might have reformed itself constructively, the nationalities might have been appeased, and 1914 might never have happened. From the point of view of liberal or democratic writers, therefore, Metternich has a lot to answer for.

METTERNICH AND HIS CRITICS

Most writers or critics of this school, however, have assumed three things: first, that Metternich dominated the Empire's foreign policy and through that the diplomacy of Europe as a whole; secondly, that he was also responsible for the main features of the Empire's domestic policy; and thirdly, that both his domestic and foreign policies were intimately related. Both, it is said, were based on the same reactionary principles and merged together in the so-called Metternich System. Put another way, these writers believe that Metternich's foreign and domestic policies were ideological and that his ideology rested on the following beliefs: that the only true form of government was monarchy; that monarchical government should be absolute; that it existed to protect the social order which, like itself, was divinely ordained; that monarchs everywhere should combine to protect this order and the political stability which it engendered; that in practice this meant rejecting the representative principle which presupposed popular sovereignty; upholding the European Concert and the balance of power; and being seen to exert authority through the coordinated use of armies and police forces, and intervening if necessary to save fellow rulers from the Revolution. The practical manifestations of this System were to be seen, therefore, in the Karlsbad Decrees of 1819, the Final Act of the Vienna Congress of 1820, the intervention in Naples in 1821, in Spain in 1823, in the Papal States in 1830, in the Berlin and Münchengraetz agreements of 1833, in the annexation of Cracow in 1846, in the 'occupation' of Ferrara in 1847 and in the imprisonment of such enemies of the régime as Confalonieri, Kossuth and Wesselényi. Yet, in spite of all this repression, the System, in the eyes of these historians, failed. In the end, the moderate reformers were forced to become revolutionaries until in 1848 the inevitable happened and Metternich was overthrown by revolution.

Many of these arguments were used by contemporary critics of Metternich, for whom he loomed very large indeed. One of these, for example, an Austrian writing in 1830, could declare: 'Never was a man more feared or detested than Metternich. From Belgium to the Pyrenees, from the frontiers of Turkey to the borders of Holland, there is only one opinion of this minister and it is one of execration. For it is he who has principally contributed to giving Europe its present political form, who has been the inventor and main spring of the Holy Alliance, that embryo of great events . . . Liberty has never had as dangerous an enemy as Metternich.'[1] Lord

Palmerston put the second half of the case to the Austrian Ambassador in London: 'Prince Metternich believes that he is a conservative by obstinately upholding the political status quo in Europe: we believe that we are conservatives by everywhere preaching and counselling reforms and improvements where these things are designated and claimed to be necessary by the public. You, on the other hand, reject everything. When order and tranquillity reign in your land, you say that concessions are useless; in moments of crisis and revolt you equally refuse them, not wishing to weaken authority by appearing to bend before the storm. You also persist in rejecting absolutely everything that public opinion demands in your country and in the lands in which you have influence and patronage; [finally you reject] everything that is granted close or far from you. No, this immobility is not conservatism. . . . Your repressive and suffocating policy is also a fatal one and will lead to an explosion just as certainly as would a boiler that was hermetically sealed and deprived of an outlet for steam.'[2] Kolowrat, the Prince's main rival within the Austrian government, said much the same to his face: 'I am an aristocrat by birth and by conviction and completely agree with you that people must strive for conservatism and do everything to achieve it. Yet we differ about means. Your means consist of a forest of bayonets and fixed adherence to things as they are. To my mind, by following these lines we are playing into the hands of the revolutionaries. . . . Your ways will lead us . . . not tomorrow or next year – but soon enough – to our ruin.'[3] After the revolutions of 1848, it became the standard view of Metternich that this was precisely what had happened and today that view remains the orthodox one. Paul Schroeder's examination of *Metternich's Diplomacy at its Zenith*,[4] for example, concludes with a chapter describing him as a statesman whose policies were neither constructive, conservative nor European. Worse still, he is now often regarded as irrelevant. His much vaunted principles are dismissed as clichés – in A. J. P. Taylor's words, 'most men could do better than this when shaving'[5] – whereas a number of studies[6] have demonstrated that in European diplomacy, his was not the decisive voice: it was Castlereagh who dominated the Congress of Vienna; it was Palmerston who solved the Belgian Question; it was Russia and Great Britain who took charge of the Eastern Question; and in the affairs of Greece or Spain or Portugal, Metternich had little say. He may have persuaded Alexander of Russia to support a reactionary Troppau Protocol, but he did this at the price of losing whatever influence he had with Great Britain and did not even manage to keep control of the so-called *Congress System* thereafter. On his own doorstep, it was Prussia which seized the leadership of Germany through the *Zollverein* and it was his reactionary allies in Switzerland who were defeated in the *Sonderbund* war of 1847. Even in day-to-day diplomacy, it can be argued, Metternich's reputation among his European colleagues did not stand high: Nicholas of Russia regarded him as 'the cohort of Satan'; Nesselrode complained of his 'lack of frankness, his panics and his jeramiads, his pusillanimity and his jealousy, his unhealthy obsession with scribbling things on paper and deliberately confusing even the most simple affairs'. Nor did he enjoy a reputation for honesty. Talleyrand, comparing him with Cardinal Mazarin, said: 'The Cardinal deceived but never lied – Metternich always lies but never deceives.' Napoleon complained: 'Everyone lies sometimes, but to lie all the time, that is too much.' Canning called him the 'greatest rogue and liar on the Continent perhaps in the civilized world', whereas the real trouble with Metternich, according to the poet Grillparzer, was that he believed his own lies in the end.[7] Altogether, therefore, there is a case to be made out that Metternich was very much a failure: repressive in both domestic and foreign policy to an extent that actually encouraged revolution; irrelevant in foreign affairs; disrespected by his diplomatic contemporaries; and even lacking consistent principles of action. What then can be said in his defence?

METTERNICH AND HIS DEFENDERS

We shall deal with his influence in domestic affairs in a moment. With regard to foreign policy, his supporters would make the following points: that in an absolutist state, his power depended on the will of the Emperor; that in foreign policy, he was handicapped by the obvious economic and military weaknesses of the Monarchy; that in spite of these, however, he still managed to exercise considerable influence in Europe, not merely in Italy and in Germany, but in Europe generally where he was recognized as the main spokesman for the conservative cause and where he did indeed pursue broad principles consistently over such a long period of time that there is justice in speaking of a 'Metternich System' or even of an 'Age of Metternich'. Let us therefore examine the positive side of this negative figure.

Not a great deal is known about the exact nature of his working relationship with Francis I, but what there is suggests that he perhaps had more influence with that monarch than at times he made out. Thus, although he told a Russian general on one occasion that were he to 'diverge' from the Emperor's will, 'Prince Metternich would not remain Foreign Minister for twenty-four hours',[8] and despite his famous statement, 'I may have governed Europe occasionally, but Austria never', there can be little doubt that he played a very powerful role in both the Empire's foreign and domestic affairs. Metternich, in any case, was given to contradicting himself. He said on other occasions: 'I rule the Russian cabinet, just as I rule the Austrian one' or 'The Emperor always does what I want, although I want only what he should want.'[9] The truth seems to be that although there were occasions on which Metternich and Francis quarrelled, their views on most issues were much the same: both were horrified by change and both were committed absolutely to the struggle against the Revolution and the *Comité Directeur* which they believed was in control of it. As the Russian Ambassador commented, 'Austria's policies [were] based on Francis's character and guided by Metternich's spirit'.[10] Or as the Chancellor himself confessed: 'Heaven has placed me next to a man who might have been created for me as I for him. The Emperor Francis knows what he wants and that never differs in any way from what I most want.'[11] It is sometimes asked, however, why Metternich did not push harder occasionally to get his own way, particularly in domestic policy, over issues on which the two men were divided. There are several possible explanations for this: probably Metternich knew that it was imposible for Francis to change his style of rule; maybe he himself lacked sufficient determination to pursue his objectives (in fact this lack of determination was often ascribed to a 'feminine' vein in his character which several contemporaries remarked upon); it could well be that he did not believe that he had the right in a monarchical state to demand that he get his own way over everything. What is very difficult to maintain is that a threat to resign on Metternich's part would have brought his instant dismissal. Francis simply had too high an opinion of his Chancellor, for one thing; on the other hand, it is known that Kolowrat threatened to resign on no fewer than twenty occasions. This part of the case for the defence is therefore perhaps not as strong as it might first appear, although it can by no means be discounted. As absolute ruler, Francis always had the last word and it was almost always reactionary.

On the matter of the economic and military weaknesses of the

Monarchy, Metternich's defenders are on much safer ground. Kolowrat, for a start, controlled the purse strings of the Monarchy and, as we have seen, he objected to Metternich's policy of a 'forest of bayonets'. In fact, he described the Austrian military budget as 'a shield which weighed down the rider'[12] and made determined efforts to reduce military expenditure wherever possible. He was anxious to keep Austria's budget balanced (something he achieved only once in 1829) and to reduce the state debt, which was enormously high. He was determined, in short, to reduce Austria's reputation for being something of a credit risk, a reputation established during the Napoleonic Wars.

In 1811 the Monarchy had had to declare itself bankrupt, yet in spite of this it had had to run up further enormous debts between 1813 and 1815. In the following years, some order had been restored into its finances but, during the period 1815–48, the annual interest paid on the state debt amounted to roughly 30 per cent of the entire state revenue. If, according to one French observer in 1846, Austrian finances were none the less 'in a truly remarkable state of prosperity'[13] (taking the figures for 1840, he calculated that the public debt amounted to not much more than one year's revenue if the sinking fund were subtracted), this was not a view which was widely shared. As Kolowrat perceived things, the army's budget for most of the period before 1848 accounted for nearly 40 per cent of government revenue and was the largest item of government expenditure. In years of crisis or, rather, of intervention, it rose enormously (troops on a war-footing were paid double wages), with the result that an active or interventionist policy on the part of the Monarchy always threatened once again to undermine the creditworthiness of the state. Treasury opposition to policies which raised the military budget from 55 million florins in 1819 to 80 million in 1821, and from 46 million in 1830 to 77 million in 1831, had therefore been expressed with vigour. Stadion had wrung his hands in 1824 on discovering that the costs of the Naples expedition had brought about a deficit of 35 million gulden which in turn had necessitated a loan of 30 million guilden. Nor had his anger abated on hearing that Metternich had had to agree on the part repayment of a British loan of 40 million gulden which the British government was now demanding in a show of disapproval. During the Greek War of Independence, therefore, Kolowrat, despite Metternich's boasts to the powers, had informed Prince Windischgraetz, the later Field Marshal, that Austria, whose military budget in 1827 had again been reduced to 48 million florins, was 'armed for perpetual peace'.[14]

He continued: 'We must do everything possible to prevent hostilities and can only pray that people do not believe our threats. Our hopes rest on the divergence of interests of the three powers who are at present so unnaturally coalesced.' The Austrian army, in other words, as far as Kolowrat was concerned, was only to be used in the last resort. Metternich realized the implications of such an attitude and at the end of the Russo-Turkish War demanded that money be spent on rearmament. But Kolowrat retorted: 'If the military authorities have not yet succeeded, during a period of fifteen years of peace which has been interrupted only by one short campaign against Naples and Piedmont, to place the army and our other means of defence on such a footing as to be able to defend the Monarchy against whatever threat . . . one begins to fear that a military expenditure which already exceeds the financial resources of the Monarchy has hitherto been insufficient to fulfil its task. It is difficult therefore to answer the question how the annual 38–46 million gulden, which sum it is now recognised is insufficient for defence purposes and for protection against internal threat, could have been spent.'[15] The army, on the other hand, had certainly not squandered its resources. Both officers and men were paid miserable wages and endured hard conditions of service. Nor could it be accused of investing its money in stockpiling: it often found that its room for manoeuvre was limited by shortage of supplies. According to one statistician, in fact, the army only survived economically in peacetime by sending home one-third to one-half of its troops: 'In peaceful times it is usual for one third or even a greater part of the men to be on leave and to keep only those who are indispensable for duty. In particular the peaceful years 1815–1829 allowed so greatly an extended use of this system which is occasioned by economy and industrial considerations, that in the years 1825, 1826, and 1828 almost one half of the men were on leave.'[16] The army, in fact, was so run-down, demoralized and ill-led that it could scarcely be described as battle-worthy. Thus when Metternich in 1831 invited the Archduke Charles to lead the imperial forces against France, the Archduke made it abundantly clear in his reply that neither the financial state of the Empire nor the condition of the army would warrant it. The Emperor himself realized this. When Radetzky asked him why there had been no war against France, Francis told him: 'I held a camp this year near Münchendorf where my troops displayed themselves so badly and apathetically that the Prussians voiced their dissatisfaction. We therefore recognised Louis Phillipe as King of France at the same time as England. Isolated I could not undertake war.'[17] Radetzky was despatched to Italy to reform the army there, but despite a number of measures he introduced and despite considerable mythology, there is little evidence that he produced outstanding results. In any case, his efforts to consolidate his position against the looming threat from Piedmont before 1848 were also undermined by Treasury control. The Emperor informed the President of the Imperial War Council at the end of February 1848: 'In future no proposition which entails additional financial expenditure is to be presented to me before a preliminary agreement has been reached with the treasury praesidium.'[18] Radetzky was informed at the same time that he would only receive more troops if a 'significant rebellion' had already broken out in Lombardy or if the French or Sardinians attacked. This was in spite of the fact that the Field Marshal's strategy was based on attacking the enemy first. Meanwhile, the Russians so despaired of Austria that the Tsar was writing to his brother-in-law, the King of Prussia, exhorting him, 'Dear Friend, be the deliverer of Germany.'[19] Metternich was therefore conducting the foreign policy of an empire whose financial weaknesses were seriously undermining its ability to secure its interests and defences, a situation which was made even worse by the low morale of its armed forces: the general staff officers were reckoned to be of poor quality; Radetzky's manoeuvres were held to debilitate the troops; there were increasing cases of suicide and indiscipline among the ranks (often occasioned by the horrific punishments meted out to the men); while last but not least, there was the problem posed by the nationality question. Any allusion to this was usually condemned as a 'violation of military honour',[20] but Radetzky himself could write to Vienna at the end of 1847 of his Italian troops: '. . . we must not expect more of them than is reasonable, particularly when they are being led into battle against their own compatriots. There can be no doubt that these troops will be subjected to all kinds of influences and will be enticed to desert; if the luck of war goes against us in the first battle, then I shall not answer for their loyalty; such an experience would not even be surprising; it is as old as history itself.'[21]

None the less, despite these weaknesses, Metternich did manage to exercise considerable influence, if not quite leadership or hegemony, over a large part of Europe. In this he was aided by the fact that many of Europe's sovereigns and leaders like himself, were old enough to remember the period of the French Revolution and Napoleon. This would be a drawback in 1848 when most of them were to lose their nerve, but until then it was an advantage. Fear of revolution kept them working in concert and Metternich was able to play upon their fears. The revolutions in Spain and Naples in 1820, for example, not to mention the revolt of the Semenovskii imperial guards, made Tsar Alexander I abandon his so-called liberalism and come running to Metternich as 'a pupil to his master',[22] while his brother, Nicholas I, in 1833 after the revolutions of 1830 used the words: 'I am come to put myself under the command of my chief.' He added: 'I look to you to give me a hint when I make any mistake.'[23] Metternich was very fortunate that matters turned out this way, for this general fear of revolution and the sects enabled him to preach his views about monarchical solidarity to an already converted audience. It also enabled him, despite Austria's weaknesses, to become the spokesman for the conservative cause in Europe. Paradoxically, it may even have been the case that the very weaknesses of the Monarchy worked to Metternich's advantage. In itself, it was a threat to no other power; as a supra-national and absolutist state, it could hardly countenance nationalism or liberalism; it was clearly also a territorially satiated state. Hence Metternich's constant pleadings to respect treaty rights, to consult diplomatically before resorting to force, to respect the claims of prescription and tradition, were obviously sincere. They had to be. The Monarchy's vital interests required peace and monarchical solidarity. Metternich, in fact, viewed the Empire as a European microcosm: a system in which a variety of nationalities coexisted within a monarchical framework based on social hierarchy and the rule of law. Placed at the centre of the continent, it was also a 'European necessity', the very pivot of the balance of power. Hence as he told Wellington in 1824, Europe was like 'a fatherland' to him. By this he simply meant that as an aristocrat he could fit into aristocratic society anywhere in Europe, while as a Habsburg minister he could, for the reasons outlined immediately above, identify the interests of Europe with those of the Habsburg Monarchy. His Europeanism, on the other hand, has been challenged by Schroeder[24] as a smokescreen for Austrian self-interest. Metternich himself would scarcely have been able to understand the distinction. Certainly he would have rejected Schroeder's argument that in abandoning Britain at Troppau in 1820, he abandoned European solidarity. That, he would have argued, was best displayed in resisting revolution. But as he complained: 'With such a France and such an England how is it to be withstood?'[25] For him: 'There exists in Europe only one issue of any moment and that is revolution.'[26] Europe was a political and social order which had to be protected against it. If the British were unwilling to join in, then *they* had abandoned Europe. There was little point in abandoning it also merely for the sake of diplomatic conferences. As he told Apponyi: '. . . from the time Liberalism gained the upper hand in France and England this kind of meeting began to degenerate for it is an attempted compromise between the temper of the Right and the temper of the Left and these two powers are mutually destructive of each other.'[27] Roy Bridge, on the other hand, has argued that even on a factual level, Schroeder is wrong regarding events at Troppau: 'In terms of the practical issues of the day, the fundamental community of interests between Britain and Austria had not been affected at all. . . . British observers had after all gone to Laibach; Castlereagh had done nothing to hinder Austria's progress in Naples; and over Piedmont he had coldly rebuffed French criticism of Metternich. As the Greek Question arose to the fore in the summer so too did the Anglo-Austrian community of interests. . .'[28] It was Canning, not Metternich, who made the breach irreparable.

With England abandoning the struggle against the revolution and France forever damned as being the homeland of it, Metternich's diplomacy became increasingly dependent on Russian support. Russia was by far the mightiest of the Continental powers, despite her administrative and economic weaknesses. What the Tsar dreamed of at night, Gentz wrote, he could carry out in the morning. This power had been Metternich's greatest anxiety before the conversion to reaction of Alexander I. Between 1825 and 1833, he was to have similar anxieties regarding Nicholas I. After all, if Russia chose to destroy the Ottoman Empire, Austria would find herself either a client state of the Tsars or at war with them. The Greek revolt offered Nicholas a perfect opportunity to strike at Turkey, and after the battle of Navarino he may even have been tempted to exploit his position. Nesselrode declared: 'What will our friend Metternich say of this great triumph? He will repeat his old principles over and over again and talk of rights.'[29] To which Metternich retorted: 'Carnot, Danton and their like thought and said the same. But in spite of that, it was the boring old principles that swept them away.'[30] Nicholas, in fact, had no great love for the Greeks, whom he regarded as rebels, and no desire whatsoever to destroy the Ottoman Empire. His own one, he believed, was already too large and a weak Turkey, he understood, provided a better guarantee for Russian security than either a reformed Ottoman Empire or a partition of that state between the major European powers. He claimed repeatedly to have no territorial designs on other states, but made it equally clear that his own territories were not to be threatened; that no other power should dominate the Balkans; and that the Polish settlement of 1815 was not to be overturned. His policies, in fact, were the same as those of Metternich: to preserve peace and the 1815 treaties. When this was all cleared up in 1833 at Munchengraetz, Metternich proclaimed: 'We acquit Russia of any aggressive views with regard to the Ottoman Empire.'[31] Metternich, as a result, could, as Engel-Janosi has argued, make Western Europe his primary concern and spend most of his time attempting to split or (keep split) Great Britain and France.[32]

The solidarity of the so-called 'Northern Courts' (Austria, Prussia and Russia) was a marked feature of the period after 1833. Nor was fear of revolution its only foundation. Family ties and monarchical solidarity were also involved. Frederick William III of Prussia was Nicholas's father-in-law, Frederick William IV his brother-in-law. The Prussian monarchs, in turn, held Francis I of Austria in high esteem as the last Holy Roman Emperor, and although Frederick William believed that Prussia had special claims to hold the military command in Germany, in his dreams of a new German Empire he automatically assumed that the imperial crown should be worn by the Habsburgs. Nicholas, too, felt a special relationship towards Austria after 1835, when Francis I, before his death, extracted a special promise from the Tsar that he would protect the interests of his feeble-minded son and successor, Ferdinand. Nicholas, who was shocked by Ferdinand's physical and mental incapacities, was only too happy to oblige. He has, indeed, been accused of naïveté regarding foreign monarchs. According to Norman Rich, for example: 'Among his weaknesses as a diplomat was his predilection for dealing directly with other monarchs or their representatives, his confidence that he could solve the most complicated international problems seriously through such personal diplomacy, and his belief that he could trust his fellow monarchs as he believed they trusted him.'[33] Hence Nicholas took his commitment to protect Ferdinand very seriously. Besides, just like Metternich, he saw the Habsburg Monarchy as a European necessity, or as Nesselrode put it in a memorandum of 27 June 1848: 'The void which its disappearance would create would be so enormous and the difficulty of filling it so great, that it ought to continue for a long time yet, given the lack of anything which could be put in its place.'[34]

Given Russia's dominance in the East, Metternich's greatest influence was exercised in Italy and Germany. The Vienna settlement had made the Monarchy the leading power in both areas and Metternich had a freer hand in both, therefore, to practise what he preached. In Italy he began with a number of powerful advantages: possession of Lombardy-Venetia; dynastic links with the Central Italian duchies; the fragmentation of the peninsula into a number of weak states; the treaties which allied these to Austria; and their dependence on Austria's economy. In addition, there were certain intangible factors: a common fear of revolution on the part of the Italian sovereigns; fear of domination by France; and Austria's reputation for good government. For in Italy, Austria could really present herself as a model for sovereigns to follow: her administration in Lombardy-Venetia was by common consent the most efficiently run in the peninsula; her judicial and educational systems were the most advanced in all Italy; and the standard of living enjoyed by her Italian subjects reflected the most developed economy of the Italian states.

Metternich, in fact, was constantly forced to encourage the Italian sovereigns to reform. The chaotic state of the administration in the Papal States and Naples in particular stood in contradiction to his belief in efficient, centralized rule. Worse still, it enfeebled the struggle against the revolution in that very part of Europe where the sects were most at home. Thus he advised the Pope to create a centralized, efficiently organized administration run by a professional bureaucracy recruited from men of talent; a legal system purged of the confusion, inequity and inhumanity of the Old Regime and incorporating the principle of equality before the law and some guarantee of equal rights against arbitrary procedures; a financial system capable of providing an adequate revenue without overburdening taxpayers; and an efficient police and military capable of maintaining internal order. Similar advice was given to other sovereigns, and a programme was put through at the Laibach Congress intended to force all Italian states to reorganize their administration under Austrian supervision. Yet his efforts remained without success and in fact never really came close to achieving any.

The reasons for this are straightforward. There was, for a start, a certain distrust of Austria in Italy. This was not because – as some Italians alleged – Metternich had designs on Italian territory. The Chancellor resisted pressure to annex part of Piedmont in 1821 and part of the Papal States ten years later. There was, however, a xenophobic resistance to Austria in Italy which he exacerbated by his constant tendency to lecture Italian rulers and to insist on his advice being followed. His efforts, moreover, to negotiate postal treaties which would have brought all Italian mail under Austrian inspection and his attempts to establish an Italian League analogous to the German Confederation under Austria's presidency created resentment on the part of princes who had no objection to intervention against the revolution but who protested vehemently against any encroachment of their own legitimate rights as sovereigns. Thus the same princes who were all too content to ignore reform in the secure knowledge that Austria would intervene to save them if the worst should happen, rebuffed the Chancellor's attempts to coordinate the anti-revolutionary struggle which he was waging on their behalf. Metternich himself very often despaired of them. Thus although he was determined to intervene in Naples in 1820, by 1847 he was much more reluctant to pull the Neapolitan chestnuts out of the fire. Given the reaction of Sardinia and the Papal States to Radetzky's 'occupation' of Ferrara in 1847 – something which Metternich had originally supported[35] – he thought it best to wait for the revolution to reach Lombardy and Venetia before giving Radetzky orders to smash it. None the less, for most of the period 1815–48, Austria had the Italian situation pretty much under her exclusive control.[36]

In Germany, Metternich's task was at once easier and more difficult. It was easier thanks to the organization of the German Confederation which could pass all sorts of repressive legislation in the name of the German states as a whole; on the other hand, the more developed national consciousness of the Germans plus the growth of representative and constitutional institutions, especially in the southern German states, meant that opposition to his principles was much more articulate and widespread.

Metternich viewed Germany in much the same way as he viewed Italy – as a 'geographical expression'. Significantly, he always referred to the German Confederation as a 'European' institution – not a German one – and declared that both Austria and Prussia were European powers which just happened to be part of it, in much the same way that the kings of Holland and Denmark were represented in it through Luxemburg and Schleswig-Holstein. The Confederation itself, in any case, had no powers. Austria and Prussia fixed its business beforehand and Metternich used it as much as possible as a mere organ through which to extend his repressive policies throughout Germany. Prussia, for her part, was quite content to follow Austria in these matters and even sought Metternich's advice on constitutional reform. Predictably, he advised the Prussian monarch not to establish a central parliament and to emasculate the powers of the local diets which the king had unfortunately already promised. This advice was duly taken and in 1828 only a very few enfeebled diets were established inside Prussia. German liberalism had received a body blow.

At first it seemed as if Metternich's policies would succeed in making Germany an integral part of his system by establishing Austrian control of political life there through Metternich's usual methods. The Karlsbad decrees of 1819 – passed by the Confederation after the assassination of Kotzebue – laid down that university teachers judged to be politically unsound were to be dismissed and that student societies were to be dissolved; a press law empowered governments to control all publications of less than twenty pages; and a central investigating commission of the Confederation was established to investigate revolutionary movements and disturbances. Then by the Final Act of the Vienna Congress of the following year, Article 13 of the Confederation was modified (it empowered member states to grant constitutions) by a declaration to the effect that all sovereign power in a member state was to be united in the head of state alone and that local diets might advise their sovereigns only to a limited extent. These provisions, finally, were reinforced by the Six Acts of 1832 which, in the aftermath of the 1830 revolutions, reconfirmed the provisions of 1820 and established a commission to determine to what extent the provincial diets had already encroached on sovereign powers. It was as a result of this commission's findings that several diets and universities were in fact closed down. When the Western powers objected to this, the decrees of the Vienna Ministers' Conference of 1834 established an even more repressive censorship and spy network.

The Metternich system in Germany, however, was undermined by two developments. The first was unforeseen and the second unavoidable. In the first place, Prussia's efforts to consolidate her territories soon led to the creation of the *Zollverein* or Customs Union and, in the second, the war crises of 1830 and 1840 demonstrated Austria's growing inability to defend Germany against France.

Prussia, as a result of the 1815 settlement, had secured control of the major waterways and trading routes of Germany. In order to exploit her position as well as to consolidate her territories, she launched a Prussian customs union in 1819. This *Zollverein* first covered an area inhabited by only some 10 million Germans, but very quickly Prussia's smaller neighbours were forced to accept the Prussian tariff until, by 1833, the greater part of Germany had been absorbed within the union. The threat to Austria's interests which these developments represented had been perceived by Metternich, who had done his utmost to frustrate the Prussian achievement. Yet it was to no avail. Austrian industry was not competitive enough to allow the Monarchy itself to join, and the rival customs unions – the middle and southern German ones – eventually adhered to the Prussian system. Metternich warned the Emperor that 'a state within a state' was growing up inside the Confederation and that Prussia could use this situation 'to weaken the influence of Austria' in Germany and 'to make Austria appear a foreign country'.[37] He predicted: '. . . the links which bind Austria to the other states of the Germanic Confederation will gradually become loosened and in the end break entirely, thanks to this barrier . . . and to those machinations which tend to change a material into a moral and political separation.'[38] His counter-strategy, however, namely to construct a rival system of commerce connecting Germany with the Adriatic through Austria and Northern Italy, never achieved a significant measure of success.

In his memorandum to the Emperor, Metternich used the words: 'without Austria, Germany is incapable of meeting external danger; without the cooperation of the whole of Germany, Austria cannot find the means of developing her power'. Yet only the second half of this statement was true. For when in 1830 it looked as if a war with France was likely, Austria could match Prussia's offer of 250,000 men with only 170,000. Likewise in 1840, when war again seemed imminent, it was Prussia who took the lead. Finally, the Germans were given to understand that Austrian strategists envisaged a retreat before the French in southern Germany if and when a war should occur. Little wonder then that, when a revolution broke out in Paris in 1848, it was Prussia, not Austria, which Russia encouraged to defend Germany from attack. These potential weaknesses in the Austrian position, however, did not become fatal until the 1860s.[39] Besides, the supposed diplomatic benefits accruing to Prussia from the *Zollverein* have always been wildly exaggerated (she was deserted by most of its members in both 1850 and 1866) and even List, the German economist who was the leading spokesman for protectionism in Germany, discounted the political advantages it was held to produce for Prussia. As for the relative military weakness of Austria, this, of course, was never proved before 1866, and in 1850 seemed to be contradicted. Thus, neither of these points should count too much to Metternich's discredit. As things stood, Engel-Janosi's verdict seems acceptable: 'Metternich strove during the period of cooperation between Austria and Prussia to smooth over all possible sources of irritation between the two states with intelligence and tact. He took into consideration the sensitivities of the Prussians regarding German policy and avoided pressuring them by means of the votes of the smaller of the German kingdoms or states in the Federal Diet at Frankfurt. He always took care that Berlin and Vienna had reached agreement over important issues before they came before the Diet. Since his interest was more concerned with the European problem as a whole than with the German one, since his fears lay with the social question (in 1849 he called himself more of a socialist than a politician), Metternich was satisfied that during this period Prussia assumed the predominant position in North Germany.'[40]

Regarding Britain and France, Metternich had very little room for manoeuvre. He could only hope to exploit their differences as well as their fears of revolution. Fortunately, from his point of view, in the 1830s and 1840s these two liberal powers found much to quarrel about, so that the Quadruple Alliance of 1834 between Britain, France, Spain and Portugal, for example, never developed into a real ideological camp of any coherence. In fact, over Belgium, Spain and even Tahiti, the two powers came close to war and it proved possible for a couple of years after the dispute between them over the Spanish marriages of 1846 for Metternich to cooperate with Guizot concerning the civil war in Switzerland. Palmerston, on the other hand, was never persuaded by Metternich's jeremiads: 'If Metternich would only leave people a little alone', he wrote, 'he would find his crop of revolutions which he is nursing up with so much care soon die away upon the stalk.'[41] Hence, he had little influence in London. In Paris, on the other hand, he claimed to have a secret weapon. He told at least one ambassador that he was blackmailing Louis Philippe and that in the last resort he would therefore never have any trouble from him. Perhaps that was why France became bored with the unnaturally defeatist nature of Orleanist foreign policy. But this is an issue which will have to be investigated.[42] Certainly, many ambassadors were willing to believe practically anything he told them and, despite the previously mentioned quips about his honesty, there were many more diplomats who took him to be the very model for their profession. His diligence and negotiating skill were universally admired as well as his unequalled experience and knowledge. Berthier de Sauvigny, however, provides a very amusing example of a Russian ambassador who so emulated Metternich's convoluted manner of expression while in discussion with him that the Chancellor felt cause for complaint.[43] Not that he realized that he was being parodied. He was simply being bored. Yet it was

Metternich himself who on another occasion confessed that he could bore men to death.[44]

How successful a diplomat, therefore, was Metternich? As we have seen, there is certainly a case to be made out that he was irrelevant and boring. And there can be no doubt that the hand he had to play was as weak as that described by Gentz in 1818: '[Austria] has reduced her military resources even beyond the limits and proportions that prudence allows. She has neglected her army in all respects. . . . Her finances are recovering little by little . . . but that would not make it any easier for her to meet the costs of a serious war. She would have no liquid funds, emergency taxes would not pay for half a campaign, sources of credit are dried up for a long time to come, and nobody from now on, can count on British subsidies. Therefore, everything combines to bind Austria to a peaceful system.'[45] Yet in spite of these points, it is difficult to deny that Metternich set the tone for a whole era of European diplomacy. By preaching the sanctity of treaties (and it is noticeable that his reputation declined after the annexation of Crakow in 1846 when Nicholas I of Russia forced him to break the 1815 treaties to do so) and the need to uphold the social and political order against all challenges, he became the Robespierre of Reaction, the spokesman of all those who would not compromise with revolution or democracy. As Austrian Chancellor, he may not have had the means to achieve all his political objectives, yet it is difficult to refute the fact that the Europe of his day came closer to his ideals than to either those of the democrats or the constitutionalists. His achievement, of course, was negative: his hold on Germany and Italy was so strong that people believed that the Holy Alliance actually meant something. He may not have controlled events even there, yet his systematic call for strong monarchical governments to cooperate to preserve an aristocratic *status quo* meant that he became identified in the minds of his contemporaries everywhere with the survival of the old régime. His policies never changed; his principles never altered. He was a rock of order, he proclaimed, and even in 1848 on the steps of the British Museum, the old ideologue could still inform his fellow exile, Guizot, that it had never entered his mind that he might have been wrong. His reputation remains highest, however, less with those who sympathize with his unbending resistance to liberalism than with those who admire his ability to preserve the European balance of power. His achievement in converting Alexander I of Russia to the conservative cause after the fall of Napoleon is contrasted with the failure of Roosevelt and Churchill to convert the

Soviets in the same manner after the defeat of Hitler in 1945. Partly, this is Cold War history – one suspects that some of Metternich's admirers are equally incapable of differentiating between liberalism and communism – yet the parallel is not an altogether unilluminating one. He can certainly be defended against more particular criticisms – taking Italian territory in 1815; consenting to a Bourbon restoration in France; failing to stand up more strongly to Russia in the East; or failing to give stronger support to Louis Philippe. These criticisms fail entirely in the light of all the possible alternatives. If Austria had refused to take Lombardy-Venetia, would not France have dominated Italy? Perhaps more support could have been given to Louis Philippe but, if so, how much and at what price? Could a Bonapartist regency have really helped preserve the peace of Europe? And with what weapons was Austria supposed to fight the Russians, who after all were the most powerful supporters of reaction in Europe? From his own perspective, therefore, it is difficult to see where Metternich went wrong.

Yet doubts remain. Granted his diplomatic skills, granted that he played a weak hand very well, granted the large measure of luck he enjoyed thanks to the policies pursued by Russia, did he not, as Palmerston and so many of his contemporaries argued, merely stoke up trouble for the future by his obsession with revolution and his refusal to contemplate reform? To answer this question, we must look not merely at his foreign policy but also at his position in the Monarchy's domestic affairs.

METTERNICH AND DOMESTIC POLICY

Metternich believed, of course, that the only proper system of government was monarchy, and by monarchy he meant the pure rather than the constitutional brand. The latter might be acceptable in Britain after centuries of adaptation, but even there he distrusted it. In France, he viewed it simply as a front for revolution. Thus when he spoke about monarchy, he meant one in which a ruler ruled. A sovereign who did not exercise sovereignty he held to be a contradiction in terms. On the other hand, he was no supporter of arbitrary monarchy, which was seen as an oriental phenomenon. A sovereign had to be advised and to follow orderly practices of government. He had to uphold the laws and the social order and, of course, the laws of God. If he were not to lose respect, he would have to demonstrate his capacity to exercise justice as well as authority. In practice, this meant that there should be a powerful sovereign whose wishes, formulated in consultation with others, should be enforced by a centrally organized civil service and judiciary. Such was the system of stern paternalism which Metternich would have liked to see prevail in Europe as a whole.

In the Habsburg Empire itself there were many obstacles on the road to achieving it. Francis I, for a start – and he was monarch until 1835 – had little sympathy for organized government. His central administration lacked direction, despite his personal interference in even the smallest matters of administration. Finally, there was the problem of personalities, which became acute after the accession of the mentally retarded Ferdinand I and the establishment of the *Staatskonferenz* as a *de facto* council of regency. The result was that Metternich, for nearly the whole of his period of office, was dissatisfied with the way in which the Empire was run. He complained that 'the Empire did not have a government', or, rather, one that worked.[46] His favourite phrase was that it was 'administered' rather than 'governed'.

It is sometimes argued that Metternich hoped to improve matters by 'federalizing' the Monarchy. Yet, while it is certainly true that in 1817 he drew up plans for a reform of the administration, it is extremely doubtful whether these were really intended to devolve power away from the centre. On the contrary, these plans were intended to rationalize and increase the efficiency of the powers of central government. The theory that Metternich genuinely wanted to devolve power is in any case really the product of Cold War history. It was first put forward in a major way in the 1950s by critics in America who admired his defence of Europe against the Left and who envisaged him as some sort of nineteenth-century John Foster Dulles stemming the tide of red revolution there. For example, Peter Viereck, writing in 1951, maintained that Metternich in 1817 had 'urged freer institutions for the rest of the empire, with an embryonic parliament, which, once started, would have inevitably assumed an ever greater governing power. Possibly central Europe might even have followed England's evolutionary road of 1832 towards a freer society instead of the revolutionary road of 1848 and 1918. His plans (to summarise from two different memoranda of 1817) included a "deliberative body of notables", partly elected from provincial diets and partly appointed to represent the country in "scrutiny of the budget and every law." Far-sighted in view of the Slav and Italian revolts that were to wreck the monarchy, is his plan of separate constitutions and separate chancellors for the chief national minorities, protecting them from the oppression of Germanisation.'[47] This theme was further bolstered in 1963 with the publication of Arthur G. Haas's book *Metternich, Reorganisation and Nationality, 1813–1818*[48] which, based as it was on archival research, appeared to confirm the revisionist interpretation of the 1817 memoranda referred to by Viereck. Haas based most of his conclusions on documents referring to Lombardy-Venetia, although the book dealt also with Illyria, a subject which he treated elsewhere.[49] According to him, Metternich in 1817 had attempted 'to form the so badly shaken Monarchy into an inwardly balanced and stable union of constituent states with equal rights', something which constituted a 'notable example of statesmanlike foresight and intelligence.'[50] Haas's work was well received by a number of experts, Professor Berthier de Sauvigny in France, for example, writing in a review that it had been Metternich's aim 'to bring the turbulent Hungarian nation back into line by balancing and surrounding it with other entities endowed with the same privileges and competences'.[51] The Hungarian historian, Erzsébet Andics, was later to state quite the opposite case, namely that 'one of the fundamental aims . . . of Metternich's proposals was in reality to take away from Hungary her ancient rights; not, however, to endow other peoples with similar rights',[52] yet for many years no further analysis was made of the Chancellor's 1817 memoranda. My own conclusion, when I re-examined them for an article for a *Festschrift* for A. J. P. Taylor,[53] was that Haas had been absolutely mistaken. Far from wishing to federalize the Monarchy, I interpreted the evidence to show that Metternich had wished to centralize it, but had tried to do so behind a constitutional façade, which would have appeared to give a voice to local interests. I concluded: 'His essential function when all is said and done was to create an illusion of power on Austria's behalf in international affairs. Who can wonder that he was similarly tempted to balance appearance against reality in domestic affairs? Were he alive today he would be amused to find his method retaining effect.'[54] That he was no closet liberal can be determined by the role he played and by the policies he pursued in Austria's domestic affairs.

Reference has already been made to Metternich's relations with Francis I and to his dissatisfaction with the way in which the government was run. The problem was that Francis relied on the so called *Kabinettsweg*. This meant that the monarch commissioned reports on whatever interested him – often extremely trivial matters

– from whoever he wished and often had these supplemented by further reports, all of which might take him literally years to read and to decide upon. Metternich himself complained that his memoranda of 1817 remained in Francis's desk drawer right up until 1835, with the Emperor still unable to act upon them. Hence it was little wonder that the Chancellor wanted to bring some order and regularity into the decision-making processes of the Monarchy. He in no way, of course, wished to undermine his sovereign's right to exercise his sovereignty, but he did want him to exercise that sovereignty efficiently.

Basically, the system which Metternich would have liked to devise for the Monarchy (and which indeed he recommended elsewhere) was that the government should consist first of all of a council advising the Emperor (i.e. a *Staatsrat* or, if a few representatives were to be added from the local diets to give them a semblance of influence, a *Reichsrat*).[55] This would have had a purely consultative role. In other words, it would advise only on those issues which were presented to it, and its advice could be accepted or rejected by the monarch. Moreover, as Metternich conceived it, it would not deliberate as a full body but in sections which would deliberate orally. This, appearances notwithstanding, was to expedite its business. Once the monarch had received its advice, however, he was then to come to a decision on any particular issue in consultation with his Ministerial Conference (*Ministerkonferenz*). This, in Metternich's ideal form, would have consisted of a number of executive ministers who would have supervised the *Hofstellen* or administrative departments and who would have been responsible to the Emperor alone for enforcing imperial policy. Much of this was derived from Napoleonic administrative practice, since Metternich, as ambassador to France, had been highly impressed by the more despotic aspects of the Bonapartist régime. Napoleon, in fact, had won his eternal admiration for having imposed order on the chaos of revolutionary France.

In Austria, however, Francis I could come to no decision about reform so that for the whole of his reign Metternich was forced to operate within a system of administrative chaos. Indeed, instead of the sharp division in functions and in personnel between the *Staatsrat* and the *Ministerkonferenz*, which Metternich wished to see established, an overlapping of both was prevalent as Francis operated his system, and the *Staatsrat* functioned as the principal body advising the Emperor. The *Staatsrat* itself, however, never became an executive body, but operated rather as another part of the bureaucracy. Represented on it were most of the heads of the *Hofstellen* so that, in practice, it became a sort of coordinating body for the higher civil service. Francis, however, still managed to impede its work by demanding individual written reports from every member concerned with each and every piece of advice and very often by consulting people who were not even members at all. To Metternich's particular chagrin, he also refused to develop a proper Ministerial Conference. In fact, by 1830, Metternich himself was the only 'Minister' in the government – the post of Finance Minister had been abolished in 1829; that of Minister of the Interior had fallen into disuse almost as soon as it had been created in 1818 – and when the Ministerial Conference met, it was not really an executive conference at all. Apart from Metternich, it would be attended by the chief of police as well as by the heads of the political and financial sections of the *Staatsrat*. In any case, it was not summoned very often. Metternich was forced to accept, therefore, that the *Kabinettsweg* would continue. The best he could do was to develop *ad hoc* ways to get around the muddle which was created.

His influence was circumscribed after 1828, however, by the emergence of Count Franz Anton Kolowrat-Liebsteinsky as the dominant figure in the *Staatsrat*. Kolowrat is sometimes portrayed as a liberal and as an ideological opponent of Metternich inside the Austrian bureaucracy, but such a picture has to be modified. Kübeck, a senior Austrian civil servant of this period and one of the few of bourgeois origins, bitterly pointed out in his diaries how Kolowrat used his influence with the Emperor to have his aristocratic relatives and protégés appointed to the best administrative posts. He also quoted Kolowrat's description of his differences with Metternich as he explained them to the Chancellor (see note 3): 'You are completely wrong about me and the people with whom I mix. You think that my principles are different from yours. That is wrong.' Nor was he dissimulating. For he had originally won influence at Court when as Governor of Bohemia he had submitted a list of the best-known freemasons there with his own father's name at the top.[56] However, he did like to think that he was a much more subtle conservative than Metternich.

His opposition to Metternich's 'forest of bayonets', however, stemmed from much more than subtlety alone. Kolowrat's influence rested on the fact that he became head of both the political and financial sections of the *Staatsrat* (he later surrendered the latter post, but only to take charge of an all-powerful financial commission entrusted with the control of government expenditure) and, as such, he found himself in a constant battle with the Chancellor to balance the budget by reducing the costs of the army and the police. Given Metternich's natural inclination to expand both these bodies, not to mention his apparent lack of economic sense (he was constantly in debt and often arranged 'state' loans for himself through the Rothschilds; he also received a pension from the Tsar), it is hardly surprising that he should have encountered Kolowrat's resistance. Despite the support, however, of the Emperor's adjutant and head of the military section of the *Staatsrat*, Count Charles Clam-Martinitz, Metternich proved unable to weaken Kolowrat's hold on the purse-strings and on the police and army estimates. As has been seen, this helped undermine Austria's position in foreign affairs.

The lack of administrative cohesion became immeasurably worse after the death of Francis I. If the Empire had lacked direction under Francis, it lost much of what it had had under the rule of his son, the retarded Ferdinand I. Incapable of reading documents or of following an argument, he should never have been allowed to accede to the throne. Yet Metternich had agreed with Francis to arrange for a normal succession in the interests of 'legitimacy' – and almost certainly in the hope of achieving supreme power for himself. He certainly conspired to secure this through Francis's last will and testament and by his manoeuvrings in 1836 to circumscribe Kolowrat's influence in internal affairs. The latter had returned to his estates on the grounds of ill-health – Metternich said that he had 'piles going up to his head' – and had given Metternich an opportunity to restructure the system of government. A strong Ministerial Conference was therefore set up and separated from the *Staatsrat*, the status of which was much reduced. Metternich was to preside over the former (which would function in fact as a council of regency) and Kolowrat was given the choice of becoming either a member of the Conference or of remaining a section chief of the *Staatsrat*. He was told that he could not be both. Metternich was clearly intending to establish himself as the director of Austrian affairs.

The Chancellor, however, had reckoned without the influence of the imperial family. At this crucial moment, the Archduke John who, like his equally competent brother, the Archduke Charles, had been excluded from power by Francis and Metternich for years, returned to Vienna and upset Metternich's plans. To accommodate Kolowrat, the Archduke negotiated a scheme whereby a new Conference came into being, presided over by the Emperor and with a permanent membership of the Archduke Louis, the Archduke Francis Charles, Kolowrat and Metternich. Kolowrat was promised control of financial affairs and internal matters on condition that he surrender his membership of the *Staatsrat*. Kolowrat agreed and Metternich, clearly admitting defeat, offered neither resignation nor resistance. Thereafter the Conference in practice came to be headed by the Archduke Louis, who proved even more reluctant than the Emperor Francis to reach decisions, and whose preference for separate written reports soon reduced the flow of business to a standstill. Moreover, according to Kübeck, the Archduke Louis soon fell under the influence of Kolowrat whose position became unassailable. The Archduke John, as Kübeck interpreted it, had therefore 'effected a compromise that [was] little different from a complete defeat of Prince Metternich'.[57] He continued: '[Kolowrat] in effect is supreme head of the *Staatsrat*, master of the money power, of all employments and of the fate of all officials (through the police), head of the entire camarilla, and – through his position – the deciding spokesman in the Conference.' This has led one historian to conclude: 'Kolowrat had thus regained the greater part of the influence and power he had wielded before the crisis, with the additional advantage of being officially confirmed in much of what had been vague, undefined and contrary to regulations. He now essentially fulfilled the functions of a prime minister, an office regarded by his rival as "quite impossible" for Austria and suitable for "no sensible servant of the state".'[58] Such a conclusion, however, not only displays a certain naïveté regarding Metternich's ambitions in the years 1835–8, but vastly over-estimates the extent of Kolowrat's influence. It is true that he held control of the purse-strings in the Monarchy just as before 1835, but the man who really controlled the higher imperial police was Metternich, who likewise had the leading voice in the affairs of Italy and Hungary. There is a strong case to be made out, therefore, that, given his control of defence and foreign affairs also, Metternich's position was stronger than Kolowrat's.

Regarding domestic policy itself, Metternich did his level best to ensure that the kingdoms of Lombardy-Venetia and Hungary were run as Austrian provinces as far as possible. In the case of Lombardy-Venetia, this was easy to engineer since Francis I in 1818 had given his viceroy there, the Archduke Rainer, such little power that it was immediately clear to everyone that that this was how the kingdom was supposed to be administered. The viceroy could only mediate in (but not resolve) disputes between the governors of Lombardy and Venetia, and all important decisions were taken in Vienna. Essentially, therefore, Rainer's was a ceremonial role – as was that of the Central Congregations or diets whose wishes were constantly ignored until they lapsed into passivity from the early 1820s onwards. Austrian Italy was ruled through the *Hofstellen* and *Staatsrat* which gave the governors their orders. The governors in turn ran their provinces through delegates and district commissioners. Metternich approved of this but regretted the fact that the *Staatsrat* and *Hofstellen* would usually take ages to reach decisions and that they clogged up the administration with endless reports and paperwork.

In Italy, however, Metternich succeeded in short-circuiting the bureaucratic system. From 1826 the Emperor allowed him to attach a special agent from the State Chancellery or Foreign Ministry at the governor's office in Milan. Ostensibly his job was to expedite business with the other Italian states, but his position in fact was more important than that. His real function was to ensure that Metternich had direct control of Italian policy. Instructions drafted by Metternich made it clear that 'while paying attention to the usual diplomatic formalities and rules', his agents were 'to take note of the general political situation and do what [was] necessary in that regard'.[59] Thus they were to act as a channel between the governor of Lombardy and the State and Court Chancellery on all matters of mutual concern and especially on police affairs. Metternich underlined, however, that although they were being attached to the governor's office and would be expected to work with him, this 'in no way [altered their] relationship to [him, i.e. Metternich] . . .' and that they '[did] not cease to remain directly under [his] orders'. He used these men thereafter, therefore, as his main source of information on Italy and it was on their regular – sometimes daily – reports that he based his policies.

Most of their correspondence consisted of regular surveys of Italian opinion and of police reports on the sects, and for most of the period 1815–48 the reports they sent in were complacently optimistic. There was no attempt to deny that the Austrians were disliked by the upper classes (i.e. the local aristocracy and the bourgeoisie) and by Italian liberals, but it was always pointed out that the vast majority of the population had no political opinions and that the sects were far less active in Austrian Italy than in the rest of the peninsula. Metternich himself took pride in this. The government also consoled itself with the belief that the Italians were divided among themselves and that what Metternich referred to as *Munizipalgeist* – inter-city rivalry – would prevent any general anti-Austrian movement from emerging. There was even a reluctance to believe that Charles Albert represented a threat to Austrian rule, a reluctance which prevailed right up to 1848. Thus Metternich's agents advised the Chancellor to follow a policy of bread and circuses respecting Italy: 'At the time of the Romans, the circus was the state secret that rendered Italians submissive to the government and modern Italians are no less difficult to please or less manageable in this respect.'[60] Metternich consequently saw little need to change things. As far as he was concerned, he now had direct control of events in Italy without having to worry about the bureaucratic channels of the *Hofstellen*. He could, therefore, fob off Italian requests for change with his usual clichés, telling one visitor: 'I have not time to bother with details of administration. My job is more important than that.'[61] On another occasion (1845), the mayor of Milan was greeted by him in the following manner: 'Metternich was most amiable and received him with great courtesy, yet always avoided saying anything definite about our country. He always embarked upon generalities and what he said had no more importance than talk about the weather.'[62]

With the accession of Pius IX to the Holy See, however, and the growing anti-Austrian feeling in Italy in the years 1846–8, Metternich took slightly more interest in the administration of Lombardy-Venetia and sent his right-hand man, Count Ficquelmont, on special mission there in the autumn of 1847. This mission has given rise to the belief that, as in 1817, Metternich tried, just before the revolutions of 1848, to federalize the Austrian administration. A. J. P. Taylor, for example, supported this view in his study of the Italian Question in European diplomacy between 1847 and 1849.[63] In fact, however, Metternich did not plan to change anything in 1847–48, nor did Ficquelmont propose to federalize the Monarchy. His starting point was, rather: 'How can we go on running the Kingdom [of Lombardy-Venetia] as a province but organise it and above all govern it in such a fashion that we might present it as an Italian state to the hostile movement that the other Italian states want to stir up against us?'[64] And even his solution – a feeble attempt to bolster the position of the viceroy and his council – proved too radical for Metternich who ignored the proposals. He complained instead that 'the police department [in Vienna] [was] receiving nothing or next to nothing from Milan'.[65] Moreover, the panicky reactions of Ficquelmont and the viceroy to the so-called 'tobacco riots' in Milan in January 1848 served only to increase the Chancellor's contempt for the proposed reforms. At the price of driving Ficquelmont to submit his resignation, he made it crystal clear that a little initiative on the part of the local authorities would serve Austrian interests much better than administrative change.

Ficquelmont now told Metternich that he was deceiving himself, that despite all his agents' reports over the years, he was 'unaware of the most essential and serious matters which concern[ed] the general interests of the country as well as particular administrative, financial and judicial ones, matters which governors [had] been submitting to the competent authorities for years but which were still unexamined and unanswered'.[66] Yet Metternich would have none of it. He did not want to give more power or even more prestige to the viceroy and naturally would not accept that Austrian policy had been based on ignorance. He told Ficquelmont: 'Only by centralising the action of the various branches of authority is it possible to establish its unity and hence its force. Power distributed is no longer power.'[67] He consoled himself with the knowledge, after February 1848, that the viceroy, Ficquelmont, the governor and Field Marshal Radetzky, the commander-in-chief, were having daily conferences in Milan to coordinate whatever measures were necessary to restore order in the wake of the riots. His principle of centralizing authority was being heeded at last. He wrote: 'Here is what is needed: that we order this side of the Alps should be carried out on the other; that people there should not seek to weaken our directives but to put them into effect exactly as advised.'[68] To devolve power to Lombardy would be 'dangerous' – 'the same thing would be immediately demanded by other parts of the Empire'.[69] Thus, right until the end, Metternich was striving to ensure that Lombardy-Venetia would be treated as just another province of the Austrian Empire.

It was the Hungarians most of all, however, inside the Empire, who were to be affected by Metternich's centralizing tendencies. Hungary was the only part of the Habsburg dominions after 1815 to retain a constitutionally anomalous position, thanks to her ancient constitution. This meant that her laws had to be passed by the Hungarian Diet – albeit with royal approval – before the Vienna government could secure the Hungarian troops and revenue it sought. Hungary also retained an elective system of county administration, and representatives to the Lower House of the Diet were subject to recall by county assemblies. All this meant that the work of the Hungarian Chancellery in Vienna and the Palatine's Council in Pest could encounter stiff and vocal opposition from Magyar public opinion. Moreover, public opinion in Hungary was a genuine force to be reckoned with. In the period 1815–48, a greater percentage of its population had the vote than in France.

This was a situation which Metternich intensely disliked and was determined to alter. During the Napoleonic period he had toyed with the idea of using French troops to stage a *coup d'état* against the Hungarian constitution, and his proposals of 1817 to strengthen the central government of the Monarchy had been presented as a means by which to bring the Hungarians into line. He wrote: '. . . as a result of this reorganisation [centralizing the administration under a Minister of the Interior] the Hungarian and Transylvanian Chancelleries will sink from the high level at which they stand today to that of the administration in general.'[70] Finally, he opposed the programme of the Hungarian reform movement of the 1820s, 1830s and 1840s root and branch. Its proposals would have brought about a liberal and semi-independent Hungary and it, therefore, had to be crushed. Metternich told the Palatine, the Archduke Joseph: 'The Opposition today is a subversive one which exploits moderate constitutionalism in order to overthrow the government and the constitution. The Hungarian polity is a monarchical–aristocratic one. It cannot be accommodated to democratic institutions. Such institutions are in contradiction with the existing order.'[71] The Chancellor himself took the initiative against the reform movement both in the Diet (which financial needs forced the government to call in 1825, 1832–6, 1839–40, 1843–4 and 1847–8) and in the counties, boasting to his son in 1825 that he had taken 'things into his own hands'.[72] He was to continue to do so up until 1848. The policies he pursued, based on total opposition to Hungarian independence or initiative, took many forms: county electorates were influenced; the press was muzzled or controlled; the secret police was widely employed; and in the 1830s pure terror tactics were resorted to. Leading opponents of the régime were charged with treason and imprisoned. Wesselényi was sentenced to three years in jail, Kossuth to four, and Lovassy to ten. However, the public outcry was so great that such terror tactics had to be abandoned. Thereafter, Metternich attempted to control Hungary by backing the 'neo-conservative' party of Aurel Dessewffy, whose 'reform' programme amounted to an attack on the Hungarian county system. In 1841 he told the Ministerial Conference: 'If it is impossible to govern Hungary without a constitution based on the Diet, we are faced with the unavoidable task of so manipulating this constitution that it will become possible to govern Hungary in the regular fashion.'[73] He then outlined a plan to remove the counties from the control of their elected officials, officials who were to be replaced by administrators appointed by Vienna and backed up, if necessary, with military force. Further proposals included the abolition of county instructions to deputies and the presence of the police in the Diet during sessions. Metternich hoped in this way to be able to break the opposition. Aware, however, that there was a risk of provoking a national uprising, he declared that he was prepared to risk that. It was better that the government should press ahead with its proposals than leave the time and place of any final encounter to the opposition. Once again, therefore, Metternich intended to exert the greatest possible control from the centre. His proposals were partially introduced in the 1840s.

At the centre of Metternich's beliefs regarding forms of government was the principle that the monarch should be advised by a strong central government responsible only to himself and capable of administering all parts of the state in an orderly and uniform fashion. Although his class consciousness persuaded him that the aristocracy should be allowed to play a ceremonial role in emasculated estates, the Chancellor had no intention of compromising with the representative principle which he regarded as revolutionary. Public opinion, he believed, could be consulted and manipulated through the 'higher state police', and those of his energies which were not expended on foreign affairs were chiefly directed at controlling police matters. He completely dominated the president of the *Polizeihofstelle*, Count Sedlnitzky, and his own State Chancellery controlled the censorship. Indeed, police reports from all over the Empire had to be sent to Metternich personally and most of the key decisions regarding press censorship were taken by the Chancellor himself. He prided himself that his intricate system of press censorship, spies, subsidies and *cabinets noirs* ensured the stability of the Monarchy and boasted that within it nothing could happen without his knowledge. Outside, he corresponded with the chiefs of police of France and Russia. His greatest fear, in fact, was that the system of government which he had striven for years to build up – despite his failure with Kolowrat – would be toppled not from within but from without.

One final point has to be made about his efforts to consolidate the Habsburg Monarchy itself. Although he was often dispirited by the opposition he encountered in the *Staatsrat* or Hungary, and although he often voiced a pessimism which despaired of 'shoring up the mouldering structures' of the imperial administration, he had a genuine conviction in the value of his work which at times he could even idealize. He did believe that strong, central government was necessary in post-revolutionary Europe and he was convinced that concessions to liberal reform were the surest recipe for revolution. Nor would he accept that his policies had in any way disadvantaged the peoples his Emperor had ruled. As late as October 1847, he was telling his ambassador in Rome: '. . . if people would only view our Empire impartially: everything there is progressing; everything that is good and useful is advancing . . . all the reasonable demands preached by progressives have been fulfilled by us. Our Empire acknowledges the perfect equality of citizens before the law: we have no tax privileges or feudal burdens; in our Empire is found equality of taxation and the independence of justice. All parts of the Empire have assemblies of estates and a municipal system much more liberal than that which exists in countries ruled by the modern representative system. In no other empire are the nationalities more respected than ours; respect for the nationalities is indeed a necessary condition of our existence; nowhere is there less absolutist government than in our Empire, nor could there be any.'[74] The Chancellor was clearly exaggerating but there is no reason to believe that he lacked genuine conviction in the essential benevolence of his system.

METTERNICH: A VERDICT

How, finally, do we sum him up? In foreign affairs, it seems reasonable to admit that while there may have been an 'age of Metternich', it was one he set the tone for through his principles rather than his diplomacy. As for the principles themselves – respect for treaties, for rights, for prescription, for consultation – they may indeed have been boring, yet their abandonment after the Crimean War did indeed make room for the *Realpolitiker*, men like Napoleon III, Bismarck and Cavour, whose trademarks were to be war and the unbridled pursuit of *raison d'état*. That, at least, is one side of the story. The other is that Metternich himself was often prepared to resort to force in order to support his principles, that for him the aim of maintaining the *status quo* could also justify wars – of intervention and counter-revolution. Certainly, his disciples were never to be afraid to risk the *status quo* by starting wars. The trouble was that they would always lose. Metternich's great skill, on the other hand, lay in his ability not to become involved in wars he could not win. Peace, therefore, became his clarion call, but it was peace based on the 1815 treaties, on legitimacy, and aristocracy. In short, it was to be peace on his terms, or rather on those of the House of Habsburg. Only so long as Europe was willing to accept these terms could his system survive. For Austria, as he knew, was simply not strong enough to enforce them by herself. His main achievement, therefore, was in persuading the great powers for so long that Austria was the European necessity he genuinely believed her to be.

Domestically, he also had a very large part to play in Austrian history. He may not have had control of the Empire's purse-strings, but he had the major say in running the secret police and censorship and took the lead as far as Italy and Hungary were concerned. He also attempted to centralize the administration of the Empire to make it more efficient and uniform. In this, of course, he was thwarted by the imperial family. Yet it would be a mistake to assume on that account that his domestic policy was a failure. On the contrary, we have already seen the pride he took in its achievements. And he did not even mention the greatest of them: the fact that, unlike Western Europe, the Monarchy could totally avoid revolution for thirty-three years – that is, until his dismissal.

NOTES AND REFERENCES

1. *Tablettes Autrichiennes, contenant des faits, des anecdotes et des observations sur les moeurs, les usages des autrichiens et la Chronique Secrete des cours d'Allemagne, par un temoin secret.* Brussels, 1830, p. 191.
2. Quoted in É. Andics (1973) *Metternich und die Frage Ungarns.* Budapest, p. 274.
3. Elizabeth Herzog (1968) *Graf Franz Anton Kolowrat-Liebsteinsky: Seine politische Tätigkeit in Wien, 1826–1848.* Unpublished doctoral dissertation, Vienna, pp. 62–3.
4. P. W. Schroeder (1962) *Metternich's Diplomacy at its Zenith, 1820–23.* Texas.
5. A. J. P. Taylor (1967) *Europe: Grandeur and Decline.* Harmondsworth, p. 23.
6. See *inter alia*: Sir Charles Webster (1963) *The Foreign Policy of Castlereagh, 1812–1822, Britain, Austria and the European Alliance*, 2 vols. London; Sir Charles Webster (1969) *The Foreign Policy of Palmerston, Britain, the Liberal Movement and the Eastern Question*, 2 vols. London; Harold Temperley (1979), *The Foreign Policy of Canning, 1822–1827, England, the Holy Alliance, and the New World*, and Alan Sked (ed.) (1979) *Europe's Balance of Power, 1815–1848.* London and Basingstoke.
7. For Nicholas's view, see W. Bruce Lincoln (1978) *Nicholas I, Emperor and Autocrat of All the Russias.* London, p. 147; for Nesselrode's, see Constantin de Grunwald (1945) *Trois Siècles de Diplomatie Russe.* Paris, p. 188; for Canning's, see Ian C. Hannah (1938) *A History of British Foreign Policy.* London, p. 102; for the others, see Viktor Bibl (1936), *Metternich, Der Damon Osterreichs.* Leipzig and Vienna, p. 34.

8. E. Radvany (1971) *Metternich's Projects for Reform in Austria*. The Hague, p. 15.
9. *Ibid.*, p. 136.
10. *Ibid.*, pp. 14–15.
11. *Ibid.*, p. 14.
12. Antonio Schmidt-Brentano (1975) *Die Armee in Osterreich: Militär, Staat und Gesellschaft, 1848–1867*. Boppard am Rhein, p. 106.
13. C. A. Haillot (1846) *Statistique militaire et recherches sur l'organisation des armées étrangères*, Vol. I. Paris, p. 12.
14. Bibl, *op. cit.*, p. 208.
15. *Ibid.*, p. 230.
16. Johann Springer (1840) *Statistik des österreichischen Kaiserstaates*, 2 vols. Vienna, Vol. II, p. 254.
17. J. H. Blumenthal (1963) Vom Wiener Kongress zum Ersten Weltkrieg, in *Unser Heer, 300 Jahre osterreichischen Soldatentum·im Krieg und Frieden*. Vienna, Munich and Zurich, p. 216.
18. Alan Sked (1979) *The Survival of the Habsburg Empire: Radetzky, the Imperial Army and the Class War, 1848*. London and New York, note 47, p. 264.
19. Lincoln, *op. cit.*, pp. 285–6.
20. Sked, *The Survival of the Habsburg Empire*, p. 55.
21. *Ibid.*
22. Sorry! I have always associated this phrase with Alexander I, but, according to A. J. P. Taylor, it was actually employed by Nicholas in 1833. See his (1964) *The Habsburg Monarchy, 1809–1918, A History of the Austrian Empire and Austria-Hungary*. London, p. 43.
23. Lincoln, *op. cit.*, p. 147.
24. Schroeder, *op. cit.*
25. Webster, *The Foreign Policy of Palmerston*, Vol. I, p. 224.
26. Lincoln, *op. cit.*, p. 145.
27. *Ibid.*, p. 144.
28. Roy F. Bridge (1979) Allied diplomacy in peacetime: the failure of the 'Congress System', 1815–23, in Alan Sked (ed.) *Europe's Balance of Power, 1815–1848*, pp. 34–53, 45–6.
29. Bibl, *op. cit.*, p. 204.
30. *Ibid.*
31. G. A. Sandeman (1911) *Metternich*. London, pp. 239–40.
32. Friedrich Engel-Janosi (1963) *Geschichte auf dem Ballhausplatz. Essays zur österreichischen Aussenpolitik, 1830–1945*. Graz, Vienna and Cologne, pp. 45–6, 66.
33. Norman Rich (1985) *Why the Crimean War? A Cautionary Tale*. Hanover and London, p. 15.
34. de Grunwald, *op. cit.*, p. 191, note 1.
35. Alan Sked, *The Survival of the Habsburg Empire*, pp. 96–9.
36. Alan Sked (1979) The Metternich System, 1815–48, in Alan Sked (ed.) *Europe's Balance of Power, 1815–1848*, pp. 98–121, 108–11.
37. *Ibid.*, p. 118.
38. *Ibid.*
39. *Ibid.*
40. Engel-Jánosi, *op. cit.*, pp. 66–7.

41. Webster, *op. cit.*, p. 226. For Switzerland, see Alan Sked, *The Survival of the Habsburg Empire*, pp. 119–21, and Roger Bullen (1971) Guizot and the Sonderbund Crisis, *English Historical Review*, Vol. LXXXVI, July, no. CCCXL, pp. 497–526.
42. Aberdeen MSS, British Museum 43, 211(1), Sir Robert Gordon to Lord Aberdeen, Vienna 13 Dec. 1842.
43. G. de Berthier de Sauvigny (1962) *Metternich and His Times*. London, pp. 29–30.
44. '. . . knowing how to bore myself, I am just as capable of killing an adversary by the sheer weight of boredom.' Quoted by Berthier de Sauvigny, *op. cit.*, p. 26.
45. Quoted in Alan Sked, *Europe's Balance of Power*, p. 9.
46. See Radvany, *op. cit.*, p. 136.
47. Peter Viereck (1951) New views on Metternich, *Review of Politics*, XIII, p. 225.
48. Wiesbaden.
49. Arthur G. Haas (1958) Kaiser Franz, Metternich und die Stellung Illyriens, *Mitteilungen des Osterreichischen Staatsarchivs*, XI, pp. 373–98, and (1968) Metternich und die Slaven, *Gedenkschrift Martin Gohrung*. Wiesbaden, pp. 146–61.
50. Haas, Kaiser Franz etc., p. 379.
51. In *Revue d'Histoire*, Vol. 12 (1965), p. 72.
52. Erzsébet Andics (1973) *Metternich und die Frage Ungarns*. Budapest, pp. 24–5.
53. Metternich and the federalist myth, in Alan Sked and Chris Cook (eds) (1976) *Crisis and Controversy, Essays in Honour of A. J. P. Taylor*. London and Basingstoke, pp. 1–22.
54. Alan Sked, *Metternich and the Federalist Myth*, p. 20.
55. See Radvany, *op. cit*.
56. Herzog, *op. cit*.
57. Radvany, *op. cit.*, p. 110.
58. *Ibid.*
59. Alan Sked, *The Metternich System*, p. 109.
60. *Ibid.*
61. *Ibid.*
62. *Ibid.*, p. 110.
63. A. J. P. Taylor (1934) *The Italian Question in European Diplomacy, 1847–49*. Manchester.
64. Alan Sked, *The Metternich System*, p. 110.
65. *Ibid.*
66. *Ibid.*
67. *Ibid.*, p. 111.
68. *Ibid.*
69. *Ibid.*
70. Alan Sked, *Metternich and the Federalist Myth*, p. 11.
71. Andics, *op. cit.*, p. 81.
72. *Ibid.*, p. 31.
73. *Ibid.*, p. 116.
74. Metternich to Lützow, Vienna, 10 October, 1847, in Richard von and Klinkowström, Alfons von Metternich (eds) (1880–4) *Aus Metternichs Nachgelassenen Papieren*, 8 vols. Vienna, Vol. 7, pp. 424–5.

CHAPTER TWO

1848: the Causes

Did the revolutions of 1848 cause the fall of Metternich or did the fall of Metternich cause the revolutions? This is not a trivial question. It is rather an invitation to pause and think before falling into the traditional trap of assuming that Metternich's liberal critics were correct and that the Habsburg Monarchy in 1848 was overwhelmed by profound forces of revolution which swept away the Metternich System in some inexorable fashion. Too many historians have assumed that just because there had been a revolution in France and because there was revolutionary activity elsewhere, there was bound to be a revolution in Austria. Yet this does not necessarily follow. There were certainly forces for change in Austria in 1848 – of differing degrees in different parts of the Monarchy – yet it is enormously difficult to make out the case that in any part of the Monarchy – with the exception perhaps of Lombardy-Venetia – any real revolutionary spirit existed. A more plausible explanation of events is simply that when a street riot took place in Vienna on 13 March, the imperial family lost its nerve, sacked the Chancellor and thereafterwards lost control of events as the Monarchy plunged into a power vacuum. While this lasted, various groups made their own bids for power. Most were content to demand constitutional monarchy under the Habsburgs who, in turn, proved ready to concede many demands. Yet things began to go wrong when the Italians attempted to secure constitutional rule under the House of Savoy. This meant war in northern Italy. The consequence was that attitudes became polarized, commitments were reappraised, the army became involved in politics and the Hungarian settlement of March–April 1848 was overturned once the war in Italy had been won. Once Hungary itself had been conquered, Austria then found the opportunity to reassert her position in Germany. In short, rather than believe the old tale (a sort of a revolutionary old wives' tale) that a bankrupt system was swept away by a great revolutionary flood, which then somehow receded leaving the former landscape intact, it is easier and more realistic to assume that there was no great flood in the first place but, rather, a squall which created a number of exceedingly muddy patches, the negotiating of which led to unforeseen accidents and tragedies.

THE SECRET SOCIETIES

Who positively wanted revolution in Austria in 1848? There are a number of candidates or rather groups of candidates: members of secret societies; political liberals and democrats; the rising bourgeoisie; the impoverished masses; dissident nationalists. There is of course an overlap between some of these categories, yet it is convenient to treat them separately to clarify the argument. So let us look first of all at the secret societies. Metternich himself certainly believed that these were at the root of unrest all over Europe between 1815 and 1848. They were, he maintained, controlled by a directing committee – the *comité directeur* – and he devoted a large part of his time in a vain attempt to trace the members of it. In 1833, for example, he informed one of his agents in Italy: 'For many years all those who pointed to the existence of a *comité directeur* working secretly for universal revolution were met everywhere only by incredulity; today it has been shown that this infernal propaganda exists, that it has its centre in Paris and that it is divided into as many sections as there are nations to regenerate. . . . Everything that refers to this great and dangerous plot cannot, therefore, be observed and surveyed with too much attention.'[1] The trouble was that when put to the test, neither Metternich nor Sednlitzky, the Police Director of the Empire, could say exactly who was behind the great plot. There were, fortunately, people around who themselves claimed to head one – Buonarotti or Mazzini, for example – yet although Metternich's spies did ocasionally manage to discover lists of suscribers to Mazzinian periodicals, there was in practice little that could be done about the sects, save warn the Italian troops and others that membership was tantamount to high treason. Hence, for example, the following order to Radetzky's army in 1833:

When twelve years ago the sect called the Carbonari threatened civil order in the Italian states with its complete overthrow, His Majesty warned you, his subjects, of the harmful and seditious teachings of this sect and of their criminal and treasonous aims in order 324 of March 1821. This was made known to everybody in order to ensure that even the most inexperienced and careless men, from whom the leaders of this sect took care to conceal their aims, would know of them and hence would abstain from joining the Carbonari.

The monarch's same fatherly care now compels him in view of recent events to issue the same order with regard to a no less dangerous sect, indeed one which represents a higher form of Carbonari, called Young Italy. The aim of this society is the overthrow of existing governments and of the complete social order; the means which it employs are subversion and outright murder through secret agents.

It goes without saying therefore that anyone who knows of these aims but who, none the less, joins Young Italy is guilty of high treason. He is also guilty even if, given that he knows its aims, he merely fails to prevent its progress or to point out its members and, as guilty, is liable to punishment under Article 5 of the Articles of War. Likewise from the date of publication of this order, no one will be able to excuse himself by saying that he was a member of Young Italy and yet was ignorant of its objectives. On the other hand, anyone who, out of remorse, reveals the members of the same, its statutes, the aims and undertakings of its leaders, if these are still secret or if their work can still be prevented, is assured complete immunity from punishment and his actions will remain secret.[2]

Despite such steps, however, very few members of Young Italy were ever caught by Metternich's spies. The same had been true of the Carbonari. Metternich, in fact, could pride himself on the fact that the sects seemed to operate outside the Empire. This was due less to the fact that the police in Lombardy-Venetia were more efficient than elsewhere in Italy than to the acknowledged superior standards of nearly all branches of administration in Austrian Italy. Thus after the revolts in Piedmont in 1820 and in the Papal States in 1831, Metternich actually came under pressure from Italians to annex more territory in Italy. The same thing happened after a revolt in the Papal States in 1845, leading the US consul in Turin to report to Washington: 'It is not for liberty but for bread they rise and much as Austria is detested by all Italy, the Legations are reduced to such dreadful extremities that they would gladly seek refuge from priestly extortion in the more orderly and better regulated despotism of an Austrian Prince.'[3] Yet even outside of the Monarchy, according to modern research, the sects were much less influential, even where they existed in large numbers, than previous historians and writers had assumed. Professor Rath, for example, has demonstrated how the Carbonari, although well established in Naples, was an extremely loosely organized body with no very definite programme, containing monarchists and republicans, clerics and anti-clericals, conservatives and revolutionaries.[4] Outside of Italy, the sects had influence only in France and the Iberian ports. The Charbonnerie, the French equivalent of the Carbonari, was supposed to have a membership of some 40,000 to 80,000, but it had even less success in promoting revolution than its Italian counterpart, subverting only a few French troops in mutinies during the 1820s.[5] Like the Carbonari, it too included a wide variety of political belief and acted as a political umbrella for political groups of different kinds. Every possible variety of opponent to Bourbon rule could be found within it – not merely Bonapartists, but Orleanists and republicans. The attraction of the sects must therefore have been as much social as political. In an era of counter-revolutionary assertiveness, they formed perhaps an alternative society, providing forums where people with different values could meet and criticize the restoration régimes. They may not have been very different, therefore, from the masonic lodges of the *ancien régime* which still existed and whose membership lists were known to the authorities.[6] Many of these members were in fact aristocrats. But even Mazzini did not allow uneducated Italians to be used as proselytisers for Young Italy.[7] All in all, therefore, it is difficult to believe that the sects posed any major threat to Metternich's Austria, although they did, it must be admitted, contain some bolder spirits, the equivalents of today's terrorists and extremists, who would have liked to do so and who, like some of the Decembrists of 1825 or the Hungarian Jacobins of 1794, deliberately set out to mislead their more moderate supporters.

A POLICE STATE?

A second group of people who are often held to have worked for the overthrow of the Metternich system are the liberals and democrats who criticized the régime, particularly from the 1840s, and whose works were banned by the political censorship. These men are often seen as the opponents of Metternich's police state. Hence Robert Justin Goldstein, in his recent survey of *Political Repression in 19th Century Europe*, has written: 'The Austrian secret police were the most notorious during the 1815–1860 period. . . . Huge numbers of informants – especially in such occupations as servants, prostitutes, waiters and doormen – were hired to report to the police on the activities and conversations of Austrians, and an extremely effective shroud of intimidation was lowered over the Austrian public that was not significantly lifted until after 1860.'[8] Certainly Goldstein is able to quote from a whole list of well-known complaints against the censorship and police, from Beethoven's letter of 1794 – 'One doesn't dare lift his voice here, otherwise the police find lodging for you'[9] – to the complaint of Metternich's secretary, Gentz (the censorship invaded the privacy of even high officers of state and members of the imperial family) in 1832, namely: 'You must realise that the mistrust towards one and all, the espionage against one's own confidants and the opening of all letters without exception has here reached heights for which there can scarcely be a parallel in all history.' Goldstein does point out, however, that during the same period, 'all the other major countries, including especially France, Germany and the United Kingdom, carried out similar surveillance activities in a scaled-down form'.[10] In Britain in 1844, for example, there was a great scandal when Sir James Graham, the Home Secretary, admitted directing the Post Office to intercept the mail of the exiled Mazzini and transmitting information gained thereby to Austria. People took to marking their letters 'not to be Grahamed' and the magazine *Punch* invented 'Graham wafers' to be attached to mail, bearing messages such as 'Nothing particular inside' imprinted across a profile of Graham's head. Parliamentary inquiry discovered that the practice had been legal since 1711 and that every Home Secretary had employed it since. Graham, indeed, had had the mail of many leading radicals opened, including that of one MP and a leader of the Anti-Corn Law League.[11]

If surveillance in Austria was much more widespread than in England, some authorities, none the less, would warn against depicting the Monarchy as a 'police state'. Donald Emerson, for example, has written: '. . . the term "police state" misleads if it encourages the belief that the police dominate the state. Instances of domination are surely rare. The point is that police are restrictive, obnoxious, oppressive or powerful, not that they are dominant. In addition the government rules arbitrarily.'[12] Military leaders, he points out, have often seized power; police chiefs very rarely. He therefore concludes: 'What distinguishes the police state is that a government disregards any limits in principle on its treatment of citizens. Frequently it seeks to justify its arbitrariness and oppressiveness by claiming the necessity of the security of the state. In such a case, rulers greatly cherish a political police and encourage its arbitrary action. Yet in fact the independence and even the power of such a political police are likely to be much less than rumoured.'[13]

What then was the situation in the Habsburg Monarchy? Was Metternich's Austria really a 'police state' and did this help bring about the revolutions of 1848? Thanks to the work of a number of historians,[14] we now know a great deal about the workings of the Austrian police system. The Police Ministry (*Polizeihofstelle*) was first created 1789 by Joseph II, who placed Count Pergen at its head. It was abolished soon afterwards by Leopold II but restored in 1793 by Francis I, a most suspicious sovereign, who in 1801 also gave it command of the censorship. Thereafter, it remained more or less unaltered until 1848. In 1815, located at 38 Herrengasse, Vienna, it had twelve members, four of whom had served in Pergen's day. In addition, there were some thirteen regular censors. The Police Director, however, could call upon the assistance of all the regular police of the capital, headed by a directorate of up to ten leading officials with a staff of about twenty-five. This directorate included offices for passes and the registration of residence, employment of servants and regulations regarding Jews. There were also district police stations in the capital – four in the inner city and nine in the suburbs. The regular force included seven officers, seventy-eight NCOs and 490 men, together with a mounted force of one officer, three NCOs and fifty-six men plus a civilian guard of sixty-four men in the suburbs. Thus the police reserves of the capital were hardly large and it is difficult to believe that they could have been capable of even intermittent control of most citizens.

In the provinces the Police Ministry depended on the officials of the provincial capitals to conduct its business, although there were twelve district commissariats in Lombardy and seven in Venetia. Such commissariats could be quickly established anywhere when needed – for example, in the Bohemian spas during the season, or in Pressburg when the Hungarian Diet met. All local officials were supposed to help out when asked and everyone from the local governor to the local district commissioner might become involved in police enquiries. In Hungary, however, the Hungarian Chancellery took control when the need arose. Local police bureaux carried out both regular police duties and secret police work. Their tasks included maintaining law and order, the registration of all persons in the area, control over the movement of subjects, as well as aiding the secret policy and censors. The secret police had several tasks: surveillance of suspects; opening the mails; censoring books, the theatre, the press, drawings, paintings and even buttons; as well as positively promoting the government's point of view. The Secret Court Cipher

Office, which opened the mails, was controlled by the Emperor personally during the reign of Francis I, who enjoyed being read the choicest gossip each morning by his officials. Both Metternich and Count Sedlnitzky, the Police Director from 1816, however, also received daily reports. The rest of the work was supposed to be the official business of Sedlnitzky, but in practice he was dominated by Metternich, whose excuse was that much of the business involved touched on foreign affairs. In 1817, therefore, he demanded 'to be kept directly and uninterruptedly informed about matters which relate to the higher state police'.[15] After 1835, Kolowrat was given control of the police as part of his dominance of home affairs, but not control of the censorship. In practice, police policy remained under the control of Metternich and Sedlnitzky.

The first task of the police was to protect the security of the state. This was also the first task of the censorship. There could be no criticism, therefore, of the ruler or of the dynasty, of government decrees or of imperial policy. Likewise, no support could be expressed for liberalism, nationalism or popular sovereignty. Not even foreign sovereigns could be attacked. Indeed, Article 4 of the Karlsbad Decrees specifically laid this down as far as the German sovereigns were concerned. The second task was to protect religion, particularly Catholicism. Protestant writings, however, were severely censored for religious errors, although Jewish ones were the most strictly censored of all. Importing foreign writings on Judaism was illegal, but, thanks to the influence of the Tsar, Greek Orthodox works could be imported into Hungary for the Serbs there. The third priority was the preservation of good taste: no eroticism, *double entendres* or obscenities were permitted. Neither, for that matter, were pictures of the royal family or Metternich as a rule or, ironically, those of famous criminals.

The censorship of foreign news or reports from foreign newspapers was controlled by the State Chancellery; the Police Ministry controlled domestic news. Metternich and Sedlnitzky, working in tandem, therefore, ensured that newspapers followed the government line. In the provinces the governors did the same thing working under instructions from Vienna. Newspaper editors and publishers were harassed by numerous rules: only articles from the appropriate government bureaux might be published; those by private authors had to be approved. Only printers were allowed to see the censored proof-sheets; articles for the following day had to be submitted for censorship by noon the previous day. If an editor tried to oppose the censors, the forthcoming edition of his paper was threatened with a ban. Yet this was a weapon which had to be used very carefully, lest the next edition be too eagerly sought after. It was better, therefore, to threaten to remove the paper from the list of permitted publications altogether. On the other hand, editors, particularly those of foreign newspapers, were often bribed or otherwise persuaded to present the government's point of view. Both the *Augsburger Allgemeine Zeitung* and the *Gazetta di Lugano* were successfully converted. Many – often quite distinguished – publicists were also in Metternich's pay. As Metternich put it: '. . . the activity of a police ministry in the higher sense is not limited to the mere picking up of utterances and circulating rumours, but that, in order to fulfil the high purpose of its establishment, it must actively influence opinion, putting the actions of the government in their true light and opposing to the spread of false news the conquering power of truth'.[16]

The censoring of books, however, gave the system its worst reputation, especially as the authors had to bring in their manuscripts for censorship before publication. Moreover, since there were no published standards, they were subject to slowness, arbitrariness and uncertainty. The censors were supposed to judge each case on its merits, but since they had to pay attention to hundreds of secret regulations about precedents, their judgements were never easy to follow. Very often they were men of great learning and integrity, but since they were all closely supervised by superiors, they rarely erred on the side of broad-mindedness. All works were subject to these processes, which were controlled by the State Chancellery and the Policy ministry. Metternich himself 'took a full, often a dominant part in these matters',[17] displaying a particular interest in manuscripts concerning Hungary, foreign affairs, history – particularly Habsburg history – the affairs of the Catholic Church, political science and natural law. There was little regard for academic research. After all, Francis I had made the imperial position quite clear on that: 'I don't need scholars but good citizens. . . . Who serves me must teach as I command. Anyone who cannot do that or who comes with new ideas can go or I will dismiss him.'[18] The theatre was subject to the same imperial restrictions.

The other main job of the secret police was the supervision and surveillance of potential spies and subversives. This involved the registration of residence, regulations regarding servants and Jews, the need for permission to travel outside the Monarchy, and the registration of guests at inns and hotels. Most notoriously, of course, it involved the interception of the mails and the supervision of the international postal system. The Secret Cipher Chancellery was the body responsible for most of this, but it cooperated with the Police Ministry which used 'post-lodges' in the provinces. The whole system was run by Metternich and Sedlnitzky, although always, while he was alive, under the close eye of Francis I. The result supposedly was that 'anything in the Habsburg mails was likely to be read by the police unless negligence, effective disguise or sheer chance interfered'.[19] Nobody of rank – archdukes, generals, ambassadors or civil servants themselves – could expect to be spared, so that anyone wishing to keep his correspondence private made private arrangements to have it delivered. 'I only write through the post that which anybody could or should read,' said Gentz.[20] The interception system reached new heights during the Metternich period. For example, officials would have the mail for the 7 a.m. post brought to the Secret Cipher Chancellery and dealt with so that it could be returned to the Post Office by 9 a.m. This meant that all the tricks of the trade, involving special candles, quicksilver, special machines etc., not to mention the actual copying of the letters, had to be done within a few hours, the same restrictions applying to most other postal deliveries, including the erratic transit post from Turkey. Hence there was an imperative need for efficiency. By 1817, some 1,000 letters were arriving in Vienna daily, although only between 80 and 100 would be purloined.

To maintain the efficiency required, the staff of the Secret Cipher Chancellery were highly trained and well paid. They also tended to be members of a small number of families or 'dynasties' – Eichenfelds, Schweizers, Geitters etc. – and were expert code-breakers, since no foreign government was stupid enough to send unciphered mail through Austria. One employee boasted to Metternich in 1823 that he had broken eighty-five foreign codes. Many others could read intercepted letters as fluently in code as in their original languages. Knowledge of foreign languages therefore was clearly of great importance and 500 florins was paid out for each new one which was learned. One official, Joseph Schneid, became the master of nineteen languages, something which was said to be not very exceptional. All these people were very well paid: between 500 fl. per annum for middling ranks and up to 3,000 fl. in higher ones. Special missions during congresses and diets brought special payments, and pensions were higher than average. Code-breakers, moreover, paid no rent, no taxes, lived on the second floor of the Hofstallburg, and had immediate access to the monarch. They received free firewood for fuel and enjoyed a good, if busy, life. By

1848 there were twenty-two people (including servants) installed in the Hofstallburg.

So much then for Metternich's police state: it was one, in fact, which employed a remarkably small number of people whether one considers those involved in regular police duties or in the secret police. How successful was it? To what extent did it contain or provoke revolutionary sentiment within the Monarchy? How repressive was it? These are questions which must be considered if one is to discover whether it was responsible for the outbreak of revolution in 1848. Fortunately, they are fairly easy to answer. In the first place, especially by twentieth-century standards, it does not appear to have been cruel. True, the stories of Pellico's and Confalonieri's long incarceration within the Spielberg are well known, but there is no evidence that torture was used. Nor does it seem to have been the case that there were many political prisoners in Austria. The many rumours which went around concerning the ubiquity and omnipotence of the secret police seem actually to have discouraged revolutionary activity within the Monarchy. *The imperial government, therefore, was never threatened by revolution throughout the whole period, 1815–48.* Technically, on the other hand, the system was never as efficient as Metternich would have liked: the Russian and Hanoverian codes proved hard to crack and, despite his best efforts, he never managed to establish an Italian centre along the lines of the Investigating Centre which had been set up in Mainz in 1825. Nor, indeed, did his efforts to coordinate police activities with other powers – Bavaria, Prussia and France, for example – ever acquire the degree of routine of formality for which he had hoped. And, of course, it did not prevent revolution breaking out in 1848. Yet we still have to determine the exact relationship between the existence of the 'police state' and the outbreak of revolution. And to do that, two points have to be made.

In the first place, despite the 'Chinese Wall' which was supposed to surround Austria intellectually on account of the censorship, most people could read what they liked. Travellers' accounts and memoirs from the period all confirm this. Indeed, they praise the authorities' help in securing whatever reading material – banned or not – that was required. For example, the great Austrian dramatist Grillparzer recorded of the post-1835 period: 'In principle the censorship still remained as severe as under the Emperor Francis. But in practice it was infinitely milder, to be sure chiefly because of the impossibility of enforcing it. The reading and circulation of prohibited foreign writings was as general as anywhere in the world and the most dangerous ones were the most widely circulated.'[21] He admitted that the domestic press was closely supervised and that political writings 'could count on less consideration', but if Austrian writers wanted to publish their views on politics abroad 'they needed only in way of an open secret to shorten their name a syllable or assume a false one to spare themselves nearly all questioning and to ward off attack. Yes, the authorities were perhaps even secretly joyful, because they believed that their necessary severity did not stand in the way of the development of the more distinguished literature.' Nor were his views exceptional. Count Hartig, for example, one of Metternich's closest colleagues, recorded: 'The strictness of the censorship more especially was only exercised against works and journals published in the country and against the public advertisements of booksellers. All foreign literary productions were easily obtained in private, so that a man of any literary pretensions would have been ashamed in society to acknowledge himself unacquainted with a forbidden book or journal that had excited observation: for instance, even in the presence of the highest officials, and in the most public places, it was customary to speak of the worst articles in the journal *die Grenzboten* since no one thought it his business to enquire how the speaker became acquainted with such an article. Directions were previously given to the professors, prescribing in what manner and on what subjects they were to lecture; but if they taught differently, they incurred no censure provided their teaching impugned no dogma of Catholicity.'[22] This view of the universities under the Metternich system is upheld by a future professor, who was then a student at Vienna. At the university there, he recalled: students 'read with indescribable pleasure the prohibited writings of men permeated with a spirit of freedom'.[23] Clubs were formed to purchase the latest prohibited books, which were then circulated among members. The rules did not matter: 'The academic laws were draconian in regard to prohibited books. Whoever circulated such writings among his fellow students or even read them by himself without telling others about them was punished by being excluded from all educational institutions in the Monarchy. In spite of this, they were generally read. In the University of Vienna they even circulated from bench to bench in the lecture rooms. The liberal *Grenzboten* especially was read for entertainment during the tedious lecture hours. Many students stinted themselves to save money to join the above-named clubs.'[24] In fact, it was not merely the students who were clubbing together to circulate and buy books. From the 1840s, clubs such as the liberal *Legal-Political Reading Club* and the *Concordia* were doing the same and also discovering that the authorities were happy to turn a blind eye. For example, according to Professor Rath, the former was allowed to subscribe to such newspapers as the *Leipziger Zeitung, Le Constitutionnel, Le Siècle* and even *die Grenzboten* itself.[25] And for those who were not members of such clubs, it was also an easy matter to acquire such reading material. Copies of *die Grenzboten*, for example, were smuggled across the Austrian border from Bavaria in coachloads. The censorship, therefore, was more of a nuisance than anything else. it neither prohibited the circulation of ideas, criticism of the government or academic research. It just added to the incredible atmosphere of tedium in Metternich's Austria.

The second point to be made about the censorship, however, is that to some degree, it was supported. That is to say, there were probably only few people who supported the viewpoint that it should be abolished altogether. Religious feeling would have militated against such a view, custom also. Nor is there any evidence of widespread radicalism beneath the surface of the Monarchy at this time. Hence the otherwise perhaps curious fact that, when in 1845 a petition against the censorship was submitted to Metternich and signed by no less than twenty-nine of the leading authors of the day, it did not demand outright abolition, but merely the amelioration of the censorship laws.[26] In fact, it asked for better pay and conditions for the censors, so that they might be able to devote more time and attention, not to mention a better frame of mind, to the manuscripts which they had to consider. Perhaps then, it was hoped, they might have sufficient time to discuss these properly with the authors concerned. The logic of this request, of course, was that more censors should be appointed, not fewer. Whether the petition reflected moderate views or merely the acceptance of the fact that outright abolition would never be conceded anyway, it is difficult to tell. Yet one suspects that completely committed ideological opponents of the government's position would have felt uncomfortable associating themselves with such a step. All in all, therefore, it is difficult to believe that the existence of a 'police state' of some kind provoked revolution in 1848. Ironically, as we shall see, it was to be *the lack of adequate police forces in Vienna in March 1848* which would go far to explain the success of the revolution there, a success which was to prove absolutely crucial to the spread of revolution elsewhere in the Monarchy during the fatal spring of that year.

THE LIBERAL OPPOSITION

How strong then was liberal opposition to the Metternich system inside the Monarchy and whence did it arise? Clearly, from what has been argued already, it found expression mainly in the foreign press and in books published abroad. Moreover, it was not until the 1840s that it became important, although it is not altogether clear why this should have been the case. Most likely the reasons include a generational change, the feeling that Metternich should have departed along with Francis I (Grillparzer wrote a poem lamenting the fact that the Chancellor had not died at the same time), the influence of the new King of Prussia, Frederick William IV, the downturn in the economy and the war-scare of 1840. Like France, Austria was distinctly bored. Certainly, from the 1840s, there was a perceptible change of pace as lots of political poems began to flood the coffee houses and salons, as propaganda began to creep into plays, and as more and more writers began to make use of the German press rather than just read their works to one another. Professor Rath, whose book on the Viennese Revolution of 1848 is still the best work on the subject,[27] has mapped out the political landmarks: the founding of the *Grenzboten* in Brussels in 1841 by the Czech exile, Ignaz Kuranda, as a rallying point for oppositionist groups within the Monarchy; the publication of a whole series of important critical works in Germany (mainly in Hamburg and Leipzig) starting with Baron Victor von Andrian-Werburg's *Austria and its Future* in 1842, through Franz Schuselka's pamphlets of the 1840s (*German Words of an Austrian, Austria Rules Supreme If She Only Wills It, Austria's Forward and Backward Steps* etc.), through the most important works of 1847 (Count Schnirding's *Austria's Internal Politics with Reference to the Constitutional Question* and Karl Beidtel's *The Financial Affairs of Austria*) to Karl Moering's devastating critique of January 1848, the *Sibylline Books from Austria*. The trend in these works was an increasingly radical one. Von Andrian, for example, had been most concerned to attack the bureaucracy and to suggest as the vital remedy for Austria's misfortunes the strengthening of the provincial diets. These, he proposed, should be given the power to vote provincial taxes, choose their own officials and acquire representatives from the peasants and middle classes. They should also be able to petition the monarch. As for central government, he suggested the creation of an imperial diet to represent the Empire as a whole and to be formed from representatives of the provincial estates. It should meet once a year to apportion taxes among the provinces and to vote on the budget, and should also be able to petition the monarch. The book had enormous influence and appealed, especiallly and predictably, to the liberal nobility of the estates. Then in a second volume published in 1847 (which also advocated a free press, academic freedom and the abolition of feudal dues), von Andrian again stressed the need to reform the diets. Other writers were more radical. Schuselka, for his part, placed no faith in the aristocracy (or the church for that matter) but called for a 'citizen-king' who would rule in alliance with the people. Schnirding was even further left, calling for rights to be granted to the proletariat and middle classes. He advocated industrialization and the abolition of feudal dues. Beidtel likewise painted a grim picture of the peasantry and working class, but made his name by purporting to demonstrate how very shaky the Empire's financial situation was. According to Beidtel, the amount of gold and silver in the reserves could not cover the amount of banknotes in circulation, while the chronic inability of the government to balance the budget would undermine the financial health of the Monarchy. His remedy for the problem was simply to declare a partial bankruptcy and refund without interest only a part of the sums owed to the state's creditors. The alternative would be runaway inflation. To supervise this manoeuvre, however, it was imperative, Beidtel argued, to establish a national assembly. Needless to say, the fears aroused in creditors by this analysis did much to undermine the government's position between the fall of Louis Philippe in France and the fall of Metternich. After all, it did not take a genius to work out that if there was to be a war with the Second French Republic – and Metternich was held to be planning one – this might prove to be the final straw for Austria's apparently precarious finances. Moreover, people still remembered the bankruptcy of 1811 and, according to C. A. Macartney, 'it was indeed that memory, more than any other single factor, that touched off the revolution of 1848 in both Vienna and Hungary'.[28] Moering, however, had little to say about finance. He highlighted the lack of any Austrian patriotism due, in his estimation, to the suspicion and contempt with which the government treated the people.

The curious feature of all this literature, however, was, as Professor Rath points out, that none of these liberal writers before 1848 'expressed a desire for a constitution, a bill of rights, popular sovereignty or a genuine "liberal" parliament. Except for the Archduke Louis, no member of the imperial family was attacked.

Emperor Ferdinand was mentioned only in terms of the most flattering and obsequious adulation. In all the opposition literature not once was a demand made for revolution.'[29] These writers, rather, wanted the government to do away with the irritations of the political police and censorship, establish toleration, reform the tax system, decentralize the machinery of government and get better advisers and ministers. In particular, advice should be sought from a more representative but, on the whole, consultative assembly with a veto over taxation. There were no demands, however, for a ministry responsible to a modern parliament, which should rule while the monarch reigned. The liberal opposition was therefore both loyal and limited. Even between the fall of Louis Philippe at the end of February 1848 and the fall of Metternich in the middle of March, when petitions were pouring in profusion into the *Hofburg*, the situation did not change. Having examined these popular demands, Professor Rath concludes: 'Considered from a present day perspective the demands of the Viennese radicals expressed in these petitions were surprisingly moderate. The petition for the abolition of monopolies and for freedom of trade is mild in comparison with the position then held by laissez-faire theorists in Western Europe. Included are the usual entreaties for freedom of the press, speech and religion; but such typical "liberal" demands as freedom from search and the right of public assembly are missing. The hesitant appeals for provincial assemblies and a united diet, with members chosen by traditional Austrian, not democratic methods and with the limited prerogatives of approving taxes and the budget and sharing in the legislation, are certainly a far cry from the demands of modern liberals. Also it must be remembered that in the Austria of 1848 the person of the Emperor was still considered sacred. Even the most radical Viennese were unswerving in their loyalty to the Habsburg ruler. Not the Emperor but the bureaucracy was held responsible for the malfeasances of government. To the liberals, Emperor Ferdinand remained the good-hearted, beloved father of the Austrian people whose every command was to be obeyed. Moreover, while the political reforms requested by the Viennese liberals were numerous, they could doubtless have been granted without disrupting the traditional monarchist rule of the Habsburg government.'[30] We shall examine this conclusion later, but before then we still have to discover who the Viennese liberals were and whether their views were held in other parts of the Monarchy. Certainly, if Hans Sturmberger's investigation of political developments in Upper Austria between 1792 and 1861 is anything to go by – and his research is based on the police archives of the province – there was very little for the government to worry about: the fortunes of the Bavarian parliament were followed with great interest there after 1819; there was a general hatred of Russia and a sympathy for the Poles in 1833; but the revolutions of 1830 aroused little interest.[31] Books and pamphlets were smuggled in and agricultural and industrial societies were founded after 1839, but most controversy appeared to centre on the activities of the Archbishop of Linz, a former Benedictine monk named Thomas Ziegler, who was a prominent supporter of the Catholic Restoration movement. He made life particularly difficult for the Protestants of the province and introduced the Jesuits in 1837. But all in all, there seemed little cause for the authorities to feel concerned. Even the local diet posed no challenge to the government and was treated by the locals as something of a joke. According to the theatre director of Linz, the estates constituted 'the most bitter caricature of a representative constitution' and 'met only once in a whole year and convened from only 9 a.m. till noon on one day'.[32] Ceremonial, moreover, took up two out of these three hours. The other hour was taken up by the provincial governor reading out the government's demands and by the estates replying 'yes' to them. After that they were dismissed.

The whole question of the powers of these estates or diets, on the other hand, was becoming an extremely controversial one in Austria by 1848. This was not merely because von Andrian had suggested that they should form the basis for a new constitutional order, but because they were in fact becoming the political arena for aristocratic opposition to the Metternich system. This, of course, had long been the situation in Hungary, where the Diet, especially after 1790, had acted self-consciously as the guardian of the constitution, a constitution which placed it at the very centre of national life. But the emergence of opposition to – or rather criticism of – the government in the estates of Lower Austria, Bohemia and even in the so-called Central Congregations of Lombardy and Venetia in the months immediately before the revolutions certainly represented a new phenomenon in Habsburg affairs. For it was in the Diet of Lower Austria that the liberal writers who were so well represented in the German press – Baron von Doblhoff, Count Albert Montecuccoli and Cavalier Anton von Schmerling, for example – organized real political criticism for the first time, helping to pass motions calling for among other things the abolition of peasant dues and services, a reduction of all taxes, the establishment of a credit bank, municipal reform, the introduction of an income tax and the extension of elementary education. Early in 1848, the Diet even petitioned for the abolition of military conscription, while on various occasions it asked for the budget to be made public, for the non-privileged classes to be represented in the estates, and for it to be consulted whenever the affairs of the province warranted. In Bohemia, too, in the later 1840s the Diet demanded to be consulted more often and quarrelled with the government over the levying of local taxes while, finally, the Central Congregations of the kingdom of Lombardy-Venetia came to life in the winter of 1847–8, petitioning their monarch for reforms after a period of suspended animation which had lasted for almost a quarter of a century. Some historians, none the less, write off these developments as having been of no significance. According to Macartney, for example, the reform party in the Bohemian estates was 'in a small minority',[33] while the Czech historian Polišensky, in his account of the revolutions, ignores it altogether.[34] Like most Marxists, he is content to fit developments within the paradigm of the 'bourgeois revolution', a paradigm which is also employed by the British historian, Paul Ginsborg, in his account of the revolution in Venetia in 1848.[35] Ginsborg argues that events there were caused by the emergence of a new bourgeois class of commercial lawyers whose leading figure was Daniele Manin – this, despite the fact that there were only fifty-eight lawyers in the whole of Venice, some of whom were aristocrats.

A REVOLT OF THE NOBILITY?

At the time, however, it seemed fairly obvious to those in power where the main challenge to government policy was coming from. Metternich, for example, in a memorandum composed in 1850 entitled 'the nobility', declared: 'To the list of symptoms of a sick, degenerate age belongs the completely false position which the nobility all too often adopts. It was they nearly everywhere who lent a hand to the confusion that was being prepared.'[36] Hartig echoed these sentiments in his own account of the revolutions, writing: 'The greater or less importance of the insurrection against the government was in proportion to the weight which was possessed by these provincial estates, or by the aristocracy, who always considered themselves bound to throw down the gauntlet to the so-termed bureaucracy arising partly from the extent of the privileges they possessed and partly from their connection with members of the central government.'[37] Indeed, when the army discovered in the spring of 1848 there was a need to explain recent events to the troops, it did so by telling them that the cause of the revolution had been the pressure in Vienna and elsewhere in the Monarchy for the establishment of diets with powers similar to the Hungarian one: 'The Emperor can look after lands much better and more quickly if a certain number of intelligent men are chosen to voice the wishes and requests of a country in a Diet as in the case of Hungary . . .'[38] We must ask ourselves, however, whether these views can be substantiated before concluding that Metternich and his allies were correct in seeing the aristocracy behind the revolutions. After all, we have already seen that the views of most of the Austrian liberal nobility were extremely moderate.

In the case of Hungary, there is almost no argument among historians. Everyone seems to be agreed that the revolution there was the work of the Hungarian nobility. István Deák makes this explicit in his recent study of Kossuth[39] and even communist historians appear content to accept this interpretation. For example, Professor Bartha writes in the history of Hungary edited by Erwin Pamlényi that: 'It is one of the anomalies of Hungarian social development that the change to bourgeois conditions depended little on the class which should have been responsible for the ideological transformation and for the practical realisation of the actual development, that is to say the bourgeoisie itself. It was the result of grave historical circumstances that when the time came for the actual change to bourgeois conditions, there was no bourgeois force capable of carrying out the task. The bourgeoisie of the royal towns in fact fought on the side of the court defending feudalism against national independence as represented by the feudal nobility.' Schwarzenberg had arrived at exactly the same conclusion by 1849. He told his brother-in-law, Prince Windischgraetz: 'The Hungarian aristocracy is a politically and morally degenerate body: if the government wishes to rely on the nobility in that country it can hope for no support. The role which the nobility has played in the political history of Hungary – particularly in recent times – shows clearly its true spirit. I do not believe in political conversions and since the nobility in Hungary made and executed the revolution there, I find no guarantee of its future effectiveness. One can be of old lineage, have an old title and call oneself an aristocrat but still be a supporter of revolutionary subversion.'[40] Yet this was an exaggeration. Like their counterparts in Vienna, the aristocratic critics of the Metternich system in Hungary had been in no sense revolutionary before 1848.

In fact, they were reactionaries in the truest sense of the word, since their main political aim was to restore the original powers of the Hungarian constitution. Moreover, even though they claimed that Metternich had subverted that constitution, they had worked with him throughout the 1840s to bolster the position of Magyardom and to initiate certain reforms. Yet they seized the opportunity to set up a responsible ministry in Hungary as soon as Metternich had been removed. The reason for this, however, had nothing to do with revolution: their real motive was simply to restore their constitution. This is why Deák entitles his book *The Lawful Revolution*. It was held to be lawful in two senses: first, in that it restored the constitution; secondly, in that the king agreed to it. And throughout the revolutionary struggle between Austria and Hungary in 1848–9, the Hungarians consistently based their claims on the April Laws to which the monarch had given his assent. They never saw themselves as revolutionaries in any sense at all. Their problem was that the king later withdrew his assent to the April Laws and expected them to return to the old arrangements. The Bohemian aristocracy, meanwhile, were highly impressed by what had happened in Hungary and under the leadership of the governor there, Count Thun, tried to persuade the acting head of the imperial family, the Archduke Francis Charles, that Bohemia too should be granted a constitutional existence independent of Vienna. Indeed, as soon as the opportunity arose in May 1848, Thun established a Bohemian national government, claiming that since its imperial counterpart had lost both control of the capital and its authority, it had also lost the right to govern Bohemia. On the advice of Doblhoff, however, who was sent down to Innsbruck to put the case for Vienna, the Archduke decided that acceding to Thun's plans would mean the eventual break-up of the Monarchy. The Hungarians, in any case, were already causing enough problems for the dynasty on their own. That was why the royal assent to the April Laws was ultimately withdrawn: trying to run an empire with two governments pursuing mutually hostile financial, defence and foreign policies was beyond the capacity of a dynasty's limited political and intellectual resources. Hence its decision in September 1848 to back Jellačić's attack on Hungary. But it was only then that the Hungarians found themselves in opposition to their monarch, and not at all by their own decision. It was he – or his Austrian advisers – who in their eyes had overthrown the legal order.

If the Magyar nobility cannot be characterized as true revolutionaries, despite their opposition to Metternich, the same is certainly true of the Austrian aristocrats who ran the Vienna government after Metternich's fall. They in fact had all been extremely close colleagues of the former Chancellor. Kolowrat had been his closest collaborator as well as rival; Ficquelmont had been his right-hand man and presumed successor until 1848; Wessenberg had been a colleague in the diplomatic service since the Congress of Vienna. They now tried to run the government much as before, save that they had to draw up some kind of constitution which meant co-existing uneasily with a parliament of sorts for a few months. But there was never the slightest possibility of them becoming revolutionaries, or even of opposing the wishes of the dynasty, supposing that the latter could make up its mind what to do.

Only in northern Italy were the aristocracy truly revolutionary, albeit in a purely political rather than in any social sense. That is to say, it was only in Lombardy and Venetia that the local aristocrats made a determined bid to overthrow the dynasty. The reason was quite simple: the northern Italian territories had little experience of Habsburg rule and what they had they did not like. This was particularly true since, unlike the case of Hungary, Habsburg rule in Lombardy-Venetia meant rule by German-speaking foreigners who excluded most of the local aristocrats from court, the army and the diplomatic service and most local lawyers from the law courts. Kent Roberts Greenfield and other historians discovered, therefore, to the surprise of those who relied too automatically on the paradigm of 'bourgeois revolution', that it was the Italian upper classes and not the middle ones who were at the forefront of the revolution. As Romeo was to put it in the introduction to Greenfield's book: 'It would be natural to infer that Italian liberalism reflected a movement by the middle class to gain control of society. The defect of this thesis is that the liberal programme was initiated, expounded and propagated, not by an aspiring and self-conscious bourgeoisie, with strong intellectual interests to serve, but by landed proprietors and groups of intellectuals many of whose leaders were of the aristocracy. . . . There is no evidence to colour the view that the liberal publicists were being pushed by a rising capitalistic class or were prompted to act as its mouthpiece.'[41] Previous writers had been misled perhaps by Carlo Cattaneo's classic contemporary account of the insurrection in Milan in 1848. This asserted that 'The middle class constituted the heart of the national party,'[42] although Cattaneo had to admit that at the head of that party stood 'a backward aristocracy, an absolute king and a pope'.[43] 'Why,' he asked, 'had the middle classes, who were truly revolutionary, failed to assume the direction of the movement?'[44] The answer is probably that his analysis was flawed. Luigi Torrelli, for example, in his examination of the likelihood of a revolution succeeding in Lombardy, published in Paris in 1846,[45] reached the conclusion that the most dangerous class in the country was not the professional one but the rich landowners, that is, the aristocracy and the landowning bourgeoisie. Meanwhile, Metternich's agents in Milan were reporting the same. The class of the population which the Austrian authorities feared most were the younger nobles who had travelled abroad and who on their return home felt alienated from the imperial régime.

There were indeed many reasons for such alienation.[46] For a start, although recognized as nobles by fellow Italians, many were denied this recognition by the Austrians. Imperial heraldic commissions which had toured the kingdom after 1818 had abolished the rights of all sorts of nobles to claim their titles. Moreover, many titles, even among those which had been confirmed, were often downgraded when standardized with Austrian ones. Hence certain ladies who went by the title 'princess' in Italy could not lay claim to the title in Austria; Italian 'dukes' likewise became *Grafs* or counts when they visited Vienna. Worst of all, perhaps, the strict court etiquette adhered to in Milan and Venice meant that most Italians were barred from court. Only those with sixteen quarterings could be admitted. And every visitor to court had his or her credentials checked. According to one report: 'It was taken badly when a number of ladies who had first been admitted were chased away.'[47] The viceregal court in any case was rather drab in comparison with the splendid one remembered from Napoleonic times. Then, Eugene Beauharnais had been encouraged to flatter and play up to Italian sensitivities; now these days had gone. Italians, who as a rule had no connections with the high aristocracy of Central Europe and who rarely took the trouble to acquire good German, found it difficult to get jobs in the bureaucracy. And even when they did, they discovered that the pay was modest and promotion slow. The introduction of the Austrian Civil Law Code also created difficulties, since it meant that most lawyers had to know German to understand legal precedents. In practice, this meant that the legal profession became dominated by bilingual Tyrolese. In the years before 1848, therefore, the Italian nobility increasingly boycotted the Austrian court, so that when Countess Ficquelmont, for example, joined her husband in Milan in the autumn of 1847, she could report to a relative in Russia that life was led 'in total isolation from the Milanese' – indeed, as in 'an outpost in enemy territory',[48] a description which was not far off the mark. Still, if Austrian Italy seemed dominated by a hostile and foreign régime, the same was by no means true of neighbouring Piedmont. There the king, the ambitious – and until 1848 – reactionary Charles Albert, welcomed all these nobles to court and decorated them as loyal subjects. Many, in fact, were *sudditi misti*, landowners with estates in both Piedmont and Lombardy-Venetia. Hence, they could, legitimately, send their sons to Piedmont, to find there the more glittering careers in the army or the bureaucracy which were denied them by the Austrians. Count Casati, the mayor of Milan, for example, sent his sons to the Sardinian Military Academy to become Sardinian officers, much to the disgust of the Habsburg authorities. By 1848, they regarded such behaviour as more or less treasonable.

Yet what were the authorities to do? Some of them professed indifference. General Schönhals, for example, Radetzky's adjutant, wrote: 'But he who knows the disinclination, particularly of the Italian upper classes against everything which constitutes state service, he also knows what little inclination they possess for serious study, will understand that Austria could not seek her governors, supreme judges or generals among the Italian nobility. Look through the matriculations of the universities of Pavia and Padua and see if one meets with a distinguished name there. The theatre and the cafés are not the places where statesmen are produced and tiresome working up the ladder of service posts is not to the taste of rich Italians. We do not blame them for this. But at the same time they cannot accuse the state of violating nationality, of partiality and neglect.'[49] Metternich, meanwhile, was becoming more alarmed, especially after the riots of January 1848 in Milan, which erupted when the young bloods of the Jockey Club organized a tobacco boycott. He wrote to Ficquelmont: 'What do the Lombard nobility want? Do they intend to renounce their moral and material existence? How can they do so? Yet their conduct must make one assume this. The driving force behind the unspeakable position of the country is coming without a shadow of a doubt from their side. Do they want to surrender their fortunes on the high altar of some incredible divinity and bring on the holocaust?'[50] The answer was that the upper classes wanted to be bought off. There are several reports of Milanese and other nobles informing the authorities that the problem would be resolved if only the younger nobility were found suitable posts and some of the richer landowners of the bourgeois class were ennobled. One told Metternich: 'The possibility given to Italians of occupying only middling and lower posts which demand much work, profound study and long practice and bring a minimum reward and very little influence cannot win the interest of the patrician families and the wealthy of the Kingdom. It is a short step, moreover, from being excluded from the service of the state and joining the opposition; yet by conceding modest rewards, it would be easy to attract Italians into ruling circles.'[51] This was really a demand for *trasformismo*. Yet Metternich was not prepared to concede the necessary 'modest rewards'. Any kind of concession, he believed, would be seen as a sign of weakness and would bring greater demands in its wake. This was why he rejected the extremely modest reform proposals which were suggested to him by Ficquelmont and the Viceroy at the beginning of 1848. Instead, he became convinced that a show of force was necessary. Hence his policy of negotiating new defence treaties with the Italian duchies and his proclamation to the Milanese. This had the sovereign declare his faith in the loyalty of his peace-loving subjects. But it added: 'We count too upon the valour and loyal devotion of our troops whose principal glory has always been and always will be to show themselves as solid supporters of our throne and a rampart against the calamities which rebellion and anarchy would bring upon the lives and property of peaceful citizens.'[52] Radetzky added his own gloss in a separate proclamation to his troops: 'The machinery of fanaticism,' he prophesied, 'will break upon your loyalty and valour like glass upon a rock.'[53]

Yet it was not merely confidence in the army which underlay Metternich's policy in northern Italy and elsewhere. For events had taken place in 1846 which had convinced the authorities that they had nothing to fear if the local aristocracies were foolhardy enough to push their opposition to the point of revolution. These events had been the efforts of the Polish nobles, organized from Paris, to start a revolution in Cracow, Posen and Galicia. In the latter area, which was the Austrian-controlled part of partitioned Poland, the nobles had been slaughtered in their thousands by the local peasantry, apparently under the illusion that this had been ordered by the Emperor.[54] Indeed, the rumour had got round that he had abolished the Ten Commandments to allow them to murder the local nobles and priests. In fact, the Habsburg authorities – despite later charges of connivance – knew nothing about what was going on and were appalled at the results of the blood-lust. None the less, it was very reassuring to learn that the peasantry had supported the state against their landlords. The idea took root among the army and the bureaucracy, therefore, that if revolution were to be attempted elsewhere in the Monarchy, the same thing would happen again. This, indeed, was already part of the prevailing wisdom. Ficquelmont, for example, had told the Tsar in 1837, with respect to the Hungarian opposition: 'It would need only a word from the court to wipe out this opposition by making the peasants think of an improvement to their lot, something which the nobles have no wish to grant them.'[55] In April 1848 he would tell a British diplomat the same thing about the Italian nobles: '. . . If Austria chose to avail itself of its actual power to raise the peasantry against their superiors it would have the perfect facility in procuring the ruin and destruction of these persons . . .'[56] Metternich himself placed enormous value on the Galician events. He told Radetzky: 'An extraordinarily significant event has just taken place . . . the attempt by the Polish Emigration to start a second revolution in the former Polish territories has been thwarted. This attempt was smashed by the Polish peasantry. This fact in my eyes has the full worth of an unparalleled phase in world history. . . . A new era, therefore, has dawned whose influence will not be limited to our monarchy. The democrats have mistaken their base; a democracy without the people is a chimera.'[57] The Field Marshal was ordered to ensure that word of this new era reached the Italian nobility. Meanwhile, the Chancellor sent the same warning to the Hungarians, informing one leading Magyar aristocrat: 'The example of the justice meted out [in Galicia] could easily turn against the upper classes in Hungary . . . you know as well as I do what an effect would be produced in the countryside if the king appeared to be appealing to the people.'[58] By March 1848, however, it was in Italy in particular that the nobility were being threatened with a 'Galician programme'. Army officers were telling the poor of Milan that their misfortunes were the fault of the Italian upper classes and not the Austrians. Radetzky was advocating a programme of reforms in aid of the peasants against their masters and ominous hints were being dropped in the Austrian press that the Galician horrors were about to repeat themselves in Italy. As the *Augsburger Allgemeine Zeitung* put it: 'People in Italy are making the same remarks as were made in Galicia. The masses in Italy as in Galicia are not interested . . . in [political] movements and if the Lombards are forced to pay the cost of their revolution, it will not be the farm labourers who will suffer as a class; the repayment shall be made by the landowners and the rich and since they alone are guilty, they alone should pay the price.'[59] All in all, therefore, Metternich was content to risk a hard line in the belief that, if and when it came to the crunch, a combination of the army and the masses would see off any revolutionary challenge from the dissident local aristocracies who resented rule from Vienna. His policy in Italy, as in Vienna, was one of no concessions, even though there were many indications that the Italian nobility would have been more than willing to be bought off. Yet, even so, were the Austrians correct to believe that they still enjoyed the support of other sections of society? Could they really count on the peasants in particular to remain loyal? And how soundly based was their faith in the 'Galician' threat?

In Italy, there were at least two major problems which they tended to overlook: the economic grievances of the peasantry and the influence of the church. With regard to the first of these, exact grievances differed from place to place, but basically the issue was 'free possession of land'.[60] In the mountain regions, the peasants' main demand was that the *beni communali* which had been sold off on the open market after 1839 should be restored to them; in the provinces of Brescia and Como, they refused to pay tolls and taxes on food; while in areas of share-cropping they wanted to see the system extended.[61] As far as the church was concerned – and its influence extended to all classes – the break between it and the state for a variety of reasons was almost total by 1848 in Lombardy-Venetia. For a start, it had been the priesthood which along with the nobility had been slaughtered in Galicia in 1846. About eighty priests had died in the Tarnow district alone and this had led to Europe's most famous denunciation of Austrian conduct there – Montalambert's speech of 2 July 1846 in the French Parliament. This speech had been 'the protest of the Catholic world' and 'had stiffened the resolve of every Italian'; its religious overtones had 'separated the Catholic cause from the Austrian one in the public mind' in Italy.[62] If that had not been enough, it had been followed in 1847 by a major diplomatic confrontation between Austria and the Papacy when Radetzky, who regarded the Pope as a prisoner of the Roman mob, exercised his right (as he and Metternich both saw it) to garrison the papal town of Ferrara. Unfortunately, this was done without the Pope's consent and, indeed, in such a way as to make it seem that Austria had declared war on His Holiness. Metternich backtracked to save Austria's face, but Catholic hostility to the Austrians was again increased when riots broke out in Milan upon the entry into that city of its first Italian-born Archbishop. Radetzky was forced to confess: 'the Italian clergy with few exceptions belong to our most open and dangerous enemies',[63] a fact which was underlined by the obvious contrast between the reforming Pope in Rome and Metternich's resistance to change. One complaint from an Austrian official ran: 'Their priests are the promoters of these disorders, their priests are in touch with the first priest of Rome, who is the revolutionary number one.'[64] All the authorities could do, however, was to stop Austrian troops confessing to Italian priests. There was no way in which they could limit the influence of the church among the people at large. Nor, indeed, did it try to take a neutral stand. The Archbishop of Milan would soon be blessing 'the holy work of liberation' and the revolution would witness the 'enthusiastic participation of the clergy' and take on the character of 'holy war'.[65] Indeed, there was even discussion of battalions of priests being formed to help establish a Lombard army.[66] Elsewhere in the Monarchy, although there were religious problems before 1848, there was no question of religious leaders opposing the authority of the state. Josephinism saw to this as far as the Catholic Church was concerned. As for the other churches, although some religious leaders did enjoy enormous political influence, which they were indeed to make use of during the revolutions – one thinks of the Uniate Bishop Şaguna among the Transylvanian Romanians or of the Serb Patriarch Rajačić, who was the political leader of his people in Hungary – it was only in Lombardy-Venetia that the church became actively involved in promoting revolution.

Elsewhere, too, there was less sign of peasant or bourgeois dissatisfaction with the régime. In Italy, possibly as many bourgeois as nobles were alienated and for many of the same reasons. They, too, suffered from the disabilities which prevented young nobles from making their way in the imperial service and they too were influenced by the spread of nationalism, the growth of the press, the rise of Italian literature, the scientific congresses, etc. They also followed the news of reforms elsewhere and shared the hopes invested in Pius IX. They too were aware therefore, of the benefits which might accrue to them if the Austrians were to depart. Yet elsewhere, these conditions did not apply. The bourgeoisie in Bohemia, Czech or German, were loyal to the throne and even the rising nationalist movement there was patronized by the governor. Elsewhere among the south Slavs, the Slovaks or the Romanian populations of the Empire, the throne seemed to be the only protection at hand against the Magyarizing tendencies of the new Hungarian nationalism. Hence, there was no threat of revolution from the bourgeoisie of these quarters. Besides, many of the bourgeoisie in the towns of these areas were often German anyway, something which was also true of Hungary proper. The peasantry everywhere had grievances, of course – in many cases, greater ones than applied in Italy. Feudal dues and services weighed heavily upon them in Bohemia, Austria and Hungary, but there is little evidence that they were either revolutionary or reactionary. After all, the Galician peasants had received no benefits for their loyalty in 1846; nor could they expect to be able to change anything by themselves. In short, they could only wait upon events. On the other hand, just how eager were they to take advantage of any breakdown that might occur in order to better their situation? And how far did the same apply to the masses in the towns? After all, it had been the French nobility in the eighteenth century who had spearheaded the *pré-révolution*, but they in turn had been swept away by the bourgeoisie, the *sans-culottes* and the peasants. Let us, therefore, take a closer look at the social and economic climate in the Monarchy before 1848.

ECONOMIC GROWTH IN METTERNICH'S AUSTRIA

Among economic historians, there is now general agreement that the 'pre-1848 Austrian economy showed definite signs of dynamism'.[67] More recently, American cliometricians have argued that 'sustained growth' – that is to say, growth of such a magnitude as not to be overshadowed by short-term fluctuations – set in during the *Vormärz* period. Richard Rudolph has written: 'When we place emphasis on the beginning of mechanization and the time when Austrian industrial growth became comparable with the rest of Europe, we can talk about Austria's being industrialised in the 1830s and 1840s'.[68] John Komlos has concluded: 'if industrialisation can be said to have had a beginning in Austria, the beginning occurred between 1825 and 1850.'[69] David F. Good has confirmed: 'The behavior of population, output, and output per person in the *Vormärz* strongly indicates the emergence of modern economic growth.'[70] Population grew by 1 per cent per annum between 1817 and 1845 and 'no Malthusian reaction occurred'. This was because the per capita industrial growth rate ranged between 1.8 and 2.6 per cent. The percentage of the population engaged in agriculture fell from 75 per cent in 1790 to 72 per cent by 1850; in Bohemia, the figures were 78 per cent in 1756 and 64 per cent on the eve of 1848.[71] Of the various sectors of industry, the highest growth was to be found in the mining industry (6.9 per cent annually between 1830 and 1845), according to Rudolph, and cotton, according to Komlos (7.1 per cent).[72] The iron industry grew by 5 per cent according to Rudolph, the sugar industry by 4.8 per cent according to Komlos.[73] A number of factors were behind this growth: the founding of polytechnical institutes; new patent laws; technological improvements in a variety of industries; the construction of roads, canals and railways; agricultural improvements (the expansion of acreage, the introduction of crop rotation, the introduction of new crops like the potato, sugar beet and clover); and the establishment of societies for the development of agriculture and industry.

There were, however a number of features of industrialization peculiar to Austria which we have to bear in mind if we are to relate it to the outbreak of revolution. Rudolph has drawn attention to one of these in a discussion of the previous stereotypical image of industrialization involving a clash between an urban bourgeoisie and a landed aristocracy. He writes: 'In actuality, however, the process of economic change was much more complex than some of the ideas which equate capitalism with industry and towns would suggest. What one sees in a microeconomic view of the Monarchy is less an urban pattern than a multi-faceted growth pattern of manufacture. It is true that there was marked urbanization in Lower Austria before the middle of the nineteenth century, but elsewhere one sees different patterns. In Bohemia and Moravia the origins of industry appear to have been markedly non-urban. In these regions, as well as in several in the Alpine provinces, the rule tended to be the growth of manufacture either on large estates, at the behest of the aristocracy, or else the growth of by-employment in the peasant households, gradually developing into larger scale industry.'[74] He, therefore, rejects the views of some historians that Austria could not have industrialized during the *Vormärz* period because of the lack of a developed middle class: '. . . as has already been pointed out, in the Monarchy a great deal of the growth of manufacture had rural origins and a rural nature and concomitantly groups other than the urban middle class picked up the functions of the urban entrepreneur. Thus local studies demonstrate a wide and varied origin of managers and entrepreneurs, including nobles, estate agents, German and English traders and skilled craftsmen, government officials and Jewish traders and pedlars. Special attention must be paid to the extensive role in Austrian economic development of manufacture on the large estates under the aegis of the landed aristocracy. In terms of capital investment, too, their role was great. As the Czech economic historian Arnost Klima has pointed out, their investment was large and crucial because they basically, were the people who had the funds to invest.'[75] The Austrian historian, Wolfgang Häusler, reached similar conclusions regarding the role of nobles, Jews, foreigners and others in the process of industrialization. As for the 'bourgeoisie', he concluded: 'There can be no case for saying that in Austria during the revolutionary year there was a sharply defined bourgeoisie which was distinctly cut off from the working class armed with established economic and political programmes.'[76] The situation was, rather, that society was just emancipating itself from feudalism and was only beginning to come to grips with new social and economic conditions.

Another feature of Austrian industry was its relative backwardness. People complained about this at the time. It was the major reason why Austrian industrialists, for example, objected to plans to join the *Zollverein*. It was the reason, too, why many traders neglected to turn up at Austrian exhibitions, even though they attended Prussian ones. Hence Nachum Gross's assertion that: 'During the second quarter of the century domestic and foreign observers seem to have become increasingly conscious of the fact that the Austrian economy, though moving ahead, was falling behind in its development.'[77] There were, it is true, a number of products in which the Austrians were superior to the Germans – Bohemian glassware, Styrian steel, Viennese shawls, coaches, gloves, ladies' footwear and Italian silks – while in many other branches, Austria could undersell Germany in the coarse-quality range – raw linen, coarse cloth and knitwear, cheap hardware, crude potteries and plain paper. Yet in general, German products were superior and cheaper in the higher qualities: in better textiles, earthenware, porcelain, most leather products, instruments and machinery. Austria, it was said, produced either for the very poor or for the very rich, while Germany produced for the middle classes. The reasons for this were to be found in both the demand and supply sides: wages were significantly lower in Austria and interest rates were higher. The results, though, were obvious and Gross has catalogued them for different industries and foreign trade. For example: 'The data on steam power and coal consumption . . . forcefully bring out what must be termed the technological backwardness of most Austrian industry in the 1840s. Belgium, with a population one fourth the Austrian, had five times the Austrian capacity in stationary steam engines and almost five times her coal consumption. The difference is not that extreme but still very impressive with respect to France and Germany. It is true that the per capacity unit investment in water wheels, and even turbines, was considerably lower than in steam engines. But this factor was, however, operative in France and Germany to about the same degree as in the Monarchy.'[78] The iron industry too suffered from chronic ailments: the prevalence of small units in the Alps; the scarcity and unfavourable location of cokeable coal; the vested interests of large estate-owners. in the Czech and Hungarian lands who viewed iron production merely as a means of marketing more timber. Alpine pig iron, which accounted for two-thirds of Austrian output in the 1830s and 1840s, remained exclusively charcoal-smelted as late as 1870. The engineering industry in turn suffered from the deficiencies in iron and coal production. That, in turn, explains why industry and agriculture were so slow to introduce steam power: steam engines were expensive, whether imported or domestically produced, and they faced severe problems of fuel supply. All these factors were, of course, mutually reinforcing; together they help explain industrial retardation and the relative smallness of the Austrian rail network. For here too the Austrians lagged behind. Thus while Britain between 1845 and 1850 increased her network by 160 per cent, Germany by 180 per cent, and France by 245 per cent, Austria could only manage 85 per cent. This is sometimes explained by Habsburg insistence on building strategic rather than commercial railroads, but in fact even by that criterion the performance was not impressive. Finally, Austria's backwardness was encouraged by her policy of *Autarkie*, her attempt to achieve economic self-sufficiency. There were both economic and political motives involved here: the hope that cheap wages in the East would provide cheap foodstuffs and raw materials in the West; the need to ally with feudal elements in Hungary; not to mention the need to protect emerging industries from competition and the domestic population from new ideas. Yet *Autarkie* inevitably made Austria less competitive and deprived her of alternative sources of supply.

A third factor of importance in delineating Austria's particular process of industrialization was the chronic lack of credit from which she suffered. According to Good: 'The evolution of a financial system in the *Vormärz* was certainly embryonic.'[79] The main bank was the Austrian National Bank, established in 1816 on the model of the Bank of France after the chaotic financial developments of that year. To restore stability, the Bank was given the sole right of note issue and granted nominal independence from state control. It was also allowed from the beginning to discount bills of exchange. These came to be the principal earning assets of the Bank's portfolio, but 'its overall impact on the credit market was slight – the terms of discounting were so stringent that only the wealthiest and most respected clients were permitted access to bank funds'.[80] In the period before 1848, branches were opened in many of the main cities of the Monarchy, but basically they only existed to allow payments to be made to the state, although they were also places where notes could be exchanged for coin. 'Only in the 1840s were the credit facilities of the Vienna office extended to the provincial branches, and not until 1847 did any branch (Prague) open discounting facilities.'[81] There was no involvement with mortgage finance before 1855, but involvement with state finance remained high. Inevitably, therefore, there were complaints concerning both the monopoly position of Vienna and of the Bank's limited lending facilities in general. There were also savings banks in Austria. The first of them, the *Erste Oesterreichische Sparkasse*, was established in Vienna in 1819, but the basic legislation governing their operation was not introduced until 1844. They were supposed to encourage thrift and industriousness among the lower-income classes, but gradually they became the preserve of the better-off. They invested chiefly in urban mortgages, although they also dealt with agricultural property. According to Good: 'Roughly one quarter of available funds was invested in a portfolio of high grade securities, chiefly federal, provincial and municipal debt. The banks were not permitted to finance industrial enterprise . . . the economic impact of their influence has not really been investigated.'[82]

It has long been clear, on the other hand, that the activities of the large, private banking houses were of enormous significance. These – and one thinks especially of the houses of Rothschild, Schoeller, Geymuller, Sina, Stametz-Mayer and Arnstein-Eskeles – held government debt and contracted long-term loans with the nobility. But they were also involved in aiding industrial and commercial enterprise – railways, for example – and provided discounting facilities to firms outside Vienna. They therefore 'filled the void left by the national bank's highly restrictive discounting policy'.[83] Even so, they could hardly hope to meet the demand for credit which was to be felt in Austria in the late 1840s.

It is now time to take a look at two other aspects of the economic situation in the Monarchy before the outbreak of revolution: the pattern of government expenditure and the position of the Empire's trade balance. Regarding the first, one fairly reliable estimate for 1834 (at which time figures were not published – they only became available from the early 1840s) paints the picture as follows:

Interest on the public debt	40,000,000 florins
Civil administration	44,000,000 florins
Expenses of the imperial family	3,500,000 florins
Military expenditure	60,000,000 florins
TOTAL EXPENDITURE	147,500,000 florins
TOTAL INCOME	130,000,000 florins
STATE DEFICIT FOR 1834	17,500,000 florins[84]

This deficit had to be filled by loans which, in turn, added to the interest on the state debt which was already heavy. Thus, according to the same source: 'In the year 1835 such a loan was raised to the amount of 40,000,000 florins, which was procured at an interest of about four per cent: but the contractors took that opportunity of requiring a specific engagement from the crown, that the military establishment should be forthwith reduced, as pressing too heavily on the finances of the state; and as soon as circumstances would permit, it was understood that such reductions were made, as to have effected a considerable saving in that branch of the expenditure.'[85] By 1847, however, the situation was not much better. According to the official figures,[86] the pattern of expenditure ran as follows:

Interest on the state debt	45,000,000 florins
Civil and court administration	60,000,000 florins
Military expenditure	63,000,000 florins
TOTAL EXPENDITURE	168,000,000 florins
TOTAL INCOME	161,000,000 florins
STATE DEFICIT FOR 1847	7,000,000 florins

Another way of stating these figures is to say that by 1847 the army was taking up 37.5 per cent of the state's revenue, the civil administration 35 per cent, and the interest on the state debt about 28 per cent. The state finances, therefore, were in a very bad way and were to get even worse during 1848–9. Military expenditure in 1848 was to rise to 73 million florins and in 1849 was to reach 165 million. The corresponding deficits were to be 45 million and 122 million florins, respectively.[87]

To make matters worse, the balance of payments by the late 1840s had also gone into deficit. This was largely because Austria had to import finished goods in order to industrialize, although it was also due to her exclusion from neighbouring markets. The relatively poor quality of her goods and the lack of productivity associated with her industry and commerce contributed as well. In any case, according to the Austrian historian, Robert Enderes, imports into Austria (his figures do not relate to Hungary) rose by 78 per cent in the period between 1830 and 1845, whereas exports rose by only 41 per cent during the same period.[88] As a result, Austria's trading surplus become a deficit. His figures in detail read as follows:

Imports	*1831*	*1840*	*1845*
Foodstuffs and raw materials:	38,481,871 fl.	52,759,772 fl.	54,339,269 fl.
Finished goods:	26,804,027 fl.	41,254,659 fl.	61,944,586 fl.
Total:	65,285,898 fl.	94,014,431 fl.	116,283,855 fl.
Exports			
Foodstuffs and raw materials:	18,127,379 fl.	23,156,892 fl.	25,933,632 fl.
Finished goods:	57,900,750 fl.	70,670,920 fl.	81,608,635 fl.
Total:	76,028,129 fl.	93,827,812 fl.	107,542,267 fl.

The real meaning of these figures was that as a result of government spending and the adverse trade balance, the finances of the Monarchy were in crisis. By the end of 1847, its only hope of salvation lay in securing yet another enormous loan from the Rothschilds. Metternich, with little understatement, told Solomon Rothschild that Hell was staring them both in the face: 'If the devil fetches me he will fetch you too.'[89] If there were to be no loan, he said, the Emperor would be faced with the prospect of surrendering Lombardy-Venetia to the revolution. Rothschild agreed and Kübeck therefore negotiated the terms which Kolowrat proposed to the *Ministerkonferenz* in December 1847. He said:

> The most important consideration lies in the urgent necessity of giving the financial administration the widest possible scope in its efforts to extricate itself from the embarrassments consequent upon heavy and unforeseen military expenditure. The reserve fund (i.e. the loan) to which I have referred is the last sheet anchor to which the Head of Treasury [Kübeck], who spares himself no efforts, can cling. Unfortunately, when this sum is spent there will be nothing left to deal with any new misfortune which may arise. Yet states must necessarily reckon with the possibility of such misfortune, even if they take the form of events which lie beyond the control of humanity, such as the death of the head of a state, the outbreak of an epidemic, the failure of a harvest, etc. I feel it to be my duty at the present moment to put forward these considerations without reserve, and as emphatically as I can, while it is still possible to place a limit to the excessive military preparations in Italy, and to the expenditure of our last resources; and to call attention to the fact, which will otherwise be made evident by the complete breakdown of our finances, that the Austrian government has sacrificed too much to its position abroad and has paid too little heed to conditions at home.
>
> I feel it my duty to make the grave statement that we are on the verge

of an abyss, and the increasing demands on the Treasury arising out of the measures necessary to combat foreign revolutionary elements have led to increased disturbances within the country, as is indicated by the attitude of the provincial estates, and by the literary outbursts in the press of our neighbours.[90]

This was a most amazing confession. Thanks to Metternich's obsession with the revolution and the military measures needed to sustain the foreign policy that was predicated on it, Kolowrat was admitting that the state had been brought to the very brink of bankruptcy. The Rothschild loan constituted the government's last hope, but once that ran out, there would be no money left to cope with whatever disasters, natural or man-made, arose. In fact, however, the government was already unable to cope. The natural disasters of the previous years – a series of harvest failures since 1845 – meant that Kolowrat's statement was already out of date.

THE ECONOMIC AND SOCIAL BACKGROUND TO 1848

It is now time to examine the other side of the economic crisis – the human misery – which formed the background to events in 1848. This was largely brought about by two factors: the structural changes and concomitant unemployment caused by industrialization, and the harvest failures of the years 1845–8. However, the effects of these were made considerably worse because, in the first place, the relative backwardness of the Austrian economy, not to mention the government's protectionist policies and the lack of credit, made it very difficult to gain new markets; while, as we have seen, the government's financial crisis meant that it had no extra resources to spend on combating the growing misery. Having said that, however, it is difficult to give precise measurements of the degree of misery involved. As Julius Marx has written in his exhaustive account of the economic causes of the revolutions in Austria: 'The ideal thing to have for a work of research on living conditions would of course be a calculation of price levels as well as the corresponding standards of living arranged as an index. Unfortunately all the preliminary materials are lacking.'[91] There are, of course, a range of statistics available but, as Marx points out, it is impossible to paint a true picture of living conditions without knowing about local customs, regional variations, side-payments, family arrangements, differences in taste, rooming arrangements and patterns of employment. However, there can be no doubt that living conditions were bad and getting worse. Police reports make this abundantly clear but, given the central importance of the harvest to the whole economy of pre-industrial Europe, this had to be so in any case. In Austria, long dry summers and autumns followed by cold hard winters brought a series of harvest failures which in turn meant that prices rarely fell in the years 1845–8. On the contrary, there was a continuous inflation. This meant that taxes also rose since the most important of these were based on price levels. The tax on consumables, in particular, became a focus for hatred and was condemned by Andrian as a 'blood tax on the proletariat'.[92] Yet since it brought in many times as much revenue as most other taxes, Kolowrat had no choice but to retain it. By European standards,[93] taxes were not especially high in Austria, but given the deteriorating condition of the economy, they were bound to be resented. One official reported of the tax on consumables that it was 'levied on every piece of bread, on every potato, so that a poor weaver, who along with his family was scarcely evading death from hunger, and from whom it took the army to extract the 3fl. tax on his income, if it was extracted at all, had to pay many times that through this tax'.[94] Standards of living, therefore, were certainly falling, and even by 1842 the police director of Linz could report that two-thirds of the town's 26,000 inhabitants were undernourished and that 1,842 people were living on a daily wage of between 2 kr and 16 kr. Yet by 1847 in Vienna, the price of one egg was 6–7.5 kr and a couple of potatoes were costing 3 kr in the shops. In 1846, a pound of butter was costing 66 kr, while a factory worker might be earning only 40 kr per day. The price of wood was also sky-high – it had risen 250 per cent in price over the decade 1836–46 – so that people could neither feed themselves nor keep warm. Given that women and children formed 60 per cent of the workforce in the cotton and paper industries of Lower Austria and were paid at most only about half of what men earned for their twelve to fourteen-hour day, it is not surprising that in some parts of the Monarchy by 1847 more than half the deaths being recorded were of children. The only hope was to get work in a factory, where so much of the money was now being made. Factory owners paid higher wages – although where possible they hired women and children cheaply – and they were more and more buying out the small workshops whose masters could not afford to install modern equipment and whose goods could not compete with factory prices and standards. By the 1840s, then, it was factory-produced goods which were dominating the Austrian economy. By 1848, the Monarchy had 209 cotton-spinning mills, 469 steam engines, 278 locomotive engines and 76 steamboat engines. Even in 1841, its 7,315 factories were producing 510,715,000 fl. worth of goods as opposed to the 184,896,000 fl. worth produced by the Monarchy's small workshops. Yet by 1848, even factories were at a standstill, since the high prices for food and the lack of credit meant that there was no money around to buy goods. By 1847, indeed, 10,000 factory workers had been dismissed in Vienna alone, although there were no repetitions of the riots which had broken out in Prague three years earlier when the unemployed had attacked the factory owners. Yet the outlook was grim: thousands out of work with no government aid to fall back on at a time when prices were at an historic high; and even for those still in work, wages which hardly covered the barest necessities of life. Typhoid, too, had broken out in many of the big cities, so that life for the urban poor was extremely bleak.[95]

In the countryside, too, the situation was often desperate. Here, again, it is impossible to give precise statistics since living standards varied from place to place and much would depend on weather conditions and how much in the way of domestic farm animals or poaching peasants could lay their hands on. The peasants' income, however, would have been everywhere reduced by a series of dues. These included: the robot or compulsory labour service which varied throughout the Monarchy; the *Zehnt*, tenth or tithe, which meant that the peasant had to pay his lord one-tenth of his crop or produce; as well as other payments in kind – for vineyards, for example, or when land-holdings changed hands. Then there was the land tax to the government, which amounted to 17–24 per cent of the net proceeds of the land; money for church and state employees (priests and schoolmasters); along with obligations such as maintaining roads and bridges, providing horses and conveyances for state officials, making house-room available for troops if they were quartered on him; and giving sons to the army in times of conscription. Feudal dues in one way or another took up 70 per cent of a peasant's income. Yet he was probably better off than an industrial worker in 1848 and better off than his forefathers had been.

In the *Vormärz* period as a whole, according to David F. Good's summary: 'Historians are not inclined to view the peasantry's condition . . . as unduly harsh. Komlos, relying on the contemporary John Paget, argues that "the material lot of the peasantry varied, but by and large, it was not unbearable". Blum believes that with respect to his personal status the peasant was "in a servile status" but "was not a serf". There were, of course, substantial regional differences. The German provinces – Lower Austria, Upper Austria, Styria and Carinthia – had relatively heavier payments in kind and money but lighter labour services and less oppressive personal status. In the Slavic provinces – the Bohemian lands and the Carpathian lands – the situation was the reverse. In general Rosdolski ranks the provinces according to the peasantry's burden as follows: The burden was lightest in the German provinces, somewhat heavier in Bohemia, Moravia and Silesia, and most severe in Galicia and Bukovina, where the peasants were simply "work animals".'[96]

The description of the Galician 'serfs' as 'work animals' goes a long way to explain the events there in 1846. Elsewhere, however, it is not so clear how the peasants felt regarding relations with their feudal superiors. This is important, since the impression is often conveyed in the secondary literature that the key to events in Austria in 1848 was the abolition of the robot. It may be the case, however, that in some parts of the Monarchy (although it is difficult to believe that this was generally true) the aristocracy were more in favour of this than the peasants themselves. Much, no doubt, hinged on terms of compensation. At any rate, here is the experience of one landlord as related in an English survey of the Monarchy published in 1840:

> 'I want work done', said he, 'on a part of my properties upon a Thursday but the robotters nearest at hand object that this is not their day of service. The Thursday workers live perhaps at a distance, far and wide apart; they are allowed by law so much time to come and so much to return; they arrive half-tired and bring broken carts and jaded horses and the result of the whole is, that hardly any useful work is performed. We always take money payments where we can obtain them and would willingly commute the whole of our robots in perpetuity; but to proposals of this nature the robotters will hardly ever consent. They compound with us for the work of weeks, or of months, possibly even a year (usually, however, on terms lower than the law defines), but rarely for longer periods. One reason of their refusal may be the want of cash; but another more availing one is, their knowledge of the inclination of the government in their favour and their persuasion of what must, in fact, ere long be the case, that robots will either be reduced to a formal nullity, or altogether cease.'[97]

Certainly, there was much debate in the 1840s in local diets and agricultural societies whether the robot should be abolished. Most historians believe that by 1848 the majority of aristocrats would have been happy to see it go. Yet the government did nothing. Why? To retain its ability to threaten to unleash the peasants? Or had no real consensus emerged on abolishing the robot? It is interesting to see the view confirmed that the government was believed, by both nobles and peasants, to be on the side of the latter. Indeed, Turnbull, the author of the above-cited passage, time and again describes the main object of government policy as one of aiding the peasants against the nobles: 'The policy of the crown aims steadily in this direction. Its tendency is invariably to abate feudal limitation and privilege of every description; but safety and wisdom require that its progress should be gradual and cautious, and hence the law recognises limitations and entails of various descriptions.'[98] None the less, according to Turnbull, it had already achieved a considerable amount on behalf of its poorest subjects through its policies on entails, education (free but not compulsory) and legal support. For example: 'Whenever the subject is plaintiff against the lord, he applies to the imperial procurator of the province who carries on the suit for him in the crown tribunals at very small expense; and indeed, so favourable is the general policy of the law toward the subject, that the late Emperor Francis in speaking of his private domains, used frequently to utter a half-serious complaint, of his inability to obtain from the peasants on his private domains the justice to which he was by common law entitled.'[99] Apparently, other lords felt likewise and were often prepared to make out-of-court settlements with peasants, settlements which favoured the latter, rather than submit to the judgement of the imperial courts. Thus, it would seem that the government could depend on considerable support in the countryside, at least in normal times. By 1848, however, the burdens imposed by the robot and the tenth must have felt considerably more onerous given the harvest failures and bad weather. Landless labourers, in particular, could have had no better prospects to look forward to than town labourers.

There is one other section of the population, finally, which must be surveyed before attempting any assessment of how social and economic conditions might have affected the outbreak of revolution in 1848. These are the middle classes, concerning some of whom a conclusion may be arrived at fairly quickly. As far as the high bourgeoisie were concerned, there is every reason to suppose that they would have been divided in their views. But few of them would have been revolutionary. Bankers and successful industrialists, they were often foreign or Jewish and wanted only to integrate into Austrian society. They looked to the government for ennoblement and status and they invested their profits in land (Jews, in fact, could only do so with government permission – they had no civil rights).

According to Häusler, the percentage of bourgeois landowners in one district around Vienna rose from 11 to 28 per cent between 1815 and 1848; in a second, it rose from 3 to 16 per cent; in a third, 7 to 16 per cent; and in a fourth, from 3 to 20 per cent.[100] Smaller workshop owners obviously also made up part of the middle classes but their plight, as we have already seen, was becoming ever more desperate as factories drove them increasingly out of business. The other part of the middle classes were the professionals – journalists, civil servants, school-teachers, academics, clergymen, officers, doctors and lawyers. They were obviously a varied lot, but they had one thing in common: they were dependent on the government. The government knew this and therefore did not pay them much. But it had one hold over them which they valued above all else: retirement pensions. The one thing in life which all these people knew was that if they were faithful to the government it would look after them and their wives and children. Hence officers would put up with decades of the lowest pay and slow promotions in the safe knowledge that retirement on a captain's pension was quite bearable and that even service ennoblement would follow. Civil servants (and school-teachers, clergy and academics were all civil servants) would even forgo their salaries in times of crisis (presumably taking refuge in loans or some sort of black economy) to be sure of their longer-term prospects. Thus at the end of the Napoleonic Wars, some grades of junior clerks had had to work for two to three years without pay to be sure of their future employment, while others had had to do so for five to seven years. Between 1815 and 1848, moreover, the bureaucracy became so bloated that law students, whose expectation was immediate government service, had to wait ten to twelve years before being taken on. All of these people must therefore have had a somewhat schizophrenic attitude towards the régime: discontented but dependent at the same time. They would certainly also have been influenced by the anti-government literature of the 1840s.

Students who had not yet graduated were, as students usually are, both more extreme in their ideas and less representative of society as a whole. In Austria, for most of the Metternich period they had enjoyed a reputation for moderation. This was partly because before they were allowed into university, not only did they require certificates attesting to their moral fitness but, if they were to acquire state grants of any sort, were required to compete for them in examinations to ensure that only serious candidates secured awards. By 1840, some 45,398 fl. were being spent in this way on 'poor students' at Austria's eight universities. The University of Vienna, for example, had 274 poor students out of a total of 2,000; Prague, 62 out of 1,700; Pavia had 26; Lemberg 33; Gratz 81; Olmutz 112; and Padua none. The Protestant institution in Vienna had 30 poor students out of a total of 49, so that in the Monarchy as a whole (excluding Pest) there were about 640 of this type. However, this was proportionately a much smaller figure than in Germany, and for this and other reasons – the police were allowed to maintain order in Austrian universities – there was much less trouble there than in German universities. An attempt to establish *Burschenschaften* at the University of Prague in the 1830s, for example, was immediately suppressed and the foreigners involved immediately sent home. On the other hand: 'The native pupils were merely admonished and imprisoned for a fortnight; and no attempt to establish secret societies, has, it is believed even been made since.'[101] Hence Turnbull's description of Austrian academic life in 1840: 'The universities exhibit a striking contrast with those of the rest of Germany. In them are no drunken brawls – scarcely any duels – no troops of students struggling six abreast through the streets with lengthy pipes in their mouths and fumes of beer in their heads – no popular professors descending at midnight to the street, humbly to thank the spirited youths for the compliment of their noisy serenade.'[102] Times would change, however. The students of the Monarchy, like those everywhere, would pick up the most critical ideas of the day in the most uncritical fashion and would become the social group most involved of any in the events of 1848.

THE FALL OF METTERNICH AND THE OUTBREAK OF REVOLUTION

So much then for the economic and social background to events in 1848. It demonstrates that there was a great deal of discontent due to inflation, unemployment, bad winters and food shortages at a time when the government's financial crisis meant that no money could be spared to provide direct help for the poor or to reduce taxes. Public awareness of this crisis and the memories of previous ones in 1811 and 1816 meant that people were becoming very worried about foreign policy. The great fear was that the money which the government would need to take the offensive in Italy (and the cost of providing troops had risen dramatically by the late 1840s) would bring about yet another state bankruptcy. Hence the so-called 'Bank Hullaballoo' – a run on the banks – began throughout the Monarchy, not after the fall of Louis Philippe in France, but after the Tobacco Riots and the imposition of martial law on Lombardy-Venetia. Even then, however, there was no talk of revolution, simply the feeling that the régime was doing nothing and would do nothing. There was certainly no call for a republic, no call even for judges, generals, bureaucrats or other members of the governing elite to be replaced as a class. The urban proletariat certainly had no idea of overthrowing the government. Rath quotes one memoir which says: 'They had no leaders, no programme, no theories.'[103] Karl Marx, whose views found no response when he visited Vienna in the late summer of 1848, described them as 'distrusted, disarmed and disorganised, hardly emerging from the intellectual bondage of the old regime'.[104] The real object of their hatred, it turned out, was not the government or the dynasty, but the Jews. The latter were prominent as traders of all sorts, factory owners and shopkeepers. They therefore got the blame for high prices and unemployment. They were also hated by the small workshop masters with whom they were in competition. Hence the anti-semitic riots that took place all over the Empire once revolution had broken out. Curiously, the dynasty remained unscathed. It had been popular among the ordinary people under Francis I, who had gone about the streets with his empress on their promenade without any guards. He had also spoken *Wienerisch* and one day a week had given audiences to whoever among his subjects had wished to consult him. The result was: 'In the days of Francis, every farmer or petty proprietor or shopkeeper for hundreds of miles round Vienna, who had a grievance to complain of against the government, used to get into his cart, drive himself up to the capital and tell his story to "*Kaiser Franz*" . . . (If wronged he usually got redress.) . . . Upper and Lower Austria and Styria abound with stories of simple-minded men, who in their domestic difficulties, their differences with each other, their doubts as to their daughters' marriages or their own testaments, used to go up to have a friendly consultation with the emperor, and were certain to receive from him plain, straightforward, sensible advice.'[105] His successor, the mentally-retarded, epileptic Ferdinand I, tried to do the same and he too secured the loyalty of his subjects to whom he became known as 'Ferdinand the Goodhearted' as well as 'Ferdy the Loony'. Thus although other well-regarded members of the imperial family died in 1847 (Archduke Joseph, the Palatine of Hungary, Archduke Charles, the victor of Aspern and Archduke

Friedrich, the 'hero of Acre' – the period of court mourning after their deaths actually leading to lay-offs in the fashion trade),[106] the Emperor was still able to ride out in his carriage among the Viennese at the height of the revolution to the applause of all. As far as the educated classes were concerned, it was the government who had to take the blame. And Metternich, whose name had become synonymous with the government, became the principal focus for cirticism. it was he after all who had rejected any kind of reform for Italy, it was he who was refusing concessions to the Hungarians, it was he who might go to war with republican France, and it was he whose foreign and defence policies in general had deprived the government of the means to help the poor. In short, it was Metternich's policies which now threatened the state with bankruptcy. Hence, when petition after petition was submitted to the *Hofburg* in March 1848, the underlying demand was for his overthrow and that of his system – always, of course, in favour of some mild, monarchical alternative.

In this atmosphere, all eyes turned to the estates of Lower Austria whose meeting place was in Vienna at the *Landhaus*. The estates were of no little importance, as Turnbull realized: 'Of legislative power they have none but their administrative faculties, always varying in different provinces, are always important.'[107] Members of the estates were in communication with all classes of people, had a stake in local prosperity, helped administer the provinces for the government and, therefore, had to be listened to. On 13 March they too were to present a petition just as the students had done the night before. Their deliberations, however, were interrupted by a student mob. This then made its way towards the imperial palace, where the imperial family, along with Metternich and Kolowrat, were taking stock of the situation. Two things now happened: the police in the capital lost control of the situation and the imperial family deserted the Chancellor.

One of the great ironies of the year 1848 in Europe was that when it came to the crunch, Metternich, Europe's self-styled Chief of Police, had no police to protect him. In a fascinating article, William L. Langer has shown that, whereas in 'liberal' Western Europe, Louis Philippe had the protection of 3,000 municipal guards, 84,000 national guards and a garrison of 30,000 troops, and the British government, under threat from the Chartists in 1848, had the support of 3,000 well-trained 'bobbies' and 150,000 special constables, not to mention the British army, Metternich in Vienna could rely only on a garrison of 14,000, a police force of 1,000 and a municipal guard of 14,000 men (at least in theory, since it consisted mainly of brass bands).[108] It was extremely unfortunate, therefore, that when the Viennese rioters – a mixture of nobles and students according to the report of the American consul – met up with a detachment of troops in the Herrengasse under the command of the haughty Archduke Albert, the latter, having been attacked by one of the mob, should have ordered his men to fire into the crowd. After this, chaos broke out. The municipal guard which was brought into the inner city went over to the mob, and workers in the suburbs took advantage of the situation to burn down the hated factories. Yet they were still loyal; one of them in Hetzendorf was reported as saying: 'That's an imperial palace; there's nothing for us there; we're only going to the factories to destroy the machines which rob us of bread.'[109] Meanwhile, at the Hofburg, a civic deputation had requested the Emperor to dismiss his Chancellor, and the Archduke Albert had been replaced as garrison commander by Prince Alfred Windishgraetz. Yet, for reasons which he would for ever refuse to divulge, the Prince did not impose martial law or put the city in a state of siege – presumably because his requests were refused by the imperial family. Grillparzer believed that a couple of battalions of soldiers could have restored order immediately. Instead, the imperial family – the Archduke Louis, a narrow-minded conservative, the Archduke Francis Charles, the Emperor's oldest brother and not much brighter than Ferdinand himself and the Archduke John, an old enemy of the Chancellor – met along with Kolowrat and Metternich to discuss what ought to be done. Metternich made a long and tedious speech counselling resistance, at the end of which there was no suitable response from the Archduke Louis, the president of the *Ministerkonferenz*. Deserted, he then composed a dignified letter of resignation to the Emperor. It was therefore the lack of police and the loss of nerve on the part of the imperial family – most of whose members resented him anyway – that had brought about Metternich's downfall. And it was his downfall in turn which brought about the revolutions in the Empire. When news of it spread to Lombardy and Venetia, Bohemia and Hungary, riots simply broke out everywhere. Suddenly there was a feeling of profound liberation and hope, a feeling that moderate change might be conceded at last. Spirits were much bolder in Italy, but elsewhere in the Monarchy, the general conviction seemed to be that since Metternich had been the main bulwark against reform, a new era of some kind now had to begin. It was a wonderful, but brief, illusion.

NOTES AND REFERENCES

1. Count F. A. Gualterio (1852) *Gli Ultimi Rivolgimenti Italiani, Memorie Storiche con Documenti Inediti*, 4 vols. Florence, Vol. 2, pp. 286–7.
2. Alan Sked (1979) *The Survival of the Habsburg Empire: Radetzky, the Imperial Army and the Class War, 1848*. London and New York, p. 43.
3. Howard A. Marraro (1946–7) An American diplomat views the dawn of liberalism in Piedmont (1834–48), *Journal of Central European Affairs*, 6, pp. 75–6.
4. J. R. Rath (1963–4) The Carbonari: their origins, initiation, rites and aims, *American Historical Review*, LXIX.
5. P. Savigear (1969) Carbonarism and the French Army 1815–24, *History*, LIV.
6. Some are to be found for the period 1815–48 in the Haus-Hof und Staatsarchiv in Vienna under *Provinzen, Lombardei-Venezien*.
7. Stuart Woolf (1979) *A History of Italy 1700–1860. The Social Constraints of Political Change*. London, pp. 307–8.
8. R. J. Goldstein (1983) *Political Repression in 19th Century Europe*. London and Canberra, pp. 69–70.
9. *Ibid*., pp. 70–1.
10. *Ibid*., p. 71.
11. *Ibid*.
12. Donald E. Emerson (1968) *Metternich and the Political Police. Security and Subversion in the Habsburg Monarchy, 1815–1830*. The Hague, p. 189.
13. *Ibid*.
14. Apart from Emerson, *op. cit*., see Josef Karl Mayr (1935) Metternichs geheimer Briefdienst. Postlogen und Postkurse, *Inventare österreichischer staatlichen Archive, V: Inventare des Wiener Haus, Hof und Staatsarchivs 3*. Vienna; Anna Hedwa Benna (1942) *Die Polizeihofstelle. Ein Beitrag zur Geschichte der österreichischen Zentralverwaltung*, unpublished dissertation. Vienna; Harald Hubatschke (1975) Die ämtliche Organisation der geheimen Briefüberwachung und der diplomatischen Chiffrendienst in Osterreich (Von den Anfangen bis etwa 1870), *Mitteilungen des Instituts fur Osterreichische Geschichtsforschung*, Vol. LXXXIII, pp. 352–413; Julius Marx (1959) *Die Osterreichische Zensur im Vormärz*. Munich and Viktor Bibl (1927) *Die Wiener Polizei, Eine kulturhistorische Studie*. Leipzig, Vienna and New York.
15. Emerson, *op. cit*., p. 38.
16. *Ibid*., p. 38.
17. *Ibid*., p. 138.
18. *Ibid*., p. 154.
19. *Ibid*., p. 179.
20. *Ibid*., pp. 61–2. Note however, the point made by Peter J. Katzenstein in his book (1976) *Disjoined Partners, Austria and Germany since 1815*. Berkeley, pp. 61–2, namely, '. . . this system of surveillance, impressive though it may have looked at the time, was still small if compared with the size of either the total population or the potential liberal and democratic counterelites. In 1848, for example, a total of only 15,000 letters were opened by Austrian censors, roughly 0.50 per cent of

Austria's foreign correspondence and only 0.08 per cent of the domestic mail. This is little compared with the 96 to 120 million letters and postcards inspected per year by Austrian censors between 1916 and 1918, roughly 25 per cent of Austria's foreign and about 10 per cent of its domestic mail. In other words, in this area the capacity for political control increased by a factor of 50 to 100 between 1850 and the years 1916–18, even though the Austrian war government was by no means a model of bureaucratic efficiency or totalitarian control.'

21. Quoted in R. John Rath (1957) *The Viennese Revolution of 1848*. Austin, pp. 10–11.
22. Count Hartig (1853) Genesis or details of the late Austrian Revolution by an Officer of State, translated as Vol. 4 of *Continuation* of Archdeacon Coxe's *History of the House of Austria*. London, pp. 38–9.
23. Rath, *op. cit.*, p. 45.
24. *Ibid.*, pp. 45–6.
25. *Ibid.*, p. 31, note 53. In the context of the secret police in Metternich's Austria, note the comments of one British observer, published in 1840, namely: 'Were it not for the order and security everywhere prevailing, a stranger might hardly suppose, beyond the walls of the cities, that any police existed except only at frontiers. In no continental country have I ever travelled, in which, except in the provincial capitals, is so little of it either seen or felt . . . those persons are in my mind greatly to be pitied, whose credulous imagination takes the alarm at the fancy of agents in disguise ever haunting their footsteps and watching their conduct. As regards the natives themselves (I confine myself as usual to the German provinces) no country in Europe probably, stands so little in need of secret paid police as Austria.' Public consensus, he maintained, was the real secret of order. The same observer also noted that booksellers could import and sell whatever works they pleased, although there were minor police restrictions on how they might advertise or display works critical of the regime. More fundamentally, he writes: 'That the whole police establishment of the empire is not considerable may be inferred from the fact, that its entire expense is only 1,643,500 fl. or 164,350 l. sterling per annum; although in this sum is included all charge for equipments and support of the two Italian regiments; of the armed force in the German states; all salaries from the 15,000 fls. paid to its chief at Vienna, down to that of the lowest employee; and all the pensions to retired servants, widows and orphans in this branch of the service.' See Peter Evan Turnbull (1840) *Austria*, 2 vols. London, Vol. 2, pp. 255–61, 253.
26. Marx, *op. cit.*, pp. 44–53.
27. Rath, *op. cit.*, Chapter 2.
28. C. A. Macartney (1965) The Austrian Monarchy, 1792–1847, in C. A. Crawley (ed.) War and Peace in an age of Upheaval, 1793–1830. *The New Cambridge Modern History*, Cambridge, Vol. IX, chapter XIV, pp. 395–411, p. 402.
29. Rath, *op. cit.*, p. 27.
30. *Ibid.*, p. 35.
31. Hans Sturmberger (1962) *Der Weg zum Verfassungsstaat. Die Politische Entwicklung in Oberösterreich von 1792–1861*. Vienna.

32. *Ibid*., p. 45.
33. Macartney, *op. cit*., p. 410.
34. J. Polisensky (1980) *Aristocrats and the Crowd in the Revolutionary Year 1848. A Contribution to the History of Revolution and Counter-revolution in Austria*. Albany.
35. P. Ginsborg (1979) *Daniele Manin and the Venetian Revolution of 1848–1849*. Cambridge.
36. Quoted in Alan Sked, *op. cit*., p. 167.
37. Hartig, *op. cit*., p. 70.
38. Quoted in Alan Sked (1976) Metternich and the federalist myth, in Alan Sked and Chris Cool (eds) *Crisis and Controversy, Essays in Honour of A. J. P. Taylor*. London and Basingstoke, p. 4.
39. István Deák (1979) *The Lawful Revolution: Louis Kossuth and the Hungarians, 1848–49*. New York.
40. E. Heller (1933) *Fürst Felix zu Schwarzenberg, Mitteleuropa's Vorkämpfer*. Vienna, p. 265.
41. Kent Roberts Greenfield (1965) *Economics and Liberalism in the Risorgimento. A Study of Nationalism in Lombardy, 1818–48*, revised edn with an introduction by R. Romeo. Baltimore, pp. xvii and xii.
42. Carlo Cattaneo (1848) *L'Insurrection de Milan en 1848*. Paris, p. 12.
43. *Ibid*., p. 16.
44. *Ibid*.
45. Luigi Torrelli (1846) *Pensieri sull'Italia di un Anonimo Lombardo*. Paris.
46. See Alan Sked, *The Survival of the Habsburg Empire*, pt. III.
47. *Ibid*., p. 174.
48. *Ibid*.
49. *Ibid*., p. 175.
50. *Ibid*., p. 168.
51. *Ibid*., p. 174.
52. For the proclamation, see N. Bianchi Giovini (1854) *L'Autriche en Italie*, 2 vols. Paris, Vol. I, pp. 277–9.
53. Alan Sked, *The Survival of the Habsburg Empire*, p. 110.
54. *Ibid*., pp. 165–7.
55. *Ibid*., p. 165.
56. *Ibid*., p. 272, note 17.
57. *Ibid*., p. 167.
58. *Ibid*.
59. *Ibid*., p. 184.
60. *Ibid*., p. 185.
61. *Ibid*.
62. *Ibid*., p. 186.
63. *Ibid*.
64. *Ibid*.
65. *Ibid*.
66. *Ibid*.
67. David F. Good (1984) *The Economic Rise of the Habsburg Empire, 1750–1914*. Berkeley and Los Angeles, p. 39.
68. Quoted in *ibid*., p. 42.
69. *Ibid*.

70. *Ibid.*, p. 45.
71. *Ibid.*, pp. 45–8.
72. *Ibid.*, p. 48.
73. *Ibid.*
74. Richard Rudolph (1983) Economic revolution in Austria? The meaning of 1848 in Austrian economic history, in John Komlos (ed.) *Economic Development in the Habsburg Monarchy in the Nineteenth Century. Essays*, pp. 165–82, p. 168.
75. *Ibid.*, pp. 171–2.
76. Wolfgang Häusler (1979) *Von der Massenarmut zur Arbeiterbewegung. Demokratie und Soziale Frage in der Wiener Revolution von 1848.* Vienna, p. 24.
77. Nachum Gross, Austria-Hungary in the World Economy, in Komlos (ed.) *op. cit.*, pp. 1–45, p. 9.
78. *Ibid.*, p. 14.
79. *Ibid.*, p. 68.
80. *Ibid.*, p. 67.
81. *Ibid.*,
82. *Ibid.*, p. 68.
83. *Ibid.*,
84. Turnbull, *op. cit.*, Vol. 2, pp. 323–4.
85. *Ibid.*, Vol. 2, p. 324.
86. Antonio Schmidt-Brentano (1975) *Die Armee in Osterreich: Militär, Staat und Gesellschaft, 1848–1867.* Boppard am Rhein, p. 109.
87. *Ibid.*
88. Robert Enderes (1947) *Revolution in Osterreich, 1848.* Vienna, p. 38.
89. Count Corti (1928) *The Reign of the House of Rothschild.* London, p. 258. Metternich saw Solomon Rothschild in November 1847 and January 1848 to arrange the loan. The quote actually comes from the January meeting.
90. *Ibid.*, pp. 254–5.
91. Julius Marx (1965) Die wirtschäftlichen Ursachen der Revolution von 1848 in Osterreich, *Veröffentlichungen der Kommission für Neuere Geschichte Osterreichs*, Vol. 51. Graz and Cologne, pp. 254–5, 94.
92. *Ibid.*, p. 99.
93. Turnbull, *op. cit.*, Vol. 2, pp. 21–22, 340, 344.
94. Marx, *op. cit.*, p. 99.
95. These figures come from *ibid.*, pp. 123–67 and Häusler.
96. Good, *op. cit.*, pp. 72–3.
97. Turnbull, *op. cit.*, Vol. 2, p. 45.
98. *Ibid.*, Vol. 2, p. 33.
99. *Ibid.*, Vol. 2, p. 54.
100. Häusler, *op. cit.*, p. 57.
101. Turnbull, *op. cit.*, pp. 150–2.
102. *Ibid.*, p. 150.
103. Rath, *op. cit.*, pp. 14–15. Note also Marx, *op. cit.*, p. 80: 'In no way however can material problems alone be seen as the driving force behind the revolution; the proletarian masses and the handworkers were as yet nationally and politically indifferent, scarcely aware of

socialist ideas, their numbers as a percentage of the population still small. Their discontent led at the most to local riots, such as occurred with the peasants over the tenth and the robot.'

104. Rath, *op. cit.*, p. 15, note 35.
105. Turnbull, *op. cit.*, Vol. 2, pp. 238–9.
106. Marx, *op. cit.*, p. 142.
107. Turnbull, *op. cit.*, Vol. 2, pp. 219–20.
108. William L. Langer (1966) The pattern of urban revolution, 1848, in E. M. Ancomb and M. L. Brown (eds) *French Society and Culture since the Old Regime*. New York, pp. 90–108. I have used the German translation, Das Muster der städtischen Revolutionen von 1848, in H. Stuke and W. Foestmann (eds) (1979) Die europaische Revolutionen von 1848, *Neue Wissenschaftliche Bibliothek*, Vol. 103. Regensburg, pp. 46–69.
109. Häusler, *op. cit.*, p. 150.

CHAPTER THREE

The Failure of the Revolutions of 1848

The history of the 1848 revolutions within the Monarchy can only be understood if their overall pattern is understood. As has been seen, the Empire was already in difficulty, especially in Italy before March 1848. Martial law had been declared in Lombardy-Venetia, but the government was also under attack in Hungary and Lower Austria in the local diets. Internationally, too, its position was weak. The conservative forces had lost the civil war in neighbouring Switzerland, constitutions had been granted by the kings of Naples and Sardinia, while Pope Pius IX was seen by many Italians as a national hero and an enemy of Catholic Austria. Thanks to its weak economic position, moreover, there was little that the government could do to improve its position. Lack of money meant both that it was unable to relieve the plight of its starving population and that reinforcements could only be sent to the army in Italy in dribs and drabs, despite the fact that Field Marshal Radetzky's strategy, in the case of war breaking out with Sardinia, foresaw an immediate Austrian offensive. Kolowrat had, after all, been quite blunt about the limits which financial weakness imposed on Austrian ambitions. The fall of Louis Philippe in France then made matters much worse. The revolution in Paris was seen by everyone in Europe as a challenge to the Metternich System. It was a common belief that the monarchs of the time would stand or fall together; Metternich himself believed this more than anyone else. Yet, given the Monarchy's financial plight – which was an open secret thanks to Beidtel's book – it was also reckoned that war with France would bankrupt Austria. Little wonder, then, that there was a run on the banks and that the pressure for Metternich's resignation increased. He had decided to await attack in Italy, but there was less faith that he would abjure from organizing a coalition against France. Finally, in the midst of this increasingly alarmist atmosphere, the students of Vienna rioted as a petition from the Lower Austrian Estates in Vienna was being delivered to the imperial palace. Events then rapidly went out of control. A detachment of troops under the Archduke Albert fired on the crowd and the riot spread from the inner city to the suburbs. The limited forces of law and order proved unable to cope and the loss of authority encouraged the unemployed to burn down factories. Meanwhile, petition after petition called upon the Emperor to dismiss Metternich as Chancellor. Yet there were no calls for a republic. In this situation, the imperial family, many members of which had no reason to feel grateful to Metternich, believed it expedient to let him go, and having failed to receive support at the crucial conference on 13 March from the Archduke Louis, the Chancellor submitted his resignation. As yet, however, Austria was not engulfed by revolution: the crowd was loyal; its demands were moderate. Yet the dismissal of Metternich was followed by a promise of constitutional reform. The Metternich System, therefore, fell along with the Chancellor, and the results of this were inevitable: a power vacuum in the Monarchy until a new system could emerge; and demonstrations, petitions and demands in all the provincial capitals of the Empire. The analogy is by no means exact, but one could well imagine what would occur today in Budapest, Bucharest, Warsaw, Prague, East Berlin and Moscow if the Soviet Politburo were suddenly to announce the introduction of multi-party politics and promise civil rights and a responsible government in the USSR.

THE PATTERN OF REVOLUTION

The most immediate problems arising for the court were what to do regarding the central government in Vienna, the government in Hungary and the situation in Lombardy-Venetia. In Vienna, it was announced that a constitution would be drawn up for the Empire, but in the meantime Kolowrat was simply placed at the head of a new government, soon to be followed by Ficquelmont and other former members of the high bureaucracy. There was no question of any 'revolutionaries' taking over. The old bureaucrats were merely assigned the job of drawing up a constitution which would offer the fewest concessions to the 'revolution'. From Hungary a deputation headed by the Palatine, the Archduke Stephen, managed to secure the promise of a responsible ministry, including portfolios for defence, finance and a minister at court, 'around the person of the king'. In practice, this meant that only a personal union would henceforth bind Austria and Hungary. When this was realized, an effort was made to retract the concessions and to limit the authority of the Hungarians to purely domestic affairs. But the attempt proved vain. As a result, the Hungarians were able to pursue policies in the spring and summer of 1848 which contradicted those of the Vienna ministry and which threatened to destroy the unity of the Monarchy. This was a situation which was to be resolved only by war. Meanwhile, the greatest challenge to the integrity of the Monarchy came from northern Italy. Revolutions broke out in Milan and Venice, Radetzky's forces were driven out of both cities – retreating from Milan, surrendering in Venice – while Charles Albert of Sardinia accepted the invitation of the Lombard nobility to come to the aid of his fellow Italians. By the summer, both Lombardy and Venetia had voted to become part of an enlarged Italian kingdom under the House of Savoy, and Vienna was negotiating a ceasefire, prepared to acknowledge the loss of Lombardy at least. From now on, however, there was to be a definite pattern to the story of the revolutions' defeat.

The revolutions were defeated in a series of stages. Stage one was the defeat of the Italians by Radetzky, whose success was absolutely crucial for the survival of the Monarchy. True, Windischgraetz had meanwhile bombarded Prague, but the so-called 'revolution' there was nothing more than a street riot by students and workers who had been provoked by the general's heavy-handedness, and who in no sense posed a military or political threat to the régime. If anything, Windischgraetz's actions impeded the process of counter-revolution by forcing the authorities to keep troops in Bohemia which were much more urgently required in Italy. None the less, by August 1848, Radetzky had succeeded in retaking Milan.

Radetzky's success in Italy meant that the question of Hungary could then be tackled. During the summer of 1848, it had become clear that the Hungarians were counting on the defeat of the imperial forces in Italy and that Hungarian public opinion was on the side of the Italians. Certainly, unlike the Croats, the Hungarians had refused to send reinforcements to Radetzky's army. Moreover, the Hungarians were refusing to contribute to the imperial exchequer, were attempting to establish a separate diplomatic service and were encouraging the movement in Frankfurt for German unity. Their assumption was that if the Habsburgs were to lose Lombardy and

Venetia to Italy and the hereditary provinces to Germany, then the imperial capital would move to Buda and the Monarchy would become a Hungarian one. Radetzky's victories in Italy, however, rendered this scenario impossible.

The second stage of the counter-revolution was the defeat of the Hungarians. Yet this was not accomplished speedily. Hungarian resistance proved much more successful than Vienna had ever anticipated and was to involve the humiliation for Austria of requesting Russian assistance. At first, however, it was hoped that the Hungarians might be bullied into making concessions in return for support against the Croats. Jellačić, the Ban of Croatia, in defiance of Vienna's orders, had assembled a military force which was threatening to invade Hungary. At the end of August 1848, therefore, the Austrian government warned its Hungarian counterpart that it would no longer remain neutral in the quarrel between the Hungarians and Croats if the Hungarians insisted on continuing to pursue separate defence and economic policies. When the Hungarians refused to be coerced, the court dissolved the Hungarian parliament and sanctioned the invasion of the country, which Jellačić had launched at the start of September. This decision in turn led to more unrest in Vienna, and when some grenadier battalions there were ordered to Hungary at the beginning of October, a revolution broke out in the imperial capital out of sympathy with the Hungarians. This, as it turned out, provided the perfect excuse for Jellačić, who had been defeated by the latter, to withdraw from Hungary altogether under the pretext of saving Vienna. In fact, just after he reached the city, Windischgraetz arrived from Bohemia with his army and was ready to bombard it into submission. Jellačić's task now became one of beating off a Hungarian army, which had been sent very reluctantly to relieve the rebels in the imperial capital. This he accomplished at Schwechat on 30 October after which Windischgraetz recaptured Vienna. Once again, however, this was not a decisive move as far as the defeat of the revolution was concerned. The court had already escaped to Olmütz, the parliament had not supported the uprising, and although the revolution in Vienna was a great embarrassment to the dynasty, even with the support of the Hungarians, the student and other rebels there were in no position to challenge the régime. It merely meant a greater delay before Windischgraetz could organize the invasion of Hungary.

It took, in fact, until 16 December before the Field Marshal ordered his advance. By 6 January, however, he had captured Buda. Yet success eluded him. The Hungarians regrouped in the east of their country and a spring offensive caught the Austrians unprepared. On 14 April, Windischgraetz was recalled for 'consultation', to be dismissed by the end of the month. His successor, Welden, also failed to stem the Hungarian advance and he in turn was removed on 24 May. His successor was to be the capable but ruthless Baron Haynau, known from his Italian record as the 'beast of Brescia'. Haynau, eventually, was to prove to be the man who would at last subdue the Magyars. Before then, however, on 1 May 1849, Franz Joseph had officially requested military aid from Nicholas I of Russia 'to prevent', as he put it, 'the Hungarian insurrection developing into a European calamity'.[1] Windischgraetz had been calling for such help since January and, although Schwarzenberg had been exceedingly unwilling to agree, he at last consented officially when it became clear that this was the only way to secure it (he had previously hoped to involve the Russians without the need to invite them formally). As it happened, the Hungarians were defeated before the Russians could make any significant contribution to the fighting. Yet it was to the Russian commander, Paskievicz, that the Hungarians, under Görgei, surrendered at Világos on 13 August 1849.

Radetzky, meanwhile, had once again vindicated his reputation. For on 16 March 1849, Charles Albert had renewed the war against Austria in Italy. In the words of Professor Rothenberg: '. . . on the nineteenth, in a campaign which would not have disgraced Napoleon, the eighty-three-year-old leader invaded Sardinia, defeated the Italians at Mortara on the twenty-first, and two days later smashed the main force at Novara. The Sardinian army ceased to be an effective fighting force, and Charles Albert resigned in favour of his son who signed an armistice the next day. It was a brilliant campaign. . .'[2] By the end of August, with the capitulation of both the Venetian Republic and the Hungarians, all the fighting in the Monarchy was over.

The third stage in the counter-revolution now took place: Schwarzenberg's diplomatic struggle against the Prussians over the creation of a united Germany. This, too, very nearly developed into warfare. However, the Prussian climb-down at Olmütz in November 1850 and the stalemate at the Dresden Conference at the beginning of 1851 brought about the resurrection of the Germanic Confederation.

The final triumph of the counter-revolution came about at the very end of 1851 with the Sylvester Patent of that year. Franz Joseph now dispensed with all pretence of ruling through parliaments or cabinets and took over the running of the Monarchy himself.

Having outlined the stages of the counter-revolution, it is now time to examine why it was successful, partly by re-examining some of the clichés which surround it. Was its success, for example, really due to the insubordination of the generals? Was the nationality question crucial to the defeat of the Hungarians? Was there such a body as the 'camarilla', the secret group of courtiers who supposedly coordinated the counter-revolutionary strategy? Were the prominent military figures – Radetzky, Jellačić, Windischgraetz – of equal importance? Given much of the recent research, it is time that several old myths were discarded.

THE REVOLUTION IN HUNGARY

Let us start with events in Hungary. Here the defeat of the revolution – or the war of independence as the Hungarians perhaps more accurately refer to it – is ascribed most commonly to the following causes: the refusal to grant equal rights to the 'nationalities' – particularly the Croats; the split between the civilian and military leadership, personified in the antagonism between Kossuth and Görgei; the neglect of the Hungarian peasantry, leading to a lack of popular support; and the intervention of the Russians which made any hope of victory inconceivable. Let us look at these factors in turn, leaving the purely military ones to the end.

It is a cliché in every textbook that the most significant development of 1848 was the split between the nationalities. In Hungary, in particular, this is held to have been crucial. The blame for the division is uniformly placed upon the Hungarians. Their policy of Magyarization is seen as self-defeating, intransigent and, in fact, irrational. Yet this is a difficult argument to sustain. While it is no doubt true that the neutrality of the nationalities, or, better still, their active support would have aided the Hungarians in their struggle with Vienna, it is by no means certain that even in either of these eventualities, the Hungarians would have won. Militarily the nationalities were probably not of crucial importance. Jellačić, after all, was defeated by the Hungarians in 1848 and his contribution in 1849 was not a decisive one. And Bem, with his Hungarian army, managed to remain master of the military situation in Transylvania right up almost until the end of the war. It is difficult therefore to blame the defeat of the Hungarians on the break with the nationalities. Besides, even with the support of the Croats and Transylvanian Romanians, it is almost certain that lack of ammunition, plus the intervention of the Russians, would have overcome whatever efforts could have been made on Hungary's behalf.

Nor is it correct to see Hungarian policy as irrational or intransigent. Its rationality was quite obvious. The new government believed that since the nationalities were part of the historic state of Hungary, they should recognize Hungarian as the state language, especially when that state was in the process of bestowing on them modern civil rights. And since it intended to grant Croatia the right to use Croatian for local affairs, to communicate with Buda in Croatian and to allow Croats to participate in the formulation of all legislation affecting them, it seemed irrational, if not downright treasonous, for the Croats to advocate the secession of their country from Hungary – all the more so if under Jellačić they intended to form part of an Austria which was still under the control of Metternich's former colleagues and making war on Italians who were in turn attempting to secede from Austria. It seemed obvious to the Hungarians that the Austrians would merely use the Croats and others for reactionary ends, particularly to help suppress their own new institutions, if and when Austrian forces succeeded in defeating the Italians.

Nor can there be any case for arguing that the Hungarians were intransigent. On the contrary, Croatia's objections in the diets of the 1830s and 1840s not only to Hungarian replacing Latin as the official language of the country, but to other reforms, including greater civil rights for Protestants and Jews, had so exasperated certain leading Hungarian liberals that they had already proposed the separation of Croatia from Hungary. The fact that Croatia was also seen as unwilling to pay her proper share of taxes was yet another reason they adduced to propose this course of action. Hence Szombathélyi could say in the 1836 Diet: 'If all the use we have of being united with Croatia is that our taxpayers pay taxes instead of hers, that our Protestant countrymen are disowned in part of our common homeland, and that our development as a nation meets with Croatia's hostility, I say: let there be an end to all close ties.'[3] Deák himself in the 1840 Diet stated that if the Croats thought 'it a sacrilege to bear their part of the tax burden in even the same proportion as Hungary, the desire would involuntarily be kindled in his breast that the tie should cease to be, though this would hardly be to the advantage of either Croatia or Hungary'.[4] Finally, in 1842, the electors of Pest county unanimously passed a complicated motion which had been drafted by Kossuth and which, having repudiated any intention to oppress any small nation, concluded: 'that it will be more conducive to the peaceful development of Hungary and the Hungarian nation if Croatia is separated from Hungary in respect of administration and legislation, though not from the Hungarian Holy Crown.'[5] It is true that these sentiments were not typical of Hungarian opinion in the 1840s but they do demonstrate that Hungarian liberals were not intransigent on the Croat question.

With the fall of Metternich and the April Laws, it was exactly such liberals who took charge of Hungarian affairs. Given their differences with Vienna and their knowledge that they were in competition with the imperial capital to win the allegiance of a disaffected Croatia, they consistently offered concessions to the Croats in the hope of keeping them in Hungary, or at least preserving their neutrality should a war develop with Austria. Wesselényi, for example, wrote to the Hungarian Prime Minister Batthyány in April: '. . . we must avoid everything that might serve the Ban and his Croats as an excuse to declare openly their secession and carry it through. We cannot keep Croatia for our own; let's give up all efforts to do so, which can bring no benefit but can do harm. Let's make an agreement with the Croats, one that recognises them and guarantees their independence, but guarantees also our trade and gives us joint ownership of a piece of coastline.'[6] Batthyány, for his part, was only too willing to negotiate and to make many concessions to preserve peace, and by July, Kossuth was thinking in terms of a confederation. Then on 27 August 1848 the cabinet passed a bill on Croatia drafted by Deák which left defence, foreign affairs, finance and trade in Hungarian hands, with provision, however, for the participation of the respective Croatian under-secretaries and, in some matters, the Ban, in the formulation of legislation. All other matters were put in the hands of a Minister for Croatian Affairs who was to reside in Pest or Zagreb. Laws were to be passed in both cities with Croat representatives sitting in both parliaments. Croat was to become the official language of Croatia, a university was to be established in Zagreb, Hungary and Croatia were to communicate with each other in their own languages (but with a translation enclosed), and voting rights were to be extended from Civil Croatia to the Military Border. However, the cabinet noted: 'if all this should fail to lead to a settlement, it was willing to agree to secession, and to accept a purely federal tie, keeping possession of Fiume, Hungary's access to the sea, with guarantees of free access and free trade.'[7] By the end of August, Kossuth was writing to Laszló

Csányi, the commissioner in charge of the defence of Hungary's southern border, that he was willing to allow Slavonia to secede as well, albeit without the fortresses of Pétervarad and Eszék. He told Csányi that it might be a good idea for him to contact the Croats and with the message: 'if they are really acting in the spirit of nationalism and not reaction, . . . then let them tell us what they want. We'll give Croatia everything even secession: let them go but let's be good friends . . . if they want to secede let them go ahead, let them be free and happy, but let them not bring blood and misfortune on the two countries for a foreign, reactionary power.'[8] By the beginning of September, however, Jellačić was almost ready to launch his attack on Hungary.

It was Jellačić, not the Hungarians, who was intransigent in 1848. He had no desire to work out any compromise and was perfectly well aware that there was no danger of the Hungarians attacking Croatia – something which he admitted in a letter written on 29 June to the Archduke John, who was attempting to mediate between them. This was the real reason why he could send reinforcements to Radetzky, not to mention his famous proclamation to the Croat troops in Italy, reassuring them that their relatives would be safe at home. Jellačić, after all, had been speedily appointed Ban of Croatia in March 1848 at Kolowrat's suggestion precisely to forestall any agreement between the Hungarians and the Croats. Or in Kolowrat's own words, before the Hungarians could 'entice the Croat-Slavonian lands by agreeing to recognise their local rights, language etc. etc.' For, as he saw things: 'Should this enticement, this alliance succeed, the Austrian, unfortunately heterogeneous state, would face a compact mass that might even be ready to attack the dynasty.'[9] 'Men of goodwill,' he added, 'expect salvation from a quick and determined move: the now vacant office of the Ban must be filled by an energetic and popular man.'[10]

Nor is there any reason to believe that Jellačić mistook his role. Thus while there is considerable dispute over his support of reform in 1848, there is none over his commitment to the dynasty. He consistently maintained that the Hungarians must surrender their portfolios of defence and finance and form part of a unitary state. In other words, they should repudiate the April Laws which had just brought them their freedom. Moreover, within the unitary state, Jellačić demanded, the Croats should receive the same rights as the Hungarians. It was the unity of the empire, however, which Jellačić was always at pains to stress. As he told Batthyány at a famous confrontation in Vienna: 'The conflict between us is not that of particularism, for that could be settled. You want Hungary to be a free and independent Hungary and I pledged myself to support the political unity of the Austrian empire. If you do not agree to that, only the sword can decide between us.'[11] Previously he had defined the aims of the Croatians as: 'to contribute, vying with the other peoples of Austria, by maintaining undisturbed order and regularising their internal affairs, to the restoration of a united – internally and externally organically proportioned – strong and free Austrian State and to promote successfully the consolidation of the throne.'[12] There was never any chance therefore – as both General Hrabowsky and the Archduke John discovered when they attempted to mediate – of Jellačić agreeing to any compromise with the Hungarians. Hence it is completely unfair to accuse the Hungarians of intransigence in attempting to explain the reasons behind their defeat in 1849.

It should not be thought either, on the other hand, that all the nationalities were willing dupes of the imperial court. After all, the nationalities had been led to believe that the new Austrian constitution which the Reichstag was debating would protect their interests. It was not until March 1849, with the abolition of the Kremsier parliament and the proclamation of Schwarzenberg and Stadion's 'decreed constitution', that it was clear that this had been a mistake. Besides, not all the nationalities had been opposed to the Hungarians. For example, the Romanians in Hungary (as opposed to those in Transylvania) resented the way in which their Serb neighbours dominated them and in particular the way in which the Serb Orthodox Church took precedence over the Romanian Orthodox one. The Hungarians, therefore, never faced any challenge from them. Likewise, although the Slovak intellectuals demanded all sorts of concessions from the government, the majority of Slovak peasants evinced no inclination to follow their lead. The Serbs in the south, on the other hand, along with the Transylvanian Romanians, were both to oppose the Hungarian government. The Serbs demanded an autonomous state and under the leadership of their Archbishop, Rajačić, and military leader, Suplikacs, threw in their lot with Jellačić. The Transylvanian Romanians, the vast majority of the principality's population, also demanded recognition as a separate nation, like the Saxons, Hungarians and Székelys, who were already officially recognized. They also demanded a separate parliament for Transylvania, despite the fact that the other nations had voted for union with Hungary. When this and other demands went unfulfilled, they supported the revolt of the local army units against the government in Buda-Pest. Only the Hungarians and Székelys, the

Hungarian border guards, gave their allegiance to the government. It has already been argued that even this revolt was contained by Bem and was not crucial to the Hungarians' defeat. The historian István Deák, on the other hand, might consider this judgement complacent. In a passage which does not entirely square with another view he maintains – and which will be examined later – he writes: 'The Romanian revolt in Transylvania was pivotal, for while Hungary had to defend itself against the aggressor Serbs and Croats, the war with the Romanians should and could have been prevented. Romanians in Inner Hungary were opposed to it, and so were the Romanians in Moldavia and Wallachia for whom Turks and the Russians were the problem and not Kossuth. Even the Transylvanian Romanians were no dedicated Habsburg followers, and timely Hungarian concessions could have saved the situation; but these concessions were never made because the Transylvanian nobility feared such reforms and because the Hungarian government feared the Transylvanian nobility. Further, the Magyar leaders despised the Romanians at least as much as they despised the Slovaks. Judged incapable of thinking for themselves, the Romanians were seen as marionettes of the *Camarilla* and the Tsar. One of the most vociferous in this respect was Kossuth, who had fallen into his own propaganda trap. He knew nothing about the Romanians; he hoped that repression combined with minor concessions would quiet these unruly peasants.'[13] Deák continues: 'Transylvania never became safe; the Hungarian army always had an enemy in the rear; retreat into that province became difficult; money, troops, and the best general, were wasted there. The Hungarians lost the war partly because of Transylvania.' The 'best general' – Bem – it might be added, issued proclamation after proclamation to the Romanians offering them equal rights; and negotiations continued to take place between the Hungarian government and various Romanian leaders, particularly after March 1849. However, the outbreak of war (which elsewhere in his book Deák appears to blame on the imperial military commanders in Transylvania, rather than the Hungarians) meant that the conditions in which these had to take place were always difficult and military operations, which Kossuth refused to abandon in case his opponents were merely playing for time, often sabotaged the prospects of any compromise being reached. It is extremely unlikely, in any case that, even had a compromise been reached with the Transylvanian Romanians, the Hungarians could have won their war of independence. The reasons for this viewpoint will be discussed presently.

One reason why the Hungarians failed to win over the Transylvanian Romanians was the delay experienced by the peasants there and elsewhere in Hungary regarding the agrarian problem. For despite its promises, the new Hungarian government failed to tackle the issue of peasant grievances with anything like the urgency which the question required. It was not until the end of May 1848, for example, that serfdom was abolished in Transylvania, but even then the peasantry there was in the same position as elsewhere in Hungary. In the words of one historian: 'The gravity of the peasant problem was due to the fact that the peasants had not gained anything else besides their personal freedom. As only the urbarial lands were transferred to peasant ownership, only two-thirds of peasants benefited, and only 20 per cent of the cultivated territory of the country was involved. Peasants living on domanial land and small-holdings, small vineyards and market gardens were not relieved of their obligations, and the grievances of the peasants over enclosures were not remedied by legislation either. The peasant masses were bitterly disappointed, and revenged themselves throughout the land by refusing forced labour services and the tithe on vineyards, by selling wine and meat without licence, and by occupying the landlord's grazing land. In other places the landless peasants divided up the land without consulting anybody. The nobility resisted and even contested the status of the urbarial land in order to deprive the peasant of his rightful ownership. In these questions the government acted as the defendent of the interests of the nobility. It first tried to deal with the situation by peaceful measures, then by sending out royal commissioners and troops, and ended in June by proclaiming martial law to repress the movement, referring the problem of the feudal survivals of the non-urbarial land to the next parliament.'[14] It was not until July 1849 that the government passed a resolution providing for the release of demesne land and cleared woodland and gardens. But by then the collapse of resistance meant that the war of independence was more or less over.

Would the result have been different had the government tackled the peasant question with greater urgency and indulgence? It is usual to argue that this might well have been the case. Yet Deák is sceptical as to whether this in fact would have made any appreciable difference. He writes: 'The question has been raised repeatedly whether more far-reaching agrarian reforms would have prevented the peasants from rioting and subsequently have caused the Magyar peasants – and even the Slavic and Romanian peasants – to rally en masse to the flag of Kossuth . . . because of the dearth of meticulous studies on the social background, living conditions, and aspirations of the earlier peasant rioters, or of the later peasant army volunteers, we simply do not know how the peasantry felt and behaved in 1848–9. The practice of Hungarian historians, citing isolated cases to prove either the hostility or enthusiasm of peasants, tells very little.'[15] By the end, according to Deák, peasant and nobleman could see the war was lost. 'No radical social reforms, outlined in hindsight, could have changed this basic fact.'[16]

Let us now turn to purely military factors. It is commonly stated in the textbooks that the Hungarians were defeated in 1849 thanks to the intervention of the Russians under Paskievicz. Haynau's own chief of staff, Colonel Ramming von Riedkirchen, wrote in his account of the campaign: 'The question is often raised whether the Austrian state, in that situation, without Russian aid, would have been able to defeat the Hungarian uprising which, after its unexpected successes during the spring of 1849, grew so rapidly and became so immense [?] . . . in order to attain a decisive military superiority, which was assured in all aspects of foreign relations also, the Russian armed intervention was indispensable in Hungary and Transylvania. The mighty and imposing aid of a Russian army would lead to an inevitable success, and would result in the establishment of peace in Austria and in the whole of Europe, even if Austria's performance were less energetic and meet with less success.'[17] The received wisdom ever since has been that Russian intervention does indeed account for the defeat of the Hungarians. Yet Deák, as usual, insists on testing such theses. Writing of the period at the end of June 1849, 'when the Russians were deep inside Hungary with neither the [Hungarian] Army of the North nor the population offering serious resistance',[18] he asks: 'Since the Russians were moving forward without engagement in major battles, why did the war last until mid-August, or in some places until the following month?'[19] His answer is: 'Because Paskievich was inordinately slow and cautious, because the Russians were decimated by cholera, and because the Hungarian generals – Görgei, in particular – managed to avoid the Russians almost completely in their determination to fight the Austrians. The main Hungarian army quietly manoeuvred behind the back of the Russians in search of the Austrians. As a result the war was not over until Haynau met and dispersed one *honvéd* unit after another, or until the *honvéd generals* decided to surrender. The tsarist army moved across the country like a witless but benevolent giant. It inflicted only limited harm on its opponents and in turn suffered little harm from the Hungarians.'[20] Discussing the casualties of the war, Deák reinforces this point: 'It seems that about 50,000 Hungarian soldiers died and about the same number of Austrians. The Russian expeditionary forces lost only 543 killed in battle and 1,670 wounded. On the other hand, Paskievich's army buried 11,028 cholera victims.'[21] The correct interpretation of the Russian intervention in 1849 would seem to be therefore that although it would undoubtedly have proved crucial had the war gone on (in fact, what Colonel Ramming was arguing), it was none the less the Austrians under Haynau who were really responsible for the Hungarians' defeat. This is why they – and particularly Haynau himself – were so upset when Görgei surrendered to Paskievicz at Világos.

Another factor often held to have been crucial in the defeat of the Hungarians is the rivalry of Kossuth and Gorgei, Hungary's civilian and military leaders. Indeed, there is a huge literature on this theme in Hungarian, including a great deal of partisan prose. What therefore should be said on the subject? Both men certainly made mistakes which undermined their cause. Görgei, for example, lost the only military opportunity to force Vienna to a compromise when he failed, at the end of April 1849, to pursue the Austrians, if necessary right up to the gates of Vienna itself. He chose instead to take Castle Hill in Buda and 'with this single move he threw away his already slim chance of final victory or even of a military stalemate'.[22] Kossuth, on the other hand, often had a debilitating influence on military affairs by failing to stand up for people he had appointed or to stand by his own decisions. General Moga, for example, was ordered into Austria in October 1848, but was then left to take the responsibility for the battle which he fought and lost at Schwechat; Görgei was appointed dictator at the very end of the war but was told not to surrender the army – by then his only possible course of action; before then, Kossuth had failed to protect General Dembinski, his own appointment as commander in chief, from the criticisms of his fellow generals, despite his professed faith in Dembinski's abilities. Yet, on the other hand, on the positive side, Kossuth's liberal faith had moved mountains in organizing Hungary's defences and finances, while Görgei's achievements on the field were often miraculous. The real difference between them was over Kossuth's deposition of the Habsburgs in April 1849 (Görgei in his Vác Proclamation of January of that year had already warned that the army would not tolerate 'any kind of foolish republican agitation) and the strategy required to win the war (Görgei hoped to take the offensive to defeat the Austrians; he had no hopes of defeating Paskievicz's huge army). Deák is inclined to brush their quarrel aside. He writes: 'In reality both men pursued idle fancies: Kossuth imagined that he could maintain Hungarian independence in a Europe where even such liberal powers as England were working for its suppression. Görgei thought that he could fight for limited goals: the preservation of Hungary's April constitution and its dignified place within the Monarchy at a time when the Habsburgs were no longer willing to grant Hungary its constitution or dignity. Kossuth believed that the peasants would fight to the last man in defence of liberty, if necessary without weapons; Gorgei hoped that a small professional army without the support of guerrillas and peasants could defeat the larger professional army of an industrially stronger country.'[23] From this point of view, Deák concludes: 'In the confrontation which developed in 1848–49 Hungary was the *inevitable* loser . . . [She] . . . ought not to have embarked on the great political adventure' in the first place.[24]

Two points in particular have to be enlarged here. The first concerns the difficulties Hungary faced in establishing a defence industry; the second, international affairs. Certainly, Deák is correct in pointing to both of them. For to a considerable degree they do completely overshadow, not merely the differences between Kossuth and Görgei, but the problem of the nationalities (hence my previous quibble concerning Deák's assessment of the Transylvanian campaign) and the role of the peasants.

Let us consider defence matters first. There were two problems to be resolved here: whether the new Hungarian ministry would secure control over the armed forces and their establishments in Hungary (not to mention Hungarian forces outside the country); and, later, whether, once faced with invasion, it could organize a national defence. Perhaps surprisingly, it was to experience fewer difficulties in asserting and securing control of the armed forces than it was in establishing a defence industry. And this was particularly surprising since the forces which the Hungarians claimed the right to control included both those under Jellačić's command and Hungarian troops located outside Hungary. From the Hungarian point of view, their claim was a straightforward one. Article 3 of the April Laws had run: 'All affairs, civil, military and ecclesiastic, as well as everything that concerns the finances and defence of the country shall for the future be regulated and directed by the Hungarian Ministry and His Majesty shall direct the executive power [i.e. in Hungary] through his ministry.' Despite the Pragmatic Sanction of 1723, therefore, which bound Hungary *inseparabiliter ac indivisibiliter* to the other Habsburg possessions, the Hungarians felt entitled to interpret their new constitution in line with the law of 1790 which had proclaimed Hungary a *regnum liberum independens*, i.e. a free realm bound only to the Habsburgs by a personal union, something which the Austrian government, which saw itself as the heir to the *Staatskonferenz*, refused to acknowledge. In fact, as soon as the latter ceased to be provisional, on 10 May 1848, it asked the Hungarians to reach an agreement on 'common subjects', which they, predictably, refused to do. In financial affairs they refused to return any of the money which they had found in the Hungarian Treasury; refused to take over a quarter of the national debt and its interest payments; and by establishing their own currency, violated the Austrian monopoly of note issue. Yet it was their behaviour in defence and foreign affairs which really upset the Austrians. Here the Hungarians persuaded the king to give them control over the regional army headquarters or *general commands* in Hungary and Transylvania with the result that all commanding generals (including Jellačić who was dismissed as Ban on 19 June) were supposed to take orders from Buda-Pest. The Hungarians were also given the right to supervise all military buildings and depots in Hungary and to make promotions within the army there. Then in July, when the Archduke John tried to effect some kind of compromise, he was told by the Hungarian War Minister: 'It is not my duty to analyse what our present situation would require, what it would demand from the viewpoint of unity and concord. However, there exists a promulgated law that dictates that there be a certain sphere of authority accorded to the Hungarian Minister of National Defence, who is subordinated to His Majesty, our common monarch, or to his viceroy (i.e. the Palatine) and not to anyone else. And I look upon the strict execution of this law and adherence to it as my duty.'[25] The only compromise arrived at was one approved by the king on 20 August whereby an exchange of officers was allowed (Hungarian ones in foreign regiments joining Hungarian regiments, and vice versa) along with an exchange of regiments. By the end of August, therefore, Hungarian regiments not stationed in Italy began to move home, while foreign regiments in Hungary began to move out. Those left on the southern front protecting it from Jellačić were, by and large, simply to cross over to him when he invaded Hungary on 11 September. By 31 August, however, the Austrian government had already declared that the existence of a separate Hungarian ministry was a 'political impossibility' and was demanding complete control of defence and financial policy. Meanwhile, the decision of the Hungarian ministry to recruit scores of thousands of volunteers and to organize them into regiments of national defence or *honvéds* had no doubt contributed to Austrian anger, as had the Hungarians' failure to reinforce Radetzky.

At this point, however, we must advert to difficulties regarding foreign affairs before continuing our discussion of Hungarian defence problems. Inevitably the two were inter-related. For foreign affairs was yet another area where Austria and Hungary clashed over common subjects. The April Laws had laid down that the Hungarians should have a Minister at Court, known officially as the 'Minister around the person of the king', that is the Minister *a latere*, whose duty it was to advise the king on any laws which touched on Hungarian interests and to counter-sign laws which specifically did so. He was also meant to be consulted on foreign policy and indeed the first Hungarian occupant of the post was the distinguished magnate and diplomat, the former ambassador in London, Prince Paul Esterházy. In any case, it very soon became the habit of both Viennese and Hungarian ministers to refer to Prince Esterházy as the Hungarian Foreign Minister, a situation which the Hungarian premier Batthyány exploited in order to pursue a more or less independent foreign policy. This succeeded in some peculiar ways – enabling Hungarian ships, for example, to fly Hungarian flags in the Adriatic, to avoid becoming involved in the Italian war – but failed entirely when it came to seeking foreign recognition of Hungarian diplomats. True, the French almost arranged an exchange of ambassadors, but this fell through when the Austrians protested, whereas the British never had any time for Hungarian pretensions, despite the Magyarphilia of Palmerston's officially recognized agent in Hungary, J. A. Blackwell. Palmerston's own point of view was that the Habsburg Monarchy was an essential part of the balance of power and that Hungarian attempts to achieve independence would merely undermine its role in European diplomacy. He therefore refused to offer the Hungarians any military, financial or moral support and refused to meet officially with any of their representatives. In fact he hoped that the war of independence would be won by Austria as quickly as possible. To the House of Commons, he explained: 'Austria is a most important element in the balance of European power. Austria stands in the centre of Europe, a barrier against encroachment on the one side, and against invasion on the other. The political independence and the liberties of Europe are bound up, in my opinion, with the maintenance and integrity of Austria as a great European Power; and therefore anything which tends by direct, or even remote, contingency, to weaken and to cripple Austria, but still more to reduce her from the position of a first-rate Power, to that of a secondary State, must be a great calamity to Europe and one which every Englishman ought to deprecate and try to prevent. . .'[26] The Hungarians did not realize this during the summer of 1848, due in large measure to Palmerston's Italian policy, which superficially appeared to condone the support of national liberation for its own sake. Hence they believed that, if the worst came to the worst, they would be able to rely on British support. They would soon enough be disillusioned, yet there was little fear in the summer of 1848 that British support would be necessary. For until August at least, events appeared to be going the Hungarians' way. The assumption was that Radetzky would be defeated in Italy and that the Germans in Frankfurt (to which the Hungarians had despatched a delegation) would also succeed in unifying themselves. Lacking both Germans and Italians, therefore, the Habsburgs would be forced to come to terms with the Hungarians. Or, in other words, the Habsburg Monarchy would become the Kingdom of Hungary. As long as the Italian war continued, however, the Hungarian government was in a difficult position. Public opinion in Hungary was very strongly pro-Italian, whereas Hungarian troops were fighting under Radetzky to retain Lombardy-Venetia for Austria. In Parliament the government defended itself by asserting that under the terms of the Pragmatic Sanction, it was the duty of Hungarians to defend their monarch when he had been attacked. There was no official support for calls to summon back Hungarian troops for another reason: Jellačić's borderers or *Grenzer* would then have the opportunity to return home as well. Still, the government was placed in an embarrassing position when the Austrians, at the end of April, asked it for reinforcements. It was this request which was eventually to lead to Kossuth's famous speech in parliament of 20 July in which he stated that troops would be sent to Italy only if the Italians failed to sign an honourable peace. And this, he implied, should give them 'a free and national government'. On the following day, he defined his terms as the Austrian surrender of Lombardy. By the end of the debate, in fact, the Hungarian position had come to mean that troops would only be sent to Italy once Hungary's own security had been safeguarded and once the Italians had turned down an offer of a national constitution. Radetzky, in short, would get no reinforcements from Hungary. Only a couple of days after the debate, however, the Field Marshal was to win his decisive victory over Charles Albert at Custozza.

Hungary's intransigence over finance and defence, not to mention its Italian policy, was to stretch Austrian patience to its limits. By the end of August 1848, therefore, the Hungarians had been warned that if they did not surrender the portfolios of defence and finance, Austria would no longer remain neutral in their quarrel with Jellačić. Whether Austria had ever been neutral in that quarrel is, of course, a major dispute in the historiography of the revolutions. In any case, when Jellačić's army crossed the Drava on 11 September 1848 he had already been reinstated as Ban (4 September) and on 3 October was to become commander-in-chief and royal commissioner in Hungary.

The realization that the quarrel with Austria might indeed have to be decided by arms had already led the Hungarians to form the *honveds*. At the government's disposal were also loyal Hungarian regiments of the imperial army and thousands of national guardsmen. All of these, together with foreign volunteers, were henceforth to be amalgamated into *honved* battalions of which, by the end of the war, there would be 204, or more than 170,000 men. Yet finding the men was only the start of the problem. Finding weapons with which to equip them would turn out to be much more difficult. Cut off from foreign supplies, having already seen most of the army's stocks sent to Italy or Austria, the government had precious few rifles in stock with which to arm its troops. Nor was the situation more optimistic regarding ammunition or uniforms. At the height of the spring offensive of 1849, the soldiers were to receive less than one round of ammunition per man per day. Rifles were to misfire one shot in four. Major battles were to be lost because there were simply insufficient weapons to sustain an offensive. Yet the very fact that there could be a spring offensive, during which the Hungarians would enjoy not only a numerical superiority but also one in weapons, was almost a miracle in itself and one which in no small part was due to Kossuth. In Deák's words: 'Ultimately Hungary had to equip itself, and Kossuth personally directed the endeavour. He dealt with the question daily, his concern ranging from the production of cannons to tiny quantities of undershirts. Only such an incurable optimist as he could take up this seemingly impossible task. At a time when Bohemia and Styria each produced 45,000 tons of iron annually, Hungary produced only about 30,000 tons and domestic iron production had not yet even been able to satisfy Hungary's very modest peacetime needs. Copper production amounted to less than 2,000 tons, and lead less than 200 tons. Other metals were almost nonexistent; the first sulphur mine, militarily so important, had been opened only in 1848. And the country's only armaments plant, in Pest, had produced little until November when it was nationalised by the government; thereafter it delivered up to 500 muskets a day. There were several good powder mills; but with that, the list of military plants is complete. Hungarian industry had made great strides in the preceding two decades, but there were few machine tools and even fewer skilled mechanics or trained workers.'[27] And during the war of independence, it should be added, the whole arms industry had to be moved from Buda-Pest to Nagyvárad twice in order to escape the Austrian army. These disruptions only served to exacerbate an already very difficult problem.

The main reasons for the Hungarian defeat therefore should be sought, according to the above analysis, in the backwardness of Hungarian industry and the lack of a properly trained army with which to resist the Austrians. Hungary's lack of allies did not help either. It meant that its economic and military deficiencies could not be compensated for by others. The nationality question likewise was a drawback; yet it was perhaps not as significant as was later thought to be the case, the same being true of the role of the peasants. Finally, there is the role of the Russian intervention. This used to be considered decisive – and no doubt it would have been had the war gone on. Yet it is probably time to give Haynau his due: he was the true victor in 1849 in Hungary.

Is Deák correct, therefore, in arguing that Hungary's defeat was *inevitable*? It is an extremely dangerous word for an historian to employ. And yet his case is a highly convincing one, especially given the Russian intervention. On the other hand, there might have been a chance of a compromise – admittedly a very slim one – had Görgei pressed on to Vienna in April 1849. More to the point, the Hungarians were allowed to establish their régime on account of events in Italy. Italy – not Hungary – was to be the key to events in 1848. It was only after the success of Radetzky at the beginning of August that the Austrians began to convince themselves that the revolutions could be defeated. Before then every Hungarian demand was allowed, all Batthyány's requests acceded to. Had Radetzky been defeated, it is therefore possible that the Hungarian gamble could have paid off. Events might also have taken a different turn in Germany; the king might even have come to Buda. Exactly what would have happened is of course unknowable. Yet it would have been different, and the difference might well have included the survival of Batthyány's ministry.

THE REVOLUTION IN LOMBARDY-VENETIA

How then did the Austrians succeed in defeating the revolution in Italy? As will have been grasped already, this outcome was by no means inevitable. For, despite having warned against the outbreak of revolution in Lombardy-Venetia throughout the winter of 1847–8, and despite the huge strategical importance he attributed to Milan in his military planning, Radetzky was forced to retreat from the city after only five days of street-fighting. This was a singular humiliation for a commander who had promised that such an event would take place only over his dead body. And the surrender of Venice without a shot being fired contributed powerfully to his consternation. His excuses were that in Milan he had been caught under-supplied and unawares, while the danger to Venice had never been reported to him by the commander there, Count Zichy. In any case his successful retreat with a large part of his army to the Quadrilateral (the four great fortresses of Verona, Mantua, Legnago and Peschiera) was a consolation – 'one of those sad masterstrokes of the art of war', as he himself described it in a report to Ficquelmont.[28]

His excuses do not really bear scrutiny. With regard to Milan, the basic question is why was he forced to retreat when he had superior forces in the city and others at hand not very far away? The Milanese were not armed. The countryside was relatively peaceful and the Piedmontese army was still only in a state of mobilization. Moreover, it was very scattered, with only three regiments in the immediate vicinity of the border. The initial strategic position was therefore in favour of Radetzky.

The insurrection began on the morning of 18 March and went on throughout 18 and 19 March, limiting itself for the most part to the centre of the city. Radetzky's plan, at least on the 19th, was to retain the Citadel at all costs as well as the other military buildings and barracks. Meanwhile, he would use mobile troops to quell the insurgents and maintain a defensive posture on the bastions against any external threat. More troops were called to reinforce the city, since nothing as yet was happening on the Piedmontese frontier. On 20 March, however, things got much worse for the Austrians. The insurgents gained ground, while the imperial forces began to run short of food and ammunition. Some were also cut off in about fifty-two different locations and Italian troops began to desert. Morale among the others now also began to sink: they had to remain awake all the time and make attempt after attempt to rescue those officers and men who had been isolated from the main force. An attempt was made on 20 March by the foreign consuls in the city to arrange an armistice. This was accepted by Radetzky but refused by the Italians, who sent out balloons with appeals for help with the result that the surrounding countryside now also rose up in rebellion. (The assumption that the peasants would automatically fight for Austria against their landlords was thereby proved to be false.) Meanwhile, inside the city, the rebels made for the gates and bastions while Radetzky attempted to reconquer lost ground in the centre. The Austrians were beaten back, whereas the insurgents took command of the Tosa and Ticinese gates, thus reaching the periphery of the city. Their success can be variously explained: by this time they were organized to some extent and there was some coordination; they also had shared ideals; but, more important, the barricades were providing enormously effective – by the fifth day there were 1,651 of them, some of which were fixed but some of which were mobile and behind which sheltered mobile columns of insurgents. After the 20th, Radetzky also began to receive reports of the losses and defeats suffered by his garrisons at Como, Bergamo, Cremona and Brescia. There were reports, too, of more Piedmontese activity on the frontier. On the night of 21–22 March, therefore, he took the decision to abandon the city. Probably the least important factor in his mind was the activity of the Piedmontese, about which he was not too worried. In any case, Charles Albert did not declare war until 23 March and the first vanguards of the Piedmontese army did not cross the Ticino until the afternoon of 25 March and the morning of the following day – that is, more than two days after Radetzky had left the city. Had he been able to maintain order in Milan, all the evidence suggests that he would have stood his ground and fought. He was, indeed, caught unawares and without sufficient supplies, but that was surely nobody's fault but his own, especially in view of the fact that the country was under martial law.

The excuses made by the army for the capitulation of Venice are to be found in the memoirs of General Schönhals, Radetzky's adjutant. He wrote: 'It was remarkable that shortly before the outbreak of the revolution, no reports reached the Field Marshal from Venetia. In particular no report whatsoever was confirmed from either the General Command or the two Corps Commands concerning the position of things there. One consoled oneself with the hunch that the authorities had nothing to report and that order had in no way been disturbed.'[29] What is really remarkable is not just the complacency of such a statement – 'one consoled oneself with a hunch' indeed! – but the fact that the archives contain not only the (frankly desperate) reports which Schönhals states were missing, but evidence that these were passed on to Vienna by Radetzky, accompanied by assurances that everything was in order. This was the reason why in mid-February, Zichy decided to address his fears directly to Vienna. The naval commander of Venice, Admiral Martini, wrote similar reports: the sailors in the city were Italian in their sympathies; the Arsenal workers were seething with discontent; the government had lost all authority; and perhaps only an additional 15,000 troops could save the situation. In Zichy's words on 28 February to the War Council in Vienna: '. . . how can people believe that the greater part of the navy is not evilly disposed towards the House of Austria and will not seize weapons to use against us at the first opportunity?'[30] The answer, amazingly, was on account of reassurances from Radetzky like the following: '. . . however bad the spirit of things in Venice reveals itself to be, I harbour no fears on that account, because, on the one hand, there can be no more unfavourable ground for a popular uprising, and, on the other hand, it is so easy to reinforce Venice that I myself would have no difficulties in putting down any attempt at an uprising.'[31] Martini therefore could be given the following response to one of his most pitiful reports: 'You certainly do not fail to recognise the difficulties of your present situation, but on the other hand, one expects complete pacification from the steps now being taken by the high command which entitle everybody to hope for the best.'[32] Zichy in the end did not even ask for help from the army corps stationed in Venetia; he merely surrendered.

Radetzky as a result had a credibility problem. In Vienna he was regarded as yet another failed commander. This meant that the government there would put its faith in negotiating with the Italians rather than fighting them. Meanwhile, his army was in danger of falling apart. Myth notwithstanding, there was no system in operation within the imperial forces whereby troops of one nationality were located in the homeland of another, according to some Machiavellian calculation. On the contrary: when Count Hartig, a former governor of Lombardy, on the eve of the revolutions, doubted the loyalty of the Italian troops serving in Italy, he discovered that: 'their loyalty had not only not been doubted, but every allusion to such doubts . . . was looked upon as a violation of military honour.'[33] The real system appeared to function instead on the assumption that since the empire was a supranational one and since recruits were taken from every part of it, there would always be troops of different nationalities located at any given time in any particular part, to be used as circumstances demanded. 'Thus although most regiments moved around a variety of Habsburg possessions every few years, it is difficult to conclude that the *Hofkriegsrat* had worked out any highly sophisticated or diabolical system. Those who believe otherwise would have to show why so many troops were at the wrong place at the wrong time and why many of them had been there so long.'[34] Thus, in Italy at the beginning of 1848, it turned out that of Radetzky's sixty-one infantry battalions, nine were Hungarian, six were Czech, ten were South Slav, twelve were Austrian and twenty-four were Italian. That is to say, 39 per cent of his infantry or 33 per cent of his army as a whole were made up of Italians. And this was so, despite the worries which he himself had expressed in a report of December 1848. He had then written to Vienna: 'I do not mistrust these troops in the least; they will do their duty; but we must not expect more of them than is reasonable, particularly when they are being led into battle against their own compatriots. There can be no doubt that these troops will be subjected to all kinds of influences and will be enticed to desert; if the luck of war goes against them, I shall not answer for their loyalty; such an experience would not even be surprising; it is as old as history itself.'[35] With the fall of Milan and Venice, therefore, the Field Marshal was brought up against the reality of his own prophecy, for by the beginning of April, nearly 11,000 of his Italian troops had deserted – leaving the remaining 10,000 as an extra problem. He asked Vienna: 'But where are they to be deployed? In the first line? There they could cross over, use their weapons against us and form a gap in the line of battle which would have to be dangerous. In reserve they threaten my rear; to keep them in the fortresses would be even more dangerous, since they could then deliver them to the enemy. The only thing left is to divide them up in such a way that only partial and gradual defections can result; in the worst circumstances I would disarm and dissolve them.'[36] As it happened, more desertions did take place, although several regiments, particularly those which had been stationed for a long time in Italy, remained loyal.

The rising tensions between the Hungarians and south Slavs were also to create problems for Radetzky. The Hungarians, as has been seen, refused to send reinforcements to Italy and pressed for a settlement there which would have given the Italians Lombardy. The Croats, on the other hand, remained loyal and sent the Field Marshal more troops. Yet, there were times when support from the south Slavs also seemed precarious. The Serb Patriach, Rajačić, for example, threatened to recall the Grenzer if he was not given more protection by the imperial army in southern Hungary against the Hungarians. Indeed, he even threatened to ally himself with the Sardinians, a move which the more radical south Slavs were actually advocating. Under these circumstances – made more ominous by the fact that the Sardinians refused to regard the Hungarians as real enemies – Radetzky clearly needed to be seen to be neutral as far as the Hungarian Question was concerned. In the end he managed to achieve this, although his personal sympathies lay with Jellačić who he admired and who had at one stage served in his army. Thus he told the War Minister: 'I do not wish at present to examine the question whether the over-confidence of the Hungarians in their treatment of the nationalities existing beside them has given rise to the misfortunes which now threaten us from this side. It is enough that this misfortune has arisen.'[37] Meanwhile, to Rajačić he wrote: 'I do not intend to set myself in judgement over both parties which now threaten Hungary with unforeseeable misfortunes. But their leaders, whoever they are, will be harshly judged by world history. It cannot – it must not come to a split in the Austrian army. The army is still loyal and is imbued with the noblest spirit. If it is forced to, it will take up arms to save the integrity of the Monarchy in the same way that it has triumphed over her external enemies. . . . I beg Your Excellency to mediate between the parties; employ the respect of your holy office to prevent the shedding of blood – is there no other way to reconcile the two parties apart from the most unfortunate way of all – civil war?'[38] In a number of other ways, too, the Field Marshal kept his distance from the Hungarian Question. It was perhaps fortunate that he had no spare cash and could not therefore send funds to Jellačić. Likewise, if he allowed the Serb leader, Suplikač, to return home from Italy, this was no sign of sympathy, since he had already accorded the same privilege to Colonel Mészáros, the Hungarian War Minister. His task was made considerably easier, however, when Jellačić acceded to a request from Schwarzenberg for a proclamation to calm the Grenzer. This ran in part: 'Do not allow yourselves to be diverted by reports and fears for the safety of your country . . . be assured we feel strong enough to defend our nationality without assistance from you.'[39] By November 1848, therefore, Radetzky could report to Vienna: 'If so far I have had the great luck to see unity maintained among all the nationalities in the army under my command, the greatest part of which consists of Hungarian and Croat regiments, it has been thanks only to the circumstance that the appearance of the government favouring one nationality at the cost of any other has been avoided.'[40] A British report to Lord Palmerston had meanwhile reached the same conclusion: 'With respect to the differences that existed between the Hungarians and the Croats, I understand that Field Marshal Radetzky, with his usual tact and talent, has managed to put an end to them.'[41] If this was in fact so, it was a remarkable achievement indeed and one which contributed in no small measure to his success. The other nationalities caused him little trouble.

The same could not be said, however, of Vienna. Here Radetzky's reputation had dwindled to naught after the capitulation of Milan and Venice, and on 20 April Ficquelmont had written to instruct him to prepare for a negotiated peace.[42] An uprising 'as general and decisive' as the one which had taken place, he explained, could 'be put down only by an equally decisive war or by way of negotiations'. Yet 'even if Austria had the means to wage such a war of repression', it was not at all clear whether she could do so in the light of world and Italian opinion. It had therefore been decided to pursue peace negotiations even while the war was still in progress. 'With luck', according to Ficquelmont, the struggle might be 'contained in the Venetian provinces', but (even) 'advantages in war' could 'only contribute to the restoration of peace through negotiations'. He therefore expected 'the closest identification of the military leadership with the attempts to reach a peace'. Radetzky was not informed of the details (although he might have guessed that the plan was to surrender Lombardy in the hope of retaining Venetia), save that Count Hartig was being sent to Italy as 'Peace Commissioner' with instructions to take control of whatever territories were won back by the Field Marshal. His job, in theory, was to 'pacify' the Italians, although, as might have been predicted, his main task, in practice, would be to pacify Radetzky.

Peace negotiations were conducted on three levels: through Hartig once he had joined up with Nugent's army, which proved quickly able to reinforce Radetzky; through Hummelauer, an Austrian diplomat who was sent to London in an attempt to secure British mediation; and through various emissaries who were sent to Milan in an attempt to split the Lombards from the Sardinians. Hummelauer's mission was clearly born of desperation. He was told before he left: 'We find it impossible to give you any precise instructions. It is absolutely necessary for us to bring the Italian problem to a speedy end. See what support can be got from English government. The essential thing for us is that a part of the state debt should be taken over. We lack the means to wage a war, in a sufficiently effective manner and even a battle won would not solve the problem. Let us know how you find things.'[43] Yet it proved impossible to win over the British to a reasonable compromise. When Hummelauer asked Palmerston to mediate on the basis of home rule for Lombardy-Venetia, his offer was rejected on 23 May. The next day, therefore, he suggested mediation on the basis of surrendering Lombardy and granting home rule to Venetia. Palmerston accepted this proposal, but it was turned down by the British cabinet on 3 June. Hummelauer, as a result, returned to Vienna empty-handed. Meanwhile, attempts to split the Lombards and the Sardinians were getting nowhere. Another Austrian diplomat, von Phillipsberg, was sent to Milan with the offer of a separate Lombard kingdom under a Habsburg prince to be ruled by an elected parliament. This mission, however, had an unexpected outcome. Von Phillipsberg was imprisoned on the grounds that his credentials were not in order. Undeterred, the imperial government sent yet another agent, Schnitzer-Meerau by name, this time with an offer to grant Lombardy complete independence. The 'equitable conditions' attached were 'to comprise principally of the transfer of a proportionate part of the state debt of the Austrian Empire to Lombardy'.[44] The Lombards, however, were to decline this proposal and by 25 June, Schnitzer-Meerau was reporting that they were demanding not merely Lombardy but all Austria's Italian territories as a prelude to negotiations. In fact, Wessenberg, the Austrian Foreign Minister, already knew of the union of Lombardy with Sardinia, a development which allowed him to give free rein to Radetzky.

The Field Marshal, meanwhile, had been complaining bitterly about Hartig's efforts at pacification, which he found ridiculous. They would, he protested, only be taken for weakness. In any case, he had no intention of cooperating with Hartig, telling the War Minister, Count Latour: 'I will negotiate only with the sword in my hand.'[45] He maintained that Hartig's instructions were incompatible with the last instructions he had personally received from the Emperor (to act, if necessary, according to the laws of war). On other occasions, he said he did not understand them. In any case, he believed that Hartig was being manipulated by the Italians who were receiving permission from him to publish newspapers which in turn carried false information and anti-Austrian propaganda. He therefore took careful steps to avoid meeting the man, while not neglecting to inform him – and Latour – that if martial law were lifted in Lombardy-Venetia – especially in the Quadrilateral which was in a state of siege – he would immediately lay down his sword: 'I as a loyal subject can do nothing but obey. But I would then be compelled to lay down my command.'[46]

In the middle of this dispute, however, a more serious problem arose for Radetzky. For on 11 June, Wessenberg, the new Foreign Minister, instructed him to negotiate a cease-fire with the Sardinians.[47] The war was 'costly' and the army deserved 'a well-earned rest'. The Field Marshal was thunderstruck. He wrote to Hartig: 'We have sunk low but by God not yet so low.'[48] His reaction was to send Prince Felix Schwarzenberg – Austrian ambassador to Naples when the revolutions had broken out – to Innsbruck to overturn the decision. In fact, the decisive clash between Wessenberg and Schwarzenberg was to take place in Vienna. The Foreign Minister was mainly worried by the financial costs of the war and the possibility of French intervention. But Schwarzenberg, following arguments drafted by Radetzky, countered that there was little hope of saving money by surrendering Lombardy – the Italians would merely threaten Venetia and attack at the first opportunity. Austria meanwhile would have to pay for a large standing army to defend her remaining province. Again, it was not in France's interest to create a strong state on her southern frontier. Nor was Radetzky intending to provoke French intervention by invading Piedmont – that was a danger he was well aware of. Finally, a *de facto* ceasefire already existed, since neither army was in a position to take the initiative. What was really needed, therefore, were more troops and a decisive battle. And once Wessenberg had heard of the failure of the Schnitzer-Meerau mission and of Lombardy's union with Piedmont, he was prepared to agree. Given that diplomacy had failed to bring about a compromise peace, he had little alternative but to leave the initiative to Radetzky.

The failure of Austrian diplomacy had been due, of course, in no small measure to the Italians. Their initial success in taking control of the capital cities of Lombardy-Venetia had duped them into believing that they had won the war – much as Windischgraetz had deceived himself in Hungary after his capture of Buda-Pest. Hence their over-confidence in the negotiations with the Austrians. In fact, Charles Albert was no better a commander than Windischgraetz: he too was slow at organizing and he too pursued occupation policies which aided the enemy. His taxes fell mainly on the poor and like Windischgraetz he became identified with the interests of the local nobility. He was nicknamed *il re dei signori* and presented Radetzky with the opportunity to play off the peasants against him. In the words of Franco della Peruta, 'the weight of the war was made to fall principally upon the poorer sections of the people and on the bourgeoisie employed in industry and commerce, protecting the landed bourgeoisie and aristocracy as much as possible.'[49] By August 1848, therefore, Radetzky was receiving *vivats* from the peasants all along his route to Milan, although he in turn would lose their trust. Basically, they feared that both sides wished to conscript them and that was something which had no popular appeal at all.

Yet it was not Charles Albert's policies towards the peasants which lost him the war. If anything, that was due to more straightforward errors of a military nature. For a start, he had not been planning to invade Lombardy, with the result that when he was invited by the Lombard provisional government to intervene, his army was not in a state of readiness. It had been expecting instead to have to put down a revolution in Genoa. It entered Lombardy, therefore, without sufficient maps, tents, horses or supplies. Moreover, it was handicapped by the king's deficient generalship and by the belief that the Austrians were already defeated. As a result there was no determined effort to pursue them or to engage them in battle before they could establish themselves in the Quadrilateral. Charles Albert was also terrified of using foreign or Italian volunteers for fear of contaminating his royalist troops with republicanism. Hence both his refusal to seek aid from the French (who in any case claimed Nice and Savoy) and his refusal to entrust Lombard volunteer riflemen with the task of cutting the Austrian supply lines through the Tyrol. Finally, the Polish Legion, which the poet Adam Mickiewicz had organized in Italy, was forced to stage a near revolt before it received permission to recruit from Austrian prisoners-of-war and to meet the enemy in battle.

Even once Radetzky had been reinforced by General Nugent, the outcome was by no means predictable: both sides had more or less the same number of men. Yet Radetzky's generalship proved superior and on 6 August he could re-enter Milan. Before then, on 24–25 July at Custozza, he had been allowed to fight a decisive encounter. Latour had written to him, after the fuss over the ceasefire: 'I do not hold myself entitled to decide from here in my capacity as War Minister when the right moment will arrive to give battle to King Charles Albert of Sardinia . . . this decision must be left to Your Excellency as the supreme commander who has the experience of war and the trust of the monarch, the government and of the army to so high a degree. . . . You must have freedom to decide what to do with regard to the enemy.'[50] The reply was Radetzky's report from Custozza, which read: 'A decisive victory has been the result of this hot day.'[51]

By this time, too, the Field Marshal had won his battle over internal policy in Italy. Count Hartig had resigned as Court Commissioner on 3 July. Only a few days before, Radetzky had written to him: 'I too honestly regret that there had to be differences between us in many respects concerning our views on the present state of Italy. However, I have had such bitter experiences, partly on account of the neglect of all my warnings and forecasts about conditions here, that Your Excellency will not reproach me if I now consider that out of this general wreckage I have at least kept my military honour unblemished. I also harbour the hope that Your Excellency will retain these friendly feelings towards me which you so often displayed in earlier and better times.'[52]

With the recapture of Milan, the war in Italy was more or less over. The outcome had never been predictable and, indeed, the situation was to remain uncertain for some time. In September, for example, it looked as if the French might intervene, but mediation took place instead – accepted now by the Austrians only on the condition that none of their territory would have to be surrendered. Then in March 1849, against the advice of the British and French, Charles Albert renewed the war. But, as we have seen, he was defeated by Radetzky within the week. With the defeat of the Hungarians and the surrender of Venice in August 1849, the revolutions were over.

DISOBEDIENCE AND THE *CAMARILLA*

A couple of myths connected with their defeat concern the relative roles of the commanders who have just been discussed. One states that they triumphed on account of their disobedience – a viewpoint attributed to Prince Schwarzenberg. A second concerns the existence of a *Camarilla*, a group of courtiers, members of the imperial family and the imperial commanders, all of whom are supposed, behind the backs of the Vienna government, to have coordinated a strategy of counter-revolution. In particular, Count Latour, is supposed to have played the pivotal part of coordinating the roles of all the others from the War Ministry where, for example, he is supposed to have organized money and material for Jellačić at a time when the Ban had been deprived of his title by the Emperor. As a result, the impression is conveyed in most secondary literature that the counter-revolution was an organized one, that the counter-revolutionaries had similar views and that they were indeed of similar importance. Hence the names Windischgraetz, Jellačić and Radetzky often get stuck together as if they were interchangeable parts of the same machine, under the control, in some accounts, of Latour or, later, Prince Schwarzenberg. The truth, however, is altogether different.

Take the matter of disobedience. It should now be clear that Radetzky was not guilty of insubordination. In his disputes with Hartig and Wessenberg, his line was always clear-cut. He wanted martial law to prevail and a decisive encounter to be fought, but there was never any thought of disobedience. Instead he would argue his case – forcefully to say the least – and avoid personal confrontations, albeit always with the underlying threat that if he did not get his way, he would relinquish his command. His words to Latour were: 'As Commanding General I am responsible to the War Ministry and to His Majesty; should my operations and the position of my army necessitate my taking measures which are not accounted for by the usual administrative regulations, I shall be responsible for them to Your Excellency.'[53] This was exactly the same view as he had adopted with Hartig: 'I as a loyal subject can do nothing but obey. But I would then, however, be compelled to lay down my command.'[54] In practice, the imperial government had little choice but to accept the views of the commander on the spot, unless it was prepared to risk chaos and a crisis of morale.

Windischgraetz, too, has been accused of insubordination – in his case, of refusing to send troops to Radetzky and of disobeying orders in Prague. Once again, however, the truth is rather different. For example, he failed, as has been seen, to put Vienna in a state of siege in March 1848 when he was appointed commander of the city immediately after the outbreak of revolution, this despite the fact that everybody knew it was his intention to do so. His failure to act, according to his biographer, Paul Müller, was due to his respect for the court which preferred to make concessions. He himself refused to say exactly what had happened 'until certain eyes had closed',[55] but the point to note is that he did not take matters into his own hands. His behaviour in Prague, as army commander in Bohemia, was in many respects to parallel Radetzky's.

In the textbooks, Windischgraetz is famous for bombarding Prague and thereby apparently taking the first strong step to combat revolution. In fact, Cracow had already been bombarded with little influence on events elsewhere and the same was to be true of Prague.

The truth is that there was no real revolutionary movement in the city endangering the Monarchy. The Slav Congress was a debating body, the majority of whose delegates were loyal to the dynasty and had nothing to do with the 'Whitsun Uprising' there. Besides, most Bohemians – Czechs more than Germans – had already been granted significant concessions through the 'Bohemian Charter' of 8 April. This had granted a separate administration for the province (although without a separate ministry) and had stipulated full equality for the Czech language in all branches of administration and education. Moreover, a new Diet was to be summoned – not based on the old estates – and the question of union with Silesia and Moravia was to be referred to the Reichstag once it had opened in Vienna. Given these concessions, there was hardly much need for revolutionary activity. Hence the most recent account of the Slav Congress can describe the June uprising in the following terms: 'Essentially it was a spontaneous popular reaction to the provocations of the Austrian military commander in Bohemia, Prince Alfred zu Windischgraetz. . . . As soon as he returned [to Prague on 20 May] military activity in the city intensified; patrols were doubled, and at a military review on June 7 the general made pointedly derogatory allusions to the new constitution. He increased the size of the garrison and placed heavy artillery on the . . . heights that dominated the centre of the city.'[56] On 12 June after a peaceful protest rally and a mass, scuffles broke out between the students and the troops. These degenerated into revolution when some students were killed. The barricades went up and for six days street-fighting continued until, on 17 June, Windischgraetz dislodged the insurgents by a heavy cannonade from the heights above the city. His wife (Prince Schwarzenberg's sister) had been killed by a stray bullet on the first day of the fighting and thereafter he had rejected all attempts to reach a compromise settlement. When the fighting ended he put the city in a state of siege and set up a military–civilian investigatory commission to catch the culprits who had been behind the 'revolution'. Both of these steps, however, were taken without reference to the War Ministry in Vienna.

Vienna already, in fact, had cause to be dissatisfied with the Prince's behaviour. It was an open secret, for example, that when the governor of Bohemia, Count Leo Thun, had tried in May to form a government independent of Vienna, Windischgraetz had supported him. (Thun had justified his actions on the grounds, first, that the Vienna government had lost its authority to the student mob after its failure to disband the Viennese Academic Legion on 23 May, and secondly, that the Bohemian Charter had implied a separate ministry for Bohemia, which it had not. The heir to the throne, the Archduke Francis Charles, however, had accepted the Vienna government's advice that to grant self-government to Bohemia would be to destroy the unity of the Monarchy.) Latour went so far as to demand from Windischgraetz an explanation of his actions. He replied that he too had believed Vienna to have lost control and that he had been motivated 'by the purest and most noble intentions'.[57] He had also used the May crisis in Vienna, however, to request direct orders from the Emperor in future and to seek permission to march on Vienna with 20,000 regulars and the Bohemian reserves. Latour, in a private letter, turned down these requests and so, too, did Francis Charles.

Given such behaviour on Windischgraetz's part, the Vienna government had grave doubts about his account of the June uprising. It more or less suspected that it had been provoked by him and sent both a civil and a military commissioner to Prague as soon as word of the uprising had been received to discover what had happened there. They were empowered to demand Windischgraetz's resignation and to withdraw all troops from the city, if such steps were thought necessary to restore public confidence. Windischgraetz, in fact, resigned his command to the military commissioner, Count Mensdorff, as soon as he heard of these powers but was asked to resume it when the army petitioned him to do so and when it became clear that his resignation alone would not restore order. Latour, meanwhile, on receiving news of the Prince's resignation, remarked that it was fortunate that he had resigned of his own volition as otherwise it would be difficult to get rid of him. There is no evidence that the two men were working hand in hand.

After the suppression of the uprising, Windischgraetz became a hero of the counter-revolution. He also received the personal thanks of the Emperor, and eventually (3 July) a clearance from the two commissioners. According to them: 'he only resisted the unrest, wanted not to infringe on constitutional matters and his motives were loyal.'[58] But on the same account, he now also became an even greater problem as far as Latour and the Ministry were concerned. This was to be proved first of all by his refusal to send troops to aid Radetzky; thereafter, it would be demonstrated by the running battle with him over martial law and the civil rights of political prisoners. Windischgraetz's main weapon, however, like Radetzky's, was the threat of resignation. For if that happened, rumour had it that his troops would desert Prague and leave *en masse* for Italy.

It was on 24 June that he wrote to Latour, informing him that he could not give aid to Radetzky. His letter ran: 'To weaken the armed forces stationed in Prague in order to send a part of them to Italy, would mean surrendering advantages which have been won with great difficulty and sacrifices, as well as abandoning Bohemia. This is my incontrovertible opinion based on exact knowledge of the situation and on account of which I am obliged to declare candidly that were I formally forced to send troops, neither I, still less anyone else, would be in a position to retain Bohemia and I am therefore determined to go to Innsbruck to put my case before the Emperor.'[59] Windischgraetz argued that troops could only be sent to Italy if he too were given reinforcements, otherwise he could not be responsible for maintaining order in the Bohemian countryside. The Vienna government did not believe that there was any threat to order in the Bohemian countryside. Hence Latour's reply that he had received Windischgraetz's letter 'with deep regret'.[60]

There were numerous clashes also regardng martial law and the prisoners indicted by the investigating committee. The Viennese government did not see how elections to the Reichstag could be held in July if Prague were still in a state of siege. A Hofrat Komers was sent to Prague, therefore, with powers to publish a decree abolishing martial law if he found that it was no longer necessary. Komers consulted with both Thun and the Prince and reached the conclusion that it would be unwise to upset the latter. Besides, Windischgraetz had assured him that, with a few technical adjustments, it would be perfectly possible to hold free elections. They would in fact, be better guaranteed to be free if martial law remained in force. The Ministry reluctantly agreed and it was not until after the Reichstag had met that Windischgraetz was finally persuaded to put an end to martial law. Meanwhile, he maintained that any attempt to do without it would simply lead to anarchy. And he repeated his threat to go to the Emperor if Vienna dared to override his opinion. Komers, in fact, had not seen any need for martial law at all. The ninety-four people arrested by the investigating committee seemed to him to be an indication that law and order had been restored. Yet he was afraid that the military would become unmanageable if Windischgraetz were to resign his command again. Nor did the Ministry in Vienna want to force the Emperor to choose between him and itself on this matter.

The new Reichstag met on 10 July and the Czech deputies spent much of their time thereafter attacking martial law in Prague. Since one of the people arrested by the investigating committee, moreover, had been elected a deputy, the situation became an embarrassing one for the new Justice Minister, Alexander Bach. The latter was an energetic personality and quite prepared to stand up to the army. He therefore announced that there would be no show trials and that political prisoners would be amnestied. Likewise, he refused to listen to complaints from the Prague garrison that various deputies should be arrested for slandering them. Latour persuaded Windischgraetz to accept the minister's position.

The Prince, however, was extremely shocked by proceedings in the Reichstag and felt forced to make contingency plans lest it should eventually attack the monarch. Once again, therefore, he approached the court (Francis Charles and the Empress) and requested full powers. This time he received them, backdated to 23 May, when the Ministry had been in crisis, in order to avoid the need for a ministerial counter-signature. According to these – and they were to be employed only in the most desperate circumstances – Windischgraetz received the authority to take whatever steps he thought necessary in Vienna and to raise the troops he required to do so. On 28 August he also bolstered his position by helping to get Prince Joseph Lobkowitz appointed as the Emperor's adjutant general. Lobkowitz was a devoted adherent of the Prince and was told to ensure that the Emperor was not induced to sign any documents which could imperil the throne. More importantly, he was instructed to speed the Emperor out of the capital if ever his person should be endangered. In Windischgraetz's own words: 'As soon as you notice that concessions are being extorted or that the person of the Emperor is in any sort of danger, collect as many troops as possible and take the Emperor and the whole imperial family, not in flight, but under the protection of the army, via Krems to Olmütz.'[61] He added: 'Then I shall conquer Vienna, the Emperor will abdicate in favour of his nephew, and I shall then take Ofen [Buda-Pest].' Lobkowitz, however, was instructed to say nothing of these plans to the Ministry or even to Latour who, according to Windischgraetz, 'although he certainly means well, has been totally deluded by recent events and by the Reichstag, and is in fact totally confused'. It was not, however, until the revolution in Vienna in October 1848 and Latour's murder that this plan was put into operation. Then, indeed, there was reason to fear for the Emperor's safety and nobody objected to what was done. Windischgraetz, therefore, cannot be accused of using his secret powers irresponsibly. With the defeat of that revolution, on the other hand, they made him virtual dictator – a title in fact which he refused to accept – and put him in a position both to nominate his brother-in-law, Schwarzenberg, as Prime Minister and to pursue his plans to arrange for the Emperor's abdication and the conquest of Hungary. Inevitably, he quarrelled with Schwarzenberg over almost all aspects of the new government's policy, although, perhaps surprisingly, he found himself unable to change it to any significant degree. In the end, as we have already seen, he was sacked as supreme commander in Hungary in the spring of 1849 when he proved unable to defeat the Hungarians' counter-offensive. However one finally assesses his role – and we shall attempt to do this presently – it is difficult to argue that he saved the Monarchy through disobedience. Like Radetzky, he was never afraid to argue his case and, backed by the threat of resignation, he, again like the old Field Marshal, was often successful when he did so.

Jellačić is a completely different case. There is little doubt that everything he did in the spring and summer of 1848 was illegal and insubordinate and that his whole strategy depended on the retrospective approval of his actions by the Emperor. His very appointment was arguably illegal, coming as it did before the new Hungarian ministry was formed, so as to avoid the need for the ministerial counter-signature, which Vienna knew would never be obtained. Thereafter, the Ban's refusal to take orders from Buda-Pest, his imposition of martial law in civil and military Croatia and, most of all, his assembling of an army with which to invade the neighbouring territory of a legally constituted Hungarian state – and this at a time when the Emperor had already deprived him of his title and office as Ban – all of this constituted the most monstrous example of disobedience. In the end, of course, he received the backing he had hoped for, when the Emperor on 4 September reinstated him as Ban and on 3 October made him commander-in-chief of the royal forces in Hungary, the country which he was invading.

Had all this been planned all along? Had the *Camarilla* organized it through Latour? The Hungarians were adamant that it had since letters had been intercepted which apparently proved that Jellačić had been receiving ammunition, supplies and money from Latour. On the other hand, if the state of Jellačić's army is anything to go by, Latour could not have been fulfilling his role very adequately. According to Professor Rothenberg: 'Overall the Croatian forces were short of heavy artillery, modern rifles, and field equipment. Of the Grenzer, only about half were armed and equipped as prescribed by the existing military regulations; the rest wore their national costumes and carried whatever arms they could procure: flintlocks, shotguns, even pikes.'[62] True, Jellačić had assumed that the regular forces in Hungary would desert to the imperial flag which he was flying but, even so, he must have hoped to have had a better army behind him than the one he led. As things turned out, he could not even pay his troops and, as he told Baron Kulmer, his main link with the court, '. . . it is difficult to maintain discipline when soldiers do not receive their pay'.[63] That this was indeed the case is confirmed by a letter of one of his officers, which recorded the mood and condition of Jellačić's troops. It ran: 'In four days' time we will be before Pesth, and God help the town, for the Frontiersmen (i.e. the Grenzer) are so embittered and angry that they will be awful to manage. Already, they can't be kept from excesses, and rob and steal frightfully. We order a thousand floggings to be administered every day; but it is no sort of use: not even a god, much less an officer, can hold them back. We are received by the peasants quite kindly, but every evening come the complaints, sometimes dreadful ones. I am driven desperate by this robber train and feel no better than a brigand myself; for I must look after the commissariat.'[64] How much support then had Jellačić actually received from Latour?

Much of the writing on this subject is based on the correspondence between Jellačić and Kulmer, who had probably been instrumental in securing Jellačić's appointment as Ban in the first place, and who certainly shared his belief that the new Hungarian constitution could not be allowed to continue. In his letter of 30 March, for example, congratulating Jellačić on his appointment, Kulmer wrote: 'Things look bad in Hungary. The new ministry has indeed been confirmed, although I think its effectiveness is zero. In the end Austria will have to reconquer Hungary.'[65] He believed Jellačić should assume this task and became frustrated with every delay. Jellačić, himself, was more cautious, preferring to receive prior approval from Vienna, but Kulmer insisted that approval would come once an invasion had taken place. Thus on 28 August he warned: '. . . only after you have actually crossed the Drava will confidence in you, which is now rapidly declining, be restored. Once you have successfully invaded Hungary, you will receive imperial sanction.'[66] A few days later he wrote: '. . . the highest circles in Vienna expect, hope, and desire that you will not stop until you have entered Pest. Therefore, good friend, advance!'[67] He also gave the impression that Latour was in favour of the invasion, writing, for example, on 16 August: 'I have just come from Latour who said to me: as a minister I cannot give advice to the Ban, but if I were in his place I shouldn't hesitate for so long but would have marched already.'[68]

The correspondence between Jellačić and Latour confirms that whatever private views Latour held, he did not allow them to interfere with his duties as a constitutional minister. Kulmer's comments are certainly correct, therefore, in that respect. More to the point, however, is the fact that the correspondence between Jellačić and Latour – and indeed between Latour and the other commanders in the Military Border – demonstrates that there was no secret flow of funds from Vienna to Zagreb. Latour, indeed, sent some money but he admitted this to the Hungarians and explained why it had been sent. He also sent them copies of correspondence from Jellačić and tried to get them to provide money for him instead. For Latour's main concern was for the retired officers, the wives, widows, children and orphans of the Frontier, who were being deprived of pay, pensions and subsistence funds. He feared that if they continued to lack these then the situation would deteriorate to the point where the Grenzer would be recalled from Italy in order to attack the Hungarians. But all the way through the summer – until the Emperor and the ministry decided to back Jellačić's invasion – Latour desisted as much as possible from interfering in Hungarian affairs and ordered the generals in Hungary to obey the orders of the Hungarian ministry. Nor was money moved from secret funds that were available in order to provide aid for Jellačić. Neither the records of the 'secret cabinet fund' nor those of the Habsbug-Lorraine family fund reveal that any aid was in fact dispensed. The only entry in the latter relating to Jellačić records that 1,700 gulden was given to his father to equip the future Ban as a lieutenant. His mother, apparently, had been responsible for this request.

The basic problem in Croatia was that the Croats would not recognize the legitimacy of the Hungarian government to which they had been subordinated, so that the latter would not pay them any money. The Austrians, on the other hand, despite their efforts to remain neutral in the dispute, were dependent on the Croats for reinforcements in Italy. They were therefore in no position to ignore Jellačić's demands, especially when he wrapped them up in phrases like the following: 'Without the Grenzer, the victory of Austria in Italy would not have been possible, without the Grenzer, the Austrian Monarchy would now stand on the brink of being overthrown without hope of salvation.'[69] Yet, he also made it clear that there could be no compromise with Hungary: 'It is an undeniable fact,' he wrote, 'that these Grenzer regiments will not recognise the Hungarian ministry under any circumstances and that I – even if I wanted to – could not subordinate myself to this ministry, since in that case the General Command would lose its own authority and the maintenance of law and order among the populace as among the border regiments would certainly break down.'[70] The result was that the Hungarians, in the shape of their finance minister, Kossuth, simply ignored the Border's needs for funds. Likewise, the war minister, Mészaros, neglected to administer the machinery for pensions and promotions relating to the Border regiments. Jellačić, therefore, put Latour under constant pressure to provide the money and promotions instead, requesting 148,000 florins in June, 280,000 in July and 145,262 in August. And Latour did what he could to come up with the money. For example, on 12 July, Jellačić wrote acknowledging receipt of 100,000 florins and requesting 168,107 more.[71] It was this request which motivated Latour to address a blistering letter to Esterházy. It ran in part: 'I allow myself, therefore, once again, as I did in my above-mentioned note, to refer to the fact that the steps taken by the Finance Minister to deprive the Agram Military Treasury of its regular payments can clearly only contribute to associating with the discontent in Croatia, sections of the population which have hitherto kept their distance from the prevailing troubles, people who will suffer from reduced incomes and will therefore see themselves facing the most wretched misery. It must as a result make the proposed imperial settlement of the very regrettable quarrel all the more difficult in its present aspects and in the longer term.'[72] Yet he was under no illusions and knew that his motives would be misinterpreted by Kossuth. Hence he continued: 'But if he [Kossuth] intends to characterise my note of the fourth of this month referring to the costs of meeting [Jellačić's] payments as a new example of the hostile spirit of the imperial government regarding the territorial unity of Hungary and as an attack on the legal guarantee of the independence and integrity of the Hungarian empire, I must protest in the name of myself and my colleagues most specifically against this, since I have repeatedly pointed out, that the oft-mentioned transfer of funds has taken place without any intent to support any political faction whatsoever, but only to cover the regular payments to the troops, some of which are located in the direction of Gör, others in defensive positions on the Littoral, which is threatened by the Italian enemy, as well as to satisfy the just claims of active and pensioned state servants or their dependents, widows and children, who rely on treasury support. The only considerations which have been borne in mind, therefore, are those which have undoubtedly been earned by a people which for months now has been, and still is fighting with admirable self-sacrifice and in great numbers to protect the rights of their monarch on bloody fields of battle.' Predictably, however, the Hungarians did nothing: Jellačić continued to complain and ask for funds, yet Latour still remained loyal to the new institutions. On 14 August, for example, he told Jellačić: 'The great many disadvantages which have arisen for the imperial service from the subordination of the entire Military Border to the Hungarian War Ministry and the persistent refusal of the Grenzer to recognise this position have long been regretfully recognised by me. But however much I have acknowledged the need to tackle this intractable problem, by returning matters in stages to their previous situation, under the Austrian War Ministry, I cannot oppose the absolutely categorical imperial commands which are known to Your Excellency and must subordinate my administrative authority to that of the Hungarian War Ministry.'[73] And on 20 August he issued a circular to all the General Commands in Hungary and the Border confirming that their requests and reports were to be sent directly to Buda-Pest unless they concerned foreign regiments or regiments outside of Hungary, in which case they might communicate directly with himself.

One week later, however, Latour was sending an ultimatum to Esterházy. He wrote: 'The troops, the administration must be paid; widows and orphans, pensioners, the wives of officers serving in the field who remain at home, are crying out for their means of subsistence!'[74] He then added, much more ominously: 'Every helpful intervention on the part of the Austrian ministry is interpreted as having a sinister significance. This Ministry can therefore do nothing but urgently recommend Your Excellency to rectify the recent complaints of the General Command and to bring to Your Excellency's attention what want and privation will and must finally lead to, namely the decision to seek the absolutely essential means of subsistence by force in neighbouring lands.' He concluded: 'I therefore urgently beseech Your Excellency in the name of the Austrian Ministry for immediate help and if a positive decision is not obtained within the course of this week, nothing else will remain for the Austrian ministry, but [itself] to put an end to the completely intolerable wretchedness in the Border by appropriate means.' When still nothing happened, therefore, Bach persuaded the Austrian ministry on 29 August to issue its warning that it could no longer remain neutral in the quarrel between Hungary and Croatia, unless the

Hungarians relinquished their portfolios of defence and finance. On 11 September, already restored to his dignity of Ban, Jellačić crossed the Drava. His first reports were full of optimism and on 4 October the king dissolved the Hungarian parliament and made him commander-in-chief of all armed forces in Hungary. His gamble had paid off, but it was only now that Latour could openly back him, something for which on 6 October he was to pay with his life.

The Empire, therefore, cannot be said to have been saved by disobedience. Nor can it be argued that it was saved by a *Camarilla*. This was merely the left-wing version of Metternich's *comité directeur*. Windischgraetz after all had refused to send troops to Radetzky, who had refused to take sides in the dispute between Hungary and Croatia; and Latour at various times had offended Windischgraetz, Jellačić and Radetzky by insisting on fulfilling his duties as a constitutional minister. It is also true that few of these people liked each other. Latour would have been pleased to see Windischgraetz resign; Windischgraetz himself had little respect for the military abilities of either Jellačić or Radetzky, and thought that Latour had sold out to constitutionalism; Radetzky, on the other hand, was apt to take a generous view of everybody.

There were profound differences between them also on a different level, namely with regard to politics. Those of Jellačić are most difficult to fathom. Clearly he believed in a united empire with home rule for the various nationalities, but what degree of liberty they were to enjoy it is difficult to say. Certainly, he did not allow much in Croatia during the summer of 1848, since the country was put under martial law, and Yugoslav historians today have reservations about treating him as a national hero. His rather unsympathetic description of Windischgraetz, on the other hand (whom he agreed should have been sacked during the Hungarian campaign), gives some reason to suppose he may not have been completely reactionary. He said: 'Windischgraetz is an aristocrat. He hates all revolution from inner feeling as much as from professional instinct. He squashed Frankfurt's constitutional ideas in Prague, and here in Vienna he will allow no liberties. He is always hard on the penitent revolutionary. A real republican devil finds more grace from him, for there the extremes touch. Besides being an aristocrat, he is a military pedant.'[75] Windischgraetz himself would not have disagreed with much of this, although he would hardly have thought Jellačić qualified to judge anyone in military matters. Regarding his views on aristocracy, these were well known and indeed almost a cliché in 1848. Yet it is worthwhile to remember just how deeply held they were, something which is borne out by the following exchange between himself and Count Stadion at the time of the Prague uprising. Stadion had written to him: 'The Emperor has made concessions to his peoples. Why and under what circumstances are for him to decide. They have been made and from this moment on they are the property of the people and as such holy as any other property. To attack this property and to limit it is a great injustice. It may not and cannot be admitted that the Emperor would lie to his peoples; he would never intend that an imperial present would be impugned. He who advises the Emperor so, impugns his honour.'[76] To all of which Windischgraetz replied: 'Regarding the Emperor's presents to his peoples, which presents are they? A man cannot give presents of other people's property and despite all his powers, that which is not the property of the Emperor cannot be regarded as the property of the people.'[77] Windischgraetz's reply to Stadion, in other words, was the same as that of Shakespeare's York to Richard II: 'Take Hereford's rights away and take from Time, His charters and his customary rights; Let not tomorrow then ensue today; Be not thyself, for how art thou a king But by fair sequence and succession?' Monarchy, in short, depended on the survival of that social pyramid of which the Emperor constituted the apex. Yet he could only hope to retain that position by cooperating with his nobles and maintaining them above the rest. To remove them or to abolish their rights and privileges was to invite the collapse of the Monarchy itself. Consequently, there could be no concessions to liberalism or democracy. The human race, he is once supposed to have said, began with barons; below that there were only monkeys.

Radetzky, on the other hand, was much more progressive and had very different views regarding the nobility. In the 1820s he had recorded his belief that all countries would soon have constitutions and had welcomed the imperial one of 25 April 1848, writing to the first War Minister, Peter Zanini: 'Yesterday I received the new constitution from the Minister of the Interior. It rests on so liberal a base that I take it to be the most liberal in Europe. That the press will find something in it to blame, we must of course expect, but I hope, however, that the best part of the nation will find in it a guarantee of all the wishes and ideas with which they believe their happiness is bound.'[78] The failure of the Reichstag, however, to accord a vote of thanks to his troops in Italy somewhat moderated his enthusiasm: 'Rome did not reward her army in this way; nor did Greece; nor did the bloody French Republic; it was reserved for modern Liberty to present such an unworthy spectacle to the world.'[79] On the other hand, a circular from Latour, dated 24 September, reminding commanders that obedience to orders meant 'upholding and respecting the constitutional institutions and arrangements in the state',[80] prompted a defence. 'The army', he wrote, 'has no reason to retain any predilection for the system which has fallen. This system was, if it can be called a despotism, a civil – not a military despotism. The army was neglected, slighted; it, therefore, expressed no spirit of hostility at all against the free institutions which His Majesty conferred upon his peoples.'[81] Yet the October revolution in Vienna and the murder of Latour on 6 October convinced the old Field Marshal that Austria was not yet ready for liberty. Hence in a proclamation which rebuked the Vienna garrison for failing to do its duty, he displayed a new and very different political tone: 'Soldiers! Open your eyes to that abyss that opens at your feet; everything is in flux; the mainstays of the social order have been destroyed; property, morality, religion are threatened with destruction. Everything that is holy and dear to man, everything on which the state is based and which it upholds, people are determined to destroy. That, not liberty, is the aim of every rabblerouser who wants to drag you down to your ruin and shame.'[82] When a Reichstag member later proposed that the army should also elect deputies, the troops in Italy predictably petitioned the Emperor to reject the idea. 'The army,' they declared, 'as an integral part of the executive power can never . . . take any share in the legislative.'[83] Radetzky himself was to congratulate Schwarzenberg when he dissolved the Kremsier Reichstag.

It was still Radetzky's hope, however, to win over the Italian people for the House of Habsburg. But he intended to do this after the revolution, not through liberalism, but through a paternalist version of the class war. He fervently believed that the revolution in Italy had been caused by the local nobility and planned to isolate it by appealing to the peasants. He told Schwarzenberg: 'To humble the refractory rich, to protect the loyal citizen, but in particular to *exalt the poorer classes of the peasantry as in Galicia* should be the principle on which from now on the government in Lombardy-Venetia should be based.'[84] His chief of staff, General Hess, was reported to have explained the policy even more straightforwardly: 'The people love us; the nobles hate us; we must, therefore, annihilate them.'[85] The result was that the north Italian nobles were taxed, taxed and taxed again in an effort to destroy their economic and social base. Radetzky levied special taxes, super-taxes and extraordinary taxes to force them to pay for the war. He even tried to confiscate all noble lands as early as November 1848, although it was not until after the Milan insurrection of February 1853 that sequestration decrees were put into effect. The result was that he acquired a reputation for communism. Palmerston said that his policies were conducted 'in the spirit of the most odious oppression and enunciated a doctrine which belong[ed] only to the disciples of communism'.[86] They were 'subversive of the very foundations of social order'. Yet they backfired. For a start, they managed to undermine the whole economy of northern Italy, based as it was on a prosperous agriculture. Secondly, the peasantry always suspected that the Field Marshal was preparing to conscript them, with the result that decrees intended to amnesty deserters were all misread as devious means of repairing the conscription lists. The Austrian army consequently found little support in the countryside; instead, thousands of peasants fled to Switzerland. By January 1849, therefore, the British Minister in Turin could report to Palmerston: 'It is the policy of the Austrians to declare openly that only one class of their Italian subjects, namely the nobles, are really disaffected towards them and that the measures which have been adopted are calculated only to break the spirit of the revolt in that portion of the population and to enable them to confer that happiness and contentment upon the rest of the inhabitants which it is asserted they are perfectly ready to receive at the hands of their Austrian rulers. The information which I have received leads me to form a totally different conclusion. From the reports which have been made to me by persons who have had the opportunity of studying this point I believe that one feeling of deep-rooted hatred pervades the minds of man, woman, and child throughout Lombardy and that this feeling has immeasurably increased since the reoccupation of her provinces.'[87]

Radetzky's outlook, therefore, was clearly very different from that of Windischgraetz. It was ironical, therefore, that the latter should select as Prime Minister in October 1848 his brother-in-law, Prince Schwarzenberg. No doubt he felt that Schwarzenberg, who was thirteen years his junior and who had once served as a cadet in his regiment, would follow his lead politically. But this was a mistake. Schwarzenberg had spent most of his time during the summer of 1848 with Radetzky and had come to share the latter's views on nobles and peasants. He therefore approved of the abolition of the robot (compulsory labour service) and proposed to exclude the nobility from any special role in government. Worse still, he was prepared to retain many of the constitutional ministers of 1848 and to contemplate a parliamentary régime. And he met Windischgraetz's protests with accusations that the Hungarian nobility were just as 'politically and morally degenerate' as the Italians. Indeed, unlike his brother-in-law, he could find nothing good to say about nobles in general. He wrote: 'I know of not a dozen men of our class with sufficient political wisdom or with the necessary experience to whom an important share of power could be entrusted without soon having to fear for it. I have thought a great deal about how to constitute the aristocracy of Austria as a body so as to maintain for it an appropriate political influence but the elements out of which this body consists, I have been unable to find. Democracy must be fought and its excesses must be challenged but in the absence of other means of help that can only be done by the government itself. To rely on an ally as weak as our aristocracy unfortunately is, would be to damage our cause more than to help it.'[88]

The more one examines the problem, therefore, the more convincing becomes the evidence that the Monarchy in 1848 was not saved by any reactionary conspiracy, and certainly not one composed of men united either by strategy, policy or even mutual regard. Apart from a shared hope that the excesses of the revolution might be overcome, there was little to bind these men together. It is somewhat ironic therefore that they should habitually be lumped together in the textbooks – three or four funny-sounding foreign names – as if they were equally important members of a team. Jellačić cannot really be called 'the man who saved Austria', the title so generously bestowed on him by his English biographer.[89] And Windischgraetz's significance is best summed up by Louis Eisenmann: 'Without military talent he became commander of an army corps at Prague; without political talent, he became for a moment, behind the curtain, master of Austria.'[90] Radetzky, on the other hand, appears as a major figure whose victories were real achievements and whose success was the key to the counter-revolution. Had he not succeeded in defeating Charles Albert, it is difficult to believe that Austria would have had the willpower to challenge the Hungarians. In Hungary, on the other hand, it is time to give Haynau his due. For if it had not been for him, the Russians, thanks to the incompetence of Windischgraetz and Jellačić, would really have had to finish off the war. All of these men, on the other hand, had had some part to play and all had been needed in the end to crush the revolutions. It cannot be stressed sufficiently, however, that there had been little agreement as to how to do this. Given that there was little agreement either as to what should happen next, there was no way of predicting the outcome of these events. Everything in 1848–9 was extremely confusing and contradictory so that immanent within the whole chaotic story was a whole variety of possible *dénouements*. As things turned out, Prince Schwarzenberg emerged as the strong man of the reaction, but he in turn lacked any clear-cut vision of the future. At the heart of the counter-revolution, therefore, lay not strength and direction but dissension and confusion, more of a vacuum than a *camarilla*. This vacuum, in the end, was to be filled by absolutism.

NOTES AND REFERENCES

1. Gunther E. Rothenberg (1976) *The Army of Francis Joseph*. West Lafayette, p. 35.
2. *Ibid.*, p. 34.
3. György Szabad (1984) Hungary's recognition of Croatia's self-determination in 1848 and its immediate antecedents, in Béla Király (ed.) *East Central European Society and War in the Era of Revolutions, 1775–1856, War and Society in East Central Europe*, Vol. 4. Brooklyn College Studies on Society and Change, No. 13, New York, pp. 599–609, p. 593.
4. *Ibid.*, p. 594.
5. *Ibid.*, p. 595.
6. *Ibid.*, p. 600.
7. *Ibid.*, p. 603.
8. Zoltán I. Tóth (1954) The nationality problem in Hungary in 1848–69, in *Acta Historica*, pp. 235–7, p. 257.
9. *Ibid.*, p. 243.
10. *Ibid.*
11. *Ibid.*, p. 256.
12. *Ibid.*, p. 244.
13. István Deák (1979) *The Lawful Revolution: Louis Kossuth and the Hungarians, 1848–49*. New York, p. 127; but cf. Toth, *op. cit.*, p. 268.
14. István Bartha (1975) Towards bourgeois transformation, revolution and war of independence (1790–1849), in E. Pamlényi (ed.) *A History of Hungary*. London and Wellingborough, pp. 207–84, p. 261.
15. Deák, *op. cit.*, pp. 117–18.
16. *Ibid.*, p. 280.
17. László Pusztaszéri (1984) General Görgey's military and political role: civil–military relations during the Hungarian Revolution, in Kiraly (ed.) *op. cit.*, pp. 473–518, pp. 479–80.
18. Deák, *op. cit.*, p. 305.
19. *Ibid.*
20. *Ibid.*
21. *Ibid.*, p. 329.
22. *Ibid.*, p. 268.
23. *Ibid.*, pp. 183–4.
24. *Ibid.*, p. 62.

25. Aladár Urbán (1984) One army and two ministers of war: the armed forces of the Habsburg Empire between Emperor and King, in Király (ed.) *op. cit.*, pp. 419–38, p. 431.
26. Quoted in K. Bourne (1970) *The Foreign Policy of Victorian England*. Oxford, p. 296.
27. Deák, *op. cit.*, but see pp. 187–201, and Joseph M. Borus (1984) The military industry in the War of Independence, in Király (ed.) *op. cit.*, pp. 519–37.
28. Alan Sked (1979) *The Survival of the Habsburg Empire: Radetzky, the Imperial Army and the Class War, 1848*. London and New York, p. 125.
29. *Ibid.*
30. *Ibid.*, p. 128.
31. *Ibid.*, p. 127.
32. *Ibid.*, p. 129.
33. *Ibid.*, p. 55.
34. *Ibid.*, p. 51.
35. *Ibid.*, p. 55.
36. *Ibid.*, p. 56.
37. *Ibid.*, p. 72.
38. *Ibid.*, p. 73.
39. *Ibid.*, pp. 71–2.
40. *Ibid.*, p. 73.
41. *Ibid.*, pp. 73–4.
42. *Ibid.*, p. 133.
43. *Ibid.*, p. 135.
44. *Ibid.*, pp. 161–2.
45. *Ibid.*, p. 137.
46. *Ibid.*, p. 140.
47. *Ibid.*, p. 141.
48. *Ibid.*, p. 142.
49. Franco della Peruta (1953) I contadini nella rivoluzione lombarda del 1848, *Movimento Operaio*, pp. 562–5.
50. Sked, *op. cit.*, p. 145.
51. *Ibid.*, p. 146.
52. *Ibid.*, p. 144.
53. *Ibid.*, p. 140.
54. *Ibid.*
55. Paul Müller (1934) *Feldmarschall Fürst Windischgraetz, Revolution und Gegenrevolution in Osterreich*. Vienna and Leipzig, p. 95.
56. Lawrence D. Orton (1978) The Prague Slav Congress of 1848, *East European Monographs*, No. XLXI. New York, p. 102.
57. Muller, *op. cit.*, p. 109.
58. Friedrich Prinz Prag und Wien, 1848, *Veröffentlichungen des Collegium Carolinium*, Vol. 21, p. 92.
59. Sked, *op. cit.*, pp. 145–6.
60. *Ibid.*
61. Friedrich Walter Die Osterreichische Zentralverwaltung, Pt. III, Von den Marzrevolution 1848 Bis Zur Dezembervesfassung 1867, Vol. I, Die Geschichte der Ministerien Kolowrat, Ficquelmont, Pillersdorf, Wessenberg-Doblhoff und Schwarzenberg, *Veröffentlichungen der*

Kommission fur Neuere Geschichte Osterreichs, Vol. 49, p. 192 (for both quotes).
62. Gunther E. Rothenberg (1965) Jellačić, the Croatian Military Border and the intervention against Hungary in 1848, *Austrian History Yearbook,* pp. 42–73, p. 58.
63. M. Hartley (1912) *The Man Who Saved Austria, Baron Jellačić.* London, p. 230.
64. *Ibid.*, p. 233.
65. Michaela Geisler (1968) *Joseph Freiherr von Jellačić de Buzim, Banus von Kroatien,* unpublished dissertation. Vienna, p. 38.
66. Rothenberg, *Jellačić, the Croatian Border etc.*, p. 59.
67. *Ibid.*
68. Geisler, *op. cit.*, p. 57. In fact, the Ministry in Vienna was split over what to do about Jellačić. According to Deák, *op. cit.*, Chapter 4, note 4 and pp. 363–4, the Archduke Francis Charles, the acting head of the imperial family, was definitely against supporting him, a policy favoured only by Latour and Kulmer, the Croat representative at court. However, even Latour did not wish to lend official support to Jellačić.
69. Jellačić to Latour, Zagreb, 5 August 1848, *Vienna, Kriegsarchiv,* MK(1848)4014.
70. Jellačić to Latour, Zagreb, 8 August 1848, *Vienna, Kriegsarchiv,* MK(1848)4123.
71. Jellačić to Latour, Zagreb, 8 July 1848, *Vienna, Kriegsarchiv,* MK(1848)3421 and 3547.
72. Latour to Esterházy, Vienna, 12 July 1848, *Vienna, Kriegsarchiv,* MK(1848)3421 and 3547.
73. Latour to Jellačić, Vienna, 14 August 1848, *Vienna, Kriegsarchiv,* MK(1848)4123.
74. Latour to Esterházy, Vienna, 27 August 1848, *Vienna, Kriegsarchiv,* MK(1848)4526 and 4527.
75. Hartley, *op. cit.*, p. 251.
76. Walter, *op. cit.*, pp. 190–1.
77. *Ibid.*
78. Sked, *op. cit.*, p. 158.
79. *Ibid.*, p. 160.
80. *Ibid.*, p. 159.
81. *Ibid.*, p. 160.
82. *Ibid.*, p. 161.
83. *Ibid.*
84. *Ibid.*, p. 198.
85. *Ibid.*, p. 190.
86. *Ibid.*, p. 193.
87. *Ibid.*, pp. 202–3.
88. E. Heller, (1933) *Fürst Felix zu Schwarzenberg, Mitteleuropa's Vorkämpfer.* Vienna, pp. 265–6.
89. Hartley, *op. cit.*
90. Quoted in *ibid.*, p. 251.

CHAPTER FOUR

From the Counter-Revolution to the Compromise

The Habsburg Empire came closer to dissolution in 1848–9 than at any other period before 1918. Indeed, even the First World War for most of its duration was to pose much less of a challenge to the Monarchy than the revolutions of 1848. This is why so much attention has had to be paid to them. They became in the end a dynastic struggle rather than a social or even a national one, although both social and particularly national issues were indubitably involved. Still, the fundamental question at stake – and one which is too often obscured in the textbooks – was which dynasty should rule in Hungary, Lombardy-Venetia and Germany? It was to ensure that there was only one answer to that question that the Habsburgs resorted to arms in all three contests. That is why the revolutions were defeated, not on the barricades – or not only on the barricades – but on the field of battle.

SCHWARZENBERG

The last two stages of their defeat ensured the return to the *status quo ante* both internally and externally. Since both these stages involved the statescraft of Prince Schwarzenberg, it is best to begin this chapter by examining his policies and personality. For few Austrian statesmen have proved to be more controversial; indeed, contemporaries also found it difficult to reach agreement over him. On the other hand, it cannot be denied that he made an impression. Franz Joseph called him 'the greatest minister I ever had at my side';[1] Metternich on one occasion called him 'a pupil of my diplomatic school . . . a man of firm character, genuine courage and clear vision', although he later came to regard him as a 'misguided pupil' and condemned his brusque 'oscillations' between 'too little' and 'too much'. Nicholas I of Russia described him as a 'Palmerston in a white uniform', while Bismarck bridled at his haughty, swaggering attitude towards his Prussian fatherland. Today, the main quarrel among historians is less whether he was successful or unsuccessful – the consensus is overwhelmingly that he was a great success – but whether he was a *Metternichian* or a *Realpolitiker*. This is a question to which we shall return presently. For the moment, however, it is necessary to sketch in just a little bit of background, in order to acquire some impression of the man.

Born in 1800, the nephew of that Prince Schwarzenberg who had been allied commander of the successful coalition against Napoleon, Prince Felix was assured a career in the Austrian military or diplomatic service. He was in fact, to enjoy a highly successful career in both, entering first the army in 1818 and then, in 1824, the diplomatic service. His career in the latter, however, did not necessitate his leaving the army; far from it, he continued to be promoted up the military ladder all the time he was a diplomat. And whatever his failings or misfortunes in the world of diplomacy, his charm, connections and good looks somehow conspired to rescue and promote him in this sphere too. In fact, it is extremely puzzling how Schwarzenberg ever managed to retain his position as a diplomat, for when he was sent to St Petersburg in 1824 the friendship he made there with Prince Trubetskoy led him to become *persona non grata* with Nicholas I. Trubetskoy, it turned out, was a leader of the Decembrist revolt of 1825 and fled to the Austrian embassy for sanctuary when the revolt collapsed. The new Tsar believed therefore that Schwarzenberg must have known of the conspiracy in advance. It was not until 1844 that they were ultimately reconciled. It was in England, however, where he arrived in 1828, that Schwarzenberg was to display his greatest diplomatic incompetence. For there he fell in love and conducted an open affair with Jane Digby, Lady Ellenborough, daughter of the First Lord of the Admiralty and wife of the Lord Privy Seal. The Austrian ambassador, as a result – the same Prince Esterházy who was to become Hungarian Foreign Minister in 1848 – had to arrange for his recall to Vienna. From there, astonishingly enough, he was sent to Paris, where Lady Ellenborough followed him, now pregnant with his child. By 1832, therefore, he was in Berlin, a figure more representative of the romantic age than of the diplomatic world, one might conclude.

Yet nothing, it seemed, could impede his progress, and his career continued with posts in Italy, until in 1848 he found himself overtaken by the revolutions as Austrian ambassador to Naples. From there, via Trieste and Vienna, he made his way to Radetzky's army and the resumption of his military career. And while serving in Italy he almost certainly picked up the Field Marshal's views (they were common throughout the whole officer corps) regarding the new constitution and the treacherous role of the Italian nobility.

Schwarzenberg's own views regarding the constitution and the nobility, however, were not entirely unformed beforehand. For example, before he left Vienna to join Nugent's army, he wrote an article in the *Wiener Zeitung* of 9 April replying to an attack on the Austrian nobility by Ignaz F. Castelli three days earlier in the same newspaper. Castelli had accused the Austrian nobles of making themselves scarce and of failing to support the revolution. Schwarzenberg, writing under the pseudonym of 'a nobleman', claimed that this was untrue. The nobility were only temporarily absent from the theatre, he claimed, because they were mourning some recent deaths; their lack of prominence in the newspapers meant nothing either. According to Schwarzenberg, they were both patriotic and had worked for the recent concessions which they had supported. However, the main task for everybody now was to work for a great, united and powerful Austria. Schwarzenberg's continued faith in the new institutions was proved when, on leave from the army in July 1848, he stood as a candidate for the Reichstag in his home village in Bohemia. There one of his estate workers objected to his candidature on the grounds that it would involve compromising with the masses. Schwarzenberg answered his objection with the reply: 'in a constitutional state we must now get used to compromising with the masses.'[2] Moreover, if like Radetzky he was to be disgusted with the tragic events of October 1848, he was not to draw from them the conclusion that responsible government in Austria should come to an end. On the contrary, it was thanks to him that the Reichstag, instead of being wound up as Windischgraetz desired, was in fact prorogued to Kremsier. For it was Schwarzenberg who, under pressure from Stadion and the conservative Czech deputies in the Reichstag, persuaded the Emperor to issue a manifesto on 19 October clarifying one which had been issued three days earlier. This had given Windischgraetz a free hand to deal with Vienna. The new manifesto, however, while in no way detracting from Windischgraetz's authority, made clear that the powers of the Reichstag remained intact and that it should continue its task of drawing up a new constitution, a task which received further encouragement from the prime minister when he introduced his ministers to the Reichstag on 27 November. His team was a fairly liberal one. Stadion was Minister of the Interior; Bach, Minister of Justice; Krauss, Minister of Finance; and Bruck, Minister of Commerce. Moreover, Schwarzenberg himself declared: 'The Ministry does not want to lag behind in the attempt to realise liberal and popular institutions; it rather regards it as a duty to place itself at the head of this movement. We want constitutional monarchy sincerely and unreservedly.'[3] Among his other promises were equality for all citizens before the law, equality of rights for all peoples, publicity in all branches of the administration, and the principle of the free commune in the free state. His aims towards Italy and Hungary were subsumed in his grand design: 'the unification of the Lands and races of the Monarchy in one great body politic.' It was only his German policy which remained opaque, although here too the emphasis was on change. He said: '. . . the continued existence of Austria as a political unit is a German as well as a European necessity. Permeated by this conviction, we look to the natural development of the still incomplete process of transformation. Not until rejuvenated Austria and rejuvenated Germany have achieved new and definite forms will it be possible to regulate their mutual relations on state level. Until then, Austria will continue loyally to carry out her duties as a member of the Bund.'[4]

Austria's own rejuvenation was confirmed a few days later with the news that there had been a change of monarch. Ferdinand's abdication had been discussed within the imperial family since November 1847. He himself had offered to stand down during the summer of 1848, but Windischgraetz had opposed this, arguing that the principle of hereditary monarchy ('God's grace') could not be interfered with. However, with the flight to Olmütz after the October revolution, the Empress had raised the matter once again and this time had secured Schwarzenberg's and later Windischgraetz's approval. The latter, despite some misgivings, could see the advantages of having a monarch who was not personally bound to the concessions made by his predecessor (a rather inconsistent interpretation of the hereditary principle, to say the least). Windischgraetz assumed, therefore, that when Franz Joseph ascended the throne, the ceremony would include a denunciation of the revolution and all its works. Instead, Ferdinand merely stroked the new Emperor's hair, saying: 'God bless you, be brave, God will protect you, I don't mind.'[5] Then, on the following day, Schwarzenberg read out to the Reichstag a proclamation in the new monarch's name, which went even further than his own previous declaration in extolling the virtues of free institutions. Austria, as a result, seemed well on its way towards constitutionalism. It came as a profound shock, therefore, when on 6 March, Stadion informed the Kremsier deputies that the Reichstag had been dissolved and that the Emperor had already approved a new constitution. This (dated 4 March) had been granted by God's grace and was to be implemented by decree. Yet since it never came into effect either, we must examine the question whether Schwarzenberg had ever intended to rule with a parliament in the first place. Had he ever been sincere in what he had said or was he merely a dishonest and unscrupulous opportunist?

SCHWARZENBERG AND DOMESTIC POLICY

The evidence suggests that Schwarzenberg was by no means a convinced absolutist and might well have been prepared to work with an elected parliament. On the other hand, apart from wishing a strong and united Austria, he does not seem to have had any definite political programme in mind and was probably out of his depth in many ways as prime minister. It is this curious mixture of determined patriotism and political inexperience which he represented that might well explain his statements regarding free institutions, the drafting of the 4 March constitution, and his subsequent political outmanoeuvring by Kübeck and Franz Joseph. It would also explain his reliance on ministers such as Bach and Krauss, who came from totally different social worlds from his own. Yet, that is only part of the story. The other part is that he was caught between the very extreme claims of the Reichstag, on the one hand, and, on the other, the unmistakably absolutist pretensions of the new monarch, who wanted to rule as his grandfather Francis had. Schwarzenberg, for his part, simply lacked the political ability – and perhaps the personal commitment – to manoeuvre between these forces. In any case, he was never sure what he should manoeuvre for.

When he arrived in office, according to Friedrich Walter, the new prime minister was 'extremely insufficiently informed of the internal condition of the Monarchy and consequently was scarcely capable of taking decisions in this field'.[6] Hence his reliance on Bach – 'the most active and powerful of colleagues'[7] – whose 'decisive parliamentary talent'[8] and skilled advocacy he found indispensable. Kübeck, however, who often chided the Prince on his 'lack of qualifications and ignorance', maintained that Bach was only consulted on technical details and that the Prince oversaw matters of principle himself. In Walter's words: 'However much the Prince admired the capabilities and diligence of his Interior Minister, it was always he himself who determined the general lines of the ministry's policy and through the fascination exerted by his strong personality caused Bach to follow his lead.'[9]

Were Schwarzenberg's principles constitutional ones? Certainly, he had no use for anarchy or revolt and could condemn these aspects of 1848 out of hand. Yet, as has been seen, he both stood for parliament and lent his name and voice to declarations in support of parliamentarianism. It has to be supposed, therefore, that he was not personally averse to the parliamentary system as a means of government. His correspondence with Windischgraetz during the winter of 1848 can certainly be used to support this proposition. Windischgraetz had, after all, been responsible for his appointment as prime minister, and was reckoned by many at this time to be the saviour of the Monarchy. He therefore demanded 'to be continuously informed' on 'the most important internal questions' and on 'all steps and negotiations in foreign policy'.[10] Since he insisted, moreover, that 'Ministers should desist from any open inclination towards the party of movement, not support ideas of reform too far and retain such old ways as were compatible with new circumstances',[11] he simultaneously challenged Schwarzenberg to defend his own principles if these indeed were constitutional ones. But defend both his ministers and the Reichstag is precisely what Schwarzenberg did, despite the fact that if he had chosen to agree with his brother-in-law, he could have depended on the support of both the army and the court. Yet, on the contrary, on 5 January 1849, he could write to Windischgraetz: 'Our Reichstag at Kremsier has become very docile. Every victory, every progress in Hungary, broadens its political horizons and brings its capacity for law-making to greater maturity.'[12] And two days later, defending his ministerial colleagues, he wrote describing 'the standpoint of the ministry' as one of 'maintaining regulated progress'.[13] Like Windischgraetz, he claimed to be fighting the revolution, but with other weapons.

Schwarzenberg only first broke with the Reichstag when conflict broke out there over the formulation of fundamental rights, in which conflict a very respectable number of deputies anchored themselves to the idea of popular sovereignty. Thus by 12 January 1849, he was writing to his brother-in-law: 'The Reichstag has, in the last few days, shown itself to be so naturally malevolent that the hope is progressively disappearing of reaching the planned objective, the working out by it and with it of the constitution.'[14] And on 21 January he was already reporting that the government's own draft constitution was almost ready. 'Then,' he added sarcastically, 'the whole unnecessary association will be asked to go on its way.'[15] When Windischgraetz advised him, however, to finish the job by getting rid of the 'ideologues' in his cabinet, Schwarzenberg was still prepared to defend his colleagues. 'Suitable ministers,' he replied, 'are altogether rare, especially in times when, apart from ordinary knowledge and capacity, endurance and a certain moral courage are absolutely necessary'.[16] If his present ministry broke up, he said, he would have no other men to choose from.

The debate which disillusioned Schwarzenberg with Kremsier had concerned a clause in the draft constitution which ran: 'All sovereignty proceeds from the people, and is exercised in the manner prescribed in the constitution.'[17] Stadion, in fact, had warned the deputies that the clause would be unacceptable, but his 'interference' had been unwelcome (Windischgraetz had said 'If they will not learn of the Grace of God they shall learn of the grace of cannon').[18] The offending clause was subsequently dropped but the damage had still been done. The final draft of the constitution was in any case quite radical. The monarch was left more or less in charge of foreign policy, but he was limited in domestic affairs. His ministers were to be responsible to parliament and he had only a suspensive veto over legislation. He could prorogue parliament but only for a month, and if he dissolved it, a successor had to be elected within three months. Many other aspects of the Reichstag's work were also provocative: all titles of nobility were abolished; the Roman Catholic religion was no longer to be the 'ruling' one; civil marriage was introduced; all citizens were to be equal before the law; and a long list of civil rights – freedom of speech, association, etc. – was introduced. Paragraph 21 on the rights of nationalities ran: 'All peoples of the Empire are equal in rights. Each people has an inviolable right to preserve its nationality in general and its language in particular. The equality of rights in the school, administration and public life of every language in local usage is guaranteed by the state.'[19] With regard to local autonomy, the draft refused to make provision for either Hungary (which was assumed to have its own constitution) or for Lombardy-Venetia. Otherwise, all the traditional lands – with a few geographical modifications – were given equal rights, with special courts to be created to deal with disputes between nationalities within any particular land. Moreover, all lands were to be subdivided into circles (counties), as far as possible on an ethnic basis. Parliament was to be composed of two houses, the Upper comprising three representatives from each land and one from each circle, the Lower composed of directly elected deputies, elected on a fairly low property qualification. This then was the famous Kremsier constitution.

Many of its provisions were clearly too radical for the government to accept. In particular, the position of the monarch was held to have been demeaned, despite the fact that the popular sovereignty clause had finally been dropped. Again, the refusal to include Hungary and Lombardy-Venetia within its scope meant that the constitution did not foresee a united Monarchy in the way Franz Joseph did. It was not allowed, therefore, to become reality.

A controversy has none the less developed regarding the 'Kremsier constitution'. Joseph Redlich, for example, compared it to the French constitution of 1791 and to the American constitution, declaring that it was the best that Austria was ever offered.[20] Others too have written of Austria's 'missed opportunity'.[21] C. A. Macartney, on the other hand, has registered his dissent, claiming that agreement was reached only because of the threat of dissolution. He writes: 'A legend has grown up about the proceedings of the Reichstag in this field, that once escaped from the nefarious influences of the Court, the aristocracy, and other reactionary forces, the peoples of the Monarchy found each other in mutual affection and sweet reasonableness, and would have produced a solution on the basis of which Austria would have lived peaceably, had the reaction not prevented it. Nothing could be further from the truth. The work eventually accomplished by the Reichstag was, indeed, very valuable. But the will to produce it had been generated, not by the absence of the non-democratic forces, but by their too close presence in the background, for everyone in Kremsier was acutely aware that while they worked, Windischgraetz was only awaiting his chance to sweep aside their work.'[22] Macartney's point, however, does not explain why the eventual draft was still so radical. Nor does it dispose of the feeling that, had it been tried, the constitution might well indeed have offered the Monarchy a basis for peaceful progress.

On the other hand, to return to our original discussion, the alternative to Kremsier did not turn out to be Windischgraetz and absolutism, but Schwarzenberg and Stadion who, as has been seen, was a firm champion of parliamentary institutions. And as Schwarzenberg's Minister of the Interior, it was he who had been given the task of drafting an alternative constitution to Kremsier's. Perhaps unsurprisingly, therefore, his constitution – the decreed constitution of 4 March 1849 – took several ideas from the Kremsier draft, while omitting the more radical ones. According to Stadion's version, the monarch was left with virtually unlimited powers in foreign affairs, while in domestic ones he exercised executive authority through 'responsible ministers'. Legislative authority was to be shared jointly with the Reichstag, which consisted of an Upper House composed of representatives elected by the local diets, and a Lower House, elected by direct suffrage. Bills required the assent of both Houses and the monarch to become law. In an emergency, or if the Reichstag was not in session, the monarch could rule by Orders in Council, but such orders had afterwards to be submitted to the Reichstag for approval. An Imperial Council or *Reichsrat* was to advise the Emperor, which body was to be nominated by the monarch himself. Below the Reichstag came the diets (*Landtage*), counties, districts, and communes, all directed by freely elected councils and all autonomous within their own spheres. All citizens were equal before the law, and the Kremsier principle of equality of language and nationality was repeated, although it was now no longer specifically 'guaranteed'. Inhabitants of the Austrian lands were promised freedom of conscience and the private practice of their religion, while the enjoyment of civil and political rights was made irrespective of faith. There was a long list of other civic freedoms. Yet, in Macartney's words: '. . . the real significance of the constitution, besides its character as an *octroi*, lay in its pan-monarchic scope. The Monarch was to be crowned only once: as Emperor of Austria. There was to be only one citizenship, one legal system, and one central parliament. The Monarchy was also to constitute a single Customs Union; all internal tariffs were to be abolished.'[23] Lombardy-Venetia, whose exact status was to be dealt with later, constituted the only exception – and then only nominally – to this new-found unity. As far as Hungary was concerned, its old constitution was to remain in force, save that those parts of it which conflicted with the new one were to be abolished, and equality of rights assured to every nationality and every local language in all fields of public and private life. The details were to be incorporated within a separate statute. Meanwhile, the Military Frontier was reinstated and three new 'Crownlands' – Transylvania (with the Partium), Croatia-Slavonia, and the Voivodina – were created out of the lands of St Stephen's crown. All in all, therefore, the document was by no means a reactionary one. True, it disdained popular sovereignty and left the monarch with a veto over legislation; yet it did provide for a responsible ministry, a parliamentary system and for civil rights. It cannot be used to prove that Schwarzenberg had lied to the people or that he did not believe in responsible government. Moreover, since his Justice Minister, Schmerling, enacted reforms which provided for trial by jury in major civil and criminal cases, and which for the first time provided for the public and interlocutive examination of witnesses, there is other evidence to suggest that a new constitutional era was foreseen. Yet the Stadion constitution, just like the Kremsier one, was never put into operation.

Exactly why this should have been the case is not clear. Essentially the answer is that the young Emperor, Franz Joseph, preferred to rule by himself. Whether he himself, on the other hand, took the initiative in restoring personal rule, or whether he was put up to this by somebody else, is a matter for speculation. In any case, it is well established that the man who masterminded the restoration of monarchical absolutism was Kübeck, head of the Treasury under the Metternich system, who found only limited resistance on the part of Schwarzenberg. The latter, in fact, in Friedrich Walter's words, displayed a curious 'passivity' when faced with Kübeck's manoeuvring. 'In Schwarzenberg's behaviour', he writes, 'one cannot fail to recognise a certain, hesitating uncertainty about his future conduct', whereas Kübeck 'was much aided by the superiority he gained from the fact that he was fighting for a clear concept, that he knew precisely what he wanted'.[24] Schmerling, Krauss and Bruck, on the other hand, were all to resign before the transition to absolutism was completed.

There were, of course, good reasons why the Stadion constitution could not be implemented immediately. The Hungarians, for a start, did not surrender until August 1849 (General Klapka, holding out in the fortress of Komárom until November); Venice did not capitulate until August either; much of the Monarchy therefore still required to be pacified and until the government was absolutely sure that it was in complete control there could be no case for holding elections for a Reichstag. The German Question had also to be settled and that too involved a possible change in Austria's constitutional position. Besides, even Vienna was still under a state of siege. In the aftermath of revolution, therefore, there were too many plausible excuses for delaying the implementation of the constitution. Still, the government proceeded to enact legislation on the principle that it would one day have to justify it to the Reichstag. This allowed Schwarzenberg and his team to retain the initiative; to avoid criticism; and to deprive the monarch of a dominating role in government. (Schwarzenberg said that he did not intend to become a 'hack' for the throne.) It also allowed Kübeck to ridicule the whole procedure. He simply could not be contradicted when he said that the Ministry was protecting itself with 'the shield of a theoretical responsibility, whose non-existence in reality bestows upon it complete irresponsibility'.[25] In practice, the country was being run by the army, the bureaucracy and the new gendarmerie (or police). Radetzky in 1849 was made Governor-General of Lombardy-Venetia; the Archduke Albert (in 1851) was made Governor-General of Hungary; Prince Carlos Schwarzenberg was made Governor-General of Transylvania; Franz Joseph himself took the title of Grand Voivod, but left the running of the Voivodina to yet another Austrian general; while even Croatia was brought into line in January 1853, although Jellačić was left in nominal charge as Governor. He, in fact, soon lost his faculties, and the kingdom was run by the army. In the famous words of one Croat to a Hungarian friend: 'we received as a reward what you were given as a punishment.' The rest of the Monarchy was run by bureaucrats working hand in hand with the police. The administration was totally centralized; German was the language of administration; and all education above the primary level was also given in German. In Hungary and Croatia, therefore, administrative posts had to be filled with German-speaking Czechs or Slovenes. Since in Hungary these people were fitted out with uniforms in the Magyar style, they came to be known as the 'Bach hussars'.

Kübeck's assault on the ministerial system began on 19 October 1850 when, on his return from Frankfurt, where he had been representing Austria at the Federal Diet, he was summoned to meet the Emperor. The latter informed him that he had decided to establish the *Reichsrat* provided for in the constitution and that he wished Kübeck to define its competence. He was to compose its statutes and to make proposals with regard to membership. Exactly why he had been chosen for this task is unclear. Perhaps it was because he was known to harbour a grudge against the Ministry: Krauss, not he, had been chosen as Minister of Finance. Perhaps it was because he enjoyed the support of important reactionaries like Metternich who wanted a return to the pre-March system of government. On the other hand, it may just be the case that, on account of his reputation as a financial wizard, it was hoped that his appointment to a *Reichsrat* would make the Empire more internationally credit-worthy. Moreover, it had been he, after all, who had originally suggested such a body when the constitution had been drafted in the first place. In any case, when he returned on 1 November with his first proposals for the Emperor, he was informed that he himself was to become president of the new body. He was also told a little later (19 November) that the *Reichsrat* was meant to 'supersede, and in a certain sense replace, the constitution'.[26] By now, therefore it must have been quite clear what the Emperor was intending. In Macartney's words: 'It is not our task to reconcile Francis Joseph's actions at this juncture with the punctilious sense of honour which his biographers ascribe to him, nor do we know just whose voice persuaded him that if his tongue had sworn, his mind had remained oathless. But it is quite certain that by 1850 at the latest he had convinced himself that whatever words Schwarzenberg had put into his mouth on his accession, it was both his right and duty to ignore them, and to make himself absolute ruler of his dominions.'[27] Kübeck proved more than willing to assist in this operation.

In his memoranda to the Emperor, Kübeck attacked the very concept of ministerial responsibility. It was rooted in popular sovereignty, he argued, and therefore incompatible with monarchy. Responsibility in a monarchy should be the prerogative of the monarch only; ministerial responsibility should therefore be abolished. There was no need either for a Ministerial Council. Instead, individual ministers should make proposals to the *Reichsrat* and this alone, composed of elder statesmen, should be given the task of advising the monarch. Kübeck, in fact, was proposing a return to the pre-March system, with the ministers in the position of *Hofstellen* chiefs and the *Reichsrat* the equivalent of the Staatsrat. The *Reichsrat* did eventually come into being in April 1851, although the Emperor did not push its powers too far, lest he provoke the resignation of Schwarzenberg. The latter, however, whom Kübeck had consulted, was prepared to live with the new body – the constitution after all allowed for it – but hoped to limit its authority and to secure precedence over it for the Ministry. By August 1851, on the other hand, this was no longer possible. Imperial decrees abolished ministerial responsibility to the Reichstag, and the *Reichsrat* was given the task of investigating whether the constitution was still workable. Yet neither Schwarzenberg nor Bach resigned; only

Krauss chose to do so, following the earlier examples of Schmerling and Bruck. Eventually, the Emperor put an end to all uncertainty when, on 29 December, he chaired a joint session of the Ministry and the *Reichsrat*, in which proposals to alter the constitution were read out and his intentions announced. Two days later the constitution was abolished and neo-absolutism received its basis in law with the so-called 'Sylvester Patent' of 31 December 1851.

The Patent actually comprised three documents: the first informed the Ministry that the constitution had been abolished, although both the abolition of peasant dues (see below) and the principle of equality before the law remained in force; the second cancelled the list of rights of 1849, although all churches were guaranteed their freedom of worship and the management of their property; the third outlined the new administrative organization of the Monarchy. This involved the abolition of the elected councils at land, circle and district levels; the abolition of Schmerling's legal reforms; the introduction of Austrian civil and criminal law into the Hungarian lands; and the disappearance of the principle of equality with regard to language and nationality. Finally, a commission headed by Kübeck was to go through the laws of the Monarchy, cancelling anything which smacked of the principle of popular representation or had its origins in the revolutions of 1848. In short, Franz Joseph had returned to the Metternich System, save that he had tightened it up enormously, achieved the centralization which Metternich had always desired and had even created ministers. It was little wonder therefore that Metternich himself, who was soon to return to Vienna, accorded it his approval. If the cosmetic diets which he had always favoured had disappeared, this was of little concern after 1848, given the trouble they had caused. Schwarzenberg himself probably had mixed feelings: if, on the one hand, he had been prepared to work within a parliamentary context, on the other he had got used to existing without the nuisance of having to justify himself to the Reichstag. Besides, with the return to personal rule, the battle with Kübeck was ended on the institutional level. Franz Joseph, as it turned out, was no more willing to be dominated by a *Reichsrat* than by a Ministry. In Macartney's words: 'While Kübeck lived, he was often called in to give advice, especially on financial questions, but the *Reichsrat* as such never had the slightest effect on policy.'[28] How the Prime Minister would have coped with the changes in the longer term, however, is unknown for Schwarzenberg died suddenly on 5 April 1852, only a few months after they had been introduced.

SCHWARZENBERG'S GERMAN POLICY

We must now examine Schwarzenberg's German policy before dealing with the other controversies of the neo-absolutist period. Here, too, his record is a controversial one, and once again the feeling arises that perhaps he lacked a definite objective and that perhaps, too, he was not as successful as some historians have claimed. At issue is the outcome of the Dresden Conference of 1850–1, but before one can understand the argument, the background to events must first be briefly sketched in.

The 1848 revolutions in Germany, as is well known, produced the Frankfurt Parliament, whose task it was to draw up a constitution for a united Germany. By October 1848, it was clear that this would favour a *kleindeutsch* arrangement; in other words, Austria would be told that to remain in Germany, she would either have to agree to a personal union with her non-German lands or stay out of the new Germany altogether. Since she was never going to accept such a plan, the crown of the new Germany was offered in the spring of 1849 to Frederick William IV of Prussia, already Germany's leading state in economic and military terms. He in fact turned down the offer (3 April 1849) disdaining, as he put it, to accept a crown from the gutter. On the other hand, he was to have fewer scruples about accepting one from his peers, the German princes. His Prime Minister General von Radowitz contrived to arrange exactly this, so that between January and May 1850 the Erfurt Union (subsequently the German Union) came into being, under which the King of Prussia became *Reichsvorstand* or Director of the German Empire and Germany acquired a bicameral Reichstag. Clearly this was a situation which Austria could not accept. Nor was it one which appealed to all the other German monarchs, since the Union was boycotted by the kingdoms of Bavaria, Saxony, Hanover and Württemberg, not to mention several of the minor states.

In May 1850, Schwarzenberg made clear his intention to ignore the Union, by reasserting Austria's position as President of the German Confederation and reconvening the Bund. This does not mean that he intended simply to arrange German affairs once again along the same lines as Metternich: his proposals to the Dresden Conference would prove that. In any case, he had already spoken to the Kremsier Reichstag of a rejuvenated Germany and had from the very beginning of his premiership proposed a number of schemes which would have required a reorganization of the Bund. One of these had involved the division of Germany into six circles; another the creation of a new directorate below the level of the presidency; while yet another had envisaged a chamber in which Austria would have held thirty-eight votes as against thirty-two for the rest of Germany. The Austrian government at one point, indeed, had declared the German Confederation to be at an end. Until well into 1849, however, Schwarzenberg's attention had been taken up primarily with other matters: Italy and especially Hungary. The result was that in September 1849 he had signed the so-called German Interim with Prussia, according to which both states would jointly supervise German affairs until a more permanent arrangement could be reached. This Interim ran out on 1 May 1850.

Schwarzenberg used the device of summoning the Bund as a means of demonstrating that Austria, having restored her position in Italy and Hungary, was now ready to do the same in Germany. The opportunity to do so came as a result of disputes in Schleswig-Holstein and Hesse-Kassel. In the former, the King of Denmark appealed to the Bund for a federal execution on his behalf against his German nationalist opponents; in the latter, the sovereign appealed for one against his rebellious, constitutionalist subjects. In both cases the opponents of these princes appealed for support to Prussia and the German Union. The question arose, therefore, which body would impose itself as the arbiter of Germany's affairs. The situation was complicated, of course, by the fact that in the case of Schleswig-Holstein more than just German interests were involved. The balance of power in the Baltic might be disturbed if the King of Denmark lost control of the Elbe Duchies, so that Russia – not to mention Great Britain – was averse to any change in the *status quo*. Tsar Nicholas I, therefore, was consulted by both sides and his moral support was given to Austria. However – like Palmerston – he did not understand all the details of the constitutional dispute between Austria and Prussia and let it be known that he would only actively intervene if a war broke out between the two German states over Schleswig-Holstein. In the case of Hesse-Kassel, he would remain neutral, albeit benevolently so in Austria's favour. As it happened, the Bund chose to assert its authority over Hesse-Kassel, which was crossed by Prussian military roads. The occupation of the Electorate therefore led to a skirmish between Austrian and Prussian troops, during which a Prussian horse and five Austrian riflemen were wounded. The horse lived on in legend as the White Horse of Bronzell, the scene of these events, but despite the small number of casualties, there was now a serious danger of war in Germany.

This danger was removed by the collapse of Prussia. Frederick

William had always been reluctant to challenge the claims of Austria – as a German romantic, he had too ready a knowledge of Habsburg history – and so he proclaimed the end of the German Union. Radowitz was sent to London as ambassador and his rival, the conservative Otto von Manteuffel, sent to negotiate with Schwarzenberg at Olmütz. However, the latter insisted that before any negotiations could begin, Prussia should disarm fully and Austria only partially. This was widely seen as a humiliation for the Prussians, although the final agreements (or *Punctation* as they are collectively known in German) were less humiliating in themselves than the fact that Prussia had climbed down. These agreements were that the questions of Hesse-Kassel and Schleswig-Holstein should be finally resolved by the German states as a whole and that the future of the Confederation should be decided at 'free conferences' in Dresden, in which all the German states should be allowed to participate. These conferences began on 23 December 1850 and closed on 15 May 1851.

The Dresden Conference saw Schwarzenberg make three main proposals: first, that Austria as a whole should enter the Confederation – the so-called *Gesamteintritt*; secondly, that a new executive authority should be created representing Austria, Prussia, the four other kingdoms and the rest of the German states, the ostensible purpose of which was to ensure a quick mobilization of the Bund in times of emergency; and thirdly, that the Monarchy, again as an entirety, should enter the *Zollverein* or German Customs Union. Schwarzenberg described these changes as most limited ones, yet had they come about they would have created a politically and economically cohesive 'Reich of Seventy Millions' stretching from the Baltic to the Adriatic, an early form of *Mitteleuropa*.

At first all seemed to go well for the Austrian premier. He had had good discussions at Berlin before the conference assembled and had even offered there to share the presidency of the Confederation with Prussia although, the details, he said, would have to be worked out later. Then in Dresden, difficulties arose. First, some of the German states wanted a national parliament, which Schwarzenberg, adhering to the confederal principle, was forced to oppose. Thereafter, the smaller states, secretly encouraged by Prussia, created difficulties over the proposed executive. (The Austrian scheme was to give the two great powers two votes each, the four other kingdoms one vote apiece, and leave three for the rest of the small states, to be distributed in such a way as to leave Prussia in a permanent minority.) Here Schwarzenberg showed a willingness to compromise, again offering to share the presidency with Prussia in exchange for a rather larger executive. He then returned to Vienna, rather shaken, leaving his deputy, Buol, to manage the conference in his absence. Buol then came to realize that there was little support for Austria's entry into the Customs Union and sent for an expert on tariffs (a man appropriately called Hock) to re-examine the Austrian case. Schwarzenberg returned to Dresden, however, in a more optimistic frame of mind, expecting a plenary vote on 23 February 1851. In fact, this was delayed for two weeks – Manteuffel had no faith in Schwarzenberg's promise to share the presidency – but when eventually it was taken, it produced a majority opposed to Austria's position. This allowed Manteuffel to declare that Prussia would accept only a unanimous vote. The Prussians, in fact, now demanded both *de jure* equality with Austria in all the affairs of the Confederation and an even larger executive (anathema to the middle states) as their price for the *Gesamteintritt*. Schwarzenberg offered them a legal share of all Confederate functions but insisted that Austria should keep the presidency. Deadlock ensued, all sorts of new proposals were submitted, and the middle states began to fear a deal at their expense between Austria and Prussia. The conference now appeared to be in danger of losing direction. Buol advised Schwarzenberg to return to his original position, but he preferred instead to hold more secret negotiations with Manteuffel. Finally, however, he admitted defeat and on 9 April accepted the principle of a return to the old Confederation plus an Austro-Prussian defensive alliance as a *pis aller*. He still insisted, however, on the committee reports all going to a plenary session for a final vote, his plan being to have them referred to the Bundestag in Frankfurt for further discussions. A final session was held, therefore, on 15 May, when Austria's proposals were defeated. There was not even sufficient agreement in committee to justify a plenary vote on the *Gesamteintritt* and the new executive. Only a report on trade and tariffs was approved for referral and then merely as 'valuable material' for discussion. None the less, Schwarzenberg felt obliged to praise the work of the conference before bringing it to an end. On the following day, however, before leaving Dresden along with Manteuffel, he signed a treaty of mutual defence with Prussia: This was the only real fruit of his discussions with the Prussian statesman. It was to last for three years (although it was renewable); was aimed against the threat of revolutionary upheaval; and contained no specific guarantees except mutual defence. On the other hand, it provided for some sort of *modus vivendi* with Berlin.

How then should these negotiations be evaluated? In recent years the American historian Roy Austensen has written several articles defending Schwarzenberg's diplomacy, acclaiming him a successful 'Metternichian' and disputing the claim that he was a failed *Realpolitiker*.[29] Before assessing this claim one has, of course, to explain Austensen's terminology. By a 'Metternichian' he means someone who pursues a foreign policy designed to support legality, tradition and treaty rights; to uphold the balance of power; to resolve disputes between states peacefully; and to preserve the social order – someone, in short, who is prepared to stick to the rules and cooperate with others to oppose revolution. A *Realpolitiker*, on the other hand, is someone who views the state system merely as the arena in which to pursue egoistic policies, someone for whom the struggle for supremacy can justify almost any tactic, the end justifying the means. Devotees of such a policy in the nineteenth century, according to Austensen, included Bismarck, Cavour and perhaps Napoleon III – but not Schwarzenberg.

The case that Schwarzenberg failed as a *Realpolitiker* seems very straightforward. He failed to get the Monarchy as a whole into the Confederation; he failed to get it into the *Zollverein*; he therefore failed to create his 'Reich of Seventy Millions' which might have dominated Europe. According to Austensen, however, he had never intended to dominate Europe; he had never intended even to dominate Prussia; finally, he did not even care very much about or even understand the issue of Austria's entry into the *Zollverein*. On this, his advisers were split – Bruck and Hock had different opinions – and the question had only been raised as a means to win over German nationalist opinion. In fact, the same was true of the *Gesamteintritt* into the Bund. At heart, Schwarzenberg was all too aware that in the end the leadership of Germany would mean cooperating with Prussia, so that the main aim of his policy had always been to achieve that. And, according to Austensen, he succeeded. He had after all frustrated the emergence of any national parliament or federal court, thus preserving the confederal nature of the Bund; Austria, moreover, had maintained the presidency; Radowitz had been overthrown; and the Erfurt Union had been killed. Finally, the defensive alliance of 16 May had provided a *modus vivendi* with Prussia. If there had been an attempt none the less to win even greater gains for Austria, it had not in fact been a serious one. Schwarzenberg's reform proposals had really always been modest in design and had never been meant to be pushed too far. In Austensen's words: 'His proposals for reform of the Confederation were designed in the spirit of Metternichian conservatism, to strengthen it as a weapon against revolution and to restore a balance of power in Germany favourable to Austria. The *Gesamteintritt* would give Vienna added weight vis à vis Berlin in federal institutions, thus compensating Austria for some of Prussia's political gains during the past decade. The extension of the *Zollverein* would give Austria a voice on economic and trade matters in Germany. The executive would provide a more effective central organ in the event of internal disruption of foreign invasion. Moreover, while the confederate principle was untouchable for Schwarzenberg, the "improvements" were to be negotiable points. He was reluctant to put the whole force of his and Austria's prestige behind them and was clearly willing to settle for less.'[30]

Austensen propounds his case with great plausibility, yet in the end it fails to convince. There are a number of reasons why it is difficult to view Schwarzenberg as a Metternichian. For a start, unlike Metternich, he was too ready to resort to force. His policy of forcing Prussia to disarm completely before Dresden was unnecessarily humiliating. Secondly, again unlike Metternich, he was prepared to play to the gallery. He may in the end have upheld the confederal principle and frustrated the emergence of an elected parliament, but at one point in the negotiations he had definitely been prepared to play the parliamentary card. After all, he had already played it in Austria, and he himself had stood for parliament there, albeit unsuccessfully in July 1848. From Dresden, therefore, he could write to Franz Joseph as early as 21 December 1850: 'Your Majesty knowing my sentiments concerning popular representations is aware of the fact that I do not advocate them. But it cannot be denied that the design of the Prussian plenipotentiaries will be materialised if the well-calculated plan of the King is not nipped in the bud by the suggested means.'[31] Franz Joseph's response does not survive, but Schwarzenberg's next letter tells us what it was: 'Your Majesty's renewed orders regarding the inadmissibility of a popular representation will be promptly followed.'[32] It was not the kind of reminder which would have been necessary in a correspondence with Metternich.

A third flaw in Austensen's case is his argument that Schwarzenberg never really believed in the *Gesamteintritt* so far as the *Zollverein* was concerned. In fact, the negotiations over the future of that body were conducted with at least as much energy as those over the Bund. The evidence unearthed by the German historian, Helmut Böhme, moreover, contradicts Austensen's claims. For example, in a letter to Franz Joseph, Schwarzenberg explained: 'Among the most effective means available to Your Majesty's Government towards the assertion and permanent increase of its influence throughout Germany, must be reckoned its active participation in fostering her common economic interests. The continuously growing importance of this aspect of statecraft will entail more difficulty for Austria as time goes on, in effectually and worthily maintaining her political position as the first power in the Germanic Confederation and as the basis of the whole European system. . . . This step may also be seen as a political measure, whose scope extends to the relations of power and influence among the great European states.'[33] A memorandum was also found among the Schwarzenberg papers which reads in part: 'The Customs Union is a matter of life and death to Austria. She will push it forward with greater energy than anything else and will not blench even at concessions on the purely political field in order to promote it. If the Customs Union as Austria seeks it is achieved, Prussia's influence will be utterly and completely broken.'[34] It is difficult to believe, therefore, that Schwarzenberg's position on the *Zollverein* was as accommodating or as half-hearted as Austensen maintains. Furthermore, one would like to see the evidence for the supposed clash between Bruck and Hock. Did they disagree over principles or over details? In fact, did they disagree at all? Hock later recalled these years as ones of cooperation with Bruck and among the most rewarding of his life.[35]

Yet another difficulty in accepting Austensen's case is his assertion that the *Gesamteintritt* could have been attractive to German nationalists and could have been employed, therefore, as a device to win their support for Austria over the German Question generally. This seems a highly improbable argument. As a result of the *Gesamteintritt*, after all, the situation could have arisen whereby a Magyar or a Pole could have become President of the German Confederation. This was not a situation designed to appeal to any German nationalists. It is difficult, therefore, to accept the proposition that Schwarzenberg was a Metternichian. In any case, Metternich himself, as Austensen admits, openly disapproved of Schwarzenberg's policy. It is more convincing, therefore, to view him as a failed *Realpolitiker*. Indeed, even as a Metternichian he is surely a failure, since his agreement with Manteuffel of 16 May was much more limited both in time and scope than Schwarzenberg had wanted. Thus, instead of a permanent arrangement, he secured merely an alliance for three years; instead of one which guaranteed the territorial integrity of both states, there was simply the obligation of mutual defence; and instead of being aimed specifically against French or English interference, the treaty was directed solely against the threat of revolutionary upheaval. Schwarzenberg, therefore, had won comparatively few gains, despite his defeat of the Erfurt Union. In short, in foreign as in domestic affairs, his achievement is difficult to assess. In both cases, it would seem that, after his initial successes, he failed to shape events in the way he wanted to – perhaps because he lacked a sufficiently clear idea himself of what he wanted to do. It is impossible therefore to judge him a great success. His legacy in fact, despite Franz Joseph's later praise of him as his greatest adviser, was to be a negative one. For he left the young Emperor, first, with the advice only to consult ministers individually – and then only on their own departmental affairs – and, secondly, with an unfortunate belief that in the last resort the interests of the House of Habsburg could always be defended with the sword. It took at least two wars to dissuade Franz Joseph of the utility of this policy, although in his old age he was once again to resort to it with fatal results.

THE ECONOMIC CONSEQUENCES OF 1848

About a year after Schwarzenberg's death, relations with the *Zollverein* were defined by the Commercial Treaty of February 1853. This excluded Austria from the Customs Union until at least 1860, when negotiations could begin again. Bruck, however, professed himself quite pleased with the results, a verdict which the most recent research would certainly vindicate. For, if at the time, it seemed that Austria's exclusion represented a victory for Prussia, it now appears that this was not the case. In fact, having already succeeded in recovering the political leadership of Germany through the revived Confederation, Austria now managed, through the Commercial Treaty, to derive almost all of the economic benefits which full membership of the *Zollverein* could have bestowed on her. This at least is the conclusion of the economic historian Thomas F. Huertas, who arrives at it for two reasons: 'First, [because] the foreign trade structures of the two areas were practically identical, so that little incentive for mutual trade existed. Second, [because] the February Treaty slashed duties to a minimum, so that free trade between the two areas was nearly achieved. The additional step to a full customs union was economically minuscule, although politically enormous.'[36] He explains: 'Further extension of the February Treaty into a full-fledged customs union would have generated little additional benefits for the Habsburg Monarchy since the commercial treaty had already slashed tariffs on trade between the two areas to the bone. . . Under its terms Austria already enjoyed free access to the *Zollverein* market for its most important exports such as grains, wool, wood, bed feathers, flax, linen, yarn, copper, raw linen fabrics and chemical products. These items accounted for over 70 per cent of the value of exports from the Habsburg Monarchy to the *Zollverein* in 1863. The tariffs on the remaining 30 per cent of Austrian exports to the *Zollverein* were not exorbitantly high; rates for livestock, hops, woolen [*sic*] yarn, silk, cotton yarn, fine leather, common glass, flour and fruit all lay below ten per cent ad valorem.'[37] Thus: 'The February Treaty had practically exhausted the production and consumption gains which completely free trade between the two areas would have brought.'[38] According to Huertas, the real motive for entering the *Zollverein* must have been a political one: 'the economic benefits of this policy have been exaggerated – both by the publicists of the period and by later economic historians.'[39]

The Commercial Treaty of February 1853, however, is only one of a number of economic changes of the period 1848–54 that have been re-examined recently by economic historians. Others include the tariff revisions of 1852 and 1854; the *Grundentlastung* or emancipation of the peasants which, although decreed in 1848, was actually only legally enforced in 1853; the abolition of the tariff wall or *Zwischenzollinie* between Austria and Hungary; the building of railways after 1848; and the establishment of the Creditanstalt bank in 1855. Taken together, these changes or reforms are sometimes held to have constituted a watershed in Austrian political and economic development. Marxist historians have seen them as necessary prerequisites for the development of bourgeois society within the Monarchy while others have seen them as part of a political strategy designed by Schwarzenberg to overcome political opposition with material progress. In any case, they have traditionally been viewed as significant. In Macartney's words: 'The results achieved by the various departments during the first years of Franz Joseph's near-absolutist, then absolutist rule, were, judged by any standard, impressive: for good or ill, they altered the face of the Monarchy more radically than had the whole half-century of Francis's and Ferdinand's reigns.'[40] A new generation of American economic historians, however, has cast doubts on this verdict, arguing that the reforms in question were of minor significance and altered economic trends within the Monarchy only marginally. Foremost among these historians are Thomas Huertas, John Komlos, Richard Rudolph and David F. Good. To understand their point of view, we must examine the reforms cited above one by one.

Regarding the tariff changes of 1852 and 1854, the old argument suggested that this reform, by abolishing the previous system of prohibitions and allowing foreign goods to compete with domestic ones within the Monarchy, gave a significant impetus to economic progress. The new competition supposedly forced domestic producers to be more efficient and to boost productivity and output. Yet according to Huertas: 'In fact, the extent of the tariff reform has been greatly exaggerated. For the bulk of Austrian import duties were actually increased. With respect to manufactures, the reforms at first glance reversed the century old policy of prohibition and substituted a protective tariff in its stead. However, in most cases the government set the rate so high that the resulting duty turned out to be prohibitive. . . In summary, the tariff reforms had little impact on the Austrian economy. . . . Even if one assumes that the entire increase in imports of manufactures was due to the tariff change and that the reform halved the Austrian price of these goods, the maximum welfare gain from the tariff reform was only 0.25 per cent of GNP. Substitution of legal import channels for smuggling routes may have accounted for the bulk of the increase in manufactures. If this were the case, the Monarchy had already derived most of the gain from trade liberalisation through the smugglers.'[41]

According to Macartney, 'the biggest transformation of all was on the land'.[42] And there can be little doubt that 'the single most important piece of legislation that survived the revolutionary months of 1848 was the *Grundentlastung*'.[43] The peasants were now totally freed from their previous subjection and the land which they had previously worked on their lords' demesne passed legally into their hands. In Austria, they were obliged to pay for only one-third of the value of this land, the state undertaking to pay for another third of its value, while the landlords sacrificed the remaining third in lieu of the judicial and administrative services which they were no longer obliged to perform. In Hungary, the peasants received title free of charge to the land which they had held in usufruct and the state compensated the landlords fully for the capitalised value of the rent they had previously collected (about one-third of the value of the land). The landlords were paid in interest-bearing forty-year bonds which could be traded or used to secure loans. In the Western lands, about 290 million gulden were paid out in compensation, in Hungary about 304 million.

The general assumption has always been that since *robot* labour was so much more inefficient than wage labour, the emancipation of the peasantry must have boosted agricultural productivity. Yet Komlos, even having allowed for a difference of 50 per cent in productivity between free and *robot* labour, argues that the end result was economically insignificant. He estimates the once and for all increase in output resulting from the emancipation as 1.2 per cent of GNP in Hungary and 2.4 per cent of GNP in Austria. David F. Good explains why: '. . . the lower productivity of labour during *robot* may have been matched by a higher productivity of the serfs as they applied themselves with greater effort and better tools and animals to their own plots. Thus from the standpoint of total agricultural output *robot* labour was not necessarily inefficient. In addition enforcement costs in the case of free labour are not zero. . . . However, even if one assumes that free labour was vastly more efficient than *robot* labour, the impact of the emancipation still was very small. This follows because the amount of forced labour was only a small proportion of the total labour supplied in the agricultural sector. In the case of Hungary the total number of *robot* days owed by the peasantry prior to 1848 was 24 million. This represents about 4.4 per cent of the roughly 540 million days of labour applied yearly to arable land. In Austria about 68 million days or 9 per cent of the estimated 756 million days worked were owed to the lords by the serfs under the arrangements of serfdom.'[44] Komlos also plays down the significance of capital formation as a result of the emancipation: bonds could only have been turned into physical capital, he argues, by being sold to capitalists. 'In other words whatever investments the bondholders would have undertaken would merely have crowded out investments of others.'[45] Hence he concludes: '. . . that the emancipation of the peasantry could not have had a profound immediate impact on the economy of the Habsburg Monarchy. The reform should be viewed as a purely formal act rather than a turning point in Austrian economic history. Only a mechanically deterministic view of history would consider the legal reforms of 1848 as . . . a necessary prerequisite to further economic progress.'[46]

The pattern of trade between Austria and Hungary had been fixed for about a century before 1848. For the main part, it involved an exchange of industrial goods from Austria for agricultural products from Hungary. For example, in 1846–7 the single most important Austrian export to Hungary was woven cotton goods (31 per cent of the total) while the most important Hungarian exports to Austria were raw wool (30 per cent) and wheat (12 per cent). All these goods, however, were subject to tariffs – unlike goods passing between other parts of the Monarchy. As a result, the economic significance of the tariff wall between Austria and Hungary was a matter of some controversy. Economists as well as public figures debated whether it was of greater advantage to Austria or Hungary, although until 1840 most Hungarians seemed to be agreed that it would be to their advantage if it were to disappear. It was only then that Kossuth and his supporters launched a campaign to retain it as a means of promoting Hungarian industry – a strategy which they had derived from the writings of the German economist, Friedrich List. The abolition of the tariff wall in 1850 therefore occasioned more controversy.

Until the mid-1960s, historians, particularly Hungarian ones, argued that the disappearance of the *Zwischenzollinie* had enabled Austria to keep Hungary in a sort of colonial dependency, although some were also of the opinion that it had also helped to increase economic growth. Thereafter, Hungarian historians (particularly Hanák, Bérend, Ránki and Katus) came round to the viewpoint that Hungary, on the whole, had gained from the customs union. Yet they still blamed it for the relative backwardness of Hungarian industry, particularly textiles. Komlos and Huertas now dispute this view. According to their calculations, the existence or non-existence of the tariff wall was of little economic significance. In Komlos's words: '. . . the elimination of the customs barrier enabled the Hungarian economy to produce at most seven million florins more worth of goods and services than it did before 1850. Compared with a gross national product at mid-century or perhaps 460 million florins, this would have meant a net addition of 1.5 per cent to aggregate output, a rather minuscule amount. Austria's social savings was 8.1 million florins approximately, compared with a gross national product of about a billion florins: that is, less than 1 per cent of aggregate output.'[47] Huertas makes the same point: by his calculation, the net gain to the Monarchy was a minuscule 0.2 per cent of its income in 1850. His explanation is: 'First, the tariffs on intra-Empire trade were minimal and can hardly be said to have significantly obstructed the economic interaction of the Monarchy before 1850.'[48] Secondly, the goods which Austria and Hungary exported to each other were also exported by the Monarchy as a whole to third countries. 'This indicates that each partner's exports were competitive on the world market. Consequently the Monarchy also conducted its internal trade at prices close to the world market level.

In combination these two factors assured that neither partner incurred a substantial disadvantage from granting preferential treatment to imports from the other. Nor did either partner gain significantly from having privileged access to the market of the other. For the Monarchy as a whole the elimination of the *Zwischenzollinie* brought a negligible economic gain, since its existence had not hindered an optimal allocation of its productive resources.'[49] As in the case of the *Zollverein*, however, Huertas once again notes that the political aims of the government in 1850 may have been more important than the economic technicalities: 'Although [the removal of the tariff wall] had a minimal impact on total Hungarian income, the distribution of income within Hungary may have been altered in favour of the noble owners of large estates. They formed a bulwark of Habsburg support in Hungary and controlled the local political scene there both before and after 1848. Thus the removal of the *Zwischenzollinie*, which boosted the prices they received for their grain, may be seen as the central government's reward for their loyalty in the Vormärz period and its attempt to guarantee their faithfulness in the neo-absolutist era.'[50] This is a point which merits attention.

According to David F. Good, 'the Bruckian push for the economic integration of the Habsburg lands through the removal of the Austro-Hungarian tariff wall was augmented by a new transportation policy. At mid century 70 per cent of the Empire's 2617-kilometer railroad network was under state ownership – the highest in Europe. The Railroad Concession Law of 1854 foresaw a reduction in the nature and scope of government involvement in the railroad system. The government was to sell some of its operations and to promote further development through a policy of guaranteeing interest on private investors' capital.'[51] This policy was partly dictated by economic difficulties arising during the Crimean War, it was also consistent with the liberalization policies of the neo-absolutist period and was, indeed, carried out. After 1854 the northern and south-eastern lines were sold off to a private company, founded chiefly with French capital, which in return for certain tax concessions and financial guarantees agreed to extend its new rail network into Hungary. Then in 1856, the state sold its Lombardy-Venetian line to a consortium of foreign and domestic investors; it was subsequently fused with several others. According to Good: 'By 1859 only 13.8 kilometers of the entire network remained in state hands.'[52] Finally, the new private companies which took over the railways expanded their networks, although the 'rail boom' which developed tapered off after the late 1850s. By 1860, however, the Austrian rail network had expanded from 1,300 to 3,000 kilometres, and the Hungarian one from 200 to almost 1,700 kilometres.

The significance of these developments has generally been recognized by economic historians. Good himself makes the fundamental point that railways both lowered transportation costs for customers and created demand in other sectors of the economy (coal, iron and steel, and timber). The Austrian historian, Herbert Matis, has gone so far as to describe the railways as the 'leading sector' of the economy in the 1850s, 'signifying a crucial contribution to the improvement of the economic infrastructure'.[53] His judgement would probably be backed by the Hungarian historian, László Katus, who argues that the railways were the most dynamic sector of the Hungarian economy between 1848 and 1918.[54] Richard Rudolph, on the other hand, is more sceptical about their role and stresses the continuity with the railroad building programme before 1848. He also dismisses the view that it was a new bourgeois social order created by the revolutions which made the railway boom possible. The later 'railway boom' in feudal, Tsarist Russia, he claims, disproves this.[55]

A final development which, together with these above-mentioned reforms, is supposed to have strengthened the economic position of the Monarchy at this time was the foundation of the Creditanstalt bank, designed to develop Austrian industry and trade by providing credit for long-term investment. As has already been seen, the ability of the Monarchy before 1848 to provide the capital for industrial development was woefully inadequate, a situation which the foundation of the Niederösterreichische Escompte-Gesellschaft in 1853 did little to change. However, a rumour that the Pereire brothers, founders of the Crédit-Mobilier in France, were about to establish a similar bank in Austria, led the government in 1855, under pressure from the Rothschilds and numerous wealthy aristocrats, to establish the Creditanstalt. It was 'organised on a joint-stock basis with a then enormous share capital of 100 million gulden. This exceeded the capital of the national bank (73.5 million gulden) and dwarfed that of the next largest commercial bank, the Niederösterreichische Escompte-Gesellschaft (5 million gulden) which in turn had more share capital than any single industrial firm. The size of this capital base permitted the Creditanstalt to extend its activities beyond the regular commercial banking business into those areas typical of the Crédit-Mobilier type banks – the financing of long-term capital projects and the founding of new firms.'[56] Historians such as

Gershenkron, Cameron and März have all therefore stressed the importance of this development.[57]

What then was the overall significance of these economic changes of the early 1850s for the development of the Austrian economy? As has been seen, despite positive and much-needed measures such as the expansion of the railways and the foundation of the Creditanstalt, many of the apparently more spectacular reforms did not produce the economic benefits which traditionally have been ascribed to them. Therefore, there was no great economic spurt after 1848. David Good, consequently, is quite correct to connect this discovery with the work of Rudolph, Komlos and himself in reconstructing the picture of the Monarchy's growth rates in the nineteenth century.[58] Traditionally, this had been one in which the years before 1848 had been seen as a preparatory period for a spurt in economic growth after 1848 which culminated in the *Grunderzeit* (promoter's era) boom of 1867–73. Thereafter came the great depression of 1873–9, followed by a period of sluggish growth until the mid-1890s, after which the Monarchy experienced rapid growth until the First World War. The most recent research, however, suggests that sustained growth emerged in Austria during the pre-March period, continued through 1848 and the 1850s and showed a very clear break only around 1859. The reversal was then a sharp one – a decline of 20 per cent between 1860 and 1865 according to Rudolph's index or one of 28 per cent between 1861 and 1864 according to Komlos's – but one which was followed by an equally sharp recovery thereafter. The peak of economic activity of the late 1850s was then surpassed in the period before 1873. The great depression of 1873–9 then followed a similar pattern – a sharp downturn followed by a vigorous increase in economic activity in the 1880s – leading to a resumption of the established trend of a relatively slow but steady growth right up until 1914. As Good comments: 'The year 1848 fails to mark off the beginning of sustained growth and is not associated with a sharp acceleration of the sustained growth already underway. Neither of the available production indices displays any such acceleration in the years following 1848. Instead, these years form a link in the larger pattern of a slowly accelerating trend rate throughout the nineteenth century.'[59]

The interruption of this trend in the 1860s is attributed by Huertas to the foreign policy of the Monarchy: 'the government's military struggles to contain the forces of nationalism and to maintain the Habsburg dynasty's great power status led to monetary and fiscal policies which impeded economic growth.'[60] He distinguishes four distinct periods in his account of Habsburg monetary policy: the revolutions of 1848, the Crimean War, the Italian War of 1859 and the war of 1866 against Prussia and Italy. After the 1848 revolutions, he argues, the government began to issue its own notes, thus abrogating the monopoly of note issue given to the Austrian National Bank in 1816. Yet by borrowing from the Bank at the same time, it helped increase the note issue of the latter also. The resulting increase in the money supply meant that it could no longer maintain the convertibility of the gulden into silver; the Monarchy went off the silver standard and the currency was allowed to float. Thereafter the government attempted regularly to restore convertibility, but was always foiled by its need to finance wars. In Huertas's words: 'the Empire's monetary policy can be succinctly summarised as the Sisyphean pursuit of the 1847 silver parity which the government had relinquished under the onslaught of the 1848 revolutions in favour of a flexible exchange rate. Each of its wars forced the government to abandon this aim and to tap again the National Bank for funds in order to finance its armies in the field. As soon as hostilities ceased, the National Bank began to decrease its holdings of Treasury debt and to amass silver reserves in preparation for the resumption of specie payments. The rate of money supply growth sagged sharply and in some instances became negative. The agio, the discount of the gulden from its 1847 silver parity, clearly reflected these gyrations in Habsburg monetary policy.'[61]

The first attempt at reform came between 1851 and 1853 under Finance Minister Baumgartner, but his efforts were frustrated by the Crimean War. Then in mid-1855, Bruck once again became Finance Minister. He too had a mandate to reform the monetary and fiscal systems and was fairly successful. He refused to sharply reduce the money supply, but raised the exchange rate by selling off state property and bonds and increasing the amount of specie in the Bank. Indeed, by October 1858, the latter was able to resume specie payments. By then, too, Austria was also able to form a monetary union with the *Zollverein* through a currency treaty of 1857. This required both parties to maintain a fixed silver parity, but with the outbreak of war in 1859 the exchange rate plummeted and the government again resorted to borrowing. The constitutional debate after the war prolonged the period of uncertainty, leading the exchange rate to plummet yet again. Finance Minister von Plener attempted to tackle the problem by reducing the stock of high-powered money in the economy (it fell by 29 per cent between September 1861 and December 1865) but only helped to produce a slump, although other factors – a bad harvest, for example – were also present as contributory factors.

The 1866 war once again forced the government to resort to the printing presses of the National Bank. After that there was the *Grunderzeit* boom and the money supply continued to grow until 1871. After 1871 this growth was restricted and the sudden drop in the rate of expansion helped bring on depression in 1873. Thus the gyrations in Habsburg monetary policy helped to retard the Monarchy's economic growth throughout the entire period 1848–73.

So too, according to Huertas, did the substantial increase in the government's non-monetary debt.[62] For in the period 1848–65, the amount of bond held by the public rose from 1.13 to 2.47 billion fl. CM, an average annual increase of 80 million fl. CM, or about 2 per cent of GNP in 1856–8. Huertas argues: 'To the extent that these debt issues crowded out private investment, Austrian growth would have suffered.'[63] In Germany, by way of contrast, the money supply was allowed to grow much more smoothly, and indebtedness on the part of the German states was always kept under greater control. Thus: 'The increase in the German public debt in 1849–65 was 1.25 billion marks, approximately 80 million marks per year or about half the increase in the Habsburg debt. Of course, this placed much less of a burden on the larger German economy, particularly in the earlier 1850s. In 1851–56 the increase in German debt held by the public amounted to 1.2 per cent of German net national income, while the increase in the public's holdings of the Habsburg Monarchy's debt totalled 4.9 per cent of the Empire's 1856–58 GNP.'[64] Germany, as a result, could experience a much greater rate of growth than the Monarchy after 1850. According to Milward and Saul: 'compared to Germany after 1850 the disparity in the size of per capita industrial output increases sharply until 1890. . .'[65] That this disparity was due to a number of causes cannot be denied, but Huertas insists that in the period 1848–67, Austria's economic backwardness was due in the final analysis to her foreign policy: 'both monetary and fiscal policies . . . took their cues from the Monarchy's military objectives. These led the Empire into successive conflicts which diverted resources, either through taxes or debt to the public sector. As a result, the Monarchy's economic growth may have lagged. In any case the Empire's exchange rate policy compounded the adverse impact of its military policy.'[66] On the other hand, Huertas, as will be seen, appears to go too far in blaming

Habsburg military policy on 'nationalism', which usually constituted far less of a threat to dynastic interests than imperial policy-makers were wont to assume.

BUOL AND HABSBURG FOREIGN POLICY

It is now time to examine the foreign policy of the Monarchy in the period 1853–66, although it has to be confessed there are few controversies which surround it. The failure of Habsburg policy is in all respects so obvious that there is little to add, if one does not wish to resort to narrative. None the less, there have been some attempts at revision which deserve attention. They comprise attempts to rehabilitate the reputations of failed Foreign Ministers such as Buol and Rechberg, for whom the defence is put forward that they had no alternatives, that they were in an impossible position, and that – once again – they were 'Metternichians', whose only desire was to maintain peace and the European Concert against the unscrupulous ambitions of men like Lord Palmerston, Napoleon III and Bismarck.

In the case of Buol, both Roy Austensen and Paul Schroeder have suggested mitigating circumstances for his failures. Schroeder, in particular, has written a very detailed account of Austrian policy during the Crimean War in which he blames Great Britain both for the war and for its disastrous outcome for Austria: 'the ultimate reason the war was begun was the same as would defeat all efforts to end it by negotiation before military victory – British honour and prestige.'[67] Connected to this was Whig ideology, 'the British desire to promote European progress and ordered liberty against both reactionary despotism and radical revolution, and to replace the old repressive international order with a new constitutional liberal one built around England. . .'[68] And in her fitful attempts to promote this liberal international order, Schroeder argues, Britain always came up against Austria. 'Everywhere in Europe where Britain wanted to do good – Italy, Germany, Poland, the Balkans, Turkey – Austria was there and standing in Britain's way.'[69] Hence the long series of disagreements between the two powers during the war. Their fundamental aims were completely different: Buol wanted a revised form of the old European Concert with the old rules but a new alignment (Britain, France and Austria), while Palmerston wanted to ignore the Concert and expel Russia to the frontiers of Europe by a dramatic victory. This difference of outlook made Buol's strategy a failure, even if in the short term he looked like succeeding. After all, before allying with the Western powers, he did secure guarantees of Austria's integrity from Prussia, the Germanic Confederation, France and Sardinia. And thereafter he managed to bring both sides to the conference table and to secure a peace without actually involving Austria in the war. All this, in Schroeder's view, was both Metternichian and laudable: 'Buol's ideas were wholly post-1815: confining potential aggressors within the Concert, rather than forming an open coalition against them; fighting wars, if at all, only for clearly defined, rational, calculable ends, and stopping when those ends were achieved; making peace settlements tolerable for the vanquished and enforceable for the victors; providing political rather than military solutions to basically political problems. His main purpose was to preserve the core of what Metternich had achieved in 1815, which since 1822, Britain had often opposed and now wanted to destroy: Austria's leadership of an independent centre for Europe that would serve both to check Prussian ambitions and Russian expansion and to function as the pivot of the Concert. Buol was not a great man, and perhaps not even an adequate representative of these ideas. But what he stood for deserves respect.'[70] This is a judgement which Austensen supports. In his view too: 'Buol never deviated from Metternich's basic principles. . . His own diplomacy, even in its more active phases, was defensive and usually formulated in distinctly Metternichian terms. . . His failure . . . represents more than just a personal failure; rather it was the failure of a conservative, defensive, concert of Europe diplomacy – that is, of the Metternich tradition.'[71]

There is something to be said for this viewpoint, at least with respect to Buol's diplomacy during the Crimean War. Yet there is another side to the story, one which, in Buol's own words, concerns 'the revolution (for it is nothing less)'[72] in Austrian diplomacy in 1854–5. The 'revolution' which Buol talked about was his policy of an alliance with the Western powers. This was actually concluded on 2 December 1854, but the really revolutionary decision had been taken before then – the decision of 3 June to send an ultimatum to Russia to get out of the Principalities. Moreover, the policy behind this had been debated in imperial conferences in March and May when both Buol and the Emperor had seemed prepared to allow Austria to take an active part in the war against Russia. Buol had then argued that the Russian occupation of the Principalities constituted a threat to Austrian and German interests. The Russians, he claimed, were preparing to incorporate these lands into the Russian Empire. Yet with Britain and France now at war, the ideal opportunity had arisen for Austria to ally with them to contain Russia. Moreover, if the Russians refused to withdraw, the war could be fought in the Balkans instead of in the Crimea, in this way giving Austria both a greater say in events and a better defence against the Russians. In return for allying with the Western powers, it should be added, Buol believed he could persuade them to provide guarantees of Austria's territorial integrity and perhaps convince them to allow the Principalities to come under Austrian protection after the war. He ruled out an alliance with Russia, first on the grounds that the Russians would almost certainly ignore Austria in strategic and diplomatic affairs and, secondly, on the more obvious grounds that such an alliance would be an invitation not merely for the Western powers to attack Austria, but for revolution to break out in Hungary and Italy. Even Prussia might use the opportunity to press her claims in Germany. As for neutrality, Buol ruled this out as a policy on the grounds that it would deprive him of the opportunity to influence the policies of any of the powers.

Yet there were distinct disadvantages in what Buol was proposing, disadvantages which were immediately obvious to many of his colleagues. The Master of the Ordinance, General Hess, for example, pointed out that Russia was Austria's traditional partner against revolution; that the Monarchy was neither militarily or financially strong enough to wage war against her; that such a war would immediately spark off revolution in Poland; and that the Western powers were unreliable and traditionally anti-Austrian and would redraw the map of Europe after any victory along revolutionary lines. Yet the only concession Buol made was to delay sending the ultimatum until he had renewed the defensive alliance of 1851 with Prussia and had secured Turkish agreement for Austria to occupy the Principalities during the war. He then presented the ultimatum without having received any prior assurances from Britain, France or Prussia regarding specific military contingencies. Later on, it is true, Austria became more moderate. She did not sign a treaty of alliance with Britain and France until 2 December 1854, by which time she had induced them to agree to moderate war aims (the Four Points). Nor did she become an active participant in the war thereafter, although her second ultimatum to Russia of 28 December 1855 threatened to make her one if Russia refused to negotiate a peace. By then, however, the damage had been done. Russia, which in 1849 had intervened to save the Monarchy, which between 1848 and 1851 had occupied the Principalities to put down revolution, and which in 1853 had given Austria full diplomatic support against Turkey during the Leiningen mission to Constantinople (Austria had threatened to go to war with Turkey if Turkey invaded Montenegro), felt cut to the quick by Austria's ingratitude. The Tsar gave a statuette of Franz Joseph, which had hitherto adorned his study, to his valet, and told the Austrian ambasador that he and John Sobieski of Poland were the two most foolish kings in history since they had both saved Austria. When he died a few months later, his subjects blamed his death on Austrian ingratitude. Indeed, for decades afterwards travellers from Russia were to relate how people there still denounced Austrian policy.

Buol's motives have already been discussed. There are still a few points, however, which might be mentioned in his defence. First, Nicholas of Russia did refuse to guarantee the *status quo* in the Balkans – in fact, he encouraged Austria to invade Bosnia-Herzegovina – so that he was himself responsible for making the Austrians mistrust his motives. On the other hand, since he had also offered to allow Austria to jointly administer the Principalities, there was little reason to believe that he would ignore her. A second point worth examining is Buol's fear of a French-inspired revolution in Italy. No doubt this was a possibility, yet with Radetzky firmly in control of Lombardy-Venetia, and given the defeat of Charles Albert in 1848 and 1849, surely the odds must have been that any rising would be defeated. Moreover, with the French committed to a war in the Crimea, there was less chance of them intervening to support the Italians. As things happened, the Sardinians were to play the same game as the Austrians and with better results. For in January 1855, they too signed an alliance with France to fight against the Russians in the Crimea; but, unlike the Austrians, they actually took part in the fighting. Napoleon III therefore felt no need after the war to support Austria out of any sense of gratitude; he was in greater debt to her most virulent enemy. As Schroeder and Austensen concede, it was an illusion on the part of Buol to have expected anything else. In the meantime, he had destroyed the whole basis of Metternichian foreign policy by destroying the counter-revolutionary alliance between Austria and Russia, relations between which powers were never to be the same again. The ultimatum of 3 June 1854 must therefore be seen in Norman Rich's words as 'an act of almost inconceivable folly'.[73] He adds: 'In retrospect the ultimatum can also be seen as a turning point in European history, for it marked the end of the friendship and cooperation between the two

Eastern European conservative powers and the beginning of a bitter hostility that was to culminate in war in 1914, the destruction of both imperial houses, and the liquidation of the Habsburg Empire.'[74]

One man, curiously, who foresaw some of this and who was scathing about Buol's conduct was Metternich himself. His own policy was one of strict neutrality, summed up in the advice: '. . . we must never allow ourselves to be used as the shock troops of East against West or West against East.'[75] He therefore denounced the ultimatum and the treaty of alliance, characterizing his former colleague as follows: 'The fatal consequences of any and every action are hidden from Count Buol. He sees what is right in front of him; of what is coming he sees nothing.'[76] Schroeder is reluctant to concede that Metternich's policy might have worked any better. However, he does insist that Buol was a Metternichian, albeit a failed one. And, despite Metternich's insistence on neutrality in 1854–6, we are reminded that: 'Metternich advocated in 1815 and in 1840–41 the European guarantee and a great-power alliance in favour of Turkey that Buol tried so hard to effect. In addition, his program of a Western alliance to stop Russia in 1828–29 was just what Buol and Francis Joseph tried for at this time, as they claimed.'[77] Metternich, on the other hand, had never threatened Russia with war the way Buol and Franz Joseph did in 1854. For this reason, it is better perhaps to accept the views of Bernhard Unckel who sees Buol and his Emperor as devotees not of Metternich but of Schwarzenberg.[78] The latter's policy he defines as support for a powerful, centralized Austria, an Austria which would maintain its independence and defend its own interests. Hence Schwarzenberg's bid for *Mitteleuropa*, his strong stand on the Hungarian refugee question in 1849–50, and his willingness to recognize Napoleon III, despite the Tsar's disapproval. Hence too, argues Unckel, Austria's strong stand after his death over Montenegro (the Leiningen Mission of 1853) and her willingness to face up to the Tsar in 1854. This was merely the continuation of Schwarzenberg's policy of self-assertion, a policy which also, by the way, explains Buol's hopes of retaining some sort of political and economic influence in the Principalities after the war. Buol therefore can be seen either as a failed Metternichian or a failed Schwarzenberger. In fact, he was probably a mixture of both. What he certainly was not, was a success.

That Buol was indeed a failure was not crystal clear until the Italian War of 1859. The Peace of Paris, if anything, appeared to solemnize his diplomatic revolution. It ended after all with a treaty signed by Austria, France and Great Britain which guaranteed the independence and integrity of the Ottoman Empire. Such a treaty, however, neither barred the way to a *rapprochement* between France and Russia or committed Napoleon III to the defence of the *status quo* in Western Europe. By 1858, therefore, he was contriving to carry out his old promise 'to do something for Italy'. As every schoolboy knows, this meant plotting war against Austria in alliance with Sardinia. The trap was set at Plombières and at the appointed time, Buol duly fell into it. Once again he had issued an ultimatum; once again he had not bothered to secure assurances of specific military support in advance; and once again Austria was to endanger her economy by pursuing a Schwarzenberg-type policy of asserting her rights. Indeed, she was to do so in defiance of an international conference which was about to meet to discuss Italian affairs. Yet since this had been called by Russia, now a revisionist power, there was little hope that it would support Austria's position. In any case, Austria's economy was so weak that she could not afford to keep her army mobilized for any length of time. Hence the need for a quick decision.

One other aspect of Schwarzenberg's legacy was involved in that decision: the need to protect imperial unity. Lombardy-Venetia since 1849 had been allowed no government of its own: like Hungary and Croatia, it had been run by the army, and there had been no attempts to alter this situation. By now, of course it was too late to buy off the Italians, as some of them had suggested before 1848. The leaders of Italian society were mostly in exile and many had had their estates confiscated after the abortive Mazzinian uprising in Milan in 1853. Nor did the appointment of Franz Joseph's brother Maximilian as Governor-General in 1857 make any difference, since he was given rather less powers than even the Archduke Rainer had received in 1818. The Emperor in any case was not willing to make any concessions to the Italians – it would just encourage demands for special treatment elsewhere. The furthest Franz Joseph would go by way of reform was a series of measures communicated to his brother in July 1858 in reply to his demand for change. These included a commission to discover whether the property tax in Italy was disproportionately high; the abolition of certain fiscal privileges enjoyed by the localities; the reorganization of the academies of art in Milan and Venice; better wages for district physicians; and changes in conscription regulations. On the other hand, he emphasized that there could never be a government in the Italian provinces independent of Vienna or one solely in communication with Vienna through a Ministry for Italian Affairs. 'The force of Austrian influence in Italy depended upon the solidarity of the entire Monarchy, not upon the intrinsic importance of the Italian lands and their development.'[79] Maximilian wrote in despair to his mother, declaring: 'We live now in complete chaos and occasionally I myself begin to ask if conscience permits blind obedience to Vienna's orders. . . .'[80] Yet there was nothing he could do. It remained a fact of life that institutions could not be granted to the Italians which were denied to the other peoples of the Monarchy; nor could British or other views be taken into account. As Buol had written in a despatch from the Congress of Paris: 'Once meddling is permitted in Italian affairs to an unlimited extent, what reason would there be not to extend it further?'[81] The Empire, therefore, was to remain a united whole and Lombardy-Venetia was to be run in the imperial interest from Vienna. Thus there was no possibility of dealing with the Italians themselves before 1859. Their fate could only be decided by war.

As we have seen, the decision for war was taken before a European Congress could meet to discuss the future of Italy, partly because Austria could not afford to keep her army mobilized. She had been provoked, therefore, into demanding Piedmontese demobilization through an ultimatum which enabled Cavour to engineer French intervention. The Austrians had only half expected this, although they believed that if it did occur they could rely on Prussian support. This was a mistake and a foreseeable one. Prussia after all had neither joined Austria in forcing Russia out of the Principalities during the Crimean War ('I find it incredible that I have to proceed without the support of Your Majesty', Franz Joseph had written to Frederick William IV),[82] nor had Prussia and the German states been willing to support the Four Points. Now, once again, the Prussians displayed little enthusiasm for a policy on which they had not been consulted. The result was that Austria had to face France and Sardinia on her own. Franz Joseph complained to his mother only one week before the battle of Solferino: '. . . our position is difficult . . . we have a numerically superior, very brave enemy . . . to whom even the most despicable means are welcome, who has revolution as his ally . . . we are everywhere betrayed in our own country. . . I hope that perhaps after all Germany and that ignominious scum of Prussia will come to our aid at the last moment. . . .'[83] Yet Prussia's mobilization on 24 June, accompanied by a declaration of armed mediation, came too late to save the

Austrians: on the very same day, they were defeated at Solferino by the French. Franz Joseph therefore made the Peace of Villafranca with Napoleon III and surrendered Lombardy to Sardinia.

According to some accounts, he was forced into this on account of the nationality problem, reflected at Solferino in the desertion of many of his Italian and Hungarian troops. In fact, this was scarcely the main reason for the Austrian defeat. Only about 6 per cent of the Austrian troops were involved in desertion and of these the majority were Italians. The Lombard troops were much less reliable than the Venetians, perhaps because it was much more obvious that Lombardy would become Italian before Venetia. Of the Hungarian regiments, there was in fact much less desertion than was feared. True, Kossuth and Klapka did manage to raise a Hungarian legion to aid the French during the war, a body which at one stage reached a total of 4,000 men. Yet it was largely composed of press-ganged prisoners-of-war whose nationality was unclear (the French identified Hungarian troops as those who wore tight trousers) and, besides, it never took part in any fighting. István Deák, in a review of the significance of the nationality problem in the fighting, reaches the conclusion that there was almost no nationality problem in the army and almost no policy for dealing with one.[84] He writes: 'At Magenta and Solferino, the junior officers marched to their deaths with dignity and pride, and their German, Czech, Hungarian, Croatian or Romanian rank and file marched behind them with little complaint.'[85] The real military causes for the defeat were to be found elsewhere, largely in the army's leadership. The commander-in-chief was Count Gyulai, a crony of Count Grünne, the Emperor's adjutant (and *de facto* War Minister) and a man who had no experience of active service. He was so sure of his own unfitness for the job that he actually requested to be relieved of his command; he was also on bad terms with his chief of staff. Yet he was allowed to conduct the campaign none the less. Moreover, since the ultimatum had been sent before the army had been mobilized, his army was hardly ready to begin that campaign. And, of course, shortages of money meant that it was under-equipped and suffered from lack of transport, so that soldiers arrived in Italy sick, exhausted and hungry. Gyulai then led them in an ultra-cautious fashion, allowing himself to be attacked first and forswearing any attempt to seize the initiative. Having been defeated at Magenta, he then retreated to the Quadrilateral. Here he was replaced by the Emperor himself, who had left for the battlefield accompanied by both Hess and Grünne. The former advised a defensive strategy, especially since the army was short of supplies. Franz

Joseph and Grünne, on the other hand, preferred to attack, with the result that they met the French at Solferino. Here the superior leadership, experience and training of the enemy proved their worth, although the nationality problem may have contributed in an indirect manner to the final result. For according to the military historian, Gunther Rothenberg, the Austrian high command had been 'reluctant to introduce new rifled arms, because this precision weapon would have required open-order tactics, and open-order tactics would have facilitated desertion. So the High Command found it better to do nothing.'[86]

RECHBERG, MENSDORFF AND THE ROAD TO SADOWA

Defeat in Italy brought about the replacement of Buol as Foreign Minister by Rechberg, whose main challenge in foreign affairs, as it was to turn out, was the German Question, this time in the formidable guise of Bismarck. Since the latter had already convinced himself that Germany was too small for both Austria and Prussia, the challenge was not going to be an easy one. In the end, Rechberg failed, yet, like Schwarzenberg and Buol, he has been acclaimed by Austensen and others (particularly the American historian Richard B. Elrod) as a 'Metternichian' whose honourable and European policy in Germany would have been preferable to Bismarck's *Realpolitik*. In Austensen's words: '. . . even if some elements of Austria's German policy can legitimately be characterised as narrow and self-centered, it can also be argued that, taken as a whole, it nonetheless stood for a much larger concept than Prussia's. The men who were trained in Metternich's "school" viewed German affairs in the context of maintaining a stable European system. Since Austria was the chief guarantor (as well as the principal beneficiary) of the 1815 settlement, they had to consider the effects of any changes in Germany on Europe as a whole. They knew that, if Austria were to lose her position in Germany, it would significantly lessen her ability to play a stabilising role in European affairs and would bring about a major shift in the relations among the great powers. Nonetheless, Austria could not defend her position through an aggressive policy like Prussia's because she would thereby lose her credibility as the defender of legality and tradition, which they considered to be Austria's greatest asset. By experience as well as training, they had learned to act with restraint and to try to exert a moderating influence on European affairs. For them it was a European necessity – as well as an Austrian interest. In contrast, the Prussians tended to view Germany as the arena in which they would realise their ambitions for expansion. It was a more narrow and short-sighted policy; and as Schwarzenberg correctly predicted, a Prussian Germany would eventually take the same attitude towards the whole of Europe.'[87]

Austensen defines a 'Metternichian' German policy as one which viewed German affairs, first and primarily, in a European context; secondly, as one which looked to close and cordial relations with Prussia, without whose cooperation the Confederation could not be managed; thirdly, as one which maintained Austria's primacy in Germany. In other words, if Austria sought to organize Germany in such a manner as to support a balance of power in Europe against the ambitions of either France or Russia, she also sought to do this in such a way that Germany would support Austrian interests in Europe and let Austria play the role of the leading German power. The problem was that, given the economic, military and political rise of Prussia after 1848, there were statesmen there – principally Bismarck – who saw no reason to continue to do this. From their point of view, the European balance would still be held even if German affairs were reorganized to reflect the changing balance of power within Germany itself. Nor did they see any reason to identify Austria's interests in Italy or in the Balkans with those of Europe, an identification which, by the way, by 1860 did not seem obvious to the other great powers either. Hence, the assumptions held by Austrian statesmen during this period may be regarded as anachronistic, a criticism which can also be made of historians such as Schroeder, Austensen, Elrod and others, who take up their defence. Nor is it plausible to talk about Austria's commitment to a stable European system or to the Concert when one bears in mind the ultimatum to Russia in 1854, the ultimatum to Sardinia in 1859 or Austrian attempts between 1861 and 1863 to reform the German Confederation. In all of these instances, Prussia's viewpoint was ignored or challenged. The truth was that the 1815 settlement suited Austria perfectly and she was only going to change it when it was to her own advantage. 'Metternichian' diplomacy, in other words, was really only Austrian *Realpolitik* under another name. A true policy of giving priority to European interests and the preservation of peace would have involved concessions on Austria's part, which she was never willing to make, in Italy, Germany or anywhere else.

Instead, she always expected the European powers to accept her leadership, despite the opposition it excited in Italy and elsewhere and despite the fact that it threatened to involve the German states in wars over Italy and the Balkans where they had no interests at stake. Moreover, the fact that Prussia was Germany's leading economic power, the head of the German Customs Union and the military power on which Germany (including Austria) depended in any war against France, did not seem to indicate any need to revise the German Confederal institutions in Prussia's favour. Hence when Franz Joseph met the Prince Regent of Prussia in 1860, the Austrian Foreign Office submitted the following advice: 'The Prince Regent must understand that the Imperial Court, even with the best will to further the influence, the prestige and the very power of Prussia, cannot but feel the most legitimate reluctance at this juncture in sacrificing its rights and its position in Germany. Austria has fought honourably against Germany's hereditary enemy, has suffered losses and money, has had to sacrifice a province in Italy, has seen the minor branches of the Imperial House being illegally dethroned in the peninsula: and now she is expected to retrace her steps in Germany too! The Prince must understand, as a friend of Austria, that he cannot ask such a thing, which would have a disastrous effect internally for the Habsburg Monarchy and cause it to lose face throughout Europe.'[88] Yet the equivalent Prussian memorandum, prepared for the Prussian Prince Regent, merely stated the obvious: 'It is well to be clear that it is Austria who needs help, whereas Prussia can easily find allies and is not dependent on Austrian help. . . . If . . . Austria asks us to regard an attack on the Mincio (Venetia) as an act of war, then we would have to explain the reasons which prevent us from complying with this request if our aspirations in Germany are not taken into account.'[89]

The story of the struggle for mastery in Germany is well known and need not be repeated here. After the Italian war Franz Joseph introduced certain constitutional reforms in the Monarchy – the October Diploma of 1860 and the February Patent of 1861. These did little to solve the constitutional crisis of neo-absolutism (see below) but they did allow the Emperor to make a bid to dominate Germany by agreeing to reform of the Confederation (delegates from an Austrian parliament could now join those from the other German states in a federal German parliament) and even by organising the famous *Fürstentag* of 1863. All this, of course, meant a clash with Prussia who had plans of her own for reform and who was also busy between 1860 and 1865 renegotiating the *Zollverein* in such a way as to keep Austria out. Between 1860 and 1866, therefore, the second round of the struggle for mastery in Germany was fought out and over largely the same issues as in 1848–51: reform of the Confederation, the *Zollverein*, and Schleswig-Holstein. This time Rechberg was less audacious than Schwarzenberg and when the two sides squared up militarily over Schleswig-Holstein, it was Austria who lost, despite the support of most of the states of the Confederation.

Can Rechberg be defended? That his policy was one of desperately attempting to reach a compromise with Bismarck over Schleswig-Holstein cannot be denied (he opposed the schemes for reform of the Confederation, which went ahead because Franz Joseph backed them). 'If we act calmly but firmly in defence of our legitimate rights,' he told a Bavarian colleague, 'and collect the other German governments around us, Prussia will perceive the impossibility of achieving her plans and this will facilitate the victory of the calmer and more sensible party in Berlin.'[90] On another occasion, he told a colleague: '. . . we do not wish to impose any humiliations on Prussia. We only ask that for her part she respect our dignity and the position we have in Germany as a great power and as an heir of a glorious past.'[91] Perhaps this was truly 'Metternichian'. But it was also senseless and merely led Austria into all sorts of contradictions – for example, backing Augustenburg and the Confederation over Schleswig-Holstein at one moment and offering to make, or actually making, separate deals with Prussia at the next. Yet Rechberg could offer no alternative. Meanwhile, even he realized that sticking to such a course (cooperation with Prussia for the sake of cooperation) lacked either dignity or success so long as Bismarck was in charge of foreign policy in Berlin: 'It burdens the conduct of affairs to an extrordinary degree,' he wrote after being told by Bismarck to avoid sentimentality, 'when one has to deal with a man who displays his political cynicism so openly that he replies to that part of my letter – that we must make the maintenance of the confederation and the hereditary rights of the German princes the foundation of our policy – with the hair-raising phrase that both of us must place ourselves on the practical terrain of cabinet policy and not let the situation be obscured by the fog that derives from the doctrines of a German policy of sentiment. Such language is worthy of a Cavour. Adherence to the basis of legality is a nebulous policy of sentiment! The task of keeping this man in bounds, of dissuading him from his expansionistic policy of utility . . . surpasses human powers.'[92] Others, however, including the German expert in the

Austrian Foreign Office, von Biegeleben, and the Minister of State in the Austrian government, von Schmerling, reached the obvious conclusion that a change in policy was needed. In Schmerling's words: 'Surrounded by egoists, even an honest man must pursue an egoistical policy in order not to go under.'[93] Biegeleben suggested an alliance with France, a course which Rechberg refused to consider, maintaining that ultimately it would only leave Austria isolated. Still, since his own policy was leading nowhere and was coming under increasing criticism in Vienna, he resigned in October 1864.

It was not until 1866 that Austria took up *Realpolitik*. In 1865 she turned down an offer from the Italians to buy Venetia, an offer which was deemed to be insulting to the *Kaiserhaus*, although the Finance Minister, von Plener, would have been happy, given the state of imperial finances, to have accepted it. Then in 1866 came the decisive change: aware that Bismarck had negotiated an alliance with Italy, Mensdorff-Pouilly, the new Foreign Minister, negotiated a secret treaty with France. Under the terms of this document, Austria undertook to cede Venetia, through France, to Italy in the event of her winning a war with Prussia, the understanding being that she would compensate herself in Germany. In fact, the plan was to take Silesia from Prussia and to establish one of the Habsburg branches which had been expelled from central Italy in the Rhineland. Napoleon III was to be consulted about the extent of Austrian gains in Germany, but there is probably no truth in the assertion of Prussian historians that France herself was offered German territory. Austrian *Realpolitik* did not extend so far. Instead, the French part of the bargain was that Napoleon III should remain neutral in any war yet receive the honour of transferring Venetia to Italy. The end result was a most curious situation and one which even the best efforts of Michael Derndarsky, the Austrian historian, cannot plausibly defend.[94] It meant that imperial troops would once again die on the battlefield in northern Italy, although the territory they were defending would be given away whether they won or lost. Surely this was too high a price to pay for anyone's honour. Yet Franz Joseph permitted it, although in the event the military gamble was lost. Defeat at Sadowa meant that Austria was expelled from Germany and lost Venetia as well. Von Plener wrote in his diary even before the war had started that it would have been better to have sold Venetia to the Italians. He added: 'But in the highest circles it was considered high treason even to refer to it, and now it will cost 100,000 men and millions in money. Austria will be financially and economically ruined, and the result will still be the loss of Venetia.'[95] He apparently had a shrewder view of the capabilities of the Austrian army than had his Emperor.

The diplomacy of Rechberg and Mensdorff has led to an exchange between two of the historians who recently have been most interested in this period, namely Elrod and Derndarsky. Both are 'revisionists' in the sense that both believe that Austria in the 1850s and 1860s pursued a 'Metternichian' and European policy, for which she should receive due credit. Yet Elrod is obviously more 'revisionist' than Derndarsky: hence his defence of Rechberg which he states as follows:

Rechberg correctly perceived that Austria could not beat Cavour, Napoleon III and Bismarck at their own game; that, surrounded as she was by revisionist states, Austria could not solve her problems by becoming revisionist herself. But his own general policy of passivity and moderation and opposing all change in Italy and Germany was equally untenable. His belief that the other powers should, or could, persist in principles and policies that served Austria most of all and which merely increased unrest and tension in volatile areas of Central Europe was unwarranted and patently self-serving.

Yet it is sophistic to argue that the logical third choice was for Austria simply to give in voluntarily to irresistible change. The government in Vienna certainly had many chances to do so: a variety of offers for the cession or sale of Venetian or for a deal with Prussia in Germany were received. But as Rechberg, and later Mensdorff, perceived, most of these proposals were designed not to solve problems but to open the way to further demands. Moreover, most of them involved the certain danger of further embroiling Austria with the other powers (particularly with Russia in the Balkans) or of recognising the principle of nationalism.

In November, 1863, the Austrian ambassador in London, piqued by another British discourse on why Austria ought to cede Venetia to Italy, stated categorically that Austria would always prefer to lose a province by war than to give it away around a green table. Paradoxically, he was right. Even Lord Clarendon admitted during the Austro-Prussian denouement in 1866 that for the Austrians 'a disastrous war is better than voluntary disgrace'. The decision to fight in 1866 at least enabled Austria to exercise some control over the nature of the war and its outcome, even if she lost. The secret treaty with France on June 12 was designed not only to insure Napoleon's neutrality but also to control his Italian policy in order to guard against a nationalistic war with Italy and to commit the French emperor to a non-national solution in Germany (Silesia for Austria and a neutralised Rhenish zone). Finally, the nature of the German war itself, with the south German states (and others) fighting on Austria's side, played a similar role. It prevented the war from becoming one of nationalities.

Thus, the immediate outcome of the war was not unbearable for Austria, despite her expulsion from Germany. The empire was still independent, still a European power, and still a restraint on German power. All this was dramatically changed by the Franco-Prussian War. The creation of a powerful and nationalistic German empire transformed the European international system. Admittedly, Bismarck's general policies after 1871 sought to maintain European peace and stability. But in the long run even Bismarck's ingenuity could not disguise the fact that the German empire itself was a destabilising element in European politics.[96]

Derndarsky agrees that Austria had to fight; continued passivity would only have led to a European Congress and the loss of territory. He points out, however, that the secret treaty with France was not really *Realpolitik*, merely a response to Bismarck's treaty with Italy. Even then it was hardly ideal – Napoleon III would only offer neutrality, not military support. On the other hand, to argue that the German Empire which emerged after 1870 was in itself destabilising, says Derndarsky, 'appears to be untenable ex-post-fatalism which denies the multi-causality of history and openness in principle of its course'.[97] Both historians, however, appear to overlook a number of factors in their assessment of Austrian policy. To begin with, it is difficult to understand how Austria can be portrayed as a stabilizing factor in European diplomacy in the nineteenth century and an upholder of the European interest if she was correct always to reject diplomatic solutions to her problems. It was exactly this attitude which made people like Cavour and Bismarck necessary. Again, they fail to condemn the morality of allowing thousands of soldiers to die in Italy for a province which was due to be given away in any case. This was a manoeuvre whose cynicism easily matched anything that Bismarck or Cavour had been capable of. It was also a blunder in military terms – the troops could have been used in Bohemia. In the last resort, however, the real question at stake in Austria's refusal to compromise was neither diplomatic strategy nor military preparedness, but simply the Emperor's honour. This is why men had to die in Italy; this was why Benedek was given the (risky) Bohemian command rather than the Archduke Albrecht; and this was why he was pressured into fighting at Sadowa and treated so miserably afterwards by those responsible. Imperial honour demanded that no territory be surrendered without a fight; theories concerning European interests or principles as opposed to *Realpolitik* are merely excuses and rationalizations. And imperial honour, for those who died needlessly defending it, had no higher moral worth than *Realpolitik*. Derndarsky, finally, understates his case when cautioning Elrod against determinism. The fact is – and we shall return to it later in connection with Schroeder – that not only is it wrong to describe the German Empire after 1870 as in itself destabilizing; it also misses the point, which is that the destabilizing factor turned out to be Austria. For, having failed to retain the leadership of Germany and Italy, she was to attempt to recoup her prestige by seeking a predominant position in the Balkans. For most of the time this did not matter – *she* could be restrained by Germany. Yet in 1914, when this did not happen, the result was world war and the disappearance of the Monarchy – after yet another ultimatum and yet another refusal to compromise, this time with the south Slavs. Failure to compromise, therefore, had serious long- as well as short-term consequences. However, we shall return to this point later.

Just as the loss of Italian leadership had led to constitutional reform, so too did exclusion from Germany. Partly this was the natural price of failure; more specifically, the Monarchy found that nobody would lend it the money needed to repair its economy unless constitutional changes were made. The period 1860–6 was therefore a sort of continuous constitutional crisis. In the end it was to be resolved by the *Ausgleich* or Compromise with Hungary, a deal made in a great hurry between Franz Joseph and the Magyars. Before then, the Monarchy had graduated from the October Diploma of 1860, a federalist scheme devised by Magyar and Bohemian aristocrats, to the February Patent of 1861, which revised the former in a more centralist direction. The 1860 scheme had been an echo of Metternich's proposals of 1817 and only served to show how unworkable they would have been, since it was rejected by practically all the nationalities of the Monarchy, who had no reason to feel that their interests would be represented by a few aristocratic grandees meeting together in Vienna. The February Patent therefore turned the *Reichsrat* envisaged by the October Diploma into a central parliament – something more along the lines of the Stadion constitution of 1849. Predictably, however, this upset the Hungarians. Even before 1866, therefore, Franz Joseph began negotiations with Ferenc Deák, the acknowledged spokesman of Hungary. The latter insisted on the legality of the April Laws of 1848, but in practice was prepared to modify them with regard to finance, foreign affairs and defence. Yet it still took defeat at the hands of Prussia to convince the Emperor that a compromise was necessary, demonstrating that even in internal affairs the demands of honour had to be satisfied. At heart he was an absolutist who resented the need for parliaments, but now he had no choice. He therefore got two, albeit on very good terms.

NOTES AND REFERENCES

1. For these quotes, see Kenneth W. Rock (1975) Felix Schwarzenberg, military diplomat, *Austrian History Yearbook*, Vol. XI, pp. 85–109, pp. 86–7.
2. Rudolf Kiszling (1952) *Fürst Felix zu Schwarzenberg. Der politische Lehrmeister Kaiser Franz Josephs*. Graz and Cologne, p. 37.
3. *Ibid.*, p. 52.
4. C. A. Macartney, *The Habsburg Empire, 1790–1918*. London, p. 407.
5. Kiszling, *op. cit.*, p. 55.
6. Friedrich Walter (1965) Fürst Felix Schwarzenberg im Lichte seiner Innenpolitik, in *Virtute Fideque, Festschrift für Otto von Habsburg zum fünfzigsten Geburtstag*, pp. 180–9, p. 180.
7. *Ibid.*
8. *Ibid.*
9. *Ibid.*, pp. 180–1
10. *Ibid.*, p. 183.
11. *Ibid.*
12. *Ibid.*, p. 184.
13. *Ibid.*
14. *Ibid.*
15. *Ibid.*
16. *Ibid.*
17. Macartney, *op. cit.*, p. 417.
18. *Ibid.*, p. 422.
19. *Ibid.*, p. 418.
20. Redlich's opinion is stressed by A. Murad (1968) *Franz Joseph and His Empire*. New York, p. 130.
21. For example, Robert A. Kann (1974) *A History of the Habsburg Empire, 1526–1918*. London, p. 312: 'Reaction had destroyed a great opportunity.'
22. Macartney, *op. cit.*, p. 418.
23. *Ibid.*, p. 425.
24. Walter, *op. cit.*, p. 186.
25. *Ibid.*
26. Macartney, *op. cit.*, p. 453.
27. *Ibid.*, p. 451.
28. *Ibid.*, p. 456.
29. See, in particular, Roy A. Austensen (1977) Felix Schwarzenberg, 'Realpolitiker' or 'Metternichian'? The evidence of the Dresden Conference, in *Mitteilungen des Osterreichischen Staatsarchivs*, Vol. 30, pp. 97–118; but also (1973/4) Count Buol and the Metternich tradition *Austrian History Yearbook*, Vol. 9/10, pp. 173–93; and (1980) Austria and the 'Struggle for Supremacy in Germany', 1848–64 *Journal of Modern History*, Vol. 52, pp. 195–225.
30. Austensen, Felix Schwarzenberg etc., pp. 106–7.
31. Adolph Schwarzenberg (1946) *Prince Felix Schwarzenberg, Prime Minister of Austria, 1848–52*. New York, p. 167.

32. *Ibid.*, pp. 167–8.
33. H. Böhme (1971) *The Foundation of the German Empire*. Oxford, pp. 69–70.
34. *Ibid.*, p. 70.
35. Schwarzenberg, *op. cit.*, p. 69.
36. Thomas Francis Huertas (1977) *Economic Growth and Economic Policy in a Multinational Setting. The Habsburg Monarchy, 1841–1865*. Chicago, p. 30.
37. *Ibid.*, pp. 34–5.
38. *Ibid.*, p. 35.
39. *Ibid.*
40. C. A. Macartney (1978) *The House of Austria: The Later Phase, 1790–1918*. Edinburgh, p. 131.
41. Huertas, *op. cit.*, pp. 26–8.
42. Macartney, *The House of Austria*, p. 131.
43. David F. Good (1984) *The Economic Rise of the Habsburg Empire, 1750–1914*. Berkeley and Los Angeles, p. 78.
44. *Ibid.*, pp. 92–3.
45. John Komlos (1983) *The Habsburg Monarchy as a Customs Union, Economic Development in Austria-Hungary in the Nineteenth Century*. Guildford, p. 49.
46. *Ibid.*, pp. 50–1.
47. *Ibid.*, pp. 39–40.
48. Huertas, *op. cit.*, p. 19.
49. *Ibid.*, p. 20.
50. *Ibid.*, pp. 24–5.
51. Good, *op. cit.*, p. 81.
52. *Ibid.*, p. 82.
53. Quoted in *ibid.*, p. 85.
54. László Katus (1983) Transport revolution and economic growth in Hungary, in Komlos (ed.) *Economic Development etc.*, pp. 183–204.
55. Richard Rudolph (1983) Economic revolution in Austria? The meaning of 1848 in Austrian economic history, in John Komlos (ed.) *Economic Development in the Habsburg Monarchy in the Nineteenth Century Essays*, p. 169
56. Good, *op. cit.*, p. 84.
57. *Ibid.*, p. 85.
58. *Ibid.*, p. 86ff.
59. *Ibid.*, pp. 87–8.
60. Huertas, *op. cit.*, p. 36.
61. *Ibid.*, p. 40.
62. *Ibid.*, p. 45.
63. *Ibid.*
64. *Ibid.*, p. 48.
65. A. Milward and S. B. Saul (1977) *The Development of the Economies of Continental Europe, 1850–1914*. London, p. 296.
66. Huertas, *op. cit.*, p. 46. The obvious interaction between economic and foreign policy during the period 1854–70 is also highlighted by Peter Katzenstein (1976) *Disjoined Partners. Austria and Germany since 1815*. Berkeley, pp. 87–8, where he writes: 'Between 1848 and 1866 the

national debt trebled and most of it was raised in foreign money markets. . . . To finance a policy of armed neutrality during the Crimean War, the Austrian government was forced to sell the entire Austrian railway system at disadvantageous prices to foreign bankers, most of them French. State finances collapsed completely when the government tried to raise funds for the war with Piedmont in 1859. Only half a war bond issue was subscribed and even that small fraction only at a substantial discount. In the eyes of foreign financiers and bourgeoisie the government was no longer a going concern. . . . Austria's political elite in the end regarded foreign policy as a game of roulette.' Katzenstein points out that between 1858 and 1859, military expenditure declined by 12 per cent, between 1860 and 1863 by 34 per cent. Austria as a result became technologically backward in military terms, being unable to afford modern weapons. For greater detail see H–H. Brandt (1978) *Der österreichische Neoabsolutismus. Staatsfinanzen und Politik, 1848–1860*, 2 vols. Göttingen and Zurich.. Another interesting point made by Katzenstein is the following (p. 89): 'But the Austrian problem was not merely one of financial weakness. Government inefficiency also played an important role. In 1854 Austria's army was about 1.37 per cent of its total population, while the corresponding ratio for Prussia was only 0.77 per cent. On the other hand, Prussia spent almost twice as much as Austria on each man under arms, 209 thalers compared to Austria's 109. Yet at the same time Prussia was able to mobilise a much larger proportion of its total population. Its wartime army was numbered 428,000 men, or 2.59 per cent of the total population, and additional trained reserves were available which would have brought that figure up to about 800,000. Compared with Prussia, Austria was using a larger proportion of its resources for military purposes in peacetime, but was capable of mobilising a smaller proportion in the event of war.'

67. Paul W. Schroeder (1972) *Austria, Great Britain and the Crimean War. The Destruction of the European Concert*. Ithica and London, p. 413.
68. *Ibid.*, p. 415.
69. *Ibid.*, p. 416.
70. *Ibid.*, p. 418.
71. Austensen, Count Buol etc., p. 193.
72. Quoted in G. B. Henderson (1975) Crimean War diplomacy and other historical essays, *Glasgow University Publications, LXVIII*. New York, p. 187.
73. Norman Rich (1985) *Why the Crimean War? A Cautionary Tale*. Hanover and London, p. 120.
74. *Ibid.*, p. 123.
75. *Ibid.*, p. 13. Metternich, it should be noted, had also condemned Schwarzenberg's German policy at the time, another difficulty in the way of accepting Austensen's Metternichians as the real thing.
76. Henderson, *op. cit.*, p. 187.
77. Schroder, *op. cit.*, p. 395, note.
78. Bernhard Unckel (1969) Osterreich und der Krimkrieg, Studien zur Politik der Donaumonarchie in den Jahren 1852–1856, *Historische Studien*, 410. Lübeck and Hamburg.

79. William A. Jenks (1978) *Francis Joseph and the Italians, 1849–1859*. Charlottesville, p. 145.
80. *Ibid.*, p. 146.
81. Unckel, *op. cit.*, p. 282.
82. *Ibid.*, p. 140.
83. Quoted in Murad, *op. cit.*, p. 154.
84. István Deák (1984) Defeat at Solferino: the nationality question and the Habsburg Army in the War of 1859, in B. K. Király (ed.) The crucial decade: east central European society and national defense, 1859–70, *War and Society in East Central Europe*, Vol. XIV, pp. 496–515.
85. *Ibid.*, p. 511.
86. *Ibid.*, p. 497.
87. Austensen, Austria and the 'Struggle for Supremacy' in Germany etc., p. 224.
88. Quoted in Franco Valsecchi (1966) European diplomacy and the Expedition of the Thousand: the conservative powers, in Martin Gilbert (ed.) *A Century of Conflict, 1850–1950, Essays in Honour of A. J. P. Taylor*. London, pp. 60–1.
89. *Ibid.*
90. Richard B. Elrod (1984) Bernhard von Rechberg and the Metternichian tradition: the dilemma of conservative statescraft, *Journal of Modern History*, Vol. 56, pp. 430–55, p. 44.
91. *Ibid.*
92. *Ibid.*, pp. 450–1.
93. *Ibid.*, p. 449 (Elrod gives the quote in German).
94. M. Derndarsky (1982) Das Klischée von 'Ces messieurs de Vienne. . .' Der österreichisch-französische Geheimvertrag von 12 Juni 1866 – Symtom für die Unfähigkeit der österreichischen Aussenpolitik?, in *Historische Zeitschrift*, Vol. 235, pp. 289–353.
95. Quoted in Elrod, *op. cit.*, p. 452 n. 82.
96. Richard B. Elrod (1981–2) Realpolitik or Concert diplomacy: the debate over Austrian foreign policy in the 1860s with comments by M. Derndarsky, *Austrian History Yearbook*, Vol. 17/18, pp. 84–103, pp. 95–6.
97. Derndarsky's comments on Elrod, *Realpolitik or Concert Diplomacy*, p. 103.

CHAPTER FIVE

The Dual Monarchy

Most students appear to believe that the Habsburg Monarchy was 'in decline' between 1867 and 1914. The common view among them seems to be that in 1914 it was on the brink of 'collapse' and that the First World War merely brought about the inevitable. In fact, almost nobody inside the Monarchy was working for a republic during this period and practically no one wanted to see the Monarchy break up. Ironically, perhaps the most militant dissidents were the German nationalists led by von Schönerer, who advocated that Austria's Germans should break away and join the German Empire of the Hohenzollerns. It was only defeat in war, therefore, which was to precipitate collapse, and that defeat was not certain until the early summer of 1918. Even then, the Habsburg army went on fighting until the bitter end. However, had the Central Powers actually won the First World War, the Habsburg Monarchy would have survived not merely intact, but almost certainly expanded. This chapter, therefore, will not smack of any misplaced determinism. On the other hand, given the well-known weaknesses of the Dualist system, it will examine such themes as the place of Hungary within the Monarchy, the nationalities problem, economic growth, the emergence of new political and social forces, cultural pessimism and foreign policy problems before 1914, to see exactly what state the Habsburg Empire was in before it entered its final struggle.

THE COMPROMISE OF 1867

Let us begin by looking at the Compromise. Some historians prefer to use the word 'settlement', but if it was a settlement it was hardly a popular one. The Germans of the Monarchy soon came to detest it and many Hungarians also wanted to alter it. The other races of the Monarchy – quite properly – felt cheated by it. Yet it stuck in its essentials. The Magyar leadership refused to countenance any alternative that would leave them with less power. And since Franz Joseph was not prepared to concede them any more, the Compromise was to become the sheet-anchor of the Hungarian state. Nothing could be done which might undermine it. Its terms came to be set in concrete, and only the end of the Monarchy was to bring the end of the *Ausgleich*.

Most historians, like most contemporaries, have scarcely had a good word to say for the Compromise. Nor is it difficult to understand why. In the first place, it was an agreement made, not between the representatives of the various parts of the Monarchy, but between Franz Joseph and the Magyar leadership. Having reached this agreement, he then forced it on the 'Austrian half' of his domains, despite its unpopularity with most of his subjects there. Indeed, one leading Hungarian historian has recently suggested that it was not even popular with his Hungarian subjects. According to György Szabad, the Hungarian parliamentarians who drew it up had failed to address themselves 'to the questionable legality of the 1865 elections and [had] failed also to take into account the fact that the conditions of the proposed settlement were hardly known to the electors who had given [Deák's] party its parliamentary majority. For not a word had been said in the course of the 1865 elections about revising the 1848 laws to extend the sovereign's prerogatives, and even the section of the programme discussing joint affairs had not yet been published in Hungary.'[1] This, however, is a curious view, first since nearly all elections in Hungary in the nineteenth century were of 'questionable legality' and, secondly, because it is extremely doubtful whether Deák can in any way be accused of misleading the Hungarian electorate. In the words of László Péter: 'When parliament was convoked in the autumn, neither the electorate nor the elected could be in much doubt about the kind of constitutional settlement Deák had intended to secure. His principles were above board. It was all the more noteworthy, therefore, that in 1865–66 not a single Hungarian politician raised his voice against Deák's course. . . . The unity with which parliament expressed its wish to settle up with the crown in early 1866 was impressive. *Kiegyenlités* [settlement] did not yet have the pejorative connotation which, through its artless translation to "compromise", it has come to have since. . . . Deák's authority was immense; most deputies recognised his leadership, and parties as such did not yet exist.'[2]

With or without the support of the electorate, the Hungarian leadership had obviously seen the chance to strike an excellent bargain. Franz Joseph appears to have been a man in a hurry in 1866 and may never have read the fine print of the deal which had been worked out with the Hungarians. Certainly, the Hungarian law embodying the Compromise included important clauses which suggested that Hungary not only had the right to a separate army but also to a separate foreign policy. These clauses, it is true, were excluded from the Austrian law embodying the settlement, but this merely meant that the Monarchy was to be run on the basis of two fundamental laws which were textually different. Even worse, the assumptions underlying these laws were different. The Austrians assumed the existence of some sort of 'overall state' or *Oberstaat* called the 'Austrian Monarchy' to which the two 'halves' or *Reichshälfe* would be subordinated. Yet such an interpretation was totally alien from Hungarian constitutional thought, which was still anchored to the concept of a separate, constitutional Hungarian state which shared a ruler – or rather the person of a ruler – with the Austrians, and which had merely entered into certain specific constitutional arrangements with them. The Hungarians, in fact, did not care very much that the Austrian law was different. Their version of the Compromise had been accepted first; moreover, since its preamble had asserted that the Compromise should be an arrangement between constitutional governments in Austria and Hungary, Austrian constitutionalism was seen to be at least as dependent on Hungary as Hungarian constitutionalism was on Austria.

The Compromise, finally, left a number of hostages to fortune by decreeing that the so-called 'economic compromise' between Austria and Hungary should be renegotiated every decade. This arrangement covered not merely tariffs and trade but also the amount of money each country would contribute to the joint exchequer – the so-called Quota. Needless to say, these negotiations led to regular clashes between both 'halves' of the Monarchy. By 1895, therefore, Karl Lueger's views on the Compromise, as delivered to the Lower House of the Austrian parliament, represented those of the majority of Austrian Germans: 'I consider Dualism,' he said, 'as a misfortune, indeed as the greatest misfortune which my fatherland has ever had to suffer, a greater misfortune even than the wars we lost.'[3] The spokesmen of the nationalities would have added their agreement also. The Compromise of 1867 had surrendered them to the master races, despite all their efforts on behalf of the dynasty in 1848. Andrássy is supposed to have summed up their position in his notorious words to an Austrian colleague: 'You look after your Slavs and we'll look after ours.'[4]

The *Ausgleich* consequently has had new defenders. Its main one has been Macartney who, in an extremely interesting article on the subject, adopted the viewpoint that in the first place, everything else had been tried and, secondly, that for all its faults, the Compromise had lasted for half a century: 'The proof of the pudding . . . is in the eating and by that test, the Compromise, if not generally palatable, at any rate contained enough vitamins to support fifty million people for fifty years.'[5] Yet there are two objections to his defence: in the first place, despite the constitutional experiments of 1860–1, it is simply untrue – take Kremsier, for example, or even the Stadion constitution – to suggest that everything else had been tried; secondly, there is no reason to approve of poor – or occasionally even starvation diets – in history.

Nearly all non-Hungarian historians have argued that through the Compromise the Hungarians took control of the Monarchy. For whereas the Magyars proved able to keep their Slavs under control and displayed great solidarity when faced with encroachments by, or more often resistance from, Vienna, in Cisleithania, on the other hand – one of the names for the Austrian 'half' of the Monarchy – the bitter struggle between Germans and Czechs fatally undermined the bargaining strength of the Austrian government when it came to negotiating with the Hungarians. The result in the words of one Austro-American historian was that: 'Hungary in effect ruled and exploited the entire Monarchy. . . . With every ten year reviewal of the "Settlement", Hungarian demands became bolder. . . . If it had not been for the First World War, it is likely that Hungary would have become independent by the time of the renewal of the "Settlement" in 1917.'[6] A recent study by a distinguished Austrian historian has reached the same conclusion. Under Kálmán Tisza after 1875, it claims, Hungary changed the nature of Dualism: 'According to [Tisza's] formula, Hungary took the lead in the "Dual Monarchy" and the Magyars were masters in Hungary.'[7] The same historian points out that the fall of the Badeni government in Austria in 1897, an event which practically led to the suspension of parliamentary government there (see below), came about not least as a result of Badeni's efforts to secure Czech agreement for a renewal of the economic settlement with Hungary. The general point he makes, however, is this: 'Austrian internal politics in these years cannot be understood without the permanent pressure being exerted by

Hungary. Much of what was and is chalked up to Austrian governments was none other than one of the consequences of Dualism, none other than the insidious and ominous consequences of Dualism, none other than the notion of keeping the Hungarians in the system at any price.'[8] With the outbreak of the First World War, according to this historian, Hungarian predominance in all diplomatic and economic matters became 'unambiguous'.[9] Worst of all, Tisza [István] closed Hungary off from Austria completely, ruled it almost as a foreign country, and denied starving Austria essential food supplies.

Hungarian historians, on the other hand, have painted a rather different picture of Dualism. Péter Hanák, for example, has tried to show how the situation was more complex than Austrian versions would sometimes allow. He reminds us first of all that arrangements regarding Hungary under the Compromise fell into three groups, namely (a) purely internal matters in which, according to the *Ausgleich*, Hungary was independent, in which decisions were reached by the Hungarian government, were approved by the Hungarian parliament, and sanctioned by the Hungarian king; (b) the so-called *unpragmatic agreements* (i.e. those not stemming from the Pragmatic Sanction of 1723), arrangements which represented an 'agreement of interests' based on 'common principles', and which included the Quota and the tariff and trade agreements of the economic compromise; these were to be renegotiated by the governments of Austria and Hungary every decade, after which the approved formulae were to be submitted to the respective parliaments and to the sovereign. The final group of arrangements (c) were those stemming from the Pragmatic Sanction and handled by the common imperial–royal (later, imperial *and* royal) ministry. The constitutional position regarding these was quite unclear. For legally, the common ministry was simply responsible (to separate parliamentary delegations from Austria and Hungary) for those matters which did not belong to the governments of either 'half'. Moreover, the relations of the common ministers to those of Austria and Hungary were also unclear, the common Minister of Foreign Affairs, for example, being legally obliged 'to proceed only with the understanding and approval of both parts [of the Monarchy]'.[10] Common policies were supposed to be prepared by the common ministry, then presented to the separate delegations of both parliaments for a vote, after which they were to be presented to the monarch for approval. From all this then, it might be assumed that Hungary was independent regarding its own affairs and had achieved parity in joint ones. In practice, however, as Hanák points out, the system worked very differently. In domestic affairs, for a start, there were two important divergences from the legal model. The Hungarian government had to lay its proposals in the first instance, not before parliament, but before the king – and in accordance with a very precise formula (the preliminary sanction or *élozetes szentesítés*). The monarch, in other words, had a veto on legislation both before and after it was presented to parliament. This might be regarded as a feudal survival, rather than as a sign of Hungarian dependence, were it not for the fact that Franz Joseph felt it quite within his rights to discuss proposals of his governments with unofficial groups of courtiers, especially if such proposals might affect the Monarchy as a whole. These groups of courtiers included members of the imperial family, the aristocracy and the armed forces, who served the dynasty rather than either of the governments concerned. Hence, in this way, Franz Joseph could subordinate even Hungarian internal affairs to the needs of the Monarchy as a whole.

There was a similar divergence from the juridical model with regard to common matters. Policy here was not determined by negotiations between governments and parliaments, but between the monarch and the governments concerned. If a clash took place between monarch and government, in most cases the government had to defer or to depart. In cases of a clash between Austria and Hungary, the monarch once again decided the outcome. As far as the common ministers were concerned, policy was also arrived at by discussion between them and the sovereign. The role of the delegations was purely formal and only in matters of extreme importance could the constitutional influence of the Austrian and Hungarian premiers be brought to bear. Meanwhile, the soldiers and courtiers from whom the monarch sought advice continuously influenced decision-making. The monarch, therefore, in László Péter's words, served as the 'keystone of the political structure'.[11] He continues: 'The sovereign's control over the army – operating largely outside the constitutional–legal sphere – normally enabled Franz Joseph to retain a free hand in whatever directly affected the Monarchy as a great power: foreign policy, defence, and imperial finance. In the highest sphere of state policy Franz Joseph remained an autocrat even after 1867. He took decisions after taking advice from the *Ministerrat fur gemeinsam Angelegenheiten*, sometimes referred to as the Crown Council, an advisory rather than an executive body with uncertain membership and without formal constitutional status.'[12]

Paradoxically, this was a situation which satisfied many Hungarians. One member of their delegation, for example, declared in 1906: 'I recognise only common ministers, but no common government.'[13] Indeed, Péter argues that this had been Deák's intention in 1867. According to him: 'That government should "derive" from a parliamentary majority Deák and his supporters had considered to be a *sine qua non* of the re-establishment of constitutional life; but they did not expect that parliament would be given ultimate political control. Political responsibility was strictly dualistic: the government was expected to maintain the confidence of both monarch and parliament so that, as a modern Palatine, it could successfully mediate between the two sides [i.e. the king and parliament – not Austria and Hungary]. Deák and the "67-er" majorities after 1867 believed in a balanced constitution rather than in a parliamentary system of government.'[14] Péter also stresses the fact that the authority of the monarch was boosted by 'the intense loyalty almost invariably displayed towards the sovereign by the vast majority of his subjects'.[15] '*Kaisertreue* and *királyhüség*,' he adds, 'were, in the nineteenth century, powerful sentiments.' He notes too 'the daunting effect of the monarch's physical presence on politicians, and even more, on ordinary people',[16] before concluding that: 'The magic of the office (which Franz Joseph did his best to maintain by cultivating court etiquette with obsessive scrupulousness), in addition to the remarkably effective institutional *potestas* ensured that, for half a century, a more than sufficient degree of cooperation was forthcoming from the constituent parts of the union even in times of crisis.'[17] Hanák is surely correct, therefore, in maintaining that the picture of Dualism painted by Austrian historians, i.e. one of Hungary dominating the Monarchy, is in need of modification. Finally, there are two other points which Hanák would have us bear in mind. The first is that although Hungary exercised much influence in foreign policy – about 25–30 per cent of the diplomatic corps, not to mention at least three foreign ministers of the period, were Hungarian, all following a foreign policy which in fundamentals had been established by Andrássy – the Hungarians had no influence on the army. Indeed, this body was distinctly antipathetic towards the Hungarians and often appeared to act within Hungary as an army of occupation. It was an independent power within the Hungarian state and made Hungary dependent on the dynasty. Hanák's description of it as 'the Achilles' heel of Dualism' is well borne out by the many clashes which took place between Austria and Hungary over military affairs, not to mention the constitutional crisis of 1903–6, during which a detachment of troops (albeit Hungarian *honvéds*) expelled the deputies from the Hungarian parliament, and during which also the imperial army was given orders, albeit never executed, for an invasion and occupation of Hungary.

The final point which Hanak makes is that one should always remember the emotional factors involved. Thus no matter how well Hungary did out of Dualism – and we shall investigate this issue later on – Hungarian public opinion still considered Hungary to be oppressed. Conversely, however weak the Hungarian position may have been constitutionally, in many respects Austrian public opinion resented what it took to be the sinister and predominant role of Hungary within the Monarchy.

Let us now examine these issues a little more closely. Regarding military affairs, there can be no doubt that the Emperor and his leading military advisers were extremely reluctant in 1866–8 to sanction anything which might ultimately split the army. The Archduke Albert, in particular, was suspicious of all Hungarian plans for any kind of separate Hungarian military formations. Franz Joseph, however, anxious to reach a settlement with the Magyars, agreed relatively quickly to a number of proposals from Andrássy, Deák's right-hand man and Dualist Hungary's first prime minister, proposals which were designed to put an end to the dispute. The problem in 1867, according to Zoltán Szász, was 'how to cut the Habsburg Monarchy in two while leaving it in one piece'.[18] The same applied to the army, since Kálmán Tisza and others were arguing that the Pragmatic Sanction of 1723 required only a joint defence, not necessarily a united one. It was Andrássy who found the formula to negotiate this obstacle. In János Décsy's words, he was 'the right man at the right time for the right job'[19] and according to Gábor Vermes, it was his 'brilliant and forceful diplomacy' which solved the problem.[20] Essentially what happened was that the sovereign was left in command of the common imperial–royal army (Article 11 of the Compromise stipulated that 'in accordance with the constitutional prerogatives of the sovereign, all matters relating to the unified command, control, and internal organisation of the entire army, and also of the Hungarian army as an integral part of the entire army are recognised as being reserved for the disposition of His Majesty'.) although terms of service, quartering and financial support for the Hungarian regiments would be determined by the Hungarian parliament. The language of command of this army was to be German, something which applied to Hungarian as well as other regiments. (Andrássy, who attempted to negotiate Hungarian as the language of command for Hungarian regiments, was informed that Hungarians comprised over 14 per cent of only fourteen out of sixty-four infantry regiments, and less than 10–12 per cent in *Jäger*, artillery, engineer and signal formations; in fact, only the fourteen hussar regiments were 80–100 per cent Hungarian-speaking.) On the other hand, Andrássy did persuade Franz Joseph to agree to the establishment of home defence forces in Austria and Hungary (also Croatia), the Hungarian one being christened, naturally enough, the *Honvédség*. This was to be patterned after the joint army in organizations and uniforms, but was to be authorized to employ distinctive insignia and flags, and would use Hungarian as the language of command. Its oath of allegiance was to be to the king and to the national constitution. Andrássy saw the *Honvédség* as an embryonic national army but, precisely to prevent this happening, Franz Joseph refused to allow it to have an artillery of its own. The monarch also insisted on appointing its commander-in-chief and ultimately controlled the issue of its commissions. In the final analysis, however, it was simply too small to challenge the imperial army: in 1870 there were only about 10,000 regular troops in it. According to Szasz: 'a battalion would contain a mere twenty-one to twenty-six men, sometimes even insufficient to mount a proper guard. Military bands were not allowed until the millenium celebrations of 1896, in part because it was feared that the band would outnumber the soldiers in any march it was leading.'[21]

Andrássy, however, realized that this was the best deal he was likely to get. In Rothenberg's words: '. . . always a political realist, [he] decided that he had reached the limit of the concessions immediately available, and, in order not to jeopardise the political settlement that had given Hungary complete parity within the Dual Monarchy, he rammed the military settlement through Parliament. However, and this was an ominous portent of things to come, in order to quiet the vehement objections of the opposition he had to promise that the government would continue to pursue greater military autonomy with all available means.'[22] The opposition, however, was never satisfied, and as the main weapon in its struggle for a more national army employed the parliamentary obstruction of army bills which came up for discussion every ten years. For example, the debate over the 1889 bill was extremely bitter and brought a statement from the ageing Andrássy, now elevated to the Upper House, that there had never been any thought of a separate army for Hungary in 1867. Concessions had to be made, none the less, to get the bill through, including the famous change by which the joint army became known as the imperial *and* royal, instead of simply the imperial–royal one (k.u.k. instead of k.k. in German). Then in 1898, when the joint ministry asked for a modest increase in troops, parliamentary obstruction was used once again, this time in conjunction with rioting, a situation which lasted for eight years. In the end the *Honvédség* at last received its precious artillery, but not before the dispute had provoked both Franz Joseph's famous order of the day from Chlopy on 17 September 1903 which reaffirmed his intention to maintain a united army, and the near implementation of plan-U, authorizing the military occupation of Hungary. Despite the bitterness of these quarrels, however, the *Honvédség* and the imperial army managed to cooperate smoothly both before 1914 and during the First World War itself. Certainly, Hungarian troops of both services distinguished themselves right up until the end. It has been suggested therefore that with a little bit more flexibility, the whole quarrel might easily have been avoided, a viewpoint which has been disputed by Gunther Rothenberg, today perhaps the most distinguished of all the military historians of the Monarchy. Commenting on the doubts expressed by one Austrian general whether 'the gallant Hungarians who since the days of Maria Theresa had worn special uniforms, braids and tight pants, really would have changed if they had displayed the national emblem instead of the double eagle on their helmets',[23] he insists that: 'The main issue, however, was the language question and this could not be solved. . . . To retain their dominant status within their own kingdom, the Hungarians needed the Hungarian language of command; to grant this would have meant the division of the army, something which no Habsburg loyalist could concede. Thus the settlement of the military issue was doomed from the start.'[24] Why did the Hungarians make such a fuss? The issue of jobs for the ruling gentry class appears to be a red herring. Although only 27 per cent of army officers in 1902 were from Hungary – and less than half of these were Magyar – there were even fewer scions of the gentry employed as officers in the *Honvédség*, where language of course was not a problem. The issue of the nationalities is also often raised in the context of the army problem. Yet the one demand which was never made in the Hungarian parliament was to change the *regimental language* of all regiments raised in Hungary to Magyar, despite the fact that this would have been by far the most effective way of magyarizing non-Magyar recruits. After the turn of the century, most Hungarian politicians in fact were willing to settle for the introduction of Magyar as the language of command in all

Hungarian regiments. 'Yet nobody thought,' writes Lászlo Péter, 'that the seventy-odd words and phrases drilled into Romanian and Slovak recruits would magyarise them, just as the existing language of command did not germanise them or the Magyars.'[25] The struggle over the army issue, therefore, cannot really be seen solely as a by-product of nationalism or the nationality question. At heart it was probably a constitutional one in the stricter sense of the term. For given that the Dualist system was dependent on the monarch; given that elections were managed by the government and lacked legitimacy in the eyes of the opposition; and given the weight attached by Hungarians to formality and tradition (they were often surprised that English gentlemen lacked uniforms), it became almost inevitable that the tradition of bargaining with the Crown to secure concessions would be exploited by the opposition before it would allow the army bills and other aspects of the Compromise, which had to be renegotiated periodically, to go through parliament. This was its principal means of reminding the monarch (and the nationalities too in an indirect way) of the continuing importance of the nation and of its essential place within the constitution. The fact that foreign policy problems had abated at the turn of the century (also perhaps that there had been a temporary economic downturn) may well have affected the timing of the disputes. Was the quarrel therefore really a serious one? Is Rothenberg correct in dismissing the view that a little more flexibility could have solved it easily? Norman Stone has written that: 'The crisis of 1905–6 had been largely histrionic, a mock-up of 1848 rather than an anticipation of 1918.'[26] In the same article, however, he writes that 'the eighty words of simple German involved a crisis which called in question the very existence of the Habsburg Monarchy' and reminds us that another dispute in 1911–12, again over the army, had much more serious implications at the time of the Balkan Wars. This was why István Tisza, Hungarian prime minister at the time, resorted to force to clear the obstructionists from the chamber. Stone continues: 'An army bill finally became law, although its effects came too late. If in 1914 the Austro-Hungarian army suffered great casualties and was ill-trained and ill-equipped, much of the blame lies on Hungary.'[27] Perhaps one might conclude, therefore, that while many of the issues involved in the debate over the army were not in themselves of life and death importance, their exploitation by Hungarian politicians as a means of asserting parliament's and the nation's rights within the constitution did, in fact, have consequences which were ultimately serious.

THE ECONOMICS OF DUALISM

Let us now turn to economics. What were the economic consequences of Dualism for Hungary and the Monarchy? Traditionally, the picture which has been painted has been a rather pessimistic one. Until the mid-1950s, Hungarian historians believed that Hungary had been a sort of Austrian colony under Dualism, a viewpoint with a long pedigree. Oszkár Jászi, for example, described the role of Austro-German capital as 'an economic tyranny which hindered progress in the Hungarian, Slav and Romanian territories of the monarchy and . . . obstructed the well-being of the population'.[28] Other historians have pointed to the fact that geographically the Monarchy made little economic sense: Bohemia was connected through her rivers with the economy of Germany; Galicia and the Bukovina were cut off from the rest of the Monarchy by mountains; Vorarlberg was connected to the textile-producing region of Switzerland and Swabia; the Monarchy lacked any river route to her main Adriatic ports; the Danube was extremely difficult to navigate; and two-thirds of the Monarchy was covered by hills and mountains. Finally, there is the argument that the political and economic uncertainty engendered by quarrels over the renewal of the economic and military terms of the Compromise did nothing to inspire confidence in the dual state. Yet today, the picture drawn by historians of almost all colours is basically a very positive one – hence the title of David F. Good's recent book, *The Economic Rise of the Habsburg Empire, 1750–1914*. This new picture stresses both the increasing economic unity of the Monarchy before 1914 and the advantages gained from it by both halves, but particularly by Hungary. As far as economic unity is concerned, Good lays emphasis on the development of rail networks, the expansion of the banking and credit system, and increasing regional market integration. By the First World War, for example, even the outlying regions of Hungary possessed sizeable rail networks – 96 and 82 kilometres per 100,000 people in Transylvania and Croatia-Slavonia respectively in 1910. Such levels, according to Good, compared favourably with those in the more developed regions of the Austrian lands and exceeded by a wide margin those prevailing in the independent Balkan states of Romania, Bulgaria and Serbia (49, 42 and 31 kilometres per 100,000 respectively).[29] Overall his verdict is the following: 'The quantitative evidence supports those who stress the more positive achievements of the Habsburg economic union. Judged in economic terms the Empire experienced substantial market integration in the decades before World War I. The evolution of extensive communication and financial networks broke down the barriers separating the local and regional markets of the sprawling multinational realm. The late nineteenth century was a period of increased interregional exchange of commodities as well as financial and human capital. Associated with these exchanges was a significant trend towards the equalization of commodity prices, interest rates, and wage rates on a regional level. Economic integration was under way.'[30] These points are reinforced by Good with international comparisons. For example, he shows that there was more variation in regional wheat prices in India than in Austria-Hungary; more regional differentiation in interest rates in the USA and Japan. Likewise, there was less regional variation within the Monarchy with regard to per capita income than in Italy or Sweden; in fact, Austria-Hungary was around the European average according to this index. Good reinforces these conclusions by a more detailed comparison between the economies of Austria-Hungary and the USA – an interesting exercise since the one is usually held to be an economic mess and the other an economic paradigm in the nineteenth century. In fact the parallels are quite remarkable. Both had significant regional cleavages – North/South in the USA, East/West in the Habsburg Monarchy – both of which pertained to differing social systems in the first half of the century – slavery in the American South, serfdom in the East of the Monarchy on a scale much greater than elsewhere; both also contained differing political systems, both of which were to be affected by the legacies of civil war. In any case, a comparison of the two economies reveals that while both countries experienced uneven development in the first two-thirds of the century, regional differences narrowed afterwards in the Monarchy but widened in the USA. All in all, therefore, Good appears to make his case that the Monarchy was bringing economic benefits to all its constituent parts before 1914 (even if there was less development in Galicia and the Bukovina than elsewhere).

How much growth was there and how well did the Monarchy compare internationally in terms of economic growth? According to one set of estimates, the Austrian economy grew between 1870 and 1913 at an average rate of 1.32 per cent. 'This put it among the leaders of the late nineteenth century growth league. Among the earlier developers it was matched only by Germany and among latecomers only by Sweden and Denmark.'[31] After 1871 the Hungarian lands grew at an even faster rate – about 1.7 per cent. 'Taken together, the impressive performance of Austria after 1870 and the faster growth rate in Hungary imply that the Empire's relative backwardness was less severe in 1913 than it was in 1870.'[32] Yet over the nineteenth century as a whole, the Monarchy's relative economic backwardness appears to have increased. Good's verdict is: 'Even though the western regions of the Empire more or less kept up with western European contemporaries throughout the nineteenth century, the relative economic backwardness of the Empire as a whole, probably intensified between the Napoleonic Wars and World War I. By the 1870s sustained growth had spread into the Hungarian lands. It is unlikely, however, that the Empire was unable to grow fast enough to close the gap that had widened so long as the eastern territories had not been attached to the growth process.'[33]

Good's belief that the Monarchy proved to be economically beneficial to all of its parts is shared by many other economic historians, especially those concerned with Hungary. John Komlos, for example, in his recent study of Habsburg economic development,[34] maintains that 'the Austrian economy . . . could have done as well without its Hungarian partner'.[35] In other words, Hungary exploited Austria rather than vice versa. Komlos's conclusion is that 'Hungary was not exploited economically by Austria; instead, she derived considerable benefits from her special ties to the Austrian economy. Austria provided a reliable market for her agricultural products and was more importantly even, an indispensable source of capital and skilled labour. Hungary gained much more than Austria did from the "marriage of textiles and wheat". These advantages were to a large extent instrumental in the mobilization of both agricultural and industrial sectors of Hungary. This overall pattern is perhaps to be expected as a smaller economy, especially one located geographically as inconveniently as Hungary, can stand to gain more from such ties than a larger, more advanced economy. (Austria, even at the end of our period, produced twice the value of goods and services as the Hungarian economy, and 44 per cent more even on a per capita basis.)'[36] Hungary, however, in Komlos's opinion had positively retarded Austrian economic growth in the nineteenth century. Beginning in the late 1870s, her governments had begun to issue state securities profusely; more than half of these were bought by Austrian capitalists until the 1890s. In fact, Hungary's operations on the open market in Austria allowed her to finance social overhead capital at home without diverting funds away from private investment or resorting to excessively high taxation. The result was that government expenditure and investment could grow faster than tax revenue during periods of high economic growth or, in other words, disposable income and therefore consumption could be boosted by Hungary's unencumbered access to the Austrian capital market. According to Komlos: 'The upshot of these developments was that beginning in 1878 industrial production advanced significantly in Hungary for the first time in widely diffused sectors of the economy led by flour production. Consequently in Hungary the symptoms of the "great depression" were essentially absent. In Austria, on the other hand, the diminished stock of venture capital had a negative impact on industrial production until the 1890s. By attracting large amounts of Austrian capital, the Hungarian economy was therefore influential in prolonging the depression in Austria.'[37] Elsewhere in his book, Komlos says that in the late nineteenth century 'Hungary was somewhat of a burden in that it drained the Austrian capital market of funds needed by Austrian industry'.[38]

Hungarian economic historians, needless to say, do not share this view. Péter Hanák in a paper given in 1981 and revised for publication in 1982 on Hungary's contribution to the Monarchy, argued that the Compromise 'contributed greatly to the economic prosperity of the Monarchy'[39] and that 'there were both mutual advantages and disadvantages in the trade between the complementary economies of the two countries'.[40] His case is that political consolidation promoted investments, secured international creditworthiness and stimulated the exploitation of Hungary's natural resources. But 'no less significant'[41] was Hungary's yearly contribution of 58 million crowns to the repayment of the interest on the state debt from 1867. (She also undertook the amortization of 1.4 billion crowns in 1908.) With regard to capital movements, Hanák writes that: 'Hungary provided a secure market for both the direct and indirect export of Austrian capital, and this was not merely a consequence of common statehood or the guarantee of interests for railway construction, but was also the result of the tight *link* between the banking systems and commerce of the two countries. Austrian capital placed in Hungary during this period amounted to some 3 billion crowns, which proved to be a fruitful investment for *both* parties.'[42] Finally, he argues that Hungary took an increasing share of Austrian goods as the century wore on and in particular became 'indispensable for Austria, whose industrial products hardly competed with those of Western Europe'.[43] This, he says, can be proved from the fact that, apart from textiles, Austria sold her inferior quality industrial products to Hungary, while selling her better wares in Western markets. Hanák's paper has come under severe criticism from another leading economic historian of the Monarchy, Scott M. Eddie.[44] The latter agrees with Hanák's fundamental conclusion but disputes many of his statistics and arguments (including some over tariffs which I have not mentioned). For example, Hungary did not take an increasing share of Austrian goods as the century wore on; according to Eddie, her share remained fairly steady. One surprising criticism made by him, however, is that Hanák omits altogether what is 'arguably [Hungary's] greatest contribution to overall prosperity in the Monarchy', namely her agricultural exports abroad. He writes: 'Without Hungarian agricultural exports outside of the Monarchy, Austria could not have financed her massive imports, particularly of fibres and textiles, on which much of her industrial activity was based. While common knowledge among historians of this period, a look at figures for net exports and net imports makes this contention strikingly clear. . . . Hungary's agricultural net exports not only covered the entire net export of the Monarchy in those categories, they covered Austria's import surplus as well. This, therefore, has to be a prime candidate for Hungary's principal contribution to the economy as well.'[45] It would seem, therefore, that Komlos has perhaps been too hasty in his assertion that Austria could have developed as quickly without Hungary, and that the consensus which now operates among economic historians of the Monarchy, namely that both Austria and Hungary profited economically from the *Ausgleich*, can still be supported.

A BACKWARD HUNGARY?

This picture of the Monarchy during the later nineteenth century as one which was growing relatively fast and becoming increasingly economically integrated enables us to examine the work of the political sociologist Andrew János with a degree of confidence. In some fascinating recent work,[46] he has put forward a number of controversial views on Hungary during the Compromise era. In particular, his reassessment of the nationalities problem will have to concern us. Yet his basic assumption is one that forces us to review both the economics and politics of Dualist Hungary, namely that '. . . during the period under consideration Hungary was a backward country located at the periphery of the world system and labouring under the same material and psychological handicaps as are today's emerging nations in the so-called Third World'.[47] This is an insight which he hopes can be used 'to develop a generalised concept of peripheral politics', although his work in fact turns out to be more or less a socio-political history of Hungary, concentrating on the Dualist era.

János is a scholar of impressive erudition, yet his work is open to a number of criticisms. For a start, his generalizations are not convincing. One cannot really accept that there has been such a thing as a 'Western historical experience'. Or if one must, it is surely something which relates to parliamentary government, the rule of law and the values of Christianity and the Enlightenment. But these are all matters which make Hungary an integral part of the Western tradition rather than a 'backward country located on the periphery'. It may be true that Hungary was not a model democracy under Dualism, but there were no model democracies in Europe at that time. As things were, Hungary's rulers were committed to parliamentary government under the rule of law and operated on a franchise which was not so out of line with other European states. For example, it has been estimated that whereas 6.3 per cent of the population in Hungary had the right to vote in 1890, the percentage in Austria was 7.2, in Italy 9.1, in the Netherlands 6.5, in Norway 9.8, in Sweden 6, in Belgium 2.2, and in the UK 16. True, percentages elsewhere were higher – 29 in France, 21 in Germany, 24 in Spain and 22 in Switzerland – but this merely highlights the difficulties involved in talking of a common Western experience. What did this amount to in the nineteenth century? Germany and Italy had to endure wars of unification; France experienced every sort of régime from revolutionary republicanism to military caesarism, to constitutional monarchy, to moderate republicanism; Britain meanwhile consolidated her constitutional monarchy; while finally, Germany constructed a different form of government again after 1871. If the common factor is supposed to be the accountability of governments, or the rule of law, then once again it is difficult to see where Hungary is so out of line. János himself provides evidence to show that the courts were free, the press was free and that (outside of areas inhabited by the nationalities) elections were free. Prime ministers who did not regularly consult their backbenchers lost power; the High Court freed one deputy who tried to shoot one prime minister, and backed another who had accused a second premier of fraud (the premier resigned). The same court regularly disputed election results in government constituencies, while newspapers were allowed to flourish everywhere, including socialist ones which referred to ministers as 'pigs' and 'criminals'. In fact, the liberal and parliamentary tradition in Hungary, which had been strong enough to resist Joseph II, Metternich and Franz Joseph, would also prove strong enough to resist Gömbös and Imrédy between the world wars, so that right up until 1944, as János admits, an effective parliamentary opposition and free press could survive under Horthy. Indeed, Hungary was even able to protect her Jewish population until 1944, something which the presumably less 'backward' French did not bother to do. It is difficult therefore to see why János should insist that her history is akin to those of Third World countries, which themselves have remarkably varied pasts, but most of which are not renowned for responsible government or the rule of law.

János might object that his generalizations are really meant to apply to economic and social history. Yet here again there are difficulties with definitions. He talks about the core and the periphery of Western Europe, for example, without ever making it clear whether the core in question includes the whole of France and Germany or not. This may be because he is attempting to overcome the difficulty (either surreptitiously or subconsciously) that economically advanced and backward regions existed within different European states at the same time. In other words, there were economically less developed regions in nearly all the leading states – Ireland or the Scottish Highlands within the UK, for example, or the Mezzogiorno in Italy, or the large areas of rural France and Germany which coexisted with new industrial towns. Almost everywhere in Europe, in fact, core and periphery could be found together existing within single states. Yet János never faces up to this problem and fails to see that Hungary might be better tackled from this perspective, one which, once again, would keep her within the Western tradition. David F. Good's work on economic integration within the Monarchy demonstrates the greater value of this approach.

Still on the level of what has been called 'meta-history', however, János argues that Hungary's 'backwardness' accounts for important elements in her social and political structure which again cut her off from the West. His thesis is that, lacking any entrepreneurial class, Hungary had to use the state to industrialize. In other words, the state was created before the economy, the 'reversal' of the 'normal' procedure in the West.[48] This approach is derived, one suspects, from the work of Alexander Gerschenkron[49] who argued that backward economies required the stimulation of central state banks (or cartels operating as the hand-maidens of banks) to catch up with the West. Gerschenkron's own work, however, has recently come under criticism from scholars who point out, first, that there was a re-organization of industrial management and structures throughout Europe in the late nineteenth century – in order words, that the resort to banks and cartels was not something restricted to relatively backward areas – and, secondly, in David Good's words that 'in terms of the development of modern technology, the distinction between advanced and backward areas is not particularly useful. Follower countries did not simply borrow already existing technology – they were often in the vanguard of the technological developments that supported the late nineteenth-century organizational revolution. German advances in chemicals and American advances in agriculture and food processing come easily to mind.'[50]

János, however, is less concerned with economics than with social structures. His argument that Hungary's development was the opposite of the West's – i.e. that the state was created before the economy – is supported, he believes, by the view that in Hungary a backward and declining gentry class created an inflated bureaucratic state for self-employment, leaving the Jews to dominate the economy. Hungary, therefore, should be seen as a developing country where a powerful native ruling class employed 'pariah entrepreneurs' to run the commerce which it itself disdained to manage. There is certainly something in this – as, indeed, there is something in all of János's arguments – yet once again there is exaggeration and an unwarranted assumption that matters had developed very differently in the 'West'. Just how true is it that economies there developed before states? Might it not be argued that the French state was essentially the creation of Napoleon I, whereas the French economy as such did not emerge until the rule of Napoleon III? If Eugen Weber is to be believed, it was the French state which was still responsible for turning 'peasants into Frenchmen' at the turn of the twentieth century.[51] And what of Great Britain? Her industrialization was indeed largely financed by independent entrepreneurs, but she had found it necessary to establish a Bank of England as early as 1694. Nor should one overlook the role of the Dissenters in her industrial revolution since they may well be held to have constituted a group of 'pariah entrepreneurs' comparable to the Jews in Hungary. János, finally, seems unaware of the debate concerning the role of the English establishment in the 'decline of Britain'. It too has been accused of being socially and culturally hostile to industry and opposed to the industrial spirit. The equivalent of his declining gentry class with its disdain for commerce therefore is by no means absent in the historiography of nineteenth-century England.[52] Perhaps more surprisingly, János can also be accused of overlooking the role of bureaucracies in the developed parts of Europe. Austria and Prussia in the nineteenth century were of course famous for their *Beamten*. France, however, also relied upon her bureaucrats, and prefects were under no illusion but that their job was to execute the will of Paris. In this respect it is quite interesting to compare Napoleon III and István Tisza. Both men controlled large bureaucracies of police forces and officials; both encouraged the growth of industry; both used the language of contemporary progressives; both were associated with the rise of capitalists and financiers; but Tisza was more committed than Napoleon III to a *Rechtstaat*, whereas Napoleon III introduced universal male suffrage. Great Britain, of course, never had a large bureaucracy – at least at home. Yet there is an important factor not to be overlooked here, namely that parts of the British ruling class exploited the state for their employment too, as colonial administrators and soldiers. If Bright could describe the diplomatic service as 'outdoor relief for the aristocracy', János should consider how much more relief the British Empire provided in terms of colonial governors, district commissioners, police and army officers and all the rest. One final point about the bureaucracy in Hungary is that it was not corrupt: it was well paid and kept its hands clean, as János admits. This is hardly a characteristic of officials in today's Third World – but it was said to be true of the bureaucrats of Germany, Austria and other parts of Europe in the nineteenth century.

The question of the Jews gives rise to a number of thoughts, some of which will be revealed later. First of all, they did not simply constitute a 'pariah class'. True, society liked them to convert before they became completely acceptable, but it is misleading to suggest that they were not integrated into society or that they were restricted to commerce. As János shows, they had a large stake in agriculture, the professions, the labour movement and even landholding itself. Tisza himself opened the bureaucracy and the ruling party to them; he ennobled them in hundreds; they sat in the House of Lords and in the cabinet; prime ministers and peers married them. Their position was not akin therefore to, say, Asians in modern East and South Africa. On the contrary, they enjoyed imperial and governmental protection. And this brings us to another criticism of János, namely that he overlooks factors in Hungarian history which certainly help make it unique, but which do not cut it off from that of the West.

One factor (which has already been mentioned) is the role of Hungary's parliamentary tradition. Another is the influence exercised on her by the superior power of neighbouring countries. Her domination by Austria is clear enough. Before 1848, the Diet could only meet when summoned by the Emperor-King. Then, in 1849, an independent Hungary was defeated by an Austrian army under Haynau. Between 1849 and 1867 she was ruled from Vienna and, even under the *Ausgleich*, Franz Joseph and his closest advisers determined foreign and defence policy. (The same pattern of foreign domination was to continue after 1918. By the Treaty of Trianon of 1920, Hungary was deprived by the Allies of more than two-thirds of her previous population and territory and in the same year was invaded by Romania. Between 1933 and 1944 she came under pressure from Berlin, leading to her occupation by the Nazis in 1944 and in 1945 by the Soviets, who in 1956 also crushed a bid for independence.) If all this is taken for granted by János, he is guilty of a mistake, because Hungary's insecurity about her national independence meant that she would not allow it to be risked by granting equal rights to the nationalities within her boundaries – the Slovaks, the Romanians, the Serbs and the Croats. János, however, deliberately underplays the significance of the nationality question in his writings in favour of the socio-political consequences of economic backwardness. In this he is always interesting but, finally, unconvincing. It was, after all, the nationality problem which divided, if not defeated, the nation in 1848–9; it was the nationality problem which was at the heart of the Tisza system – jobs for Magyar boys, not to mention 120 'safe' government seats in the Slovak and Romanian counties; again, it was the fact that the Jews could be assimilated which brought them government protection, since it was the large numbers of assimilated Jews which gave the Magyars their majority in Hungary; finally, it was the existence of the nationalities which deprived the vast majority of Hungarians of votes – a paradoxical situation. Still, to have given everyone a vote would have meant bringing huge numbers of Slovak and Romanian deputies into parliament, not to mention socialists and other opponents of the government. The nationality question, therefore, can explain a great deal of the phenomena in which János is interested, a great deal more easily than spurious parallels with the Third World.

THE NATIONALITY PROBLEM IN HUNGARY

The nationality problem has to be considered in more detail, however, since many people believe it to have been responsible for the downfall of the Monarchy, a view made popular perhaps by the writings of R. W. Seton-Watson more than anybody else.[53] The popular view seems to be that by alienating the south Slavs in particular, the Hungarians drove them into the arms of the Serbs, thus forcing the Monarchy into the desperate and suicidal stratagem of its ultimatum to Serbia in 1914. How true is this picture? Before a final judgement can be reached, we shall have to examine both how the Magyars treated the nationalities and to what extent their reaction was one of alienation from the dynasty. For it certainly cannot be assumed that, merely because some student radicals assassinated an Archduke in 1914, they automatically enjoyed the support of a majority of south Slavs – within or even without the Monarchy.

Two points have to be explained before we can begin our examination on these issues: the Compromise between Hungary and Croatia (the so-called *Nagodba*) of 1868 and the Nationalities Law of the same year. The first was more or less a miniature version of the *Ausgleich* between Austria and Hungary, that is to say Croatia, while forming 'one and the same state complex' with Hungary, retained her own Diet for internal affairs and was represented in the Hungarian delegations with respect to 'pragmatic' ones. When the latter came up for discussion in the Hungaran parliament, Croat deputies (up to forty in number) were allowed to attend and to speak in Croat. A Croat Minister without Portfolio meanwhile represented Croatia's interests in these fields in the same parliament. All other questions were decided by the Croatian Diet alone, which was also allowed to spend 45 per cent of the revenues collected in Croatia. In Macartney's words, however: 'the value of her independence was reduced by the fact that the Ban, who was the head of the Croat "autonomous provincial government", was, while responsible to the Croat Diet, yet appointed by the Crown on the proposal of the Hungarian Minister President.'[54] The official language in Croatia was solely Croat.

The Nationalities Law of 1868 was a rather liberal document whose preamble, which had been drafted by Eötvös and revised by Deák, ran:

> Whereas, according also to the basic principles of the constitution, all citizens of Hungary form, politically, one nation, the indivisible, unitary

Hungarian nation (*nemzet*), of which every citizen of the country, whatever his personal nationality (*nemzetiség*) is a member equal in rights:

And whereas this equality of rights can be qualified by special provisions only in respect of the official use of the different languages current in the country, and that only so far as is necessitated by the unity of the country, the practical possibilities of government and administration and the claims of the administration of strict justice, while in every other respect the complete equality of rights of all citizens remains intact: the following rules will serve as guidance in respect of the official use of the various languages.[55]

This meant that whereas the language of state, including that of parliament and university, was Hungarian, 'ample provision was made for the use of non-Magyar languages on all levels, from the Counties downward, in administration, justice and education, while the use of them in private life was entirely free'.[56] Eötvös, in fact, had viewed Hungarian as the language of merely one other *nemzetiség* within the territory of the historic, collective *nemzet*. But this was a point of view which was not shared by his fellow Magyars. Instead of providing a solid basis for a liberal nationality policy, therefore, the 1868 Law, as is well known, came to be applied in such a way as to constitute an instrument of magyarization.

This policy was reflected from the 1880s in a variety of spheres: education policy; electoral law; cultural policy; the press; political trials; and public administration. It was motivated by a sense of cultural superiority, a civilizing mission and a belief that Hungary's role in international affairs was to use the Monarchy to maintain a balance of power in Central Europe and to resist Russian or German hegemony. In practical terms, this meant the following: the Education Laws of 1879, 1883, 1891 and 1907, which together made Magyar obligatory in all state and confessional schools (including kindergarten), which laid down that all teachers had to be fluent in the language, which declared that teachers should not be hostile to the state, and which finally decreed levels of salaries for teachers so high that only the state could pay (and therefore control) them.[57] These laws also laid down that more and more subjects should be taught only in Magyar and across wider and wider levels. Electoral restrictions were also used to further the Magyar cause. Thus the franchise, given to roughly 10 per cent of the population in 1848, was restricted to about 6 per cent under Dualism. The Magyars, themselves, needless to say were massively over-represented even within this small electorate, taking over 90 per cent of parliamentary seats. Hence although Romanians, Slovaks and Serbs made up a majority in over 100 Hungarian constituencies, they never secured more than between five and twenty-five seats in parliament – less than 10 per cent. The government also sought to control the press, first by demanding that high deposits should be made before permission could be granted to found a newspaper and, secondly, by using laws of 1878 which forbade anyone to incite any class of the population, any nationality or any religious community against another. Offenders could be punished with fines or put in jail. In this way, not only newspapermen but politicians could be harassed. For example, the Serb deputy in the Hungarian parliament, Svetozar Miletič, was jailed as early as the 1870s, despite his parliamentary immunity. Then in 1892, after students and other Romanian nationalists had signed a petition of grievances to Franz Joseph, the Hungarian government instituted charges against a number of the signatories, who were found guilty by the courts, despite an international outcry. (Franz Joseph himself declined to receive the petition.) The Slovaks, of course, fared no better. The priest Andrej Hlinka, for example, was put on trial in 1906 for supporting the Slovak National Party at an election and condemned to two years' imprisonment. He was also suspended as a priest by his local bishop. However, his parishioners rioted when he was not allowed to dedicate their new church, leading to the deaths of fifteen people and the imprisonment of forty more. Once again these events were internationally condemned. Finally, administrative measures were taken to bolster the Magyar position. For example, the Saxons of Transylvania lost all their ancient rights in 1876, a year after the Slovaks were forced to witness the closure of the Matiča Slovenška, their cultural organization. The Slovaks by then had also lost their three confessional, Slovak-speaking high schools. Again, everything was done to restrict the powers of local authorities. Since the central government now represented Magyar interests, there was no longer any need to defend local autonomy as under the Metternich or Bach systems. By the end of the nineteenth century, therefore, it had practically disappeared. Each town or village, for example, under a law of 1898 could have only one official name, which was to be approved by the Minister of the Interior; this meant, of course, that it would be a Magyar one. Local cemeteries had also to ensure that tombstones were engraved in Magyar.

What does all this add up to? How repressive actually was the policy of magyarization? János for his part has his doubts. He writes: 'According to the careful documentation of Robert Seton-Watson in one critical decade (1898–1908) 503 Slovaks were indicted on charges ranging from incitement to riot to abusing the Hungarian flag, and in 81 trials drew a total of 79 years and 6 months. During the same period 216 Rumanians were sentenced to 38 years and 9 months. These aggregate figures were impressive but a division of years by sentences yields averages of 1.6 and 2.2 months. . . . The records of the Socialist movement, as published by one of its leading members, show 916 indictments in the pre-war period resulting in an aggregate sentence of 24 years and 11 months or an approximate average of 12 days.'[58]

János almost certainly underestimates the harm done to the nationalities by policies of magyarization in his concern to demonstrate the benefits available through assimilation. The thought of a couple of months in prison for employing one's own language or of a couple of years in jail for supporting a particular party does not seem to worry him. On the other hand, although pointing out that the working class comprised only 10 per cent of the population, he is prepared to concede the harshness of the official reaction to social democracy by the end of the century: '. . . workers associations were harassed, their leaders arrested and hauled into courts, and their members placed under police surveillance. Riots were put down by gendarmes and soldiers firing into crowds or charging them with fixed bayonets. Repression reached a peak under Bánffy's premiership (1895–1899) when a recently published source claims 51 workers were killed and 114 wounded in pitched battles with law-enforcement authorities.'[59] We may conclude therefore that to oppose the régime brought unpleasant consequences.

How then did the nationalities react and how successful was government pressure to assimilate? Let us attempt to answer the latter question first. According to the Austrian historian, Horst Haselsteiner, the most likely candidates for assimilation were the educated classes and the prosperous bourgeoisie who could relatively quickly – within a generation or so – become members of the dominant nation in the state.[60] Hence in the era of the Compromise it was scions of the educated German and Jewish bourgeoisie who became the spearhead of the drive towards magyarization – people with names like Falk, Rákosi, Agai, Horn, Helfy and above all Grünwald. After them came the mass assimilations of the turn of the century. According to the same historian, relatively large numbers of people were involved – no less than between 2.5 to 3 million people between 1787 and 1910. It is not clear just how many of these were forcibly assimilated (perhaps 50 per cent) but Haselsteiner believes that two conclusions concerning their numbers before 1914 can be drawn with confidence: first that the number of assimilated Magyars was scarcely less in number than the natural growth of the Magyars themselves; and secondly, that on the eve of the First World War the proportion of assimilated Magyars accounted for more than a quarter and indeed almost a third of all Magyars.[61] In any case, the 1910 censuș put the percentages of the various nationalities as follows: Magyars 48.1; Germans 9.8; Slovaks 9.4; Romanians 14.1; Ruthenes 2.3; Croats 8.8; and Serbs 5.3. This represented an increase of 2.7 per cent over 1900 for the Magyars, of 0.1 per cent for both the Croats and the Ruthenes, and a decrease of 1.3, 1.1, 0.4 and 0.2 per cent for the Germans, Slovaks, Romanians and Serbs respectively.[62]

How did the nationalities react to Hungarian policy? This question can be answered by looking at the political situation in Transylvania, the south Slav lands and Slovakia in turn. In Transylvania there was no separate Diet to voice the wishes and aspirations of the predominantly Romanian population. The 1865 Diet, in which the Magyars, representing merely 29 per cent of the population, had received eighty-nine delegates, had voted for union with Hungary, despite the opposition of the thirteen Romanian delegates who represented 54 per cent of the population. Then in 1874 a new electoral law, by setting high property and educational qualifications, effectively disenfranchised the Transylvanian Romanians, the great majority of whom were illiterate peasants. It was no accident, therefore, that Franz Joseph's threat to introduce universal manhood suffrage into Hungary in 1905 should have solved the constitutional crisis there. In Transylvania, meantime, there was little resistance to Magyar predominance. The small intellectual class, plus church leaders, hoped for some sort of franchise reform plus the same degree of autonomy that Croatia had achieved with the *Nagodba*. Yet there was little prospect of acquiring this. The Nationalist Party formed in 1881 did eventually hit on the idea in 1892 of sending a petition to Franz Joseph but, as we have seen, the signatories were arrested and in 1894 received prison sentences of up to five years. Only in 1905 did the National Party change tactics and decide to contest elections. In 1906, therefore, fifteen Romanian deputies were elected to the Budapest parliament. There they cooperated with Serb and Slovak colleagues, but achieved very little; the Hungarian government ignored them in favour of increased magyarization. In reality, therefore, despite an increased national awareness (especially among the educated), an impasse had been reached as far as the Transylvanian Romanians were concerned. The franchise was not going to be reformed (Tisza was adamant about that); the Diet was gone; and there was no hope of Austria's weak ally, Romania, taking any steps to improve their lot. In Barbara Jelavich's words: 'Transylvania had no important group standing either for an independent state or for union with Romania. Such a policy was not practical given the international conditions of the time. Romania, in alliance with Germany and Austria-Hungary in 1914, was unwilling and unable to foster Romanian nationalism in Transylvania. No power, including Romania, desired or foresaw the breakup of the Habsburg Empire. The Monarchy was regarded by most statesmen as necessary to political equilibrium on the Continent. Although some Romanians in Transylvania and the independent kingdom looked to union in the distant future, few considered it a possibility close to realisation.'[63] It is difficult to believe, therefore, at least as far as the nationality question in Transylvania was concerned, that Hungarian policy between 1867 and 1914, despite its ruthless programme of magyarization, can really be accused of having brought the Monarchy to the brink of dissolution. On the contrary, it is the lack of organized opposition, the lack of any real movement towards unification with Romania, and the apathy of large sections of the population which is more striking. What then was the situation in the south Slav lands?

Not all the south Slavs, of course, came under Hungarian rule. The majority of Slovenes, for example, lived in Carniola, Styria, Istria, Gorizia and Gradisca, territories which formed part of Cisleithania. The same applied to Dalmatia, whose population was mainly Croatian, although it also included Serbs and Italians. Thus the potential political influence of the south Slavs was diminished from the fact that they were divided between the two parts of the Monarchy. Moreover, the acquisition of Bosnia- Herzegovina (occupied by Austria-Hungary in 1878, annexed by her in 1908) made no difference in this respect, since these provinces were joined to neither 'half' of the Monarchy, but run by the imperial Finance Ministry in a deliberate attempt to maintain the ethnic balance of the Dualist system (see below). The Slovenes in any case were a peasant population, strongly conservative politically and deeply attached to the Catholic Church. They may not have inhabited the richest part of the Monarchy but, in general, they owned their own farms and were better off than the other peoples of the Balkans. According to one authority: 'By 1914 the Slovenes were culturally and economically by far the most advanced South Slav nation.'[64] According to another: 'In fact, the average Slovene peasant was much better off than his equivalent elsewhere in Eastern Europe.'[65] The result was that they were politically moderate. True, a nationalist movement developed after 1848 which sought to advance the use of the Slovene language and true, too, the Slovene political parties opposed the *Ausgleich*, yet the electoral reforms in Austria in the 1880s and 1890s and in particular the introduction of universal manhood suffrage in 1907 meant that the Slovenes could protect their nationality. On the other hand, this did not mean opposition to the Habsburgs, partly because the Slovenes were opposed to Italian nationalism in Gorizia and Istria. Instead, the Slovenian clericals, finding themselves unable to work with the German conservative parties, began to cooperate with the Croatian Party of Rights and in 1912 a declaration of mutual support was signed at Ljubljana. It must be stressed, however, that neither party was Yugoslav in orientation, and both were opposed to cooperation with the Orthodox Serbs of the Monarchy. There were other parties among the Slovenes too, but none of them desired the breakup of the Empire. 'The only truly radical faction was the youth group *Preporod*, which favoured the dissolution of the Monarchy and the joining of Slovenia, Croatia and Serbia to form a Yugoslav state. This organisation represented, however, only a small minority of the conservative, Catholic and peasant population. Prior to 1914 there was no Slovenian movement of consequence that stood for the breakup of the Habsburg Empire and the formation of a Yugoslavia.'[66]

In Dalmatia for most of the period up until 1860, political influence rested with the very small minority of Italians (2 per cent) and Italian-speaking Slavs in the coastal towns. After Italian independence, however, the government began to favour this group less. The result was that the Slav majority acquired more influence. Still there was a rivalry between the Autonomists who wanted home rule for Dalmatia (and who were sympathetic towards the professional, Italianate class) and the Nationalists who wished to be united with Croatia in a reconstituted Triune Kingdom (Croatia–Slavonia–Dalmatia). The Nationalists by the 1880s, however, had won the upper hand and in 1883 the official language of the province was changed from Italian to Serbo-Croat. The political situation was further complicated by the rivalry between the Serbs and Croats (16 and 82 per cent of the population respectively according to the 1910 census). The major source of difficulty was the future of Bosnia-Herzegovina after 1878, since the Serbian National Party, which had been organized in 1879, opposed Croat plans to unite the province with Croatia and Dalmatia. As a result the Serbs cooperated with the Autonomists and the Croats with the

Croatian Party of Rights, with its clerical, conservative and Croat nationalist stand. Yet at the beginning of the twentieth century, events were to lead to the formation in Dalmatia of a Serbo-Croat coalition which was to influence developments in Croatia itself.

As has been noted, Croatia had succeeded in retaining a certain degree of autonomy with regard to Hungary through the *Nagodba* of 1868. None the less, the Hungarian government had been able to keep control there by appointing the Ban and by controlling Croatian finance. Furthermore, only 2 per cent of the Croatian population had the right to vote, although that percentage was to rise to 8.8 from 1910. Thus politics was the affair of only a small and wealthy élite. It was dominated by two issues: the relationship with Budapest; and the rivalry between the Serbs and Croats, which was exacerbated by their differences over the future of Bosnia-Herzegovina. In Croatia-Slavonia the population consisted of 62.5 per cent Croats and 24.6 per cent Serbs. The main spokesman for the Croat nationalists was Ante Starčevič, leader of the Party of Rights. His ideal was a Croat state comprising the triune kingdom and Bosnia-Herzegovina and, according to Barbara Jelavich, he regarded the Serbs as merely 'second-rate Croats' who could be 'croaticised'.[67] The Serbs, for their part, resisted this political pressure and looked to some extent towards the government for protection. (Until 1903 there was little forthcoming from Serbia, since that country, like Romania before 1914, was an Austrian ally and indeed a satellite.) Under these circumstances, Budapest found it fairly easy to maintain control. The Ban between 1883 and 1903 was Count Khuen-Hédervâry who, with the support of the Unionist party (those in favour of the link with Budapest) and some nationalists, won elections in 1882, 1884 and 1892. The régime was further strengthened by the fact that the Serb proportion of the population had increased after 1881 with the incorporation of the Military Frontier into civil Croatia.

After 1894, Starčevič's party split in two, with a Pure Party of Rights emerging under Josip Frank. This was more anti-Serb but more pro-Habsburg than the parent party and called for a Trialist reorganization of the Monarchy – i.e. the creation of a Croatian state including Dalmatia and Bosnia-Herzegovina with the same status as Austria or Hungary within the Monarchy. The proposal also called for the Slovenes of Austria to be included in the new Croatian state. As for the Serbs of the Monarchy, it was clear that they would become the losers under any such scheme. Yet such a scheme was also demanded by the Croatian Social Democratic Party founded in

1894 and the Peasant Party founded in 1904. The result in Barbara Jelavich's words was: 'The emphasis on Croatian political rights was accompanied by growing animosity between the Serbs and Croats by the end of the century. Riots occurred, and the press of both sides exchanged violent recriminations. The major focus of Serbian and Croatian discontent was thus directed against each other and not against the dualist system.'[68]

Yet the year 1903 was to bring many changes. In Serbia, to begin with, the royal family was murdered and replaced with a dynasty which was hostile to Vienna. In Croatia, Khuen-Hédervâry left Zagreb to become prime minister of Hungary. In Bosnia-Herzegovina, Kállay, the head of the administration there since 1882, died. A new generation of politicians also came to prominence in Croatia, including some who had been educated at Prague under Thomas Masaryk, a strong supporter of Slav unity. The year 1905 also brought about a major change. In Dalmatia the south Slav leaders came together in an attempt to exploit the constitutional crisis in Hungary over the army question. They offered to support the Hungarian opposition to Vienna in return for Hungarian agreement to revise the *Nagodba* and restore the triune kingdom. Later on in the year a variety of Serb and Croat parties in Croatia approved a similar programme. The Serbs agreed to work for a triune kingdom, so long as they were to be granted equal rights within it. The principal objective was to secure the unification of Dalmatia and Croatia; the issue of the future of Bosnia-Herzegovina was avoided. The new Croatian–Serbian coalition thus took on a Yugoslav hue as Croats and Serbs now promised to work together and respect each other's rights. One immediate result was the winning of forty-three out of eighty-four seats in the Croatian Sabor (May 1906). However, the Hungarians were not impressed. Presented with Franz Joseph's threat to introduce universal manhood suffrage, their problems with Vienna were resolved. The policy of magyarization was then intensified and a law was passed concerning the use of Hungarian on the state railroads which contradicted the *Nagodba*.

Nevertheless, the coalition continued to play a major role in Croatian politics before 1914, albeit often in an opportunistic fashion. Nor can there be any doubt that its activities upset the authorities. In 1909, for example, they put a number of its leaders on trial (the Agram and Friedjung trials) in an attempt to prove subversive links with Serbia. However, the use of forged documents and improper evidence merely brought the proceedings into disrepute, consolidated the coalition and left the Monarchy with the reputation of behaving like a banana republic. In 1910, on the other hand, agreement was reached between the coalition and the government to reform the electoral law, increasing the number of voters from almost 50,000 to 190,000. Between then and 1914 it worked, sometimes with, sometimes against the government, but always within the dualist system hoping to reform the *Nagodba*. It was opposed by both branches of the Party of Rights and by the Peasant Party, all of which favoured trialism and were anti-Serb. It itself, in contrast, stood for cooperation with the Serbs *within* the Monarchy. All the major political parties in Croatia, therefore, were working within a political framework which assumed the continued existence of the Empire. It was only the students of the secret terrorist societies who favoured union with Serbia and who tried to bring this about by political murder. In aims and methods they were almost certainly totally unrepresentative. In 1912, none the less, the constitution of Croatia was suspended by the Ban against whom a couple of assassination attempts were made. According to A. J. P. Taylor, the consequences were ironic: '. . . South Slav idealism was confined to a few middle-class intellectuals. The Croat gentry and army officers, organised in the Party of Pure Right, though hostile to Hungary, were yet more fanatically anti-Serb and devoted to the Monarchy. Moreover the Croat peasant party now developing a mass following, took the same line, though with more democratic phrases. Radič, its leader, preached the "Austrian idea"; the task of the Monarchy, he said, was to be "neither German nor Magyar nor Slav but Christian, European, and democratic." The South Slav idea, synthetic and intellectual, won only the educated middle class, which looked at Strosmajer's collection of pictures; mass nationalism, in Croatia as everywhere else, sprang from the soil and hated its nearest neighbours. In Austria, universal suffrage weakened national enthusiasm, though it did not kill it; in Croatia universal suffrage would have thrown up a Catholic peasant party favourable to the Habsburgs and hostile to Hungarian rule. In any case, the Magyar gentry, dodging universal suffrage by every expedient in Hungary, could not introduce it in Croatia. Thus, they denied themselves the only decisive weapon and had to perpetuate the *imaginary* danger of a widespread South Slav movement.'[69] (Author's italics).

The third area affected by Hungarian magyarization policy was Slovakia. Here, cultural life by 1914 had come to a virtual standstill and the only hope available to Slovaks seeking an escape from magyarization was emigration. According to one historian: 'In the first years of the present century, Slovak emigration, particularly to the United States, reached the proportions of a mass flight. This further weakened the Slovak people by depriving them of their most enterprising elements.'[70] Politically, too, the situation, was pretty bleak. According to the 1910 census, the Slovak population was 1.95 million or about 10 per cent of the Hungarian population. This should have allowed them about forty seats out of the 413 in the Lower House of the Hungarian parliament. Instead, thanks to the restricted franchise, only seven Slovak deputies were elected in the elections of 1906 and only three in 1910. Even then, one of the latter was soon forced to resign. The inevitable result was that political life had to be conducted outside parliament. The main vehicle for political debate was the Slovak National Party, 'a loose political organisation of leaders without a mass following' which 'reflected several political trends, from liberal-democratic to conservative clerical'.[71] It also suffered from the traditional division between Catholics and Protestants. Hence Hlinka in 1912 took the lead in founding a clerical Slovak People's Party. No Slovak politician, however, before 1914 had any plan either to dismantle the Monarchy or even to seek unity within it with the Czechs. Altogether, therefore, there can be no case for arguing that by 1914 the Hungarians had brought the Monarchy to the brink of dissolution on account of their treatment of the nationalities, however unjust it may have been. The role of Hungary in the Monarchy between 1867 and 1914 may have been a depressing one in many ways, involving regular squabbles over the army and the Quota and international condemnation of magyarization. Indeed, all this was to form an essential part of the *Kulturpessimismus* for which the *fin de siècle* Monarchy was to become so famous. Yet Hungary did contribute to the Monarchy's economic growth, was becoming more economically integrated within it, and played an important part in formulating and determining its foreign policy. Its contribution, therefore, was not simply a negative one.

THE NATIONALITY PROBLEM IN CISLEITHANIA

The nationality problem, of course, was not one which was peculiar to the Hungarian part of the Monarchy. In Cisleithania, it was equally in evidence, determining the whole course of political life there. For the Austrian Germans found it much more difficult to control their Slavs than the Hungarians after 1867. The result was that government fell into the hands of the bureaucracy, as parliamentary life became paralysed and Franz Joseph selected premiers from the ranks of the high civil service. There is no controversy surrounding the course of events. Basically the Czechs and Germans were unable to reach any agreement over the issue of national representation and public education in the Czech Lands (Bohemia, Moravia and Silesia) and (less well known) in Lower Austria. The dispute took place on two levels – in the local diets and in the *Reichsrat*. Very often it seemed as if a compromise might be reached (as one was in Moravia in 1905) – yet at the crucial moment hard-line pressure from political radicals always succeeded in sabotaging agreement. Nor was there any way to force a solution: even after the introduction of universal manhood suffrage in 1907, both sides were in a minority in the *Reichsrat* – 232 German Austrians and 107 Czechs out of a Chamber of 516 deputies. As for the others – Poles, Slovenes, Ukrainians, Italians, Croats, Serbs – they could not agree on anything either. The result was bureaucratic rule. What then did the Czechs want? Clearly their differences with the Germans were constitutional ones. The Czechs appeared to desire the restitution of their 'ancient liberties', i.e. the unity and independence of the Bohemian crownlands as guaranteed by the Habsburg king in 1526 and disregarded thereafter. In practice, this meant 'federalism' – a position in the Monarchy for Bohemia like that enjoyed by Hungary. Yet even that, by the 1880s, no longer seemed to be a practical proposition. The last federalist proposal from the Czechs was actually put forward in 1903 but one authority has doubted its seriousness. She writes: 'This proposal never became the subject of official negotiations: therefore, it may be doubted that it was meant to be more than a trial balloon. Kramář, the recognized leader of the Czechs, used to characterize similar proposals by other parties as unrealistic; it was never quite clear whether his attitude was motivated by a realization of the almost insurmountable obstacles to such reform, or by a reluctance to grant the German *conditio sine qua non* in Bohemia, or by a conviction that eventually the Slavs would capture the apparatus of the state and thus dominate all Austria. His speeches in the *Reichsrat* seemed to indicate one or the other consideration at various times. Whatever their reasons, throughout the period under investigation the government as well as the national parties restricted their efforts at reconciliation to Bohemian affairs and to the central administration so far as it concerned Czechs and Germans.'[72] In other words, the Czechs had abandoned any attempt to alter the dualist system but were attempting to dominate the Bohemian lands.

The antagonism between Czech and German was fought out over constitutional matters but arose from intellectual and social factors. The Czech middle class had become nationally conscious by the middle part of the century, largely as a result of a cultural renaissance: the Bohemian Scientific Society had been founded in 1784; the Bohemian National Museum in 1818; the *Matice ceska* – a cultural society with its own publishing house – in 1834. Reading societies and salons had also sprung up; and the first volume of Palăcky's history of Bohemia (or of the Bohemian *people* as later volumes – now in Czech rather than in German – were entitled) appeared in 1836. As the century wore on, however, important social changes took place. The Czech population, which during the earlier part of the century had been engaged mainly in farming, turned increasingly to industry, made its way more and more into the towns and gradually prospered. It began therefore to move into areas and jobs which had been previously occupied by Germans. Prague, for example, became overwhelmingly a Czech rather than a German town, and even Vienna felt threatened by Czech immigration. By 1900 the Czech minority there represented about 4.3 per cent of the population. This may not appear to be many (in fact, it represents about the same percentage as the number of blacks in England today) but it was enough to persuade the diets of Lower and Upper Austria, Salzburg and Voralberg to pass laws, which were sanctioned by the Emperor, making German the exclusive language of these diets, the local administration and, in practice, education. As a result, Czech pupils living in Vienna had to travel to Moravia to be taught Czech in school, something which caused deep resentment, since it was held to be unconstitutional.

The problem was that the constitution was unclear. Article 19 of the German version of the *Ausgleich* promised the equality of all colloquial languages in school, office and public life and obliged all crownlands inhabited by more than one nationality to provide education in their own language for all inhabitants. However, the constitution failed to define nationality or to state whether equality was to be assured to the individual, to an organized body of members of each nationality, or to the territories predominantly inhabited by one nationality. The constitution also failed to provide any definition of 'colloquial', which might refer to every language spoken in a crownland or only those spoken in a specific location. Nor, finally, was it clear who was to enforce the law: the central government, the crownlands or some administrative agency or court. Interpreting the constitution therefore became a purely political matter with different interpretations themselves being interpreted as examples of discrimination and illegality. But since no government was strong enough to impose a single interpretation and since no compromise was ever reached, the matter evaded solution.

That there was little likelihood of a compromise being reached can be demonstrated by listing the different interpretations: (a) the Czechs insisted that Article 19 granted national equality to every individual anywhere in the Monarchy; the Germans recognized Czech equality only in territories which were predominantly Czech; (b) the Czechs regarded any language as colloquial if it was spoken in any crownland, meaning that a Czech should be able to use his language in public life wherever he found himself; the Germans wanted to restrict the term to languages spoken in a specific district by a specific percentage (10–35 depending how it suited them) of the population; (c) the Czechs interpreted national equality as the right to use their language in communication with as well as within the public services, i.e. as a language of internal as well as external administration, to have schools teach Czech to all Czech children, wherever they might be, and to have the same proportion of posts in the civil service as the proportion of Czechs in the relative population; the Germans insisted on keeping German as the only official language for German areas of Bohemia and on retaining it as the exclusive language of internal administration in Cisleithania.

Successive governments, none the less, did try to arrange a compromise if only to persuade the Czechs to enter the Vienna *Reichsrat*, which at first they boycotted. In 1871, for example, Count Hohenwart amended the *Ausgleich* to please them. Fundamental articles were drawn up whereby the Czechs recognized the *Ausgleich*, but which altered the workings of it with respect to Cisleithania. First, the Bohemian Diet was promised fifteen places on the Cisleithanian delegation supervising common affairs; secondly, all legislation which did not relate to common affairs but which affected Bohemia was to be submitted to the Bohemian Diet for the protection of Bohemian interests; thirdly, administrative matters concerning tariffs, trade, monopolies, posts, telegraphs, railways, military affairs and other matters which were not deemed common were to be supervised in Cisleithania by a committee comprising government ministers, top civil servants and the respective ministers from each crownland; finally, instead of the House of Lords, a Senate was to be erected in Cisleithania, half the membership of which would be appointed by the Emperor himself, the other half, however, at the suggestion of the diets. These proposals, however, aroused great opposition, not only from the Bohemian Germans, who quit their diet, but from the army, the bureaucracy and the church, not to mention the Moravian and Silesian diets (the latter, given that the Germans were the largest nationality in the province, rejecting any tie to Bohemia). Yet the decisive opposition came from the Hungarians under Andrássy, who protested that the 1867 arrangements were inviolable. Given that the Slovenes, Ruthenes and others also objected, the Emperor felt constrained to withdraw the proposals.

It was only under Taaffe (prime minister between 1879 and 1893) therefore that the Czechs re-entered the *Reichsrat*. He made Czech and German equal as languages of external administration in Bohemia and Moravia in 1880; established a Czech university in Prague; and widened the franchise in 1882. The result was that a new majority was established in Vienna of Poles, Czechs, clericals and conservatives, while in 1883 the Czechs won a massive majority in the Bohemian Diet. From now on it was the Germans who were on the defensive. This almost led to a compromise in Bohemia in 1890, which opposition from the Young Czechs frustrated. In 1896 a reform of the franchise reduced the strength of the Germans further, leaving them with only 47 per cent of deputies in the *Reichsrat* compared with two-thirds in 1873. The result was growing despair. In 1897 this exploded, when the Prime Minister, Badeni, in order to win Czech votes to renew the Compromise with Hungary, agreed to give Czech equal status with German as the internal language of administration in Bohemia and Moravia. This meant that all German civil servants would henceforth have to be bilingual. The result was riots all over the Empire; Germans everywhere protested against the decrees. Yet the only Czech response was to demand that they should be extended to Silesia in which there were twice as many Germans as Czechs. Badeni fell from power and the decrees were withdrawn. Between 1900 and 1904 a new premier Ernst von Koerber tried to reconcile both sides and, according to Alexander Gerschenkron, hoped to do so through 'the primacy of the economic factor'.[73] Gerschenkron however, overrates Koerber's importance (he sees the premier's public works programme as a significantly innovative way to reconcile the two sides by giving them common economic interests), which in any case was undermined by his inability to win the support of his Finance Minister. The real hope before 1914 was that the so-called Moravian Compromise of 1905, negotiated by the Gautsch ministry, might provide a model for Bohemia. For the relative proportions of Czechs and

Germans in Moravia was 71.3 to 27.9 per cent of the population. The basis of this deal was an electoral arrangement whereby the Czechs would get 73, the Germans 40 seats in curia other than those elected by landowners and members of the chambers of commerce. This, it was hoped, would put an end to all the national agitation, by guaranteeing a Czech majority while leaving the Germans well represented. In fact the Compromise had little impact on Bohemia. Differences which emerged between the two sides after the 1908 elections there led the Germans to obstruct the Bohemian Diet, while the Czechs took to obstructing the *Reichsrat*. In 1914, therefore, the constitution of the former was suspended and the latter was prorogued.

Should the imperial government be blamed for this situation? One historian thinks not: 'The governments patiently but unsuccessfully searched for a middle way acceptable to both, and the nationalists acquired the habit of blaming the government for the failure to achieve the settlement which they themselves had prevented. The moderates among them, however, expected to reach an agreement eventually and struggled for the best terms obtainable in the inevitable redistribution of power in the state and in the crownlands. In the process the radicals aroused the emotions of the masses with promises of untold economic and social advantages to derive from the fulfilment of their national program. This agitation increased the radicalism of the voters and not only frightened the Vienna ruling class but made a national compromise ever more difficult of achievement. Without it, constitutional reform was impossible, the *Reichsrat* remained paralysed, and government by bureaucracy was all but inevitable.'[74] There is perhaps much truth in this viewpoint, yet the core of the problem was the Germans. It was they after all who objected to complete equality with the Czechs, out of an anachronistic sense of cultural and political superiority. Why should not they have had to learn Czech in the Bohemian lands? Fortunately for them, Franz Joseph could see no great reason to insist either. His Empire may have been a *Hausmacht* but the *Haus* concerned had traditionally been a German one. Besides, he needed his German alliance and had always preferred to run the Monarchy through the bureaucracy anyway. Finally, the Czechs themselves were scarcely a threat to the dynasty. One future Czech prime minister said in 1906: 'We wish to save the Austrian parliament from utter ruin, but we wish to save it for the Slavs of Austria, who form two-thirds of the population. The empire is ours by right.'[75] No less a person than Masaryk himself said in 1909: 'We want a federal Austria. We cannot be independent outside of Austria, next to a powerful Germany, having Germans on our territory.'[76] Finally, Kramář said in 1914, after the assassination of the Archduke Franz Ferdinand: '. . . we protest most resolutely against anyone thinking that because of our sincere Slavism, we are hostile to the empire . . . We lean in no direction outside the empire.'[77] The American historian Victor S. Mamatey has, therefore, concluded: 'On the eve of World War I the Czechs, though deeply frustrated in the Habsburg empire, could not conceive of living outside of it.'[78]

In Galicia, the Polish province of the Monarchy, the nationality problem proved much more manageable. The Poles, who numbered almost 5 million and constituted 17.8 per cent of the population of Cisleithania in 1910, regarded Austria as the main defender of Polish interests after the suppression by Russia of the rebellion in Congress Poland in 1863. The year 1868 therefore brought an effusive declaration of loyalty to the Monarchy and to dualism, in acordance with which the Poles proved themselves the staunchest pillar of the new political system. Equally, they never hid their support for the resurrection, in the long term, of an independent Polish state. Their reward in the meantime, however, was to be allowed to dominate the political life of Galicia: here the population was 46 per cent Polish and 42 per cent Ruthenian. Yet the Poles, thanks to the electoral system, controlled the overwhelming majority of seats for both the *Reichsrat* and the Diet. In the latter, for example, between 1877 and 1908, the Ruthenes managed to win only between 8.6 and 14.2 per cent of the seats. The official language in the province was Polish and the two universities (Cracow and Lvov) were also Polish. Moreover, Polish schools and cultural institutions received official support while Ruthenian ones did not. Needless to say, this fed the sense of grievance of the Ruthenes and led to clashes between them and the Poles. Some of them were tempted to look to Russia for help (ethnically they were the same people as the Ukrainians), yet since Russian policy was consistently more oppressive than Austrian, she was hardly an appropriate alternative. With the introduction of universal manhood suffrage, Ruthenian representation increased. By 1914 a quarter of the *Reichsrat* deputies from Galicia were Ruthenes and so too were one-fifth of the representatives in the Diet. This did not solve the problem – there was obstruction in the Diet and a Ruthenian boycott of the universities in the province – but by the eve of the First World War, the situation had improved. An electoral compromise had been agreed, which would have given the Ruthenes 27.2 per cent of the seats in the Diet, and the government had begun to prepare plans for the establishment of a separate Ruthenian university. A compromise was also worked out in the neighbouring province of Bukovina. There in 1910, there were 305,000 Ruthenes, 273,000 Romanians, 168,000 Germans and 102,000 Jews, together with sizeable numbers of Poles and Hungarians. A new constitution in 1910 gave personal autonomy to these six nationalities. Moreover, to quote Barbara Jelavich: 'The fact that this region was relatively remote from the centre of the Austrian state appears to have been an advantage; it was never the scene of the bitter national conflicts that took place elsewhere.'[79]

The smallest nationality in the Monarchy before 1914 – if one does not include Bosnian Muslims, Galician Jews, Greeks, Armenians, Albanians and Bulgarians – were the almost 800,000 Italians who did not yet form part of a united Italy. They inhabited the South Tyrol and the Adriatic Littoral making up the populations of three provinces, Gorizia-Gradisca, Trieste and Istria. In the South Tyrol they sought their own assembly to free them from the domination of Innsbruck. In the Littoral they sought to retain their privileged position in government, since they were outnumbered there by Slavs by almost two to one. In fact, they were a favoured rather than an oppressed nationality in the sense that, especially after 1907, they had more representatives for their numbers than any other national group. Most historians, in fact, tend to treat them as part of Austria-Hungary's foreign policy problems – *Italia irredenta* – rather than part of the nationality problem. Only occasionally did they cause any problems as, for instance, when the student, Guglielmo Oberdan (in fact, Wilhelm Oberdank, a Slovene from Trieste who converted to the Italian cause), sought martyrdom on behalf of Italy and was hanged for rather incompetently setting out to assassinate the Emperor.[80]

Ironically, as opposed to the Magyars in Hungary, it may even be possible to treat the Germans in Cisleithania as part of the nationality problem. They formed only 35.6 per cent of the population of Cisleithania in 1910, 9.8 per cent of that of Hungary and 23.9 per cent of the Monarchy as a whole. Their problems in the Czech lands have already been examined, but also relevant was their knowledge that next door existed the new and dynamic German Empire. Hans Kohn has therefore written: 'The position of the Germans in Austria could be compared with that of the Austrian Poles or Italians. They felt part of a larger national entity the majority of whose people lived outside the Habsburg Monarchy. The Austrian Germans had more recent memories of community with the Germans beyond the border, whereas the Italians of Trieste or of Trentino had never formed part of any Italian state and Polish statehood (with the exception of the Republic of Cracow) had gone out of existence by the end of the eighteenth century. But the Austrian Germans had been part of the German Bund until 1866 and participated in the National Assembly at Frankfurt am Main. Thus the situation of the Germans in the Habsburg Monarchy was in the age of nationalism not so fundamentally different from that of the non-Germanic elements.'[81] German grievances in fact were to lead to the establishment of a Pan-German movement inside Austria, led by Georg von Schönerer. Along with others (among them such famous future personalities as Heinrich Friedjung and Viktor Adler), he was an author of the Linz Programme of 1882 which called for the separation from Cisleithania of such non-German territories as Dalmatia, Galicia and the Bukovina, as well as the raising of German to the status of sole official language in the remainder of 'Austria'. Various steps were also recommended whereby a German economic and cultural life could be organized for this same 'Austria'. Von Schonerer's own plans, however, were more extreme. He wanted a break with both the Catholic Church and the Habsburg dynasty and saw the future of Austria's Germans as lying within the German Empire. His chosen enemies within the Monarchy were the Slavs and the Jews; his supporters, apart from nationalist students and extreme anti-semites, mainly Germans who lived along the fault-lines between the ethnic groups. In 1884 he unsuccessfully led a campaign to nationalize the Nordbahn, a railway which had been financed by the Rothschilds. The issue, he claimed, was one of the Jews versus the people. In 1898 he called on the German army to invade Austria to save its German population. One of his followers, the deputy Franko Stein, declared in the *Reichsrat* on 1 March 1902: 'I say it aloud, we want to belong to the German Empire', adding, 'Today anyone who is a patriot in Austria is a fool.'[82] On 13 March he told a Young Czech deputy: 'We are just as anti-Austrian as you are.'[83] Schönerer, therefore, was a forerunner of Hitler, who glorified him in *Mein Kampf*, but who also criticized his lack of organizational talent. The Pan-Germans, in fact, remained a quite small parliamentary group split between a number of warring factions.

Want of organizational talent, on the other hand, was not a charge which could be levied against Karl Lueger and his Christian Social Party, which also took up the cause of anti-semitism among Austrian Germans at this time, although it always supported the dynasty. Lueger, in fact, was a political operator of the first rank who, by spell-binding oratory and sheer hard work on behalf of the shopkeepers and artisans of Vienna, came to dominate entirely the political life of the imperial capital. At first he was suspected of being a revolutionary, having challenged the leadership of the city council, and four times between 1895 and 1897 the Emperor refused to confirm his election as mayor. Yet his majority always increased and there was no escaping him. Thereafter, he ruled the city until his death in 1910. His politics were those of city boss and social reformer. Nor can it be denied that the Viennese benefited from his efforts, in terms of roads, houses, sewers, parks and other public amenities. Hitler admired him too and declared in *Mein Kampf* that he had been profoundly moved by his funeral. Yet he called his anti-semitism a sham, a view which has been partly upheld by historical research. Lueger, in fact, employed his anti-semitism less as a racial doctrine than as a political expedient. 'Who is a Jew,' he said, 'is something I determine.'[84] Once established, his Christian Social Party became a conservative one, partly due to the realization that the city's artisans could not hope to escape the consequences of industrialisation; partly because, as the party outgrew Vienna, it became more and more interested in the peasants and the countryside. Indeed, one of Austria's leading landowners, Prince Alois Liechtenstein, became one of the party's leaders. By the time of Lueger's death, therefore, the Christian Socials were no longer seen as the enemies of big business, but were noted for their loyalty to the dynasty, resistance to Magyar interpretations of the *Ausgleich*, and support of political and social paternalism.

One party which might have been expected to help reconcile the nationalities in Austria were the socialists, who had emerged united from their Hainfeld conference of 1889. In 1907 they won eighty-seven seats and became the largest party in the *Reichsrat*. Before then, at their conference in Brunn in 1899, they had affirmed their loyalty to the dynasty – at least indirectly – and had called for a solution to the nationality problem by recasting the Empire as a federation of autonomous national groups. Two of their leaders, Karl Renner and Otto Bauer, were advocates of 'personal autonomy' and wrote influential books on the problems posed by the nationality question for socialists. Their solution was to separate the cultural issue from the territorial one and to allow people wherever they were to register as voters of a particular national group. They could then vote in a separate curia for a predetermined number of deputies of their particular nationality. Educational and other matters could be administered by nationally homogeneous agencies. This policy, it should be noted, was never officially adopted by the Socialist Party in Austria. However, as can be seen, it was similar to the Compromise worked out in Moravia in 1905, in the Bukovina in 1910, and in Galicia on the very eve of the First World War. The Socialist Party itself, ironically, was to prove unable to avoid the consequences of the nationality issue as far as its own organization was concerned. In 1911 the Czech branch of the party broke away from the main Cisleithanian body, complaining of the overwhelmingly German character of its leadership. Marx and Engels's prejudices, in truth, were still apparent. The German historian, Hans Mommsen; has confirmed this, writing: 'Renner's cultural nationalism and Bauer's Greater German attitude became apparent, if only indirectly, in the arguments between Social Democrats over nationality policy after the first Russian revolution of 1905.'[85] He adds: 'Their position regarding national assimilation, the problem of minority schools, and the economic implications of the nationality question, clearly show that they had not remained uninfluenced by the national attitudes of their time. Their proposed solutions to the nationality problem amounted to the illusion (Aporie) that persistent national conflicts, which increasingly took on the character of an imperialist power struggle, were paving the way for democratic reforms, which represented the preconditions for any lasting compromise over nationality.'[86] Robert A. Kann's verdict, though critical, is different: 'The principle of personal autonomy,' he writes, 'even though it was a more sophisticated instrument of national justice than that of territorial autonomy, would not in the long run have resolved the problems of national conflict. In the last analysis most national groups in the Habsburg empire, like any other who were or felt to be oppressed, wanted statehood and not just national equality based on a perfect legal structure. Personal autonomy, though more equitable than territorial autonomy, actually seemed rather far removed from the semblance of the desired identity of nation and state. The nation appeared to be anchored in the public records rather than in conspicuous territorial jurisdiction, however limited. Nevertheless, as long as the empire lasted within the strong setting of the centralistic systems in the dual states, personal autonomy could have provided national justice to a degree which no other institutional system could grant under existing conditions. Moreover, reforms on this basis precluded the sweeping innovations of a federal structure, which probably could not have been brought about without conflicts with Hungary and ensuing intervention from neighbouring countries. Thus, although the personality principle would not have solved the Austrian national problems, it might have helped to arrest the creeping disease of national disintegration for some time. This, however, was the most a desperately sick patient could have hoped for.'[87]

Yet just how desperately sick had the nationality question made Austria-Hungary by 1914? There can be no doubt that there were genuine grounds for despair: the obstructionism in the *Reichsrat* after the Badeni crisis; the failure of electoral reform in 1906 to change matters; the crisis in Hungary for almost a decade after 1898; and the nationalist revival among the nationalities there. In fact, a great many people had already written the Monarchy off. The future German emperor, Wilhelm II, for example, had given rather tactless expression to just this view in 1887, when the Archduke Rudolf reported him as follows: '. . . he remarked that things were doing well only in Prussia: in Austria the whole state was rotten, near to dissolution, that it would break up, that the German provinces would fall like ripe fruit into Germany's lap, that [Austria] as an insignificant duchy would become even more dependent on Prussia than Bavaria was.'[88] Wilhelm had continued: 'The Emperor of Austria can, if he wishes, live out his life as an insignificant monarch in Hungary. Prussia will do nothing to bring this about quickly, it will happen in any case by itself.' Surprising as it may seem, the Habsburgs themselves may even have shared this view. Franz Joseph had written to his mother in 1866: 'One just has to resist as long as possible, do one's duty to the last, and finally perish with honour.'[89] He had only been thirty-three at the time. Over the years, however, he had become no more optimistic. In his will he made arrangements in case 'the crown should no longer remain with our House' and advised his daughter, Gisela, to claim her fortune on his death, since 'it would be safer in Germany than in Vienna'.[90] Likewise, the Archduke Rudolf, before committing suicide at Mayerling, wrote to his sister Maria Valerie, advising her to leave Austria 'when papa passes away' since, as he put it, 'only I know what will happen then'.[91] In Germany itself, meanwhile, Pan-Germans were openly advocating the annexation of the German parts – sometimes the non-German parts too – of the Monarchy as a German colony. For example, one book published in 1899 and entitled *Osterreich's Zusammenbruch and Wiederaufbau* (Austria's Collapse and Reconstruction) suggested that 'the Austrian littoral with the southern portion of Dalmatia, Ragusa and Cattaro, Trieste and Pola, should constitute, as Alsace-Lorraine, a Reichsland . . . which would serve as a base for the maritime power of Germany in the Adriatic and Mediterranean'.[92] R. Tannenberg's much-read book *Grossdeutschland* (Greater Germany) published in 1911 went even further, advocating the division of the Monarchy between Prussia, Baden, Bavaria and Saxony, and arguing: 'every insult offered to a German student at Prague, every popular riot at Laibach, is an affront to German honour and a sufficient . . . reason for us to occupy the territories in question.'[93] Yet it was by no means only German commentators, politicians or dynasts who expected the Habsburgs to lose their Empire. One of the most influential works on this theme was A. Chéradame's *L'Europe et la question d'Autriche au seuil du XX-e siecle*, which was published in Paris in 1901.

The pessimism concerning the future of the Monarchy from the 1890s onwards can be linked perhaps with the great cultural effervescence which was taking place there at the same time. This was the period after all of Schnitzler and von Hofmannsthal in literature; Freud in psychoanalysis; Mahler and Schoenberg in music; Klimt and Schiele in painting; and Kraus in satire. Carl Schorske has suggested that the connection is to be found in a flight into art and aesthetics as a reaction against the political sterility of the times,[94] while others have stressed the darker side of this cultural climax itself: the obsession with the ego; with sensuality; with ideology; and with death. William Johnson's study of *The Austrian Mind*, it will be recalled, has chapters entitled *Death as a Bulwark against Change*, *Death as Ephemerality*, and *Death as Refuge: Suicide by Austrian Intellectuals*.[95] Karl Kraus, it will be recalled, saw the intellectual ferment of his day as a sign of cultural decay or mental hysteria in an Empire which he damned as a 'research laboratory for world destruction'. Yet none of this need be accepted. It can be argued with equal plausibility that the cultural developments of the time had less to do with local politics than with a basically healthy environment created by Viennese cosmopolitanism, cultural freedom and Jewish emancipation.

Again, the pessimism regarding the nationality question must also be put into perspective. Thus although Berthold Sutter, for example, stresses that in Austria after the Badeni crisis, no government could ever again take it for granted that the Germans within the Monarchy would automatically identify their interests with those of the state, that indeed they 'disavowed the state which had denied them',[96] he also writes that 'in the last decade before the World War the return to Austria had begun again among ordinary Germans',[97] even if it was strongly coloured by the *Wacht am Rhein*. Regarding the other nationalities in the Monarchy and their loyalty to the dynasty, we have already seen that in almost all cases, despite political and cultural grievances, there was no desire to destroy the

Monarchy or to break with the dynasty. Indeed, compromises of some kind had already been worked out in Moravia, the Bukovina and Galicia before 1914. The Hungarian historian, István Diószegi, has therefore written: 'Nationalism did not work towards the destruction of the Monarchy. Of the nations inside the Habsburg Empire only the Italians aimed unconditionally at breaking away; the others from considerations of economics, politics and foreign policy, were led, not disinclined, to see the Monarchy as the appropriate area in which to fulfil their national aims.'[98] Barbara Jelavich stresses the same point: '. . . the national leaderships had to concentrate on the immediate questions of the day. Most of these concerned practical questions such as the franchise and the language of administration and education. Thus, despite the fact that there was indeed much dissatisfaction with Habsburg rule, the nationalities directed their attention primarily to the issues that directly affected their daily lives. No major leader or party called for the destruction of the monarchy.'[99] Regarding the nationalities in Hungary in particular, she points out: 'It is a great impediment to understanding the national developments that in the Hungarian kingdom the majority of the inhabitants were excluded from the political process by the restrictive franchise. The spokesman for all of the national movements, and, of course, for the Hungarian government, came from a small percentage of the population. They claimed to speak for the "nation" and the "people", but they were often in fact personally as divided from the peasants of their own nationality as they were from those of another ethnic background. What the people really thought could not be determined until after the war, when peasant parties first came to power.'[100] It is very important, therefore, not to allow one's judgement to be clouded by hindsight, not to assume that, because the Habsburg Monarchy did not survive the First World War, it was bound not to survive in any case. Again, it is equally wrong to assume that, because it did not survive, it was already in decline and that this decline had been a progressive one. At no point between 1867 and 1914 did the Monarchy even vaguely face the sort of challenge to its existence that it faced in 1848–9. The truth is that there was no internal pressure between 1867 and 1914 for the breakup of the Monarchy; no repudiation of the dynasty; while in some areas problems were actually being solved or compromises reached. At the same time, economic growth was continuing and the Monarchy was becoming more and more integrated in terms of living standards, infrastructure and finance. Indeed, as contemporary observers suggested, there was a feeling, especially after 1906 or thereabouts, that things were positively improving. Hence, for example, Louis Eisenmann, the great French observer of the Monarchy, could write in 1910: 'On December 2, 1908, Franz Joseph I celebrated the sixtieth anniversary of his accession to the throne. On the occasion of his Jubilee [December 1898], Europe had viewed with fear and distrust the future of the monarchy, which seemed inevitably doomed to dissolution at the death of Franz Joseph. But ten years have elapsed since then and the prognostications are completely different. The acute crisis has been dispelled solely by the internal forces of the monarchy. . . . There is still the violent struggle between the nationalities, but the inevitable solution is in sight. . . . It seems as though all the Austrian, Hungarian, and Austro-Hungarian questions could be settled from within. It is in this that the progress consists; herein lies the great security for the future . . . fifty years of national and constitutional life have endowed the people of the monarchy with the strength to enforce their wishes side by side with those of their sovereign, and, if necessary in opposition to him. They are of age, and can control their destinies if they wish to do so, provided only that they agree amongst themselves. They have come to realise the common interest which keeps them united in the monarchy and in time they will become conscious of the strength by means of which they can govern it in accordance with their own interests. The monarchy no longer rests on the power of the dynastic tie alone, but also on their conscious desire for union. Herein lies its mighty new strength; this is the great, the enormous result of the reign of Franz Joseph.'[101] Coming from the author of a critical account of the Compromise which had been published in 1904 and which A. J. P. Taylor was later to call a 'work of superlative genius' ('no greater work of history has been written in this century'),[102] Eisenmann's revised opinion of the Monarchy's prospects deserves to be treated with respect, despite its exaggerations. His grounds for optimism were the introduction of universal suffrage in Austria ('the dawn of a new Austria – an Austria which was stronger than the old one, and quite determined to live')[103] his belief that it would also be introduced in Hungary ('The King will certainly not give up universal suffrage');[104] and the conclusion of a new economic compromise between Austria and Hungary in 1907. This in particular he saw as an act of statesmanship with very positive implications for the future. He wrote of it: '. . . on this occasion, neither country profited at the expense of the other, the Compromise being in conformity with the interests of both countries, as conceived by them. This Compromise did not, like those which had preceded it, give rise to bitterness and malice. It was adopted by both States before the end of 1907. On January 1, 1908, the constitutional interregnum that had lasted ten years came to an end.'[105] What had happened was that the Austrians had traded economic advantages for political concessions to the Hungarians. Most of the economic differences between the two countries – save the problem of the Bank which was reserved for future negotiations – were now resolved. Austria gained the declaration and confirmation of the principle of commercial freedom between the two countries and of equality of their respective subjects before the fiscal laws; the institution of arbitration to settle any differences which might arise regarding the economic compromise (she had been demanding this in vain for forty years); the recovery of her liberty in the matter of railway tariffs which for the last ten years had been curtailed to the advantage of Hungary; and finally, a favourable settlement over the Quota, or the proportional contribution towards the common expenditure, which henceforth was to be set at 36.4 per cent for Hungary and 63.6 per cent for Austria. (In 1867, the proportions had been 30 and 70 per cent respectively.) Hungary, in turn, was gratified by the form of an international treaty instead of that of a union, by a guarantee that, in future commercial agreements with foreign countries, her independence and sovereignty should be more clearly emphasized and, lastly, that the Austrian market should be opened without restriction to her loans.[106] Eisenmann, finally, was impressed by the outcome of the Bosnian crisis which he felt had given both parts of the Monarchy a common interest: '. . . the annexation is irrevocable. Austria and Hungary are at one in their desire to maintain it.'[107]

The whole question of foreign policy, in fact, was one which did much to convince foreign observers that the Monarchy would hold together. The President of Harvard University, A. Lawrence Lowell, for example, wrote a survey in 1896 of *Governments and Parties in Continental Europe*, much of the second volume of which was devoted to the Monarchy. His conclusion was that: '. . . the forces that have made the dual system work smoothly in the past are likely to produce the same result in the future.'[108] Exactly how smoothly they had worked before the mid-1890s is debatable and, as will be seen, Lowell did not really exaggerate them, but the point to note is that the main force he was referring to to explain the 'strange connexion' between Austria and Hungary was the need for a common foreign policy: 'The explanation of the strange connexion,' he wrote, 'is to be found in the fact that the two countries are not held together from within by any affection or loyalty to a common Fatherland, but are forced together by a pressure from outside which makes the union an international and military necessity. Austria, on the one hand, would not be large enough alone to be a really valuable ally to Germany and Italy; and if not an ally, she would likely become a prey, for she contains districts which they would be glad to absorb. Moreover, there would be imminent danger of some of her different races breaking into open revolt if the Emperor had not the Hungarian troops at his command. On the other hand, the Magyars without Austria would not be sufficiently strong to block the ambitions of Russia, or resist the tide of panslavism. They would not only have little influence outside their own dominions, but they would run the grave risk of foreign interference in favour of the Slavs in Hungary. The union, therefore, is unavoidable, and it is very little closer than is absolutely necessary to carry out the purposes for which it exists.'[109]

NOTES AND REFERENCES

1. György Szabad (1977) *Hungarian Political Trends between the Revolution and the Compromise (1849–1867)*. Budapest, pp. 166–7.
2. Lászlo Péter (1984) The dualist character of the 1867 Hungarian Settlement, in György Ránki (ed.) Hungarian history – world history, *Indiana Studies on History*. Budapest, pp. 85–164, p. 118.
3. Quoted in B. Sutter (1968) Die Ausgleichverhandlungen zwischen Österreich und Ungarn, 1867–1918, *Österreichisch-ungarische Ausgleich von 1867 etc.*, pp. 71–111, p. 90.
4. The saying is apocryphal.
5. C. A. Macartney (1970) The Compromise of 1867, in R. H. Hatton and M. S. Anderson (eds) *Studies in Diplomatic History; Essays in memory of David Bayne Horn*. London, pp. 287–300, p. 229.
6. A. Murad (1968) *Franz Joseph and His Empire*. New York, p. 176.
7. Sutter, *op. cit.*, p. 81.
8. *Ibid.*, pp. 92–3.
9. *Ibid.*, p. 106.
10. P. Hanák (1967) Die Stellung Ungarns in der Monarchie, in F. Engel-Jánosi and H. Rumpler (eds) *Probleme der Franzisco-Josephischen Zeit, 1848–1916*. Vienna, pp. 79–93, p. 88.
11. Péter, *op. cit.*, p. 147.
12. *Ibid.*, pp. 147–8.
13. *Ibid.*, p. 151.
14. *Ibid.*, p. 150.
15. *Ibid.*, p. 151.

16. *Ibid.*, pp. 151–2.
17. *Ibid.*, p. 152.
18. Zoltán Szász (1984) The founding of the Honvédség and the Hungarian Ministry of Defence, 1867–70, in B. K. Király (ed.) The Crucial Decade: east central European society and national defense, 1859–70, War and Society in East Central Europe, Vol. XIV, pp. 533–9, p. 533.
19. János Décsy (1984) Gyula Andrássy and the founding of the Honvédség, in Király, op. cit., pp. 540–50, p. 540.
20. Gábor Vermes (1983) Hungary and the common army in the Austro-Hungarian Monarchy, in S. B. Vardy and A. H. Vardy (eds) *Society in Change, Studies in Honour of Bela K. Kiraly*. New York, pp. 89–101, p. 95.
21. Szász, *op. cit.*, p. 358.
22. Gunther E. Rothenberg, The Military Compromise of 1868 and Hungary, in Király, op. cit., pp. 519–32, p. 526.
23. *Ibid.*, p. 259.
24. *Ibid.*
25. László Péter, *The Army Question in Hungarian Politics, 1867–1914*, p. 24. Unpublished paper, a copy of which was kindly given to the author.
26. Norman Stone (1966) Army and society in the Habsburg Monarchy, 1900–1914, *Past and Present*, Vol. 33, pp. 965–111, p. 106.
27. *Ibid.*, pp. 104, 106.
28. Oscar Jászi (1961) *The Dissolution of the Habsburg Monarchy*. Chicago and London, p. 206.
29. David F. Good (1984) *The Economic Rise of the Habsburg Empire, 1750–1914*. Berkeley and Los Angeles, p. 104.
30. *Ibid.*, p. 124.
31. *Ibid.*, p. 240.
32. *Ibid.*
33. *Ibid.*, p. 241.
34. John Komlos (1983) *The Habsburg Monarchy as a Customs Union, Economic Development in Austria-Hungary in the Nineteenth Century*. Guildford.
35. *Ibid.*, p. 218.
36. *Ibid.*, pp. 219–20.
37. *Ibid.*, p. 218.
38. *Ibid.*, p. 218.
39. Peter Hanák (1984) Hungary's contribution to the Monarchy, in G. Ránki (ed.) *op. cit.*, pp. 165–80.
40. *Ibid.*, p. 169.
41. *Ibid.*, p. 166.
42. *Ibid.*
43. *Ibid.*, p. 169.
44. Scott M. Eddie (1984) On Hungary's economic contributions to the Monarchy, in Ránki, *op. cit.*, pp. 191–207.
45. *Ibid.*, p. 195.
46. See both his essay (1971) The decline of oligarchy: bureaucratic and mass politics in the Age of Dualism (1867–1918), in A. C. János and

W. B. Slottman (eds) *Revolution in Perspective. Essays on the Hungarian Soviet Republic*. Berkeley, pp. 1–60; and his (1982) *The Politics of Backwardness in Hungary, 1825–1945*. Princeton.
47. János, *The Politics of Backwardness etc.*, p. xxi.
48. *Ibid.*, p.314.
49. Alexander Gerschenkron (1965) *Economic Backwardness in Historical Perspective*. New York.
50. Good, *op. cit.*, p. 192.
51. Eugen Weber (1976) *Peasants into Frenchmen, Rural France, 1870–1918*. London.
52. For a brief survey, see Alan Sked (1987) *Britain's Decline, Problems and Perspectives*. Oxford.
53. For Seton-Watson's writings and career, see the book by his sons, H. and C. Seton-Watson (1981) *The Making of a New Europe*. London.
54. C. A. Macartney, *The Habsburg Empire, 1790–1918*. London, p. 558.
55. *Ibid.*, p. 165.
56. *Ibid.*
57. For an excellent summary of the nationality problem under Dualism, see Barbara Jelavich (1983) *History of the Balkans, Vol. II, Twentieth Century*. Cambridge, chapter II. The most thorough, up-to-date account in German is to be found in the two relevant and massive volumes of the Austrian Academy's survey of the Monarchy, namely A. Wandruszka and P. Urbanitsch (eds) (1980) *Die Habsburger Monarchie, 1848–1918*, Vol. III, Pts I and II, *Die Völker des Reiches*. Vienna.
58. János, The decline of oligarchy etc., pp. 18–19.
59. *Ibid.*, p. 43.
60. Horst Haselsteiner (1984) Das Nationalitätenproblem in den Ländern der ungarischer Krone, in E. Zöllner and H. Mocker (eds) Volk, Land und Staat, Landesbewusstsein, Staatsidee und nationale Fragen in der Geschichte Osterreichs, *Schriften des Institutes fur Osterreichkunde*, 43, pp. 118–37, p. 132.
61. *Ibid.*, p. 133.
62. *Ibid.*, p. 132, notes 36 and 37.
63. Jelavich, *op. cit.*, p. 76.
64. Jozo Tomasevich, quoted by Jelavich, *op. cit.*, pp. 55–6.
65. Jelavich, *op. cit.*, p. 55.
66. *Ibid.*, p. 57.
67. *Ibid.*, p. 66.
68. *Ibid.*, p. 68.
69. A. J. P. Taylor (1964) *The Habsburg Monarchy, 1809–1918, A History of the Austrian Empire and Austria-Hungary*. London, pp. 240–1.
70. V. S. Mamatey (1973) The establishment of the republic, in V. S. Mamatey and R. Luža (eds) *A History of the Czechoslovak Republic, 1918–1948*. Princeton, pp. 3–38, p. 7.
71. *Ibid.*, p. 8.
72. Suzanne G. Kornish (1949) Constitutional aspects of the struggle between Germans and Czechs in the Austro-Hungarian Monarchy, *Journal of Modern History*, Vol. 21, pp. 231–61, p. 239.
73. The main theme of his last book, i.e. A. Gerschenkron (1977) *An Economic Spurt That Failed*. Princeton.

74. Kornish, *op. cit.*, p. 261.
75. Mamatey, *op. cit.*, p. 5.
76. *Ibid.*
77. *Ibid.*, p. 5.
78. *Ibid.*
79. Jelavich, *op. cit.*, p. 58.
80. Alfred Alexander (1977) *The Hanging of Wilhelm Oberdank.* London.
81. Hans Kohn (1975) The viability of the Habsburg Monarchy, in Peter N. Stearns (ed.) *A Century For Debate, 1789–1914, Problems in the Interpretation of European History.* New York and Toronto, pp. 466–71, p. 469.
82. *Militär und Zivil. Zeitgemässe Betrachtungen von einem Osterreicher.* Vienna and Leipzig, 1904, p. 15, note.
83. *Ibid.*
84. 'Wer ein Jude ist bestimme ich.' See Menachem Z. Rosenhaft (1976) Jews and Antisemites in Austria at the end of the nineteenth century, *Leo Baeck Institute Yearbook*, pp. 51–86, p. 83. See also Peter G. J. Pulzer (1964) *The Rise of Political Antisemitism in Germany and Austria.* London.
85. Hans Mommsen (1979) *Arbeiterbewegung und Nationale Frage, Ausgewählte Aufsätze.* Göttingen, p. 216.
86. *Ibid.*, pp. 216–17.
87. R. A. Kann (1974) *A History of the Habsburg Empire, 1526–1918.* London, pp. 442–3. See also Arthur G. Kogan (1949) The Social Democrats and the conflict of nationalities in the Habsburg Monarchy, *Journal of Modern History*, Vol. 21, pp. 204–17.
88. Quoted in Georg Markus (1984) *Der Fall Redl.* Vienna, p. 109.
89. A. Wandruszka (1968) *Finis Austriae?* Reformpläne und Untergangsahnungen in der Habsburger Monarchie, in *Der österreichische Ausgleich von 1867. Seine Grundlagen und Auswirkungen*, Buchreihe der Südostdeutschen Historischen Kommission, Vol. 20. Munich, p. 119.
90. *Ibid.*
91. *Ibid.*
92. Quoted in W. W. Gottlieb (1957) *Studies in Secret Diplomacy During the First World War.* London, p. 261.
93. *Ibid.*
94. Carl E. Schorske (1981) *Fin de Siècle Vienna, Politics and Culture.* New York.
95. W. Johnson (1972) *The Austrian Mind: an Intellectual and Social History, 1848–1938.* Berkeley.
96. B. Sutter (1980) Die politische und rechtliche Stellung der Deutschen in Osterreich, 1848–1918, in A. Wandruszka and P. Urbanitsch (eds) *op. cit.*, Pt. I, pp. 154–239, p. 239.
97. *Ibid.*, p. 304.
98. István Diószegi (1985) *Die Aussenpolitik der Osterreichisch-Ungarischen Monarchie, 1871–1877.* Vienna, Graz and Cologne, p. 10.
99. Jelavich, *op. cit.*, p. 77.
100. *Ibid.*, p. 78.
101. Louis Eisenmann (1910) Austria-Hungary, in The Latest Age, *The Cambridge Modern History*, Vol. XII, pp. 174–212.

102. A. J. P. Taylor, *op. cit.*, p. 292.
103. Eisenmann, *op. cit.*, p. 208.
104. *Ibid.*, p. 210.
105. *Ibid.*, p. 211.
106. *Ibid.*, pp. 210–11.
107. *Ibid.*, p. 212.
108. A. Lawrence Lowell (1896) *Governments and Parties in Continental Europe*, 2 vols. London, Vol. 2, pp. 70–179, p. 179.
109. *Ibid.*, Vol. 2, p. 177.

CHAPTER SIX

The Road to Disaster

It is now time to examine the foreign policy of the Monarchy under the dualist system. Once again, there is no space to resort to narrative; we shall have to examine it, rather, in the light of the dualist constitution and in light of arguments put forward by Paul W. Schroeder concerning Austria-Hungary's role in international affairs before the First World War. There are, in fact, very few controversies surrounding Habsburg foreign policy in the dualist era, but Schroeder's writings force one to consider the question whether Austria-Hungary was basically a force for peace or a force for war between 1867 and 1914.

DOMESTIC ASPECTS OF HABSBURG FOREIGN POLICY

Let us start with the domestic factors which impinged on foreign affairs. As far as public opinion is concerned, István Diószegi, the leading Hungarian historian of the Monarchy's foreign policy, has summarized the viewpoints of the various nationalities involved as follows: the Germans concentrated on the German question and were indifferent to other problems, including the Balkans.[1] If they were Liberals, they did not like Russia, yet they did not want to take action against her. The Hungarians opposed a Western emphasis in policy; they shared the Germans' friendship for Germany, albeit with greater reserve and wanted to make Austro-German relations dependent on the development of German–Russian ones; they wanted an active anti-Russian policy and saw the East as the main field for foreign policy; they watched nationalism in the Balkans with interest and were prepared to back it against Russia. The Czechs, on the other hand, had views which were opposed to those of both the Germans and the Hungarians. They were anti-German and pro-Russian and wanted Austro-Russian cooperation in the Balkans. The Serbs and Romanians were similar to the Czechs in their views regarding Russia and the Balkans, but were not anti-German. The Poles were both anti-German and anti-Russian. These differences of outlook were not always a source of weakness for the Empire's diplomats – they could often be exploited as an excuse for inaction. 'However,' writes Diószegi, 'in the nationalism of the people of Austria there often prevailed an indifference towards imperial interests or even foreign policy which had profoundly negative consequences.'[2] On the other hand, Hungarian opinion, as will be seen, was never slow to assert itself.

This leads us on to the second dimension of domestic politics which has to be explored, namely the institutional arrangements concerning foreign policy which were established in 1867. According to most views, including Diószegi's, these left the Emperor quite firmly in control, yet a study by János Décsy of *Prime Minister Gyula Andrássy's Influence on Habsburg Foreign Policy During the Franco-German War of 1870–1871*[3] forces one to reconsider this viewpoint. Décsy argues rather persuasively in his book that: 'The Compromise of 1867, particularly the powerful position Hungary attained in the Austro-Hungarian partnership, profoundly affected the foreign policy of the Dual Monarchy. As a result, Andrássy who weighed the security of Hungary and the Dual Monarchy in terms of foreign policy, could successfully impose his views on the common government. The basic aim of Andrássy's foreign policy was to prevent developments that were contrary to particular Hungarian national interests. . . . So from the beginning of his prime ministry [*sic*], Andrássy strove to achieve this. Between 1867 and 1870, with his well-planned, single-minded and aggressive drive, Andrássy succeeded in establishing Hungary's right to parity in internal affairs and to decisive influence in the external affairs of the Dual Monarchy.'[4]

In order to understand how Andrássy could impose his will, it is necessary to remind ourselves how the machinery established in 1867 for the exercise of foreign policy actually worked. Article 8 of the Hungarian Compromise Law made provision for a common foreign minister who was to be responsible to the king and to the delegations. He was to supervise the diplomatic service and trade delegations and was to negotiate international agreements. Yet Article 8 also laid down that he was to carry out these duties 'in accordance with the ministries of both halves [of the Monarchy] and with their consent'. This imposed on him, therefore, the obligation to consult and reach prior agreements with both prime ministers on foreign policy. Moreover, on account of the tenuous nature of the control exercised by the delegations, it was to acquire great importance. It allowed Hungarian premiers to express their views on all essential matters of foreign policy. It also allowed them to be questioned in the Hungarian parliament. For this reason alone, they tended to take an active part in debates on foreign policy when they arose in the Crown Council. In Décsy's words: 'Without their cooperation not a single important move could be made.'[5] Burián, one of the Monarchy's foreign ministers during the First World War, was later to write: 'The Prime Ministers . . . had a very considerable voice in foreign policy, for they assisted not only in determining its general lines but were also the leaders of the two parliaments or delegations . . . and provided the Minister of Foreign Affairs . . . with the necessary majority. If he could not arrive at agreement with either one of the Prime Ministers, the position of the joint minister became untenable. A good understanding with the two Prime Ministers was, therefore, of primary importance in the conduct of foreign affairs.'[6] According to Décsy, it was Andrássy's achievement to make the influence of Hungarian premiers on foreign affairs effective from the very start. In his view, the decisive moment came during the Franco-Prussian war, when Andrássy forced the Crown Council to accept a policy of declared neutrality against the wishes of Beust, the Chancellor and Foreign Minister, who would have preferred to keep a free hand in case it was possible to intervene against Prussia later on.

According to the old textbooks, Beust, the former foreign minister of Saxony, had been appointed by Franz Joseph after Königgratz to pursue a policy of revenge against Prussia. Diószegi and others, however, have shown that this is untrue. His policy, rather, was to assert Austrian leadership over the south German states in order to retain a tripartite division of Germany. He knew that neither the Liberals in Austria nor the Hungarians would support a war of revenge against Prussia, since both feared that an imperial victory would restore absolutism. In 1870, moreover, it was impossible to expect Austro-German support on behalf of a France which was at war with the whole of Germany. Still, the Emperor wanted war, the Archduke Albert, the Inspector General of the army, wanted war and the Minister of War also called for intervention. Under these circumstances, Beust's views came close to those of Andrássy, but did not coincide. He wanted a full mobilization of the imperial army to allow for a possible future intervention. Andrássy, on the other hand, ruled out any intervention in support of France unless the Russians intervened on the side of Prussia; and demanded a policy of declared neutrality, as well as partial mobilization, to deter Russia, the power he saw as the real enemy of the Monarchy. He had no desire whatsoever to seek revenge for 1866 and told the Hungarian parliament on 28 July 1870: 'There is no such intention, either on the part of the government or decision-making circles, to restore the position abandoned in 1866, which would in my opinion be detrimental to the realm.'[7] Yet, as has been seen, this had not really been true. And before the outbreak of war, Andrássy had warned Paris not to place false hopes in Austro-Hungarian intervention; assured Berlin that there would be no intervention; and in 1869, during negotiations between France, Austria and Italy, had vetoed a project for a contractual anti-Prussian alliance. Décsy, therefore, rates Andrássy very highly – 'unquestionably one of the outstanding statesmen of the nineteenth century' – and ascribes his success in 1870 to his self-confidence and lucidity. 'By that time Andrássy had emerged as the most powerful politician of the Dual Monarchy.'[8] Yet Décsy is wise enough not to overlook two or three factors of great importance. First, Andrássy was powerful because in 1870 his views were backed by public opinion in both parts of the Monarchy; secondly, the French collapsed so quickly that intervention became inoperable – after all, Franz Joseph at the Crown Council had decided on a policy of only 'neutrality for the time being'; finally, the Emperor had been able to see that Andrássy's policies had been right for the Monarchy – defeat in 1870 would almost certainly have meant its end. Hence his views had prevailed for reasons which were neither constitutional nor personal; in the end. they had prevailed because Franz Joseph believed they were correct. Beust himself, moreover, after the French defeat and Russia's successful renunciation of the Black Sea clauses in 1871, advised the Emperor to accept the new situation in Europe and pursue a policy of reconciliation with Germany and Russia.

THE OCCUPATION OF BOSNIA–HERZEGOVINA

Andrássy's reputation, however, does not rest simply on his role in 1870. It remains high because he was one of the main architects of the Compromise; and because as Foreign Minister between 1871 and 1879 he negotiated the Three Emperors' Alliance (1873), helped overturn the Treaty of San Stefano at the Congress of Berlin (1878), and negotiated the Dual Alliance of 1879 with Bismarck on terms favourable to Austria (i.e. Germany promised to come to Austria's aid if she were attacked by Russia, but Austria was not obliged to support Germany if she were attacked by France). He was also responsible for the occupation by Austria-Hungary of Bosnia-Herzegovina in accordance with the Treaty of Berlin. Behind Andrássy's diplomacy, however, there lay a particularly Hungarian view of foreign policy, according to which the Monarchy's main enemy was Russia whose support of Panslavism in the Monarchy and in the Balkans had to be resisted at all costs. The Prussian consul at Pest reported of Andrássy that 'Russia is on his mind day and night'.[9] A Hungarian deputy even complained that the Eastern Question was an 'absurd infatuation' for him.[10] Yet the phenomenon was a national one among the Hungarian ruling classes and, particularly after 1878, became an imperial one also. The Monarchy simply had no other sphere but the Balkans in which to attempt to exercise hegemony.

The Monarchy's obsession with the Balkans – and with Russian influence there, not excluding imperial territory – was cemented by Andrássy's apparent triumph at Berlin, when he secured the agreement of the great powers to the Monarchy's occupation of Bosnia-Herzegovina. In fact this was a most unpopular triumph. Inside the Monarchy, practically nobody wanted these territories since they threatened to upset the delicate balance erected by dualism. That is to say, if they were to be incorporated into either part of the Monarchy they would give the Slavs there an overwhelming preponderance. This problem was to be a recurring, and finally an insoluble one for the Monarchy, given the Hungarians' iron determination never to alter the dualist system. What was to happen if Serbia were ever conquered? Or Poland? Or Romania? How could these non-German and non-Magyar nations be absorbed into the Monarchy without upsetting the dualist system? Much of the Empire's diplomacy during the First World War would be devoted to this conundrum. In 1878, however, the solution found to the problem of Bosnia-Herzegovina was to place the provinces under the rule of the common finance minister. This was indeed an anomaly, highlighted by the fact that even after annexation in 1908 the new subjects of the Emperor could acquire neither Austrian nor Hungarian citizenship. Franz Joseph himself, on the other hand, was happy enough simply acquiring new territory; however poor it was, to some extent at least, it helped make up for the lands which he had already lost. His grievance, therefore, was that Andrássy had failed to secure an outright annexation of the provinces. Instead, the foreign minister had actually written a memorandum suggesting that one day they might be returned to the Sultan.

What then was the point of taking the provinces? For Andrássy and the military, there was the straightforward argument of military security. Control of the provinces would protect the Habsburg territories of Croatia-Slavonia and Dalmatia from attack by Serbs, Russians or Panslavs and help the Monarchy dominate the rest of the Balkan peninsula. There was no plan, on the other hand, to march on Salonika, despite Russian propaganda. In fact, this never ever became an Austrian objective. Can the move be interpreted none the less as part of the contemporary history of imperialism? According to Robert A. Kann, this is 'highly problematical'.[11] He argues: 'Imperialism, it is true, while not prevalent was certainly not absent in Austro-Hungarian Balkan policies with regard to Bosnia. But it was on the whole so ineffective and so haphazardly pursued that it is difficult to identify it with the kind of imperialism which built colonial empires beyond the seas. Thus the charge of colonialism or pseudo-colonialism just does not stand up.'[12] He bases his case on a number of grounds, first financial: 'In a financial sense the acquisition was considered not only no gain but a definite loss, a prediction which could be proved convincingly throughout the entire history of the occupation and annexation era. Occupation was considered the lesser of two evils. It would mean bad business economically but it might offer some relief against the threat of Balkan nationalism and Russian-inspired Panslavism.'[13] Andrássy, according to Kann, was no imperialist: he merely thought that with the Balkans out of control between 1875 and 1878, it would be better to occupy the provinces to gain some security. Given German and Magyar domestic opposition, Russian suspicion, Serb nationalism, Turkish dissatisfaction and the acceptance of a possibly only temporary occupation when annexation had been there for the asking, 'it is difficult', writes Kann, 'to speak of a colonial policy'.[14] On the other hand, he does not attempt to defend the annexation of 1908.

The *modus procedendi* then adopted, he admits, involved the violation of the Treaty of Berlin and helped push Europe closer to war.

Kann also examines the views of leading authorities regarding the economic development of the provinces between 1878 and 1914. One of these, Peter F. Sugar, notes that the Austrians gave the provinces thirty-six years of peace, maintained law and order, built a network of roads, constructed public buildings, and left some railways and factories behind them; they also attempted to raise living standards. Overall progress, he admits, was limited, but this was largely on account of the Hungarians, who blocked the construction of badly needed railway links with Dalmatia, western Croatia and Austria. They also prevented the linking-up of the provinces' railway line with those of either Turkey or Serbia – all this in order to protect the tariff policy of the Hungarian state railways and the one Hungarian seaport of Fiume. Finally, the Hungarians blocked all attempts at land reform in the provinces in case a precedent was set for similar reforms within Hungary itself.[15] Kurt Wessely is more critical: he too stresses the lack of any land reform and in particular the failure to emancipate the *kmets* or peasant subjects of the Mohammedan landlords. According to him, however, the motive was political, the *kmets* being largely Serbs and, therefore, considered disloyal, whereas the landlords tended to favour the régime. There were some attempts, he admits, to improve the economy, but the refusal to introduce land reform meant that they were unlikely to make any difference.[16] The British Foreign Office, according to Kann, thought the Austrian régime had been largely progressive, but believed that little could be expected given the lack of native capital and the dependence on the harvest. Kann therefore concludes that 'colonial trends had no place in the history of the administration from 1878 to 1914, unless one considers the Habsburg empire as a whole a residuum of the age of colonial administration'.[17] One need not go so far as that to disagree; but one can point out that taxes increased fivefold under Austria's administration and that the bureaucracy which had comprised only 120 men under the Turks rose to 9,533 in 1908. Moreover, under the terms of the Land Statute introduced to give the provinces some sort of constitutional structure after 1908, the diet, elected on an extremely limited franchise, had only limited powers. The common finance ministry could veto any legislation which it did not like. Finally, the administration played off Croats against Serbs and encouraged Croats and Mohammedans to cooperate. If all this did not represent imperialism, it is difficult to know what it did represent. Given the armed resistance of the population to the Austrian take-over, given the large-scale presence of the military thereafter, given the lack of real, popular representation, the limited economic and social progress, the disaffection of the Serbs (42 per cent of the population in 1910, as opposed to 21 per cent Croats and 34 per cent Mohammedans), the large bureaucracy and tax bill, it is almost a classic case of imperialism. Kann disputes this, probably because he is out of touch with modern research on the subject. Hence his argument that the provinces cannot be considered colonial dependencies, since they did not pay for themselves, made no profit and had some form of representation. Yet the British Empire had many colonies which fitted precisely that pattern. Austrian rule, we may conclude, may not have been totally unenlightened by the standards of the time, but it amounted to imperialism none the less.

AUSTRIA-HUNGARY AS A FACTOR FOR PEACE OR WAR IN EUROPE

We shall return to the Balkans and to Bosnia-Herzegovina shortly, but we shall do so in the context of yet another argument concerning Austria's international position in the period leading up to 1914, namely Paul Schroeder's thesis that, in the main, thanks to Great Britain, Austria's position at the centre of the European balance of power was undermined, forcing her to provoke a war against Serbia in 1914 which turned into a world war. This in turn left a vacuum in Central Europe, which Hitler was allowed to fill. If the Monarchy had not by then disappeared, Schroeder suggests, the tragedy of the Second World War might never have happened. This thesis has been presented by Schroeder in a number of articles and with his accustomed verve and brilliance but, as will be seen, it is ultimately unconvincing.

The following quotes will give the flavour of Schroeder's arguments. He writes: 'The threat to Austria's existence . . . was primarily international rather than internal in character, a product in great part of Entente policy. . . . Of course there was no great anti-Austrian plot. The British did not think of Austria as their enemy; they tried not to think of her at all. They did not concern themselves (as they never had earlier in the nineteenth century) with the question of whether the concessions and defeats forced upon Austria before the war, and the territorial sacrifices to be imposed upon her during and after it would leave her viable. Britain undermined Austria's position before the war – indeed throughout the nineteenth century – and assisted in her destruction during it, in a fit of absence of mind. . .'[18] At fault was Britain's defective conception of the role of Central Europe in the European balance of power. This was based on: '. . . the concept of Central Europe as useful primarily for checking France and Russia; the concept of the balance of power as essentially mechanical and operating more or less automatically, because of the natural desire of all states for independence, irrespective of the particular territorial or political arrangements for Central Europe; and the belief that Britain had only a limited and contingent interest in Central Europe.'[19] The result was that when eventually Hitler made his appearance, there no longer existed a balance of power and in particular 'a specific system of containment of German power *within* Central Europe. . . . *Austria-Hungary had been more important to Britain and Europe for checking Germany than for restraining Russia and France* [author's italics]. . . . What had worked with some success before 1914 was the existence of a great power in the area, Austria-Hungary, which simply could not survive the triumph of either Pan-Germanism or Panslavism and had to resist both ideologies.'[20]

Schroeder appears to believe therefore that in order to uphold the European balance of power it was the task of Britain to defend Austria's interests, because Austria provided a check on Germany in Central Europe. When Britain failed to do so, Austria-Hungary disappeared and Britain had to face the consequences in the shape of Nazi Germany: the result was Munich, appeasement and ultimately the Second World War. This is an interesting speculation but also a fantastical one. The answer to Schroeder is that, with regard to the Hitler period, he fails to put Munich and appeasement into its proper context – the world balance of power. Britain's main worry during the 1930s was of becoming involved in a three-front war against Germany, Japan and Italy which, given her economic and military position, she could not possibly hope to win, especially if, as was likely, she could count on no support from America, Russia or perhaps even her Dominions. The existence of Austria-Hungary in this context would hardly have counted for much. But let us return to the nineteenth century. Here the Schroeder thesis fails on a number of counts. For a start, it refuses to acknowledge that Britain had different interests from the Habsburg Monarchy and that there was no reason to put those of the Monarchy first if and when they clashed. It was the task of the Monarchy to protect her own interests and, as will be seen, she simply failed to analyse these properly and managed her foreign affairs incompetently. This in fact made *her* one of the principal threats, if not *the* principal threat to the European balance of power before 1914 – a much greater threat, indeed, than either Pan-Germanism or Panslavism. She herself, however, ignored the trouble she caused and blithely assumed that her geographical position made her a European necessity. This in turn encouraged her to believe that other powers would always come to her assistance. In fact, these assumptions were out of date after 1870 – she was no longer a European necessity – and Schroeder is wrong to resurrect them. In any case, Schroeder also overestimates the extent of Britain's capability to uphold a balance of power in Continental Europe. Britain could really only operate by sea power. This was why she had never really been able to influence events in Central Europe, and this weakness became even more apparent after 1893 when the Admiralty concluded that the Royal Navy could no longer force the Straits. Thereafter, there was little point in Austria-Hungary relying on British aid. Her true interest lay in coming to a *modus vivendi* with Russia, against whom Britain could offer no help. Otherwise, if help should be required, her main ally would clearly have to be Germany. Here, in fact, we come to the crux of the debate over the Schroeder thesis. For when we examine the evidence, it becomes immediately clear that, far from having to restrain Germany, it was Prussia or Germany in the nineteenth century who had, consistently, to restrain Austria. It was Prussia or Germany after all who had to restrain Austria in 1830, 1854, 1878, 1887 and during the Balkan Wars of 1912–13. Again, it was Austria who issued the ultimatum of 1859 to Sardinia, sought German backing for her breach of the Treaty of Berlin in 1908 and for her ultimatum to Serbia in 1914, which was deliberately designed to start a war and probably a world war. It was Bismarck who said: 'So long as I am minister I shall not give my consent to a prophylactic attack on Russia, and I am far from advising Austria to make such an attack . . .'[21] It was Bülow who said: 'Do not repeat the Bosnian affair.'[22] It was the Kaiser who told Austria that she would be crazy to become involved in the Balkan Wars, but it was Berchtold's wife who later said: 'poor Leopold could not sleep on the day he wrote his ultimatum to the Serbs as he was so worried that they might accept it. Several times during the night he got up and altered or added some clause, to reduce this risk.'[23] One might be forgiven for suspecting, therefore, that had the Monarchy survived the First World War it would almost certainly have been supporting Hitler rather than restraining him. It did not, after all, have a very good record regarding either Slavs or peace. And in any case, Hitler himself was a Habsburg product.

Why did it not prove possible to reach some *modus vivendi* with Russia? Why did the Germans not do more to restrain Austria-Hungary? These two questions arise immediately from the previous criticism of the Schroeder thesis. Regarding the first, it should be pointed out that there was in fact quite a lot of cooperation between the two powers before 1914. During the Great Eastern crisis of 1875–8, for example, there had been the Reichstadt agreements of July 1876 and the Budapest Convention of January 1877. In accordance with the former, the two powers had agreed that if Turkey won the war against Serbia and Montenegro which was then going on, they would insist on the restoration of the *status quo ante* plus the introduction of reforms in Bosnia-Herzegovina. If Turkey lost, they agreed on the partition of the Turkish Empire: a Bulgarian and a Rumelian state would be formed; Greece would receive Epirus and Thessaly; Constantinople might become a free city; Russia would acquire Batum and the southern Bessarabian lands she had lost in 1856; and Austria-Hungary would receive part, if not all, of Bosnia-Herzegovina. There was later some dispute over the last part of the agreements (they had not been written down). What is clear, however, is that Austria-Hungary was not prepared to stand by Turkey at all costs, the policy which Schroeder states that Britain should have followed later. She preferred, instead, in the name of the European balance, of course, to carve Turkey up. In Barabara Jelavich's words: 'In this agreement the Habsburg government reversed its former policy of the conservation of the empire and instead joined with Russia in a program for its destruction.'[24] Andrássy at least, therefore, cannot be claimed as a Metternichian.

Despite these agreements, however, things went wrong. Russia went to war with Turkey and, in contravention of the Budapest Convention, created a huge client state of Bulgaria by the Treaty of San Stefano. Encouraged by British policy, Andrássy now pressed for war with Russia. On 24 February he presented a clear-cut war proposal to the common cabinet meeting, arguing that the last chance had come for the Monarchy to settle her differences with the Slavs with the aid of Europe. He also stated that such a war would be popular with the peoples of the Monarchy. Yet only the Hungarian premier, Kálḿan Tisza, supported him. In Diószegi's words: '. . . the Hungarian national policy manifest in anti-Russian feelings was backed by none of the Monarchy's peoples, except the

Poles. The Czechs and the South Slavs were manifestly pro-Russian, and the Austro-Germans remained basically indifferent. The representative of the Austrian Liberal Party who was present at the common cabinet meeting expressed his doubts about the inevitability of an Austro-Slavic clash. Court circles likewise adduced numerous military and diplomatic arguments, and under such circumstances their standpoint prevailed. Andrássy's war motion was rejected.'[25] Hence it was internal opposition which was responsible in the first instance for restraining Andrássy from starting a war with Russia in 1878. This was reinforced none the less by Bismarck's diplomacy and by his offer to be an 'honest broker' at the Congress of Berlin. His solution to the Eastern Question was the straightforward one of getting Russia and Austria to divide the Balkans into spheres of influence.

For much of the *Bismarckzeit*, this almost proved possible. The Three Emperors' League of 1873 and its renewal in 1881 meant greater cooperation between both powers. In 1881, for example, the Austrian Foreign Minister, Kálnocky, flatly refused a Turkish proposal for an alliance directed against Russia. His commitments under the terms of the League meant that he had promised neutrality in the event of a Russo-Turkish war. (Russia had promised to conclude separate agreements with her partners prior to the outbreak of any such war.) None the less, another Eastern crisis arose in 1885–8 over Bulgaria, which once again put an end to good relations. The story is well known and need not be repeated here, except to point out that it was Hungarian pressure inside the Monarchy which precipitated the breach between the two countries. In September 1886, Russia sent a commissioner to Bulgaria and threatened to occupy it. Neither Kálnocky nor Bismarck made any objection. However, the Hungarian premier, Kálmán Tisza, made a speech in the Hungarian parliament stating his opposition, something which Kálnocky felt unable to ignore. In October 1886, therefore, he issued a statement publicly backing Bulgaria's independence and, in Diószegi's words, 'this amounted to a break with the Austro-Russian sphere of interest policy that had jointly been pursued for five years'.[26] By January 1888, Tisza was again advocating war with Russia, just as he had done in 1878, this time complaining to the common cabinet about 'artificial means' which had been taken to preserve the peace. According to Diószegi: 'The entire Hungarian Liberal Party backed Kálmán Tisza's policy of war, and the camp of the sabre-rattlers was greatly fortified by the support of former foreign minister, Gyula Andrássy. Contrary to the situation ten years earlier, the bellicose position of the Hungarian liberals was no longer an isolated phenomenon.'[27] Austria's military leaders also argued for war; so too did the Crown Prince. The greater part of court circles, however, were against it, as were Taaffe, the Austrian premier, and Kálnocky himself. The latter pointed out that everything would depend on Germany and that under the terms of the Dual Alliance of 1879, Germany was bound to come to Austria's assistance only if Russia attacked her first. Bismarck, however, wanted no war with Russia, although he did agree to publish the terms of the Dual Alliance in February 1888 as a warning to Russia. But that was a good step short of war and so ended the debate inside the Monarchy; no one proposed to go to war without Germany. Hence the crisis passed off peacefully due to German restraint.

Germany's attitute towards Russia was modified after Bismarck's fall from power; for example, the Reinsurance Treaty was not renewed. However, there was still no support for any armed clash with Russia, something which in Berlin was 'regarded as undesirable as before, and Kálnocky's recommendations and hints in this regard were flatly refused'.[28] An active policy against Russia in the Balkans, moreover, could not count on domestic support within Austria-Hungary either: 'Although the basis of anti-Russian feeling continued to be fairly broad, the camp of the adherents of Balkan expansion remained small and hardly extended beyond court circles.'[29]

The 1890s proved yet again that cooperation with Russia was possible. To begin with, this did not seem necessary. In the Balkans, Bulgaria was anti-Russian, and Serbia, under King Milan, had become an Austrian satellite. Under the terms of a treaty of 1881, he had agreed to suppress all anti-Austrian conspiracies in his realm and had also undertaken only to sign treaties which had received Austria's prior approval. A treaty signed with Romania in 1883 had provided yet more security for the Monarchy. This had created a defensive alliance of the two states against Russia and was renewed regularly up until 1916. It also provided some sort of guarantee that Romania would give up irredentist propaganda over Transylvania. More important for good relations with Russia was the fact that the latter power was distracted by Far Eastern affairs. This, too, took the pressure off Austria's position in the Balkans. Finally, a system of Mediterranean Agreements had been constructed between Austria, Britian, Italy and Spain to preserve the *status quo* in the East Mediterranean. Then in 1896, the British Prime Minister, Lord Salisbury, unsure of Italian policy and unwilling to enter firmer arrangements with Austria over the defence of Constantinople, allowed the Mediterranean Agreements to lapse. The result was that, with the backing of Berlin, Austria turned to Russia. In 1897 an agreement was reached to 'put the Balkans on ice', meaning that both powers agreed to maintain the *status quo* there or only to change it after prior agreement. For almost eleven years, consequently, the Balkans remained outside the sphere of great power conflict. In 1903 in fact, at Mürzsteg, both powers were able to draw up a programme of reforms for Macedonia, while in the following year they agreed to remain neutral if either power became involved in a war with a third – so long as it was not a Balkan state. This gave Austria security against Italy (nominally an ally, but a distrusted one) and Russia security against Japan. The difficult internal position of the Monarchy, of course, also helped dictate a peaceful foreign policy – particularly the quarrel with Hungary over the size and constitutional position of the army. The result of all these factors and measures in any case was that between 1897 and 1908, Russia and Austria managed to coexist quite peacefully. Indeed, in 1906, Aerenthal, shortly before he became Foreign Minister, could even propose the re-establishment of the *Dreikaiserbund* between Austria-Hungary, Germany and Russia.

During the first decade of the twentieth century, on the other hand, events conspired against continued cooperation. In 1903 the Obrenovič dynasty was overthrown in Serbia and replaced by a more independent one. In 1905, Russia lost the war with Japan; in 1907, she signed an entente with Britain over the Middle East. Inevitably, therefore, her attention returned to Europe. Still, the results need not necessarily have been dangerous. Aerenthal, who had been in Russia in 1905, believed that the Tsarist Empire was still weak: his Balkan railway programme showed that he had little fear of her. The trade war with Serbia in 1906 (known as the 'Pig War' given that 80 per cent of Serbia's exports were livestock), on the other hand, was an ominous development which alienated not only the educated classes but also the peasant ones in Serbia from the Monarchy. The outlook, in any case, was for further cooperation. In 1908, talks took place between Aerenthal and the Russian Foreign Minister Izvolsky at Buchlau on a deal whereby Austria could annex Bosnia-Herzegovina in return for a revised Straits convention. These talks were a success, but while Izvolsky toured the European capitals in search of support for his convention, Austria, fearful that the Young Turks were about to proclaim a constitution in the Ottoman Empire, annexed Bosnia-Herzegovina suddenly and without any prior warning. This blow was compounded for the Russians by the fact that Britain and France turned down their proposals for a revised Straits convention. Yet Austria, in defiance of the Treaty of Berlin, refused to discuss her actions at an international conference. Instead, Serbia was sent an ultimatum when she protested, and Russia received similar treatment from Austria's ally Germany. Both states were in fact humiliated: Russia since she was too weak to fight and Serbia because she was forced to promise to display good behaviour in future. Moreover, she received none of the financial compensation offered to Montenegro. Even so, the Bosnian crisis still left room for cooperation between the powers. In the years after 1909 Aerenthal, despite heavy pressure from the Austrian Chief of Staff, Conrad von Hötzendorf, refused to attack Serbia since he saw no place for Serbian territory within the Monarchy. His policy instead became one of consolidating Turkey and maintaining the *status quo* in the Balkans. If that could not work, then he aimed to establish a new independent state of Albania and to prevent Serbia and Montenegro acquiring access to the sea. The Emperor approved of this policy and in 1911 dismissed Conrad from his post for continuing to attack his foreign minister. Aerenthal was certainly correct not to press for a forward policy. Neither the Austrians, the Poles or the Czechs inside the Monarchy had identified themselves with the annexation, and as for the Hungarians, even they were unenthusiastic: 'it was characteristic that the greatest concern of the Hungarian delegation meeting at the time of the crisis was how to increase the Hungarian ratio within the diplomatic corps.'[30] In any case, the Russians, once the crisis was over and Izvolsky had been replaced by Sazanov, once more reverted to cooperation. They had always reckoned that the Monarchy would annex the provinces sometime. It was therefore the Slav inhabitants of the Balkans, not the Russians, who refused to forgive Austria for her actions in 1908. Worse still, it was they, against the advice of Russia, who in 1912 took advantage of the Italian attack on Libya to launch an attack of their own on European Turkey. Once again, therefore, Austria was forced to decide whether to intervene. Once again, the military pressed for action (Conrad was even recalled) yet, once again, no intervention took place and Berchtold, Aerenthal's successor, continued his policy. Belief in monarchical solidarity and Russian military weakness helped. In any case, Berlin showed no sign whatsoever of wishing to become involved.

The Balkan Wars again showed that there was room for cooperation with Russia. St Petersburg demonstrated that it was quite aware of Habsburg interests and was willing to consider Austria's programme for the establishment of an Albanian state. At the same time, however, it demanded an Adriatic port for Serbia, something which the Austrians resisted. This led to border reinforcements and trial mobilizations in 1912, but the Hohenlohe mission to Russia secured a compromise: Serbia was to get more Albanian territory rather than access to the sea. However, this temporary resurrection of good relations with the Russians was wrecked when Austria, using a cannon to shoot a sparrow in the words of the King of Montenegro, sent a naval squadron to block Scutari and oust the occupying Montenegrins. The Second Balkan War – which again took place despite the warnings of both Russia and Austria – brought more dilemmas for Austria. Once again she decided against intervention – Tisza, the Hungarian premier, the Emperor and Franz Ferdinand were all against it – but again she resorted to arms to enforce the territorial settlement. Serbian troops held on to Albanian territory to build a corridor to the sea, and an Austrian ultimatum proved necessary to ensure their withdrawal. On the other hand, whatever satisfaction may have been found in this was overshadowed by the results of the Treaty of Bucharest which ended the war. Both Serbia and Romania emerged with substantial increases of territory, battle-hardened armies and soaring morale. The reaction of the Monarchy became increasingly irrational.

Austria-Hungary gave an impression of growing desperation after 1913 concerning her position in the Balkans. It became a cliché in military circles that Serbia would have to be dealt with sooner or later. The memory of Scutari and of the ultimatum to Belgrade more than whetted the appetite to use force. This was the only language, it was said, which the Serbs would understand. The breach with Russia was now also considered irreparable, despite the fact that the Russians had done nothing to start the Balkans Wars, had agreed to the establishment of Albania and had given up their support for a Serbian seaport on the Adriatic. Nor could Austria claim to be a greater defender of the balance of power and the *status quo*, since she, for her part, had done nothing to aid Turkey against her ally, Italy.

In spite of this, the leaders of the Monarchy expressed anxiety at their position. A reconciliation between Romania and Russia in 1914 was seen as extremely menacing, but most worrying of all the attitude of Germany had apparently changed since 1909. She now seemed to have forgotten about the Dual Alliance, having in fact become the Monarchy's main economic competitor in both Turkey and the Balkans. She had also failed to lend support in the diplomacy of the wars. Instead, she had advised against intervention and had refused to support Bulgaria after the First Balkan War as Austria had done. She had also refused to take any responsibility for enforcing the territorial settlements arrived at. By July 1914, therefore, the Austrian Foreign Office was drawing up a list of grievances to send to Berlin with the implied threat that if Germany did not change her ways, the Dual Alliance would not be renewed. Before the memorandum could be sent, however, a new crisis occurred, the assassination of the heir to the throne, the Archduke Franz Ferdinand, and his wife at Sarajevo, the Bosnian capital

The assassination in itself was not something which upset the Austrian Emperor: Franz Joseph had not liked the imperial couple and shed no tears over their deaths. However, since the Bosnian students who had murdered them were held to have been the agents of Belgrade, the crime did offer an excuse for a declaration of war against Serbia. The case against this was the lack of evidence that Serbia had been involved. Nor were the Austrians ever to discover any. In fact, the Serb prime minister, who had got wind of the plot (it had been organized by his political enemies in the army), had tried to warn Vienna to take precautions. His message, however, had failed to get through – he forgot that the Finance Ministry ran Bosnia under dualism – so that the visit had gone ahead. There were of course other reasons for keeping cool. For a start, a war could not solve anything. Serbia could not be incorporated into the Monarchy without upsetting the Compromise and, besides, a war with Serbia would almost certainly involve a war with Russia. That meant that German support would also have to be secured. But even with German support, hostilities would spread: Russia's ally France would become involved and probably Britain too. Meanwhile, Austria's other allies, Romania and Italy, were totally unreliable. To cap everything, neither Austria's finances nor her army were in any condition to endure a war of any length, especially if another great power were involved. The decision to provoke one therefore cannot really be considered rational.

What can be said in favour of the decision? In the first place, the assassinations provided Austria with a moral advantage. Yet the month which elapsed before war was declared, plus the lack of evidence, soon detracted from this position. There was also some hope of localizing the war, yet once again the delay made this unlikely. The real reason to decide for war was that the Germans offered their support. This was something which it was thought might never happen again as far as the Balkans were concerned. In fact there was a curious symmetry involved. Germany too was afraid of isolation; she was also afraid that if she did not take the opportunity to crush her rivals she too would lose her military freedom of action in Europe once Russia's rearmament programme peaked in 1917. In a sense, therefore, Austria's perceived position in the Balkans was the same as Germany's in Europe as a whole. Thus, faced with enemies which were growing in strength, both powers decided in favour of war while they were still in a position to do so. That they should both have been reduced to this strategy, it should be added, was largely the result of their own diplomatic incompetence.

Let us return to Austria-Hungary, however. Just as Fritz Fischer has suggested that Germany went to war because of the *Primat der Innenpolitik*, it is often assumed that Austria did so for the same reason. Yet this is difficult to accept. As we have already seen, no major party or politician was in favour of destroying the Monarchy, the nationality question did not threaten its existence and, if anything, the situation was improving domestically before 1914. Hence Roy Bridge is correct when he writes: 'The view that the Dual Monarchy was by 1914 in a critical state bordering on dissolution, which rendered some foreign action imperative as a diversion or as a solution is not without a certain plausibility'; however, it was her position as a great power which was at stake and 'in this situation the domestic, economic and military situation in the Monarchy could hardly have any really determining effect on the government's decision either way'.[31] Bridge's statement, however, should be modified in the following ways. First, it should be remembered that the threat perceived in Vienna to the Monarchy's great power status in the Balkans was wildly exaggerated. Secondly, war was hardly the only way out. What made it seem so was the need to maintain prestige, along with the fear that relative military decline would close all options in the future. This combination of a need for prestige plus fear of the future meant that a basically irrational view of the Monarchy's interests could prevail. The element which served to obscure this irrationality was dynastic honour. An Empire according to contemporary values could only defend its interests honourably by force of arms; to compromise or give way without a struggle was to invite dishonour. War after all was simply the 'duel of the nations' and if gentlemen were still expected to preserve their honour and that of their class by challenging their opponents, the same held true for sovereigns and states. To refuse a challenge would be to give up the rank of a great power. Hence Austria's wars over Italy and

Germany, and the decision for war over Bosnia. Nonetheless, even this explanation pushes contemporary values to the limits. If every power had always acted on these values, no diplomatic settlement would ever have been possible without recourse to war. Yet this was something which happened fairly regularly among the powers of Europe. Perhaps, therefore, one should place more weight on the more rational critique put forward by István Diószegi when he writes: 'The situation after the Balkan Wars showed much similarity to the transformation that had taken place in Italy and Germany. The Monarchy was ousted from this area of interests also. She preserved only the remnants of her influence, but her territorial integrity was not affected by the changes. Serbia set as her aim the unification of the ethnic stock as a whole and Austria's South Slav population also gravitated towards this strengthened national state. Yet this attraction was not stronger than that of the Austro-Germans towards an emerging national Germany and was far behind it in respect to the importance for the Monarchy as a whole. Although Serbia kept the idea of South Slav national unity alive, she could not think of realising her plans unaided, without external help. The hope offered by a Great Power, namely Russia's war against Austria for promoting Serbian interests, did not count as a rational contingency. Acquiescence in the Balkan transformation would probably not have had worse consequences than the recognition of the Italian and German *fait accompli* at the time.'[32] The men who refused this alternative were few in number: the Emperor, the War Minister, the Finance Minister, the Chief of Staff, and the premiers of Austria and Hungary. Franz Ferdinand, who had in fact been the leader of the peace party in Vienna, was now dead. Yet only Tisza, the Hungarian premier, hesitated. He restated the old argument that Serbia could not be incorporated into the Monarchy for fear of upsetting the Compromise. But he too soon fell into line thanks to a number of reasons: the fear that German support would not be forthcoming in the future; the decision to send an ultimatum before declaring war; the news that Romania would not enter, at least immediately; the agreement not to incorporate Serb territory within the Monarchy; and, the knowledge that Franz Joseph had been converted to war. Bilinski, the common Finance Minister, actually put it to the Emperor that war with Serbia, would mean a European war. Franz Joseph's reply was: 'Certainly, Russia cannot possibly accept this note.'[33] One Hungarian historian has argued that Tisza believed that the Serb reply would be negotiable. Apparently, Berchtold gave him no reason to believe anything else. Yet Berchtold had taken great care to ensure that the ultimatum would be rejected. And just to ensure that there would be war, he specifically instructed his ambassador in Belgrade to demand acceptance 'pure and simple'.[34] Of all the issues concerning the outbreak of the First World War, this one at least is totally uncontroversial: the Austro-Hungarian ultimatum to Serbia was deliberately designed to start a war. It did not begin by accident.

AUSTRIA–HUNGARY AND THE FIRST WORLD WAR

Ironically, perhaps, nearly all the research on the Monarchy's performance during the war itself leaves practically no room for controversy. The course of events was dominated by a few very fundamental factors. In the first place, the war was fought from the Austrian viewpoint to preserve the Monarchy. The result was that no concessions could be made to states like Italy or Romania to keep them out. This was very annoying for the Germans, who had had their own reasons for entering, but who discovered after 1916 that they had acquired two new enemies on account of Austrian intransigence. Yet the Austrian position was a logical one: there was little point in fighting to keep one's south Slav subjects merely to surrender one's Transylvanian or Italian ones. The second point to remember is that from the Hungarian point of view, the Monarchy was only worth preserving if it remained the Dual Monarchy; any change in the imperial constitution, therefore, was ruled out of order. This upset many democrats during the war, as well as Franz Joseph's successor, the last Habsburg Emperor Charles, who would have liked to federalize the Monarchy. But the Hungarians were insistent, Tisza most of all. There could be no federalism and no franchise reform in Hungary either and that was that. This severely limited the political flexibility required during wartime, especially after 1916 when the solidarity of the nationalities began to be undermined. The third point to note is that almost half of the regular army was killed in the campaigns of 1914. Conrad had bungled the mobilization and had not received the support from Germany which he believed he had been promised. From the start of 1915, therefore, the army was more or less a militia. Even before then, it had been badly equipped, under-financed, technologically backward but splendidly uniformed. From now on, however, it would be dependent on Germany. Even on the Italian front, regarded by the

Austrians as peculiarly their own, German help would be needed to win the campaign of Caporetto. The Italian front, however, was the easiest to defend: the Italians had been sent into war against their wishes; the Austrians were sitting on top of the Alps shooting down on them; and there was a tradition of defeating Italians. Elsewhere – in Poland and Romania – victory depended entirely on the Germans. Finally, the Monarchy depended on Germany just as much for food and hard currency as she did for troops. The result was diplomatic dependence too: Germany claimed the right to decide the future of Poland and Romania, despite the Austrians' assumption that these countries should be associated in the future with the Habsburgs. The Germans also created, by the Treaty of Brest-Litovsk at the beginning of 1918, a Ukrainian state which was recognized by the Austrians in the (vain) hope that they could requisition its grain supplies (Romanian grain had already proved elusive). The only result was that the Poles of the Empire accused the Habsburgs of betraying them. In this, moreover, they were not alone, for by the spring of 1918 even the Germans of the Monarchy distrusted the dynasty: the Emperor Charles, in an astonishing piece of family diplomacy (the Sixtus affair), was revealed by Clemenceau as having recognized France's right to Alsace-Lorraine and having offered to end the war by compensating the Germans with Galicia. It was Europe's last example of purely dynastic diplomacy and failed, as it was doomed to, by excluding the Hohenzollerns. Thereafter, to prove his good faith, Charles was obliged to act as Germany's poodle; the Monarchy now agreed to participate in schemes for *Mitteleuropa*, a Central European Customs Union. The details, it is true, were to be worked out later, but the significance of the agreement was clear. The Monarchy, already a military appendage of the German Empire, would become an economic one also; in fact, she was almost one already. By 1918, therefore, the Habsburg Monarchy had little future as an independent state, even if Germany won the war; German victory, on the other hand, would still ensure that it could leave the war intact.

Even the Allies, however, supported the territorial integrity of the Monarchy until almost the end of the struggle. President Wilson's Fourteen Points of January 1918 called only for its reorganization along federal lines, not its disappearance. Point Ten ran: 'The peoples of Austria-Hungary, whose place among the nations we wish to see safeguarded and assured, should be accorded the freest opportunity for autonomous development.' The British at this point were still considering a Monarchy, enlarged with Polish territory, as a counterweight to both Germany and the newly created Soviet Union. With the failure of the Sixtus mission, however, Charles's submission to the Germans at Spa and the Austrians' decision to stake all their hopes on a German victory, Allied opinion swung towards recognizing the national committees of the Czech and Yugoslav exiles. Even so, it was not until September 1918 that the Czechoslovak national committee was accorded recognition as a belligerent government-in-exile. This decision, however, was a crucial one, for it was incompatible not only with Dualism but with the territorial integrity of the Monarchy.

Domestic developments, meanwhile, were pointing in the same direction: by the spring of 1918, most of the population were war-weary and starving; the Monarchy was convulsed in strikes; the Czechs, Poles and south Slavs inside the Empire were calling for its dissolution. Franz Joseph had died (21 November 1916) and, although his successor was well-liked, the old Monarchy seemed to have died with the old Emperor. The Russian revolution, moreover, had shown not only that dynasties could be overthrown, but that the territorial map of Eastern Europe was bound to be redrawn. Worse still, it had returned to Austria thousands of prisoners-or-war, mainly Czechs, who wished to redraw it. The Austrian parliament by May 1917 was once again in session, but that in itself solved nothing. Parliamentary life in Austria had long been discredited, and for the first three years of the war the parliament building had been used as a hospital. Franz Joseph had seen no need to consult the people's representatives. One result was that in October 1916, Friedrich Adler, a Socialist deputy, had shot the Austrian prime minister in an attempt to draw attention to this strange state of affairs. His trial, in fact, became a trial of the government. The last Emperor, Charles, therefore, had had an incentive to recall parliament. Under wartime conditions, however, with the army – often the German army – running large parts of the Monarchy, its role was bound to be a limited one; its constitutional powers, in any case, had not been enlarged. In Hungary, meanwhile, dualism was rigorously upheld. The franchise remained restricted and the Hungarian bureaucracy ensured that Hungarian grain reserves supplied Hungarian needs first. The Austrian government, as a result, became even more dependent on Germany to feed an increasingly starving population. This was a situation which undermined its authority both in diplomatic negotiations (Poland, Romania, *Mitteleuropa*) and in military strategy, so that Conrad, who had greeted the outbreak of hostilities with the hope that 'if the War ends in victory, then Austria-Hungary will be so much strengthened that she will be able to face Germany as an equal',[35] was soon reduced to referring to Germany as 'the secret enemy'.[36] Yet it was on her – as had been the case since 1915 – that everything depended. The fate of the Monarchy was determined, therefore, by the failure of the German and Austro-Hungarian offensives in the spring and early summer of 1918. In September, Bulgaria left the war while in October, Germany, Turkey and the Monarchy sued for peace on the basis of the Fourteen Points. On 16 October, the Emperor issued a manifesto designed to restructure the Monarchy as a federal state. The initiative proved irrelevant and on 27 October a new cabinet was sworn in to preside over the dissolution of the Empire. By now everyone was declaring their independence – Czechs, Yugoslavs, Hungarians and Poles – and on 11 November the Emperor eventually abdicated. Right to the very end, however, his troops had been fighting and when the Italians took the surrender of between 350,000 and 400,000 of them on 3 and 4 November, they discovered that only about one-third were German Austrians. The rest included 83,000 Czechs and Slovaks, 61,000 south Slavs, 40,000 Poles, 32,000 Ruthenes, 25,000 Romanians and even 7,000 Italians. In István Deák's words: 'this was the final irony: the last fighting forces of the Habsburg monarchy were to a great extent Slavs, Romanians and Italians, all theoretically the allies of the Entente armies.'[37] The Hungarians had eluded capture almost entirely.

The Habsburg army then had done well in certain respects. All authorities are agreed that it remained a praiseworthy and effective fighting machine until the summer of 1918, with even the south Slavs fighting for the most part until the end. It was not therefore overwhelmed by the nationality question. It also survived enormous casualties, for when the final tally was taken of the eight million men mobilized throughout the war, 1,106,200 were found to have died, about half of them in action, the rest of wounds, sickness or starvation. The small regular officer corps had lost 13.5 per cent in action, while the enlisted ranks had suffered 9.8 per cent battle casualties. The Germans and Hungarians, perhaps appropriately, had lost more men per thousand than any of the other nations fighting for the Empire. Taken altogether, the losses had, in Gunther Rothenberg's words, been 'equal in scale to those of any of the major combatants in the war. They clearly show that the Habsburg army knew how to fight and to endure.'[38] Its record was all the more remarkable considering the handicaps under which it had entered the war. By 1914, the Monarchy had fallen behind all the great powers in military terms. After the onset of the economic recession of 1873, its armed forces 'were treated like orphans'.[39] According to A. J. P. Taylor, the Monarchy in 1914, 'though ranking only after Russia and Germany in population . . . spent less than any Great Power [on defence] – a quarter of Russian or German expenditure, a third of British or French, and even less than Italian'.[40] Roy Bridge has pointed out that 'by 1913 Franz Joseph's subjects were spending more than three times as much money on beer, wine and tobacco than on the entire armed forces of the Dual Monarchy',[41] while Norman Stone has noted the low level of manpower conscripted: 'Before 1914 the Monarchy trained 0.29 per cent of her population per annum, France trained 0.75 per cent, Russian 0.35 per cent, Italy 0.37 per cent. In 1914 the war strength of the Austro-Hungarian army was 2,265,000, the war strength of the French army, which was based on a population ten millions lower than that of Austria-Hungary, was almost four millions.'[42] Technologically, the army was also backward: it remained overwhelmingly an infantry force; its artillery was fast becoming obsolete; is infantry was under-equipped with machine-guns compared with Italian or Russian divisions; Franz Joseph spurned armoured cars as of no military value because they frightened horses (in the civil administration, he likewise spurned typewriters, telephones and elevators); and there was even a shortage of uniforms. To quote Norman Stone again, it had been with justice that Conrad had opposed the Monarchy's participation in the Hague disarmament conference on the grounds that 'the present condition of our army has already an appearance of permanent limitation of armament'.[43] Franz Ferdinand had perhaps seen its real role, declaring in 1896 that: '[its] main task is not the defence of the fatherland against an external enemy, but the protection and maintenance of the dynasty against all internal enemies.'[44] In international terms, it was fit only for fighting Serbia.

How then did it survive so long? Certainly matters did not get easier. Almost half of it was killed by the end of 1914, with the result that it had to be rebuilt and reorganized. Then in 1915 and 1916 new enemies, Italy and Romania, entered the war. Casualties remained extraordinarily high and practically every battle fought unaided by the Germans was lost. Even when it won, the price to be paid was subordination to its ally. At home, things were no better. There was growing friction between Austria and Hungary and between the various nationalities. 'A particular sore point was the uneven social and ethnic distribution of battle casualties. It was no secret that certain social classes, particularly the peasants, who made up the bulk of the infantry, were forced to pay an inordinately high tribute in blood. Likewise, certain nationalities, especially the German-Austrians, Hungarians, Slovenes and Croats, lost far more men than the others.'[45] Industrial production, it is true, picked up from a sluggish start, but by 1917 was in decline, thanks to shortages of raw materials, manpower and rolling stock. In fact, transportation has been described as 'the Achilles' heel' of the Monarchy during the war.[46] The difficulties did not stop there, however. The rural population suffered from brutal requisitioning, the urban population from hunger, which by 1917 also began to affect the troops: 'Before the war, per capita consumption of flour was 380 grams a day. In April 1918 the supply was 165 grams a day for Austrians and 220 grams for Hungarians without any private food resources. Daily per capita meat consumption, around 82 grams before the war, was in 1918 some 17 grams in Austria and 34 grams in Hungary.'[47] The whole population likewise suffered from inflation, particularly the working classes. Taking the cost of living index as 100 in 1914, the figure for the general population had reached 1,082 by June 1918; for the workers it was 1,560. By 1917, therefore, the army was discovering that thousands of young men were fleeing to the woods or hiding in the cities rather than fight in the war. They would rather risk the execution squads than fight in the trenches for a régime which they were growing more and more to despise. Two things, however, kept the army from falling apart: 'First, despite all its difficulties, the army remained a remarkable fighting machine, clearly superior to the far better-equipped and better-fed Italians. Second, and this is the real paradox, it appeared by the spring of 1918, that the Central Powers had won the war. This must have been the main reason why the army did not simply fall apart. As far as Austria-Hungary was concerned, practically all its war aims had been achieved: Serbia and Romania had been punished and occupied, Russia lay prostrate, and even Italy had been humiliated, its troops driven back to a line dangerously close to Venice.'[48] The same author, István Deák, adds: 'By the summer of 1918, the Habsburg army faced the enemy in only two relatively narrow areas: a small sector of the Balkan front (the rest was held by the Bulgarians and the Germans) and northern Italy. Gone were the vast and bloody Russian and Serbian fronts. Casualties had been declining since late in 1916: in the fourth year of the war they amounted to only half of what they had been in the first year. . . . There were now far fewer soldiers at the front. In fact, by 1918 the vast majortiy of Austro-Hungarian soldiers were no longer involved in fighting: they were either at home or, if with the field armies, far from the combat lines.'[49]

Despite all the problems associated with the war, therefore, the imperial army managed to survive until the end. The spring offensives of 1918, however, did not bring the desired results. Instead of final victory, there was the shadow of defeat. As it spread, the Monarchy disintegrated. Its dissolution was not brought about by the Allies, who hoped until almost the last that it might endure. Instead, the peoples of the Monarchy at long last demanded their rights: democracy and independence became their clarion calls and they put down their national markers long before the Allied troops appeared on the scene. The peace treaties, in many instances, therefore, merely approved their *faits accomplis*. Later on, after more catastrophes, it would become fashionable in certain circles to bemoan what had been done, and certainly there were grounds enough to feel nostalgia for the Monarchy. Yet, at the time of its passing, the majority of its inhabitants were hoping for better things.

CONCLUSIONS

Let us now conclude. There are several points which have emerged from this survey. First, to speak of *decline and fall* with regard to the Monarchy is simply misleading: it fell because it lost a major war. Yet almost until the very end of that war there was no question but that it would survive, even if it failed to secure victory. A win for Germany, on the other hand, would certainly have ensured its survival in some form or other. Secondly, it is by no means obvious that the nationality problem was the reason for its fall. Most nationalities fought for it during the First World War right up until the end. Before 1914, if anything, the nationality problem seemed to be abating. Its real weaknesses in 1914 were military and financial, and this, in fact, had been the case throughout the nineteenth century. If these had been remedied, Habsburg history would have been very different. This leads on to a third point: why was there such a need to fight so many wars? To cite the rise of nationalism in Europe is no answer to this problem. The real question is why did the Habsburgs fail to come to terms with the challenge posed by nationalism? And here one comes to the crux of the matter, which turns out to be the very nature of the Monarchy itself. The Habsburg Empire was first and foremost a dynastic power, a *Hausmacht*. Its *raison d'être* was to provide a power base for the political ambitions of whichever Habsburg Emperor inherited it. It was his duty to ensure that no territories were lost – at least none without compensation; to fight to keep those which he had inherited; and, if possible, to add to the imperial patrimony. Since the territories involved were so many and varied, it was also his duty not to identify himself with any one group of his subjects. As the Archduke Albert once said: 'In a polygot Empire inhabited by so many races and peoples the dynasty must not allow itself to be assigned exclusively to one of these. Just as a good mother, it must show equal love for all its children and remain foreign to none. In this lies the justification for its existence.'[50] The best way to live up to this ideal was for the Emperor to run the show himself. The imperial ideal, therefore, was always the establishment or re-establishment of a centralized, unified state run by the sovereign in collaboration with the army and the bureaucracy. This was the ideal of Francis I, Metternich and Kollowrat, Schwarzenberg and Franz Joseph.

It was not possible after 1859 and 1866, however, to stick to this ideal; instead, Franz Joseph had to accommodate himself to dualism. Since this left him in charge of foreign affairs and the army, and still allowed him enormous influence in domestic affairs, he learned to do so remarkably easily. Yet there was a price to be paid. Internally, the Magyars insisted that there could be no change in the system, which meant that there could be no domestic political development. Externally, the price was an increasingly anti-Russian stance. The national prejudices of Hungary now poisoned the well of Habsburg diplomacy. Perhaps this is an exaggeration: after 1866 the Monarchy was bound to pay more attention to the Balkans anyway, since there was no other outlet for its dynastic ambitions; moreover, a final clash with Russia was by no means inevitable. Indeed, there was much cooperation between the two powers right up until 1914. With the assassination of the Archduke Franz Ferdinand, however, the Monarchy insisted on war, an irrational decision but an explicable one.

Among some historians there has been a tendency to adopt an 'either or' attitude to explain the Monarchy's supposed decline. That is to say, either its foreign policy or the nationality problem is given the blame, while the interconnection between the two is overlooked. Yet the two were intimately connected, and it is precisely this interconnection which gives Habsburg history its structure. For example, the *Gesamteintritt* inevitably became part of Schwarzenberg's German policy given his previous commitment to the Stadion constitution with its emphasis on a united Empire. Franz Joseph, likewise, could only resume his struggle for the German crown in the early 1860s once constitutionalism had been reintroduced into the Monarchy. It was the foreign policy consequences of the *Ausgleich*, however, which were to be most ominous for the Monarchy, since the anti-Russian prejudices of Hungary now secured a voice in the formulation of the Empire's foreign policy. Andrássy established this tradition, but it was continued by Kálnocky and others. As has already been pointed out, this need not have been fatal: public opinion in the Monarchy was not interested in the Balkans; besides, there was plenty of scope for cooperation with Russia. Yet it was a factor which cannot be ignored. Finally, although it is true to say that the nationality problem was abating before 1914 and that the nationalities fought for the Monarchy during the greater part of the First World War, it cannot be denied that the position of the nationalities both influenced Austrian thinking about the Balkans in a dangerous way and did, in 1918, help bring about the breakup of the Monarchy. Had the Habsburg Empire enjoyed an homogeneous population, there is no reason to suppose that it would not have left the war intact.

The key to the connection between foreign and domestic policy was of course the monarch himself or, for short periods, those who acted on his behalf, people like Metternich and Schwarzenberg. It was they who personally *made* the connections between domestic and foreign policy. For most of the period under review in this book, however, the man in charge was Franz Joseph and it is to his views that we must now turn.

In terms of domestic policy, it is clear that Franz Joseph's ideal was a centralized, unified and Germanized monarchy. That is what he set about establishing as soon as he was able to undermine Stadion's constitution. In foreign affairs, he wanted the Monarchy to be a leading power on the level of France, Britain or Russia. And having come to the throne at a time of Habsburg military success, he believed that this aim was a practical one. Schwarzenberg's humiliation of Prussia merely reinforced this illusion. Hence his willingness in 1854 to stand up to the Russians. 'It is hard,' he wrote to his mother, 'to have to stand up to former friends, but there is no alternative in politics, and in the East, Russia is always our natural enemy.'[51] With Russia's defeat, he was ready to negotiate a permanent alliance with the Western powers: 'he thought Russia would long bear ill-will to Austria for the part she had taken, and he wished to be united in a Treaty with the Maritime Powers, with a view to a permanent political system.'[52] He took it entirely for granted, of course, that Prussia would follow his lead. It was to take not only the Italian and Prussian wars, therefore, but also the Franco-Prussian one, to disabuse Franz Joseph of his illusions about Austria's position. Thereafter, however, he settled down to a pattern of supporting dualism within the Monarchy and the German alliance outside it. For long periods there was also cooperation in foreign affairs with Russia. None the less, there could be no permanent *modus vivendi* here since, as he said, Russia was Austria's 'natural enemy' in the East.

The real problem was the Balkans. Since Franz Joseph was always prepared to stick to the spirit and letter of dualism, he had no means of reconciling his south Slav subjects with the Magyars. In fact, he did not much care about them, since dualism allowed him to retain control of the defence and foreign policies of his Empire. Compared with this, the need to remedy the local grievances of his Serb and Croat subjects carried little weight, especially since these same Serbs and Croats could be easily played off against each other. He could not escape the fear, however, that their dissatisfaction might one day convert them to Panslavism, a fear which naturally increased after the occupation and annexation of Bosnia-Herzegovina. So long as Serbia was under control, however, all appeared to be well. As Kálnocky put it in 1881: 'If Serbia, by whatever means, is subordinate to our influence, or better still, if we are the masters in Serbia, then we can be at ease concerning our possession of Bosnia and its appendages and our position on the lower Danube and in Romania. Only then will our power in the Balkans rest on a firm basis which accords with the important interests of the monarchy.'[53] But with the overthrow of the Obrenovič dynasty in Belgrade in 1903, the outbreak of the Pig War in 1906, the annexation of Bosnia-Herzegovina in 1908 and the humiliation of Serbia and Russia in its wake, the Monarchy was clearly no longer in such a position. Given this, the military, particularly in the person of Conrad, pressed for preventive war, a policy which was resisted by both Franz Joseph and Franz Ferdinand. Indeed, Franz Joseph made it absolutely clear to Conrad that the peace policy, identified with his Foreign Minister Aerenthal, was, in fact, his own. He said: '. . . I make this policy, it is my policy. My policy is that of peace. To this policy all must adjust themselves.'[54] Yet in 1914, Franz Joseph changed his mind and we must ask ourselves why.

Imperial honour and prestige were certainly involved, and may have been crucial. Equally important were the memories and fears generated by the Balkan Wars and their results: the performance of the Serbian army; Serbia's large increase in territory; her link with a rapidly rearming Russia; the feeling that after Turkey, Austria-Hungary was inevitably next in line as a victim of Balkan nationalist aggression; not least was the lesson that was supposed to have been learned in 1912 and 1913 – that the threat of force paid dividends. Finally, there was the assurance of the German support which had been lacking in 1912–13. It was the combination of all these factors which made Franz Joseph accept war in 1914. The price paid was a horrific one; indeed, given the financial and military weaknesses of the Monarchy, the decision was more or less suicidal. Yet it was not inevitable. If Franz Joseph had been prepared to bother about the nationality question, had he retained his sense of proportion about Serbia, had he listened to Tisza, had he been prepared to compromise, he could still have strengthened his position in the Balkans without recourse to war. Besides, Serbia was never going to be in a position to challenge the Monarchy without the support of Russia, which support was unlikely to be forthcoming. The war, therefore, was an unnecessary one brought about by an irrational policy. In the words of Count Polzer Hoditz, cabinet chief to the Emperor Charles: 'Nobody thought of revising our Balkan policy, for this would have involved a complete change also in the inner policy. The understanding that the hatred of Serbia and Romania . . . was caused by ourselves, by our customs policy, that the Southern Slavs did not want anything else than to unite themselves and to get an outlet to the sea, that by our unfortunate Albanian policy we closed the last valve and therefore an explosion became inevitable, this understanding was never attained by the ruling elements.'[55]

Destruction, even with the onset of war, however, was not inevitable. The Monarchy had often depended on being rescued by others and, given its status as a European necessity, this was a strategy that had often worked. This time the Germans were cast as saviours but, alas, they too made avoidable mistakes. In particular, as Lothar Höbelt has pointed out, they invaded Belgium in 1914 and declared unrestricted submarine warfare three years later. The result of these two decisions was to embroil the Anglo-Saxon powers, Great Britain and the USA, in the conflict. And according to Höbelt, it was the intervention of the Anglo-Saxon powers which tipped the balance in what would otherwise have been a

Continental stalemate between France and Russia, on the one hand, and Austria-Hungary and Germany, on the other. In his view, therefore, the Monarchy's destruction must be blamed on Germany's military strategists.[56] There is definitely something in this, yet had the war not been started in the first place, German military decision-making could not have taken its toll and Austria-Hungary would not have lost control of her own destiny. Höbelt, therefore, like many American historians whose views have been discussed – e.g. Schroeder, Austensen, Elrod, Haas, Viereck and János – falls into the trap of making excuses for the Monarchy: it meant well; it was not particularly oppressive; reforms almost happened, potential saviours went unheeded or died; other powers failed to come to the rescue or made the wrong decisions when they did. A lot of this amounts to sentimentality based on the feeling that the successor régimes, especially those created after 1945, were even less successful in resolving the problems of East–Central Europe than the Monarchy itself. It is certainly no coincidence that much of the writing on the Monarchy has come from those who suffered, or from the sons of those who suffered, at the hands of these régimes.[57] This combination of hindsight and subjectivity, however, should not be allowed to obscure the fact that the Monarchy deliberately started a world war rather than compromise internally or externally on the south Slav question. It should also not be overlooked that starting or being prepared to start wars had become a Habsburg habit in the nineteenth century. Yet it was probably unnecessary: the Italians might have been reconciled before 1848; the Prussians before 1866; the south Slavs and others after 1867. What failed was Habsburg statecraft, which assumed that the *status quo* was eternal and that the duty of everyone and every power was to uphold it. Otherwise, as Franz Joseph wrote in 1866 and still obviously believed thereafter: 'One just has to resist as long as possible, do one's duty to the last, and finally perish with honour.'[58] This was all very well, and perhaps even a trifle romantic, but just as he had allowed tens of thousands to die needlessly for his honour in Italy in 1866, so too in 1914 did he overlook the fact that the millions who would now die in what he almost certainly knew would be a world war, would not be consulted either. In the same spirit, the last Habsburg Emperor was to leave his throne without even issuing a proclamation of official gratitude to his troops. That old phrase *the thanks of the House of Habsburg* was thus to preserve its irony.

NOTES AND REFERENCES

1. István Diószegi, *Die Aussenpolitik der Osterreichisch-Ungarischen Monarchie, 1871–1877*. Vienna, Graz and Cologne, p. 10.
2. *Ibid.*
3. New York, 1979, East European Monographs 11, *Studies on Society in Change*, No. 8.
4. *Ibid.*, p. 113.
5. *Ibid.*, p. 114.
6. *Ibid.*
7. *Ibid.*, p. 102.
8. *Ibid.*, p. 115.
9. *Ibid.*, p. 32.
10. *Ibid.*
11. Robert A. Kann (1977) Trends Towards Colonialism in the Habsburg Empire, 1878–1918, the case of Bosnia-Hercegovina, 1878–1914, in D. K. Rowney and G. E. Orchard (eds) *Russian and Slavonic History*. New York, pp. 164–80.
12. *Ibid.*, pp. 166–7.
13. *Ibid.*, p. 168.
14. *Ibid.*, p. 170.
15. *Ibid.*, pp. 171–2.
16. *Ibid.*, pp. 172–3.
17. *Ibid.*, p. 178.
18. Paul W. Schroeder (1972) World War I as Galloping Gertie: a reply to Joachim Remak, *Journal of Modern History*, Vol. 44, pp. 319–45, pp. 341–2
19. Paul W. Schroeder (1976) Munich and the British tradition, *The Historical Journal*, Vol. 19, pp. 223–43, p. 237.
20. *Ibid.*, p. 240.
21. A. J. P. Taylor (1965) *The Struggle for Mastery in Europe*. London, p. 322.
22. *Ibid.*, p. 456.
23. C. A. Macartney, *The Habsburg Empire, 1790–1918*. London, p. 808, note 1.
24. Barabara Jelavich (1975) *The Habsburg Empire in European Affairs, 1814–1918*. New York, p. 117.
25. István Diószegi (1983) *Hungarians in the Ballhausplatz, Studies on the Austro-Hungarian Common Foreign Policy*. Budapest, p. 55.
26. *Ibid.*, p. 82.
27. *Ibid.*, p. 84.
28. *Ibid.*, p. 88.
29. *Ibid.*
30. *Ibid.*, p. 210.
31. Roy F. Bridge (1972) *From Sadowa to Sarajevo: the Foreign Policy of Austria Hungary, 1866–1914*. London, p. 370.
32. Diószegi, *Hungarians in the Ballhausplatz*, pp. 228–9.
33. Robert A. Kann (1973) Kaiser Franz Joseph und der Ausbruch des Weltkrieges in *Mitteilungen des Osterreichischen Staatsarchivs*, XXVI,

pp. 448–55, pp. 449–50. The Emperor had also favoured war in 1913 over Scutari according to Bilinski.

34. On Tisza, see Gábor Vermes (1985) István Tisza, The Liberal Vision and Conservative Statecraft of a Magyar Nationalist, *East European Monographs CLXXXIV*, New York, Chapter IX. On Austria-Hungary's determination to have a war, see especially William Jannen Jr. (1983) The Austrian Decision for War in July 1914, in S. R. Williamson Jr. and P. Pastor (eds.) Essays on World War I: Origins and Prisoners of War, *War and Society in East Central Europe*, Vol. V, New York, pp. 55–81. On page 58 he writes. "Even at the July 19 Council of Ministers . . . . there was no discussion of the possible consequences of Russian intervention." Cf. p. 60: "The monarchy's leaders appear to have paid virtually no attention to the likely response of other powers." See also Sam Williamson's article in the same collection, which makes similar points.
35. W. W. Gottlieb (1957) *Studies in Secret Diplomacy During the First World War*. London, p. 263.
36. The title of the most recent and comprehensive study of Austro-German relations during the war, namely Gary W, Shanafelt (1985) The secret enemy: Austria-Hungary and the German Alliance, 1914–1918, *East European Monographs*, CLXXXVII. New York.
37. István Deák (1985) The Habsburg army in the first and last days of World War I: a comparative analysis, in B. K. Király and N. F. Dreisiger (eds) East Central European society in World War I, *War and Society in East Central Europe, Vol. XIX, East European Monographs, CXCVI.* New York, pp. 301–12, p. 310.
38. Gunther E. Rothenberg (1985) The Habsburg army in the First World War: 1914–1918, in B. K. Király and N. F. Dreisiger, *op. cit.*, pp. 289–300, p. 297.
39. János Décsy (1985) The Habsburg army on the threshold of total war, in B. K. Király and N. F. Dreisiger, *op. cit.*, pp. 280–8, p. 281.
40. A. J. P. Taylor (1964) *The Habsburg Monarchy, 1809–1918, A History of the Austrian Empire* and Austria-Hungary. London, p. 247.
41. Bridge, *op. cit.*, p. 23.
42. Norman Stone (1966) Army and society in the Habsburg Monarchy, 1900–1914, *Past and Present*, Vol. 33, p. 107.
43. *Ibid.*
44. Gunther E. Rothenberg (1976) *The Army of Francis Joseph*. West Lafayette, p. 129.
45. Deák *op. cit.*, p. 307.
46. J. Robert Wegs (1977) Transportation: the Achilles heel of the Habsburg war effort, in R. A. Kann, B. K. Király and P. S. Fichtner (eds) The Habsburg Empire In World War I, essays on the intellectual, military, political and economic aspects of the Habsburg war effort, *Studies on Society and Change, 2, East European Monographs, XXIII*, pp. 121–34.
47. Richard Georg Plaschka (1985) The Army and Internal Conflict in the Austro-Hungarian Empire, 1918, in B. Király andd N. F. Dreisiger (eds) *op. cit.*, pp. 338–53.
48. Deák, *op. cit.*, pp. 307–8.
49. *Ibid.*, p. 308.

50. Quoted in Brigitte Hamann (1982) Die Habsburger und die Deutsche Frage im 19 Jahrhundert, in H. Lutz and H. Rumpler (eds) *Osterreich und die Deutsche Frage in 19 und 20 Jahrhundert, Probleme der politisch-staatlichen und sozio-kulturellen Differenzierung im deutschen Mitteleuropa*. Munich, p. 222.
51. G. B. Henderson (1975) Crimean War diplomacy and other historical essays, *Glasgow University Publications, LXVIII*. New York, p. 21: 'Es ist hart gegen frühere Freunde auftreten zu müssen, allein in der Politik ist dies nicht anders möglich, und im Orient ist Russland jederzeit unser natürlicher Feind.'
52. *Ibid.*, pp. 53–54.
53. Quoted in Solomon Wank (1967) Foreign policy and the nationality problem in Austria-Hungary, 1867–1914, *Austrian History Yearbook*, Vol. 3, pp. 33–56, p. 44.
54. E. C. Count Corti and H. Sokol (1955) *Der Alte Kaiser*. Graz, Vienna and Cologne, p. 363.
55. Oscar Jászi (1961) *The Dissolution of the Habsburg Monarchy*. Chicago and London, p. 420.
56. Lothar Höbelt (1982) Österreich-Ungarn und das Deutsche Reich als Zweibundpartner, in H. Lutz and H. Rumpler (eds.) *op. cit.*, pp. 256–281, 278–9.
57. On this theme, see Alan Sked (1981) Historians, the nationality question and the downfall of the Habsburg Empire, *Transactions of the Royal Historical Society*, 5th series, Vol. 31.
58. A. Wandruszka (1968) Finis Austriae? Reformpläne und Untergangsahnungen in der Habsburger Monarchie, in *Der österreichische Ausgleich von 1867. Seine Grundlagen und* Auswirkungen. Buchreihe der Südostdeutschen Historischen Kommission, Vol. 20. Munich, p. 119.

Appendix

1. CHRONOLOGY OF EVENTS

1804	14 August	Proclamation of Austrian Empire
1806	6 August	Abdication of Francis (II) I as Holy Roman Emperor
1809	8 October	Metternich appointed Foreign Minister
1814–15	September–June	Congress of Vienna
1818	September–November	Congress of Aix-la-Chapelle
1819	August	The Karlsbad Decrees
1820	July–August	Revolts in Spain, Naples and Portugal
1820	October	Congress of Troppau
1820	19 November	Protocol of Troppau
1821	January–May	Congress of Laibach
1821	March	Revolts in Piedmont and Greece
1821	28 May	Metternich appointed State Chancellor
1822	October	Congress of Verona
1827	20 October	Battle of Navarino
1828–9	May 1828 – September 1829	Russo-Turkish War
1830	3 February	Greece becomes independent
1830	July–November	Revolution in France. Revolts in Belgium, Poland, the Papal States and parts of Germany

1833	8 July	Treaty of Unkiar Skelessi
1835	2 March	Death of Francis I of Austria; accession of Ferdinand I
1839	19 April	Holland accepts Belgian independence
1840		War scare with France over Mehemet Ali crisis
1841	13 July	Straits Convention
1846	10 October	The Spanish Marriages
1846	6 November	Austria annexes Krakow
1847	November	Sonderbund War in Switzerland
1848		Revolutions in Italy, France, Germany, the Habsburg Monarchy and elsewhere
	24 February	Abdication of Louis Philippe in France
	13 March	Resignation of Metternich in Vienna
	23 March	Piedmontese troops invade Lombardy
	11 April	Ferdinand approves Hungarian Laws granting a separate Hungarian government
	1 May	Slav Congress opens in Prague
	6 May	Radetzky defeats the Piedmontese at Santa Lucia
	18 May	St Paul's Assembly opens in Frankfurt
	15 June	Windischgraetz bombards Prague
	10 July	Reichstag open in Vienna
	25 July	Radetzky defeats Piedmontese at Custoza
	6 August	Radetzky re-enters Milan
	11 September	Jellačić invades Hungary
	6 October	Uprising in Vienna
	28 October–1 November	Windischgraetz storms Vienna; Jellačić defeats the Hungarians at Schwechat, outside Vienna
	21 November	Schwarzenberg named Prime Minister

	22 November	Reichstag meets at Kremsier
	2 December	Ferdinand abdicates in favour of Franz Joseph
	16 December	Windischgraetz invades Hungary
1849		Triumph of counter-revolution
	March	Kremsier Reichstag dissolved; Stadion's octroyed constitution promulgated; Piedmont resumes the war against Austria and is decisively defeated at Novara
	28 March	Frankfurt Assembly votes German crown to Prussia
	3 April	King of Prussia rejects the Assembly's offer
	14 April	Kossuth deposes the Habsburgs in Hungary
	14 April	Windischgraetz relieved of command of imperial troops
	1 May	Nicholas I of Russia is asked by Franz Joseph and agrees to aid Austria against Hungary
	August	Gorgei surrenders to Russians at Világos; Venice surrenders to Radetzky
1850	December	*Punctation* of Olmütz; start of Dresden Conference on the future of Germany
1851	May	Failure of Dresden Conference to alter German affairs; return to old German *Bund* arrangements
1851	31 December	Sylvester Patent restores absolutism in Austria
1852		Metternich returns to Vienna; death of Schwarzenberg
1854		Britain and France enter Crimean War; Franz Joseph issues ultimatum to Tsar to quit the Principalities
1856	February–March	Congress of Paris

1859	April–July	Austro-French Piedmontese War. Austria loses Lombardy
1860	20 October	October Diploma
1861	26 February	February Patent
1863	14 August	Franz Joseph convokes a meeting of the German Princes at Frankfurt. The King of Prussia refuses to attend
1864	February–October	Danish War
1865	20 August	Convention of Gastein
1866	June–August	Austro-Prussian War; Austria is expelled from Germany and loses Venetia to Italy
1867		Austro-Hungarian Compromise; Andrássy becomes first Hungarian prime minister; Franz Joseph crowned in Budapest
1878	June–July	Congress of Berlin; occupation of Bosnia-Herzegovina
1879	7 October	Dual Alliance of Austria-Hungary and Germany
1897	April–November	Badeni crisis
1905–6		Hungarian crisis
1907	26 January	Universal suffrage in Austria
1908	5 October	Annexation of Bosnia-Herzegovina
1913	18 October	Austria-Hungary sends ultimatum to Serbia over Albania
1914	28 June	Assassination of Archduke Franz Ferdinand and wife at Sarajevo
1914–1918		First World War
1915	23 May	Italy declares war on Austria-Hungary
1916	21 November	Death of Franz Joseph; accession of Emperor Charles, the last Habsburg Emperor
1918	3 March	Peace of Brest-Litovsk
1918	11 November	Renunciation of Emperor's executive powers; proclamation

	of the Austrian Republic; breakup of the Monarchy

2. HABSBURG FOREIGN MINISTERS, 1809–1918

Clemens Wenzel Lothar von Metternich	8 October, 1809–13 March, 1848
Karl Ludwig Ficquelmont	20 March–4 May, 1848
Johann von Wessenberg	8 May–21 November, 1848
Felix zu Schwarzenberg	21 November, 1848–5 April, 1852
Karl Ferdinand von Buol-Schauenstein	11 April, 1852–17 May, 1859
Johann Bernhard von Rechberg	17 May, 1859–10 October, 1864
Alexander von Mensdorff-Pouilly	27 October, 1864–30 October, 1866
Frederick Ferdinand von Beust	30 October, 1866–8 November, 1871
Julius Andrássy	8 November, 1871–8 October, 1879
Heinrich von Haymerle	8 October, 1879–10 October, 1881
Gustav Kálnoky	20 November, 1881–2 May, 1895
Agenor von Goluchowsky	16 May, 1895–24 October, 1906
Alois Lexa von Aehrenthal	24 October, 1906–17 February, 1912
Leopold Berchtold	17 February, 1912–13 January, 1915
Stefan Burián	13 January, 1915–22 July, 1916
Ottokar Czernin	22 July, 1916–16 April, 1918
Stefan Burián	16 April–24 October, 1918
Julius Andrássy (the son)	24 October–2 November, 1918
Ludwig von Flotow	2 November–11 November, 1918

3. POPULATION AND NATIONALITIES IN THE EMPIRE, 1843–1910

The Empire in 1843 (millions)

Slavs	15.5
Germans	7.0
Magyars	5.3
Romanians	1.0
Italians	0.3
Total	29.1

(Source: F. Schuselka (1843) *1st Osterreich Deutsch?* Leipzig)

The Empire in 1910 (millions)

Germans	12.0
Magyars	10.1
Czechs	6.6
Poles	5.0
Ruthenians	4.0
Croats	3.2
Romanians	2.9
Slovaks	2.0
Serbs	2.0
Slovenes	1.3
Italians	0.7
Total	50.8

(Source: 1910 Census)

The Empire 1880–1910 (percentages)

	1880	*1910*
Cisleithanian Austria:		
Germans	36.8	35.6
Czechs (incl. Slovaks)	23.8	23.0
Poles	14.9	17.8
Ruthenians	12.8	12.6
Serbo-Croats	2.6	2.7
Romanians	0.9	1.0
Hungarian Crown Lands (incl. Croatia-Slavonia)		
Magyars	41.2	48.1

Romanians	15.4	14.1
Germans	12.5	9.8
Slovaks	11.9	9.4
Croats	9.0*	8.8
Serbs	6.1*	5.3
Ruthenians	2.3	2.3
Bosnia-Herzegovina	1880	1910
Croats	—	21
Serbs	—	42
Mohammedans	—	34

* Figures for 1890
(Source: Official Nationality Statistics)

Map 1 General map of the Empire

R U S S I A
Troppau
SILESIA
Cracow
GALICIA
Lemberg
(Lwow)
CARPATHIANS
Czernowitz
(Cernauţi)
Munkács
ratislava)
BUKOVINA
Debrecen
Budapest
R. Tisza
Klausenburg
(Kolozsvár)
H U N G A R Y
TRANSYLVANIA
Hermannstadt
(Sibiu)
Temesvar
Kronstadt
(Brassó)
Esseg (Osijek)
R. Sava
ROMANIA
R. Danube
Sarajevo
SERBIA
ostar
BULGARIA
ERCEGOVINA
MONTENEGRO
0
100 mls
0
100 kms

Map 2 Gains and losses in the Empire

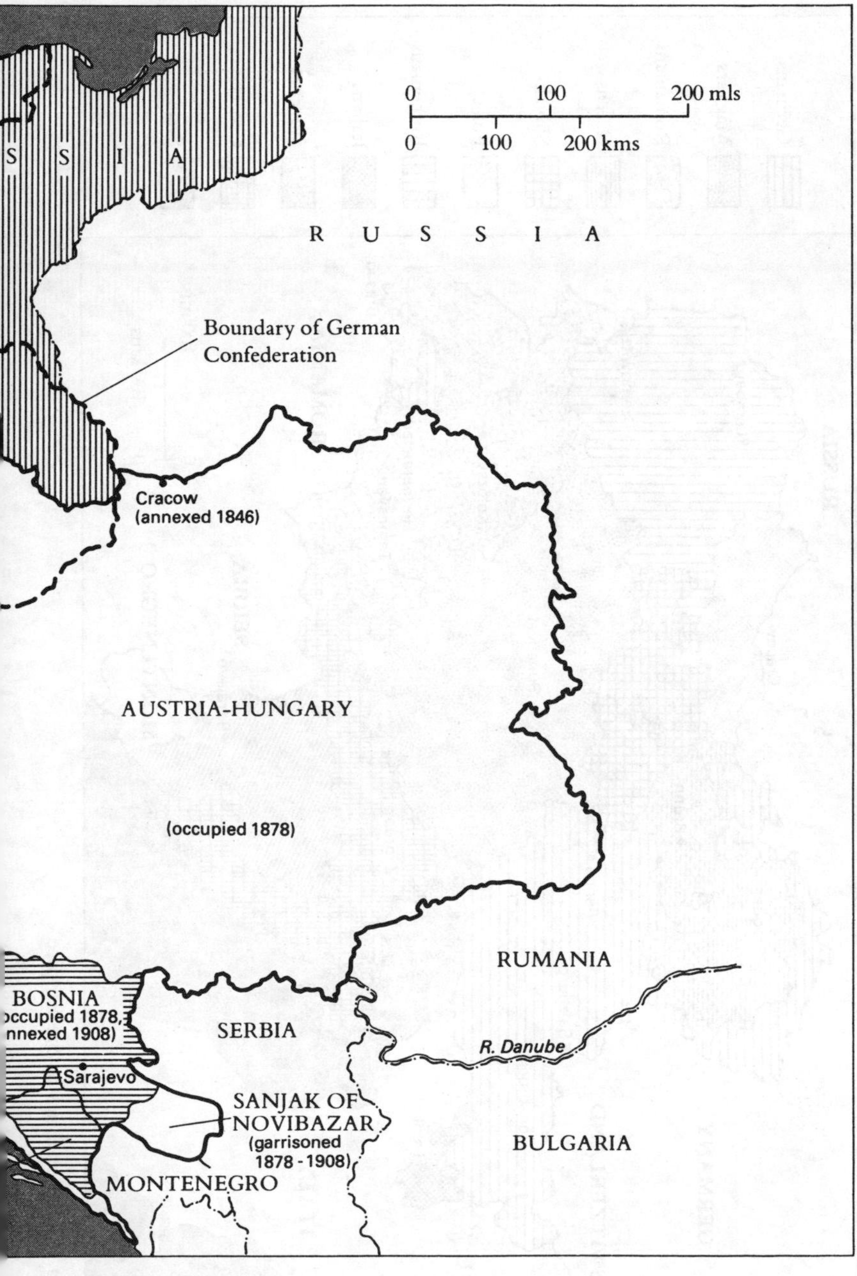
0
100
200 mls
0
100
200 kms
S S I A
R U S S I A
Boundary of German
Confederation
Cracow
(annexed 1846)
AUSTRIA-HUNGARY
(occupied 1878)
RUMANIA
BOSNIA
occupied 1878,
nnexed 1908)
SERBIA
R. Danube
Sarajevo
SANJAK OF
NOVIBAZAR
(garrisoned
1878 - 1908)
BULGARIA
MONTENEGRO

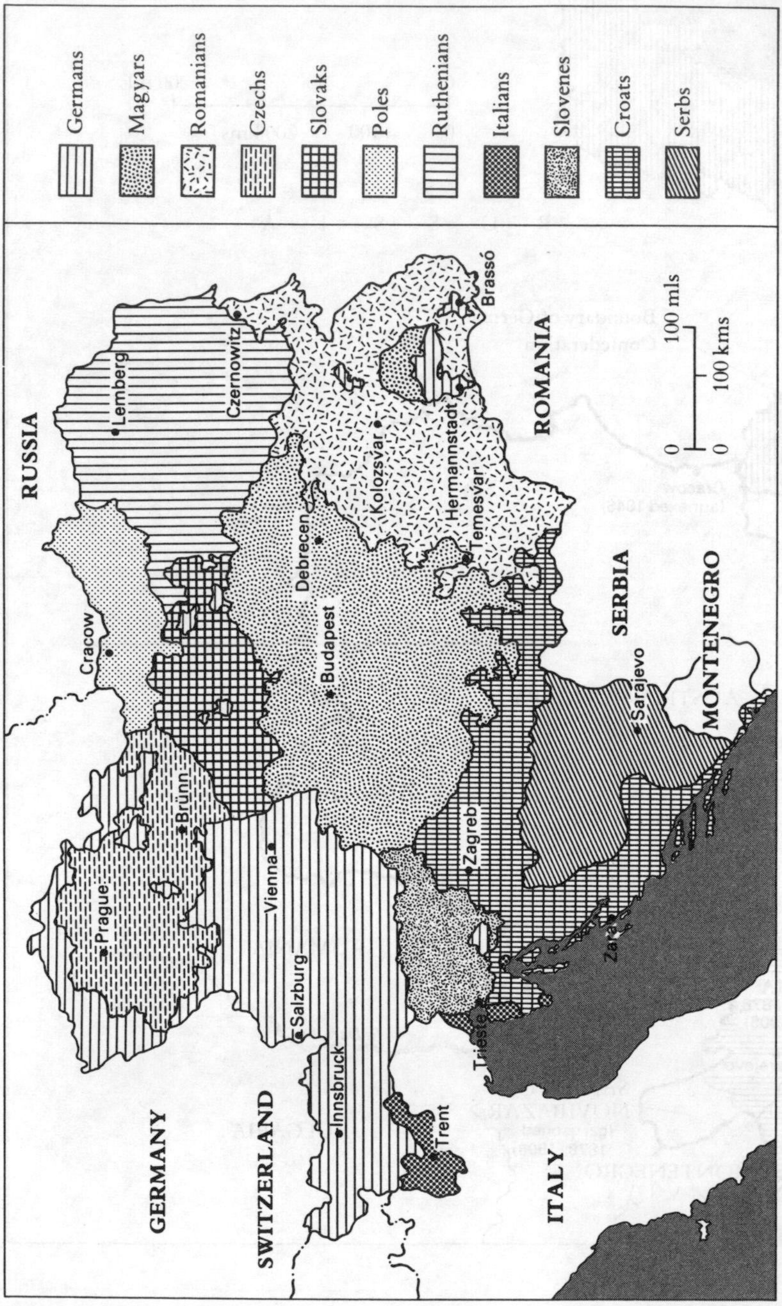
Germans
Magyars
Romanians
Czechs
Slovaks
Poles
Ruthenians
Italians
Slovenes
Croats
Serbs
RUSSIA
GERMANY
SWITZERLAND
ITALY
ROMANIA
SERBIA
MONTENEGRO
Lemberg
Czernowitz
Cracow
Prague
Brünn
Vienna
Salzburg
Innsbruck
Trent
Trieste
Zagreb
Zara
Sarajevo
Budapest
Debrecen
Kolozsvar
Hermannstadt
Temesvar
Brassó
0 100 mls
0 100 kms

Map 3 Nationalities in the Empire

Index